IFIP Advances in Information and Communication Technology   378

IFIP – The International Federation for Information Processing

IFIP was founded in 1960 under the auspices of UNESCO, following the First World Computer Congress held in Paris the previous year. An umbrella organization for societies working in information processing, IFIP's aim is two-fold: to support information processing within its member countries and to encourage technology transfer to developing nations. As its mission statement clearly states,

> *IFIP's mission is to be the leading, truly international, apolitical organization which encourages and assists in the development, exploitation and application of information technology for the benefit of all people.*

IFIP is a non-profitmaking organization, run almost solely by 2500 volunteers. It operates through a number of technical committees, which organize events and publications. IFIP's events range from an international congress to local seminars, but the most important are:

- The IFIP World Computer Congress, held every second year;
- Open conferences;
- Working conferences.

The flagship event is the IFIP World Computer Congress, at which both invited and contributed papers are presented. Contributed papers are rigorously refereed and the rejection rate is high.

As with the Congress, participation in the open conferences is open to all and papers may be invited or submitted. Again, submitted papers are stringently refereed.

The working conferences are structured differently. They are usually run by a working group and attendance is small and by invitation only. Their purpose is to create an atmosphere conducive to innovation and development. Refereeing is also rigorous and papers are subjected to extensive group discussion.

Publications arising from IFIP events vary. The papers presented at the IFIP World Computer Congress and at open conferences are published as conference proceedings, while the results of the working conferences are often published as collections of selected and edited papers.

Any national society whose primary activity is about information processing may apply to become a full member of IFIP, although full membership is restricted to one society per country. Full members are entitled to vote at the annual General Assembly, National societies preferring a less committed involvement may apply for associate or corresponding membership. Associate members enjoy the same benefits as full members, but without voting rights. Corresponding members are not represented in IFIP bodies. Affiliated membership is open to non-national societies, and individual and honorary membership schemes are also offered.

Imed Hammouda   Björn Lundell
Tommi Mikkonen   Walt Scacchi (Eds.)

Open Source Systems:
Long-Term Sustainability

8th IFIP WG 2.13 International Conference, OSS 2012
Hammamet, Tunisia, September 10-13, 2012
Proceedings

 Springer

Volume Editors

Imed Hammouda
Tommi Mikkonen
Tampere University of Technology
Korkeakoulunkatu 1, 33101 Tampere, Finland
E-mail: {imed.hammouda, tommi.mikkonen}@tut.fi

Björn Lundell
University of Skövde
Högskolan i Skövde, 541 28 Skövde, Sweden
E-mail: bjorn.lundell@his.se

Walt Scacchi
University of California
Institute for Software Research
Irvine, CA 92697-3455, USA
E-mail: wscacchi@ics.uci.edu

ISSN 1868-4238   e-ISSN 1868-422X
ISBN 978-3-642-42879-1   ISBN 978-3-642-33442-9 (eBook)
DOI 10.1007/978-3-642-33442-9
Springer Heidelberg Dordrecht London New York

CR Subject Classification (1998): D.2.7, D.2.13, K.6.3, D.2.0, D.2.3, D.2.9, D.2.11, K.4.1, K.3.1, H.5.4, H.3.4, D.1, D.3

Typesetting: Camera-ready by author, data conversion by Scientific Publishing Services, Chennai, India

Printed on acid-free paper

Springer is part of Springer Science+Business Media (www.springer.com)

General Chairs' Foreword

Over the past two decades, Free/Libre Open Source Software (FLOSS) has introduced new successful models for creating, distributing, acquiring, and using software and software-based services. Inspired by the success of FLOSS, other forms of open initiatives have been gaining momentum. Open source systems (OSS) now extend beyond software to include open access, open documents, open science, open education, open government, open cloud, open hardware, open artworks and museum exhibits, open innovation, and more. On the one hand, the openness movement has created new kinds of opportunities such as the emergence of new business models, knowledge exchange mechanisms, and collective development approaches. On the other hand, the movement has introduced new kinds of challenges, especially as different problem domains embrace openness as a pervasive problem solving strategy. OSS can be complex yet widespread and often cross-cultural. Consequently, an interdisciplinary understanding of the technical, economic, legal, and socio-cultural dynamics is required.

The goal of the 8th International Conference on Open Source Systems, OSS 2012, the first to be held in Africa, was to provide an international forum where a diverse community of professionals from academia, industry, and the public sector, and diverse OSS initiatives could come together to share research findings and practical experiences. The major conference theme was long-term sustainability with OSS, with related themes addressing OSS as innovation, OSS practice and methods, OSS technologies, and more. The conference also aimed to provide information and education to practitioners, identify directions for further research, and to be an ongoing platform for technology transfer, no matter which form of OSS is being pursued.

The choice to focus the conference on open source *systems*, rather than just on open source *software*, enables us as a community to better serve our established and emerging research agendas through discovering, exploring, and comparing the similarities and differences between open source systems whose openness arises from features not necessarily in software, but in open practices, methods, technologies, and governance patterns that are informed by what we have already learned about open source software. For example, open source hardware projects often share hardware designs from which users can make the hardware package, or embed it within some other hardware system, rather than sharing and modifying the hardware itself. Should we expect to see the rise of open source hardware repositories or repositories of repositories, as we have seen in the world of open source software? The development of open source hardware systems, and other kinds of open source systems, may follow different processes than open source software. Similarly, are open source hardware projects organized and hosted in online communities in a manner that strongly or weakly follows the practices we see in open source software project communities? Again, the choice we face as a research community is whether to embrace the diversification of the openness movement into new kinds of open source systems, or whether to maintain and further explore the world that focuses primarily on open source software. Such diversity helps outline the freshness and vitality of future research in both open source software and open source systems.

Putting together this conference this year, with a multitude of parties contributing to its success, required considerable effort and contribution of time from the program chairs, Imed Hammouda and Björn Lundell. Without their work, the event would have been impossible to organize. Sincerely, thank you both very, very much for everything!

We are also grateful to the local conference organizers, Said Ouerghi and Khaled Sammoud, without whom it would have been impossible for us to organize the first OSS event on the African continent, thus further expressing the global nature of the topic of this particular conference series. In addition, we wish to thank Syrine Tlili and Nizar Kerkeni, who acted as the public sector and community liaison chairs, respectively. Moreover, the work of industry chairs, Slim Ben Ayed and Stephane Ribas, is gratefully acknowledged.

Sincere thanks also go to Jonas Gamalielsson and Chuck Knutson for their work as proceedings chairs, and to Charles M. Schweik, Cornelia Boldyreff, Klaas-Jan Stol, Chuck Knutson, and Yeliz Eseryel for managing the doctoral consortium, which has become one of the key elements of the OSS conference series. In addition, we wish to thank Mona Laroussi, Pekka Abrahamsson, and Greg Madey for their roles as tutorial, panel, and workshop chairs. Sincere thanks also go to Alexander Lokhman, our web master, for his maintenance of the web site.

The team of publicity chairs, led by Sulayman K. Sowe, our publicity and social media chair, and constituted by Nnenna Nwakanma (Africa), Tetsuo Noda (Asia), Greg Madey (North America), Carlos Denner Santos Jr. (Central and South America), Stefan Koch (East Europe), Faheem Ahmed (Middle East), Jonas Gamalielsson (West and North Europe), did a tremendous job in promoting the conference, thus ensuring a wide interest in the event in the form of submissions as well as participation.

We also wish to thank the two universities involved in the organization, Tampere University of Technology, Finland, and the University of Monastir, Tunisia, for their support of the event – these universities administered great help and financial assistance. In addition, we wish to thank the sponsors of the event, the IFIP Working Group 2.13, and past conference organizers, who provided a great deal of assistance during the preparation of the program as well as the actual event.

Finally, we humbly wish to thank the authors and the members of the Program Committee without whom there would have been no technical program.

July 2012   Walt Scacchi
                                                               Tommi Mikkonen

Program Chairs' Foreword

It is a great pleasure to welcome you to the proceedings of the Eighth International Conference on Open Source Systems, OSS 2012. The conference program and papers published here reflect the main goal of OSS 2012: to provide an international forum where a diverse community of professionals from academia, industry, and the public sector, and diverse OSS initiatives could come together to share research findings and practical experiences.

The maturity of research in our field is also reflected in the range and number of excellent contributions received. The technical program committee worked very hard to put together an outstanding program which included research papers, industry papers, formal tool demonstrations, lightning talks, and posters. The papers published here reflect the international communities of active OSS researchers. We received and reviewed 63 contributions (54 research and 9 industry) with an acceptance rate for full papers of 33%. This enabled us to offer sessions on a variety of topics, which included: collaboration and forks in OSS projects; community issues; open education and peer-production models; integration and architecture; business ecosystems; and adoption and evolution of OSS.

This year's keynote addresses came from six distinguished members of the OSS community. Italo Vignoli (The Document Foundation) gave the keynote address: The Sustainability of an Independent Free Software Project. This was followed by Simon Phipps (Open Source Initiative - OSI) who delivered a keynote on the OSI Reform, and Michael Widenius (Monty Program AB) with the keynote: The MySQL and MariaDB Story. Following this, Nasser Kettani (Microsoft) gave a keynote on experiences from Microsoft, followed by Mikko Kurunsaari (Gurux Ltd) with the keynote: Gurux - The Open Source Experience. Finally, Carol Smith (Google) provided the keynote: Google Summer of Code, Open Source, and Education.

Furthermore, there were two workshops on OSS education and mobile OSS, a special session on sustainable development and open source, a panel on OSS business, a doctoral consortium, and a business networking event collocated with the main conference. Overall, the program reflected a very relevant perspective on contemporary issues related to the conference theme for this year, which is long-term sustainability with OSS. In addition to the technical program, the conference also included an interesting social program. The conference also hosted the traditional Women@OSS and Nordic@OSS breakfast events.

We want to give special thanks to all the people who allowed us to put together such a topical and outstanding program, and we would especially like to mention: the program committee members and additional reviewers; the session chairs; all the authors who submitted their papers to OSS 2012; the general chairs (Walt Scacchi and Tommi Mikkonen), the local conference organizers

(Said Ouerghi and Khaled Sammoud) together with their local team, in particular Nizar Kerkeni, as well as all the other people who worked hard to make the conference a great event. Because of all of your efforts, the conference program was very rich with exciting papers and events. We hope that you enjoyed this program and that the conference provided you with a valuable opportunity to share ideas with other researchers and practitioners.

July 2012

Imed Hammouda
Björn Lundell

OSS 2012 Conference Organization

Conference Officials

General Chairs

Walt Scacchi   University of California, Irvine, USA
Tommi Mikkonen   Tampere University of Technology, Finland

Program Chairs

Imed Hammouda   Tampere University of Technology, Finland
Björn Lundell   University of Skövde, Sweden

Organizing Chairs

Said Ouerghi   University of Manouba, Tunisia
Khaled Sammoud   University of Tunis el Manar, Tunisia

Proceedings Chairs

Jonas Gamalielsson   University of Skövde, Sweden
Chuck Knutson   Brigham Young University, USA

Doctoral Consortium Chairs

Charles M. Schweik   University of Massachusetts, USA
Cornelia Boldyreff   University of East London, UK
Klaas-Jan Stol   Lero, University of Limerick, Ireland
Chuck Knutson   Brigham Young University, USA
Yeliz Eseryel   University of Groningen, The Netherlands

Industry Chairs

Slim Ben Ayed   TMI, Tunisia
Stephane Ribas   INRIA, France

Public Sector Liaison Chair

Syrine Tlili   Open Source Software Unit – Ministry of
                                 Communication Technologies, Tunisia

Community Liaison Chair

Nizar Kerkeni   University of Monastir, Tunisia

Tutorials Chair

Mona Laroussi   INSAT, Tunisia

Panels Chair

Pekka Abrahamsson   Free University of Bozen-Bolzano, Italy

Workshops Chair

Greg Madey   University of Notre Dame, USA

Publicity and Social Media Chair

Sulayman K. Sowe   United Nations University Institute for
                                 Advanced Studies, Japan

Publicity Co-chairs

(Africa)   Nnenna Nwakanma, FOSSFA
(Asia)   Tetsuo Noda, Shimane University, Japan
(North America)   Greg Madey, University of Notre Dame, USA
(Central and South America)   Carlos Denner Santos Jr, University of Brasilia,
                                 Brazil
(East Europe)   Stefan Koch, Bogazici University, Turkey
(Middle East)   Faheen Ahmed, United Arab Emirates
                                 University, UAE
(West and North Europe)   Jonas Gamalielsson, University of Skövde,
                                 Sweden

Web Portal

Alexander Lokhman   Tampere University of Technology, Finland

Advisory Committee

Giancarlo Succi   Free University of Bozen-Bolzano, Italy
Walt Scacchi   University of California, Irvine, USA
Ernesto Damiani   University of Milan, Italy
Scott Hissam   Software Engineering Institute, USA
Pär J. Ågerfalk   Uppsala University, Sweden

Program Committee

Alberto Sillitti   Free University of Bozen-Bolzano, Italy
Andrea Capiluppi   University of East London, UK
Andreas Meiszner   SPI - Sociedade Portuguesa de Inovação,
                                 Portugal
Anthony Wasserman   Carnegie Mellon Silicon Valley, USA
Antonio Cerone   University of East London, UK
Barbara Russo   Free University of Bozen-Bolzano, Italy
Björn Lundell   University of Skövde, Sweden

Bruno Rossi	Free University of Bozen-Bolzano, Italy
Charles Knutson	Brigham Young University, USA
Chintan Amrit	University of Twente, The Netherlands
Daniela Cruzes	Norwegian University of Science and Technology, Norway
Davide Tosi	University of Insubria, Italy
Diomidis Spinellis	Athens University of Economics and Business, Greece
Dirk Riehle	University of Erlangen-Nürnberg, Germany
Ernesto Damiani	University of Milan, Italy
Etiel Petrinja	Free University of Bozen-Bolzano, Italy
Fabio Kon	University of São Paulo, Brazil
Filippo Lanubile	University of Bari, Italy
Francesco Di Cerbo	SAP Labs, France
Francesco Lelli	European Research Institute in Service Science (ERISS), The Netherlands
Gabriella Dodero	Free University of Bozen-Bolzano, Italy
Giancarlo Succi	Free University of Bozen-Bolzano, Italy
Gregorio Robles	Universidad Rey Juan Carlos, Spain
Guy Martin	Red Hat, USA
Imed Hammouda	Tampere University of Technology, Finland
Ioannis Stamelos	Aristotle University of Thessaloniki, Greece
Jaco Geldenhuys	Stellenbosch University, South Africa
Jay Kesan	University of Illinois at Urbana-Champaign, USA
Jean-Michel Dalle	Université Pierre et Marie Curie, France
Jesus M. Gonzalez-Barahona	Universidad Rey Juan Carlos, Spain
John Noll	Lero, the Irish Software Engineering Research Centre, Ireland
Joseph Feller	University College Cork, Ireland
Joseph Jackson	Open Science Alliance, USA
Juho Lindman	Hanken School of Economics, Finland
Karim Chine	Cloud Era Ltd, UK
Kevin Crowston	Syracuse University, USA
Klaas-Jan Stol	Lero, University of Limerick, Ireland
Luigi Lavazza	Università degli Studi dell'Insubria, Italy
Maha Shaikh	London School of Economics, UK
Mohamed Amine Chatti	RWTH Aachen University, Germany
Netta Iivari	University of Oulu, Finland
Patrick Wagstrom	IBM TJ Watson Research Center, USA
Reidar Conradi	Norwegian University of Science and Technology, Norway
Roberto Di Cosmo	Université Paris Diderot and INRIA, France

Sponsors

Table of Contents

Integration and Architecture

Business Ecosystems

Adoption and Evolution of OSS

Part II: Lightning Talks

Community Issues

OSS Quality

OSS in Different Domains

Development Practices

Business Ecosystems

Part III: Tool Demonstration Papers

Part IV: Short Industry Papers

Product Development

Industrial Experiences

Part V: Posters

Part VI: Workshops

A Comprehensive Study of Software Forks: Dates, Reasons and Outcomes

Gregorio Robles and Jesús M. González-Barahona

GSyC/Libresoft, Universidad Rey Juan Carlos
{gregorio.robles,jesus.gonzalez.barahona}@urjc.es

Summary. In general it is assumed that a software product evolves within the authoring company or group of developers that develop the project. However, in some cases different groups of developers make the software evolve in different directions, a situation which is commonly known as a fork. In the case of free software, although forking is a practice that is considered as a last resort, it is inherent to the four freedoms. This paper tries to shed some light on the practice of forking. Therefore, we have identified significant forks, several hundreds in total, and have studied them in depth. Among the issues that have been analyzed for each fork is the date when the forking occurred, the reason of the fork, and the outcome of the fork, i.e., if the original or the forking project are still developed. Our investigation shows, among other results, that forks occur in every software domain, that they have become more frequent in recent years, and that very few forks merge with the original project.

Keywords: free software, open source, forks, forking, social, legal, sustainability, software evolution.

1 Introduction

Issues related to the sustainability of software projects have historically been studied in software engineering in the field of software evolution. However, research on software evolution has always implicitly assumed that development and maintenance of a software is performed by the same organization or group of developers. It is a task of the creators of the software to make it evolve [13].

But in some cases a software project evolves in parallel, lead by different development teams. This is known as "forking". The term fork is derived from the POSIX standard for operating systems: the system call used so that a process generates a copy of itself is called `fork()`. As a consequence, there exist two copies of the process that run independently and may perform different tasks. In analogy to this situation, a software fork happens when there exist two independent software projects, deriving both from the same software source code base.

Forking may happen in proprietary environments, but it is *natural* in free software as the freedom to modify a software and redistribute modifications is part

I. Hammouda et al. (Eds.): OSS 2012, IFIP AICT 378, pp. 1–14, 2012.

of the freedoms that it grants. However, the free software movement has traditionally seen forking as something to avoid: forks split the community, introduce duplication of effort, reduce communication and may produce incompatibilities.

To the knowledge of the authors, no complete and homogeneous research on forking has been done by the software engineering research community. This paper has as main goal to raise a point of attention on this issue. The contributions of the paper can be summarized as follows: first, it offers a wide perspective of forking, identifying all significant forks. Second, it enters into detail in the reasons given for forking, presenting and classifying them. Third, it provides information on the outcome of the forks, in order to see if forking undermines the sustainability of the projects.

The structure of the paper is as follows: next, we will propose some definitions of forking and related concepts. Section 3 contains the related literature on software forking. Then, we introduce with detail the research questions that we target in this paper. Section 5 describes the methodology used for the identification and the study of forks. Results are shown in Section 6. Finally, conclusions are drawn and further research possibilities are offered.

2   Definitions

In this section we define a series of concepts used in this paper.

2.1   Clone

Cloning is the action of creating a software system designed to mimic another system. This can be done by reverse engineering or completely reimplementing from documentation or source code, or by the observation of the behavior and appearance of a software. Cloning is a common practice in free software [2].

2.2   Branch

Branching refers to the duplication of source code in a version management system. When branching occurs, parallel threads of development will take place. It is a common practice in free software projects to have branches. Software projects use branching for instance when developers do not want new features to be included in the stable branch. The popular GitHub service, which uses the `git` distributed versioning system, refers to branching as forking.

2.3   Fork

Forking occurs when a part of a development community (or a third party not related to the project) starts a completely independent line of development based on the source code basis of the project. To be considered as a fork, a project should have:

1. A new project name.

2. A branch of the software.
3. A parallel infrastructure (web site, versioning system, mailing lists, etc.).
4. And a new developer community (disjoint with the original).

2.4 Derivation

A derivation is the process of forming a new software system on the basis of an existing one, but ensuring compatibility between both systems. Derivations are common among Linux-based distributions[1]; new systems assemble software software programs and libraries that can and will be used in the other distributions without problems.

2.5 Mod

A mod is an enhancement made by enthusiasts to existing software. Mods are not standalone programs and require the user to have the original release in order to run it. They are specially popular in personal computer games. Scacchi has studied the culture of mods [19].

3 Related Literature

3.1 Software Engineering Related Research

The software engineering research literature on forking is, to the knowledge of the authors, very scarce. We have only found a technical report by Ernst *et al.* that looks specifically at forking [5]. They analyze a case study of a project forked because different requirements wanted to be met.

If we focus on software evolution articles, we find some related research. For instance, Xie *et al.* talk about parallel evolution of some free software projects in [22]. While analyzing the validity of Lehman's *laws* of software evolution on several free software projects, they discover that projects tend to have several branches (although the authors use the term *fork*) of the source code tree, one that is used for the correction of errors and another one for the inclusion of new features.

Although forks have not been specifically the matter of research *per se*, there have been some publications where notorious forks have been used as case studies for software evolution studies. In this sense, Fischer *et al.* studied the evolution of what they call a *product family*, three variants of the BSD kernel [7]. The BSDs are studied as well by Yamamoto *et al.* to measure the similarity of the source code [23], and by Yu *et al.* to analyze their maintainability [24].

There have been some efforts to study copying of source code in free software projects. Mockus performed a massive survey of free software code and found that many projects shared files [15]. Germán *et al.* analyzed the legal consequences and issues that code being copied (*reused*) raises [10].

---

[1] A complete graph on the various families of Linux-based derivations can be found in the Wikipedia at http://en.wikipedia.org/wiki/File:Gldt.svg

3.2   Related Free Software Literature

Forking has been widely discussed outside the research literature in the free software community. In Raymond's Hacker Dictionary we can find that "[f]orking is considered a Bad Thing not merely because it implies a lot of wasted effort in the future, but because forks tend to be accompanied by a great deal of strife and acrimony between the successor groups over issues of legitimacy, succession, and design direction. There is serious social pressure against forking. As a result, major forks (such as the Gnu-Emacs/XEmacs split, the fissionings of the 386BSD group into three daughter projects, and the short-lived GCC/EGCS split) are rare enough that they are remembered individually in hacker folklore." [17].

Di Bona mentions the possibility of forking as a fear of losing control of individuals and especially companies [4]. Eric Raymond argues in [18] that the free software movement has *an elaborate but largely unadmitted set of ownership customs* that include the possibility, but mainly avoidance of forking. As Feller *et al.* put it, "[t]here is a strong taboo against forking" [6]. Neville-Neil agrees with this position and recommends to *think before you fork* [16]. He notes that only abandoned projects should be forked as developers who fork may be taken as *a petulant and spoiled child who wants to take your toys and go home*. Bezroukov indicates that ego-related issues can lead to forking, and that forking can cause the death of both initial and forked projects [1]. In Fogel's "Producing OSS" book [8], the topic is handled in detail. First, some sections are devoted to the consequences of *forkability*, what the author calls the mere possibility of doing a fork. Then, in a very practical way, he discusses how to manage a fork when it occurs.

3.3   Related Research from Other Areas of Knowledge

There are other areas of research beyond software engineering that have put some attention on forking. So, from the economics literature, Lerner and Tirole [14] identified as one of the four main roles of a leader in an FOSS project to keep the project together and prevent forking (also pointed out by Germán [9]), Weber *et al.* analyze forking from the software business perspective [21], Kogut *et al.* look it from the point of view of distributed innovation [12], and Karpf *et al.* have had some thoughts on governance, although they discuss them not using a software project but Wikipedia [11].

4   Research Questions

In this study, we have targeted following research questions:

4.1   How Many (Significant) Forks Exist?

The aim of this question is to obtain the number of significant forks. When we started with this study, we had the impression that forking -being discouraged by the community- is seldom performed, but the exact number of projects that had been forked was unknown.

To answer this question we will have to identify all significant forks that have occurred in the history of free software. When identifying the forked projects, we will record the software domain in order to determine if forking is more common in certain types of software projects. Our initial (probably naive) assumption was that forking is more frequent in some domains.

4.2 Is Forking Becoming More Frequent?

With this question we want to verify if the number of forks per year has been growing. Our initial (again naive) assumption is that forking is becoming more frequent in the last years. The first reason for assuming this is that nowadays more companies are leading free software projects; in such cases, *organizational and strategic tensions* between the goals of the company and the rest of the community may appear. If members of the community think that the company does not take their contributions and requirements into consideration, a fork may happen. The second reason is that the number of projects has grown exponentially [3], so we assume that the probability of having forks increases.

4.3 What Are the Main Reasons for Forking?

When reading the literature, and especially if we have in mind the recommendations given by the free software community, forking is a very sensitive topic. Those who create a fork have to argue that forking was a last resort [8]. With this question we want to know which are the most frequent circumstances for forking. We part from the following classification of reasons, that is derived from our knowledge of very known forks:

- Technical (addition of functionality): Some developers want to include new functionalities into the project, but the main developer(s) do not accept it. As an example of this type of fork we have xpdf and Poppler.
- More community-driven development: This occurs when the original leaders, whether a company, an institution or an independent group of developers, does not take into account the community. Then developers seeking for more open and public development practices create a fork. Examples of this type are following well-known forks: EGCS from GCC, and XEmacs from GNU Emacs.
- Discontinuation of the original project: The original project is unmaintained and a new developer community takes it over. The Apache web server project would be such a fork.
- Commercial strategy forks: This type of forks happens when a company forks an existing project to meet some commercial strategy. Commercial strategy forks include those where a software is released as free software by the company, or when the company creates a proprietary version of a free software. Examples of this type are OpenOffice.org from StarOffice, and Webkit from KHTML. In the opposite situation, when the community has

concerns about the commercial strategy of a company, the fork belongs to the *More community-driven development* category; the `LibreOffice` fork from `OpenOffice.org` when Oracle took over Sun would be such a fork.

- Legal issues: Legal aspects such as disagreements on the license, trademarks or changes to conform laws (encryption) are included here. An example of such a fork is `X.Org`, that originated from `XFree`.
- Differences among developer team: The developer team disagrees on fundamental issues (beyond mere technical matters) related to the software development and the project. The `OpenBSD` fork from `NetBSD` is an example of such a type of fork.

4.4   What Is the Outcome of Forking?

David A. Wheeler notes that there are four possible outcomes of a fork[2]:

1. The discontinuation of the fork.
2. A re-merging of the fork.
3. The discontinuation of the original.
4. and successful branching, typically with differentiation.

Wheeler provides an example for each of the cases, and adds that in his opinion, the discontinuation of the fork is the most common case as it is easy to declare a fork, but continuation requires considerable effort.

To Wheeler's classification we will add the situation where the original and the forked software projects have both been discontinued.

5   Methodology

Our intention is to document all significant forks. At first, we started performing Google searches for the term *software fork*, but the number of responses (in the range of 45,000,000) showed that this would be not embraceable.

However, one of the first terms appearing in the Google search was a page with a list of software forks in the English Wikipedia[3]. The web page contained around 30 software forks.

In addition, we have searched for *software fork* using the English Wikipedia search box. As of August 2011, the result offers 1500 Wikipedia pages. After manually inspecting all these pages, a list of 235 potential forks was obtained.

So, for the purpose of our paper, we assume that a fork is significant if a reference to it appears in the English Wikipedia. We have partially tested this assumption by looking at the 300 top-positioned results of searching for *software fork* in Google, and have not found forks we did not already have on our list.

The analysis procedure we used for each potential fork was following:

1. Locate the main website of the original software.

---

[2] http://www.dwheeler.com/oss_fs_why.html#forking
[3] http://en.wikipedia.org/wiki/List_of_software_forks

2. Locate the main website of the forking software.
3. Identify the software domain of the project. This information can be obtained by using the software classification of the Wikipedia, SourceForge or Free(Code).
4. Identify the reason of the fork. We inspect the website of the forking software for any information on this. In general, in its main page or in an "About" or "History" section an explanation can be found. If not, we analyze the original software web page and the Wikipedia pages of the projects for any reference. If none of the previous is successful, we perform a Google search.
5. Identify the date of the fork. Usually a date can be found together with the reason. In some cases the registration date in a software forge, the first release or the first commit in the versioning system of the forking project has been considered. The error of the dates obtained may be in the range of months, although for our purposes this is assumable.
6. Identify the outcome of the fork, including dates. Usually we have looked for the last release or the last activity on the versioning system. If there has been no activity since mid-2010, we have labeled the project as discontinued.

All this information, including any other extra relevant facts that help understanding the reason of the fork, has been written down in a log file (our research script). The research script is publicly available for replicability purposes, and for further analysis and research[4]. We have tried to indicate always the original URL where the information has been taken from. Our intention, as well, has been to use primary sources, avoiding thus Wikipedia pages, although this has not always been possible.

During August 2011 we obtained the list of significant forks. We analyzed the forks on an individual basis during a two-week period in August, and a final set of projects during one week in March[5]. The analysis was performed at a pace of 5 to 8 forks per hour.

6 Results

6.1 Number of Forks

The total number of forks we have been able to identify is 220, as from the total number of potential forks (235) some of them were clones, branches or derivations. For instance, `Wireshark` appears as a fork of `Ethereal`. However, investigating this case, we found that what happened was a renaming due to trademark problems with the Ethereal name; it was the same community that was developing the software under a different name. Another example is `Gereqi`, a multimedia program that is considered in Wikipedia as a fork of `Amarok`. In its main web page, the author of `Gereqi` states that the software does not contain a single line of `Amarok`, and demonstrates it with the fact that `Gereqi` has been implemented using a different programming language.

---

[4] http://gsyc.urjc.es/~grex/oss2012forking
[5] The research script includes the dates when the forks were analyzed.

Table 1. Forks by software domain

Software category	Frequency
Networking (servers, clients, p2p...)	52 (23.6%)
Web applications (CMS, LMS, blogs, wikis...)	34 (15.5%)
Development (IDEs, libraries...)	29 (13.2%)
Multimedia (audio, video...)	18 (8.2%)
Games/Entertainment	18 (8.2%)
System (kernel, file systems...)	17 (7.8%)
Desktop	16 (7.3%)
Utilities	12 (5.5%)
Graphics	7 (3.2%)
Databases	6 (2.7%)
Business (ERP, CRM...)	5 (2.3%)
Security	3 (1.4%)
Package Management	3 (1.4%)

While inspecting the list of forks, we have found projects where forking is common (e.g., MySQL[6], Tux Racer, DC++, WakkaWiki, L2J...). It seems that once a fork has occurred, more forks are *cheaper*, in the sense that minor reasons have to be provided to start a new fork.

Table 1 provides information of the software domains where forks have occurred. Our initial assumption was that forking was more specific to certain domains. Our results shows that this is not true, and that we have found projects forked from operating system kernels to end-user software.

We have not studied in detail if these results are proportional to the share of free software projects, for instance in Debian, Free(Code) or SourceForge. But a fast inspection of the most prominent tags at Free(Code)[7] reveals that the most popular software domains are Internet, software development, web, and multimedia, in line with our results.

Observation #1: We have found 220 significant software forks. Forking occurs in every software domain.

6.2   Temporal Evolution of Forks

From the 220 forks, we have only identified the forking date for 210 of them. For 10 of the forks we could not obtain the date when the fork occurred, while for another 28 projects we could only find the year of forking, not the month. For the year 2011 we have only partial data, as our list of forks had been obtained August 2011.

---

[6] See "A look at the MySQL forks", http://lwn.net/Articles/329626/
[7] http://freecode.com/tags

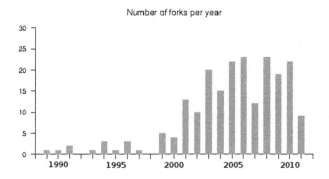

Fig. 1. Number of forks per year

The result of the temporal evolution of forks is shown in a histogram in Fig. 1. Prior to 1998, the number of forks is testimonial (13 in total), while the number increases in recent years, with around 20 forks per year since 2003.

Interestingly enough, the number of forks does not follow the exponential growth path described by Deshpande and Riehle [3], so the total number of free software projects seems not to be related with the amount of forks. Maybe a proportionality is given with company-led free software projects, although this is something that we cannot state from our study and is left for further research.

> **Observation #2: Forks have become more frequent in recent years, but the number of forks does not grow proportionally with the number of free software projects.**

6.3 Reasons for Forking

The free software community is sensible about the problem of forking, as it can be seen from the fact that we have been able to find a reason for the fork for 9 out of 10 forks.

While inspecting the forks and assigning them to the categories of reasons, we included a new category -*experimental forks*- which might be seen as a subcategory of *technical* reasons. These type of forks occur when some of the developers -usually a minority- want to introduce major changes into the project, while many others prefer a more conservative approach. In this cases, instead of just opening a branch that would have it very difficult to become the future main branch, a fork is created. These types of forks could be labeled as *friendly forks*, as many of them come with the approval of the original community.

Table 2 shows the result of classifying the main reason given for the forks. We had problems to discriminate among some categories, especially between "technical", "differences among the developer team" and "more community-driven

Table 2. Main reasons for forking

Reason	Frequency
Technical	60 (27.3%)
Discontinuation of the original project	44 (20.0%)
More community-driven development	29 (13.2%)
Legal issues	24 (10.9%)
Commercial strategy forks	20 (9.1%)
Differences among developer team	16 (7.3%)
Experimental	5 (2.3%)
Not Found	22 (10.0%)

development". This is because in many of the forks two of the reasons, or even the three of them appeared in some way. So for instance, `Carrier` (formerly `Funpidgin`) was set up because the main developers of the `Pidgin` instant messaging client refused to introduce a functionality that allowed to manually resize the text input area. Although this has been sorted as a *technical* reason, a closer inspection showed that the argumentation had a more profound basis.

All in all, as observed from Table 2 although the major force for forking is of technical nature (27.3%), the main reason to fork is very distributed among the various categories under consideration.

> **Observation #3: For most of the forks it is possible to find the reason of forking.**

6.4 Resolution of Forks

We have inspected the outcome of all forks following Wheeler's (augmented) classification. The results are shown visually in Fig. 2.

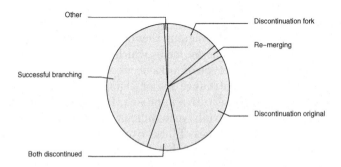

Fig. 2. Outcome of the forks

Wheeler hypothesized that most forks do not survive their original projects. Our results throw the contrary situation: the percentage of discontinued original projects doubles the discontinued forked projects.

The results may change radically if we consider apart those forks that are a continuation of a discontinued original project. This is for instance the case for the `Apache` fork of the `NCSA HTTPd` server or the `RedDwarf` fork of the `Project Darkstar`. In both cases, the institutions behind the original projects (the NCSA and Sun, recently taken over by Oracle) ceased development and support, and a fork was created. 44 forks are a *continuation forks* (see Table 3).

Table 3. Outcome of forks, considering if the cause of the fork is the possible or actual discontinuation of the original project

Outcome	Frequency
Successful branching, typically with differentiation	95 (43.6%)
The discontinuation of the original	65 (29.8%)
Fork was response to (possible or actual) discontinuation of original	44 (20.0%)
Fork was due to other reasons	21 (9.8%)
The discontinuation of the fork	30 (13.8%)
None of them currently under development	19 (8.7%)
A re-merging of the fork	7 (3.2%)
Other	2 (0.9%)

These numbers show that the amount of original projects and forked projects that are discontinued is similar, being the discontinuation of the forking project slightly more frequent than the one of original projects. Nevertheless the difference is not important enough to meet Wheeler's hypothesis. We interpret this as a consequence of developers being aware of the implications of forking, including the disadvantages of competing with the original project (the need for making the fork reasonable to the community, the use of a new name for the forked software project, etc.). Only if they consider that they have enough reasons and good changes of success, a fork is done.

From Table 3, we can also interpret that when forking occurs the sustainability of the software is ensured. Our argument to sustain such a claim is that forked projects survives for long time - whether original or as the fork. The number of projects where both, original and forked, projects are discontinued is very low compared to the usual numbers of abandoned projects in free software [20].

The number of forks that merge with the original project is very low. In addition, merging often happens by dismissing one of the projects as developers report that integrating changes is not a simple task. In the case of GCC and EGCS, the technical superiority of the fork made it become the *official* compiler of the GNU project, discontinuing the GCC source code base. The opposite happened with the `libc` Linux fork from GNU `libc`; with a new, enhanced version of GNU `libc`, Linux stopped using its own `libc`. The authors report that "changes that had been made in Linux libc could not be merged back into glibc because the authorship status of that code was unclear and the GNU project is quite strict about recording copyright"[8].

Observation #4: Most of the forks evolve in parallel to the original project. The chance of discontinuation of a fork is almost the same as the original, even if they have a disadvantageous starting situation. Software that forks ensures sustainability. Few forks re-merge, and when this happens, fewer integrate source code.

---

7   Conclusions and Further Research

In this paper we have presented to the knowledge of the authors the first comprehensive study on software forks. We have provided some insight into the temporal patterns of software forks, the reasons for forking and what the outcome of the forking has been for the original and forking project.

In the opinion of the authors, forking is going to be a more relevant and frequent situation in the next future. Free software is nowadays already the root of many other software project which build on top of it (for instance Android); the disparity in goals among the root project and others building on top of it will produce more forks.

On the other hand, technology is lowering the technical barrier of creating a fork. For instance, distributed versioning systems such as `git` are more suitable to forking, as they provide a copy of the complete history of the project; not only a branch can be built, but a complete copy of the infrastructure is provided. However this is still not the case for bug-tracking systems and mailing lists, which are not distributed and difficult to fork. In our opinion, technology should make forks easier; the convenience of forking should just be a strategic matter that allows to maintain balances among the stakeholders of a project. On the other hand, lowering the technological barrier to fork may increase the number of *friendly* experimental forks that boost innovation.

There are several topics related to forking that further research should target. First, it would be interesting to find out how much original and forking projects collaborate, even in an involuntary way, by exchanging code, bug reports and fixes. Second, parallel software development should be devoted a closer look; technology and processes should facilitate integration. Third, further research should focus on understanding how the community moves when a fork occurs. This would include among others answering questions such as where the key developers go, how many of the developers are active both in the original and forking projects, or if there is any correlation between a *positive resolution* of the fork and who pushed for it. Fourth, we think that it would be valuable to focus on how the socioeconomic and technical context may influence the probability and the type of a fork. So, for instance, if project maturity boosts forking or not.

---

[8] http://blogs.fsfe.org/ciaran/?p=85

And fifth, we think that a study on forking in projects led by software companies could answer many interesting questions that have not been addressed in our work.

Acknowledgements. The work of G. Robles and J.M. González-Barahona has been funded in part by the European Commission under project ALERT (FP7-IST-25809) and by the Spanish Gov. under project SobreSale (TIN2011-28110). We would like to thank the anonymous reviewers for their insightful comments.

References

1. Bezroukov, N.: A second look at the Cathedral and The Bazar. First Monday 4(12) (1997)
2. Capiluppi, A., Boldyreff, C., Stol, K.-J.: Successful reuse of software components: A report from the open source perspective. In: International Conference on Open Source Software Systems, pp. 159–176 (2011)
3. Deshpande, A., Riehle, D.: The Total Growth of Open Source. In: Proceedings of the Fourth Conference on Open Source Systems, pp. 197–209. Springer (2008)
4. DiBona, C., Ockman, S., Stone, M.: Introduction. In: DiBona, C., Ockman, S., Stone, M. (eds.) Open Sources. Voices from the Open Source Revolution, pp. 1–17. O'Reilly (1999)
5. Ernst, N.A., Easterbrook, S.M., Mylopoulos, J.: Code forking in open-source software: a requirements perspective. CoRR, abs/1004.2889 (2010)
6. Feller, J., Fitzgerald, B.: A Framework Analysis of the Open Source Software Development Paradigm. In: 21st International Conference of Information Systems, Brisbane, Australia, pp. 58–69 (2010)
7. Fischer, M., Oberleitner, J., Ratzinger, J., Gall, H.: Mining evolution data of a product family. ACM SIGSOFT Software Engineering Notes 30(4), 1–5 (2005)
8. Fogel, K.: Producing Open Source Software - How to run a successful free software project. O'Reilly (2005)
9. Germán, D.M.: The GNOME project: a case study of open source, global software development. Journal of Software Process: Improvement and Practice 8(4), 201–215 (2004)
10. Germán, D.M., Di Penta, M., Guéhéneuc, Y.-G., Antoniol, G.: Code siblings: Technical and legal implications of copying code between applications. In: International Working Conference on Mining Software Repositories (MSR), pp. 81–90. IEEE (2009)
11. Karpf, D.: What Can Wikipedia Tell Us about Open Source Politics?. In: Conference Proceedings of JITP 2010: The Politics of Open Source, pp. 2–31 (2010)
12. Kogut, B., Metiu, A.: Open-source software development and distributed innovation. Oxford Review of Economic Policy 17(2) (2001)
13. Lehman, M.M., Belady, L.A. (eds.): Program evolution: Processes of software change. Academic Press Professional, Inc., San Diego (1985)
14. Lerner, J., Tirole, J.: Some simple economics of open source. Journal of Industrial Economics 50(2), 197–234 (2002)
15. Mockus, A.: Amassing and indexing a large sample of version control systems: Towards the census of public source code history. In: MSR 2009: Proceedings of the 2009 International Working Conference on Mining Software Repositories, pp. 11–20 (2009)

16. Neville-Neil, G.V.: Think before you fork. Commun. ACM 54, 34–35 (2011)
17. Raymond, E.S.: The New Hacker's Dictionary, 3rd edn. MIT Press, Cambridge (1996)
18. Raymond, E.S.: The Cathedral and the Bazaar. In: Raymond, E.S. (ed.) Musings on Linux and Open Source by an Accidental Revolutionary pp. 79–135. O'Reilly (1999)
19. Scacchi, W.: Computer game mods, modders, modding, and the mod scene. First Monday 15(5) (2010)
20. Schweik, C.M., English, R., Paienjton, Q., Haire, S.: Success and Abandonment in Open Source Commons: Selected Findings from an Empirical Study of Source-forge.net Projects. In: Proceedings of the Sixth International Conference on Open Source Systems 2010, pp. 91–101 (2010)
21. Weber, S.: The Success of Open Source. Harvard University Press (April 2004)
22. Xie, G., Chen, J., Neamtiu, I.: Towards a better understanding of software evolution: An empirical study on open source software. In: Proceedings of the International Conference on Software Maintenance, pp. 51–60. IEEE (2009)
23. Yamamoto, T., Matsushita, M., Kamiya, T., Inoue, K.: Measuring Similarity of Large Software Systems Based on Source Code Correspondence. In: Bomarius, F., Komi-Sirviö, S. (eds.) PROFES 2005. LNCS, vol. 3547, pp. 530–544. Springer, Heidelberg (2005)
24. Yu, L., Schach, S.R., Chen, K., Heller, G.Z., Offutt, A.J.: Maintainability of the kernels of open-source operating systems: A comparison of Linux with FreeBSD, NetBSD, and OpenBSD. Journal of Systems and Software 79(6), 807–815 (2006)

A Model of Open Source Developer Foundations

Dirk Riehle and Sebastian Berschneider

Friedrich-Alexander University Erlangen-Nürnberg, Computer Science Department,
Martensstr. 3, 90158 Erlangen, Germany
dirk@riehle.org
http://osr.cs.fau.de

Abstract. Many community open source projects are of high economic relevance. As these projects mature, their leaders face a choice of continuing the project as is, making the project join an existing foundation, or creating their own foundation for the project. This article presents a model of open source developer foundations that project leaders can use to compare existing foundations with their needs or to design their own. The model is based on a three-iteration qualitative study involving interviews and supplementary materials review. To demonstrate its usefulness, we apply the model to nine foundations and present their organizational choices in a comparative table format.

1 Introduction

Community open source projects are open source software projects that are owned by a community of stakeholders [10]. The Linux kernel, the Apache projects, and the Eclipse platform are examples of community open source software. Community owned projects are to be viewed in contrast to single-vendor open source projects like MySQL, SugarCRM, or Alfresco [8] that are owned and managed by a single stakeholder, the company. As community open source projects mature and become increasingly economically relevant, they face a choice: Continue as is, seek the protection of an existing open source foundation, or create their own foundation.

The benefits of an open source foundation for the projects are manifold [9]. Most notably, the foundation acts as the legal representative of the projects. Thus, it can represent the projects' interests in court and protect the individual contributing software developers. Also, a foundation increases the projects' credibility and makes them less dependent on individual people, which in turn increases industry involvement and makes the projects more sustainable. Thus, the creation of a foundation is a natural step in the life-cycle of successful maturing community open source projects.

Open source foundations are similar to traditional consortia. In fact, many foundations chose to incorporate using legal forms typically chosen for consortia. The main difference is the choice of an open source license for the software being developed. By using an open source license, a foundation cannot exclude non-members from utilizing the software. Thus, the software is typically not considered competitively differentiating. This is most forcefully demonstrated by some foundations choosing a for-public-benefit organizational form rather than the for-member-benefit form that traditional consortia typically take.

I. Hammouda et al. (Eds.): OSS 2012, IFIP AICT 378, pp. 15–28, 2012.
© IFIP International Federation for Information Processing 2012

Today, dozens if not hundreds of such open source foundations exist. Next to large well-known foundations like the Linux Foundation, Apache Software Foundation, or the Eclipse Foundation, many smaller niche foundations exist, catering to the specific needs of their projects. These specific needs may be country, culture, or jurisdiction-specific (e.g. OpenPlans, Kuali, or WorldVistA), or they may be specific to a particular industry (e.g. TOPCASED, GENIVI, OpenAPC), or they may be specific to a particular horizontal layer in the technology stack (e.g. Drupal Foundation, Document Foundation, KDE e.V.) or any combination thereof.

Joining an existing foundation or creating a new one is a daunting task. First, a project considering joining an existing foundation has to ask itself whether the foundation matches the project's interests. Second, if the answer is no, the project has to consider creating its own foundation. For these processes, there is no guidance, yet the compatibility of a foundation with the projects' needs is a crucial factor in ensuring the project's sustainability.

In our analysis of open source foundations, we need to distinguish between developer foundations, created by software development firms, and IT user foundations, created by users of the software who are using open source to avoid vendor-lock-in and keep prices down. This paper is only about developer foundations.

This paper presents a qualitative analysis of the structure and processes of existing open source developer foundations. A three-step process of analyzing existing foundations led to a model of open source foundations that project leaders can use to compare existing foundations with their needs or design their own. The paper's resulting contributions are:

- A model of community open source developer foundations that has been derived from a three-step qualitative study process
- The comparison of nine open source foundations using this model and demonstrating its ability to capture the complexity of existing foundations

The paper is structured as follows. Section 2 outlines our research process. Section 3 presents a model of community open source developer foundations. Section 4 applies the model to nine existing open source foundations and demonstrates its usefulness. Section 5 reviews related work and section 6 concludes the paper.

2   Research Process

This paper shows the result of an exploratory theory generation process for developer foundations; it does not yet quantitatively validate this theory. We use the terms "theory" and "model" of developer foundations interchangeably in this article. The theory was generated in a three-step iterative process. The first step created the first model, the second and third step created refined models based on additional qualitative research. The first and second step were performed by the second author under the guidance of the first author, the third step was performed by the first author alone. The second author is a student of the first author.

2.1   First Iteration: Initial Model

For the first iteration, the first author chose six different foundations for initial analysis. These six foundations were the Free Software Foundation, the Linux Foundation, the Apache Software Foundation, the Eclipse Foundation, the GENIVI consortium, and the Albatross community. These foundations were chosen for their breadth and maturity. The second author then gathered and analyzed these foundations, using the following data:

* Telephone interviews with foundation representatives
* Email exchanges to clarify issues from the interviews
* By-laws and other materials from the foundations' websites

The second author analyzed the materials using an open coding approach. He grouped the codes into initial categories that then became the building blocks of the first model [4]. This led to the definition of sub-categories like "membership" and their possible values like "person" or "corporation".

2.2   Second Iteration: Qualitative Validation

For the second iteration, the first author provided four more foundations to the second author that were supposed to serve as a qualitative validation of the first-iteration model: Would the initial model be able to capture the complexity of these four new foundations? The four new foundations were the KDE, Mozilla, OpenAPC, and TOPCASED foundations.

The attempt to describe these four new foundations using the initial foundation model surfaced several problems with the initial model. For example, the initial model had not captured the possibility of financing a foundation through a for-profit subsidiary (Mozilla). Thus, the result of the second iteration was a revised model that enhanced several of the original model dimensions and added one more.

2.3   Third Iteration: Categorization and Review

For the third iteration, the first author took over and created a stringent categorization hierarchy from the available data. For example, the rather broad single category Intellectual Property was split into subcategories Project License, Patent License Grant, and IP Ownership. The accompanying attribute values were rearranged accordingly and in-line with the original coding. The Albatross community was recognized as single-vendor-owned open source rather than community open source and consequently removed.

The resulting hierarchy of concepts and categories is called category, attribute, and possible value in Tables 1 and 2, the final analysis result after the third iteration. We found this nomenclature to be more useful than the general terminology of categories and sub-categories. The resulting model was presented to the original correspondents of the second author from the first iteration of this research process. While not a representative survey, the generally positive feedback confirmed the quality of the model. A few minor corrections, mostly renaming of codes, was applied to the model. The result is the model presented in Section 3.

3   Model of Developer Foundations

3.1   Model Overview

Tables 1 and 2 show the final result of the combined three-step exploratory analysis using interviews and supplementary web and literature research. It presents the model as a stringent category hierarchy with

- column 1, "category", being the top category,
- column 2, "attribute", being the first layer of sub-categories, and
- column 3, "possible values", being a third layer of categories.

Column 4 contains short codes for the possible values provided in column 3. Column 5 describes constraints between the categories, providing a short form of capturing category interactions. Column 6 then provides some explanation of the meaning of the attribute (the first level of sub-categories).

The following Subsections explain the model categories.

3.2   The General Model Category

The **General:Purpose** of a developer foundation is to benefit the public (G:PB) or its members (G:MB). Member benefit does not exclude public benefit, however, it is not a primary goal of the foundation then. This choice of public vs. member benefit strongly influences how the foundation incorporates.

The **General:Incorporation** of a developer foundation is typically as a non-profit foundation (G:F) or a non-profit consortium (G:C). The difference is that a foundation serves the public and a consortium serves its members. The actual choice of the corporate form depends on the jurisdiction of incorporation. In the U.S.A., for example, the Apache Software Foundation is a 501(c)3 non-profit foundation, while the Eclipse Foundation is a 501(c)6 non-profit consortium. In Germany, they might have chosen the form of an e.V. or a GmbH. Most countries have forms of incorporation that support for-public-benefit or for-member-benefit organizations.

The **General:Members** of a developer foundation can be both natural persons (G:NP) or juristic persons (G:JP). Natural persons are people, and juristic persons are incorporated organizations. Any combination is possible, as are many restrictions. For example, the Mozilla Foundation has no members, the Free Software Foundation only has natural people (developers) as members, and the Linux Foundation has both natural and juristic persons as members.

3.3   The Philosophy Model Category

The **Philosophy:Commercial Stance** of a developer foundation can be that of a free-software-enforced (P:FSE) or closed-software-allowed (P:CSA) stance. Taking a free-software-enforced stance prevents taking enhancements to the open source software private, thereby limiting the business models possible with the software. Taking a closed-software-allowed stance allows a much broader range of business models, including those in which the open source software is enhanced without those enhancements being open sourced as well. The stance strongly determines the choice of a license.

This is an abbreviation of a more complex discussion carried out elsewhere in more detail [11]. The Free Software Foundation and the KDE e.V. are examples of foundations that take the more restrictive free-software-enforced stance, while the Apache Software Foundation and the Eclipse Foundation are examples of foundations that take the more permissive closed-software-allowed stance. In general, the more commercially minded, the more likely a permissive stance.

The **Philosophy:Development Model** of a foundation can be open (P:OD) or closed (P:CD). In the case of open development, all or most of the development artifacts are available in public as they are being developed. In the case of closed development, the project communities keep the project artifacts to themselves and only release them to the public in major increments, if they release them at all. Legally, in the restrictive sense of a license choice, the software may still be open source, though. Closed development is fairly uncommon but it does happen; an example is GENIVI, a consortium developing a Linux-based stack for in-vehicle infotainment.

3.4 The Intellectual Property Model Category

The **Intellectual Property:Project License** that a foundation chooses can be any of the 50+ open source licenses that have been officially accepted by the Open Source Initiative (OSI) as such [6]. Sometimes, foundations develop their own license, which then has to pass the OSI's license review process. Simplifying, we reduce the choice of license to either a reciprocal (e.g. GPL or AGPL) (IP:RL) or a permissive license (e.g. BSD or Apache license) (IP:PL).

- A reciprocal license forces software developers who are embedding the reciprocally-licensed software in a product to open source the embedding code when distributing the product.
- A permissive license does not force the developer to open source the embedding software code when distributing the software.

There are many options, and this simplification does not do justice to the wealth of choices one faces in choosing or designing a license. German et al. discuss some these issues and their implications [5]. In general, a free-software-enforced stance (P:FSE) goes well with a reciprocal license, and an closed-source-allowed stance (P:CSA) goes well with a permissive license.

A foundation has the option of providing the same source code under multiple licenses to increase flexibility. Contributors typically are required to accept all licenses, as enforced through a contributor agreement, see below. The Mozilla Foundation, bundles three licenses (the foundation's MPL, the LGPL, and the GPL) into its so-called tri-license. Derivative projects can then chose which license to utilize.

Table 1. Model of Open Source Developer Foundations, Part 1

Category	Attribute	Possible Values	Value Short Code	Constraints	Comments
		Model of Open Source Developer Foundations 1 / 2			
General	Purpose	• Public benefit • Member benefit	PB MB	Single choice	Implies form of incorporation
General	Incorporation	• Foundation • Consortium	F C	Single choice	E.g. 501(c)3 vs. 501(c)6 (United States) or e.V. vs. GmbH (Germany)
Philosophy	Members	• Natural persons • Juristic persons	NP JP	Multiple choice, including none	Any possible number of restrictions
Philosophy	Commercial stance	• Free software enforced • Closed software allowed	FSE CSA	Single choice	Implies license choice, including patent grant regulation
Philosophy	Development model	• Open development • Closed development	OD CD	Single choice	
Intellectual Property (IP)	Project license	• Reciprocal • Permissive	RL PL	Multiple choice; at least one	May or may not use their own license; may provide multiple licenses
Intellectual Property (IP)	Patent license grant	• No grant • Grant for use • Grant for use + embedding	NPG UPG EPG	Single choice	Usually regulated through project license
Intellectual Property (IP)	IP ownership	• No IP ownership required • Relicensing rights grant • Copyright assignment	NIP RRG CA	Single choice	Realized through contributor agreement

Continued in Table 2

Table 2. Model of Open Source Developer Foundations, Part 2

			Model of Open Source Developer Foundations 2 / 2		
Category	Attribute	Possible Values	Value Short Code	Constraints	Comments
Governance	Board membership	• Democratic (elected) • Meritocratic (earned) • Autocratic (self-appointed)	DB MB AB	Single choice	Actual value set can be much larger
Governance	Project membership	• Democratic (elected) • Meritocratic (earned) • Autocratic (appointed)	DP MP AP	Single choice	Actual value set can be much larger
Governance	Natural member career	• User/developer/committer • Project manager/leader • Officer, board member	UDC PMC BRD	Multiple choice, in-cluding none	Typically applies to natural persons only; actual career steps can be much more fine-grain
Governance	Juristic member level	• Financing level • Developer level	FL DL	Multi-dimensional choice	Typically applies to juristic persons only
Financing	Foundation	• Membership fees • Sponsorship • Gifts and grants • For-profit subsidiary	MF S GG FPS	Multiple choice, at least one	
Financing	Projects	• Foundation • Members	PFF PMF	Multiple choice, at least one	Typically only single choice though
Operations	Infrastructure	• Foundation • Members	IFO IMO	Multiple choice, at least one	
Operations	Back office	• Volunteers • Employees	BOV BOE	Multiple choice, at least one	

The **Intellectual Property:Patent License Grant** can be none (IP:NPG), for-use (IP:UPG), or for-use and embedding (IP:EPG).

- If no patent license grant is provided through the project license or a contributor agreement (see IP ownership below), then users may have to pay royalties to the patent holder. This option is uncommon, because one of the reasons for creating a foundation is to avoid such legal uncertainty.
- If a patent license grant is provided for-use, then the software can be used without paying royalties under the original open source license. A software developer who wants to sell software that embeds the open source code under a different license may have to pay the original patent holder royalties.
- If a patent license grant is provided for use and embedding, a software developer can embed the open source code in a commercial product and sell the software under a commercial license without having to pay royalties to the patent holder.

The **Intellectual Property:IP Ownership** determines the rights the foundation wants to acquire of the software code. It may be none (IP:NIP), a relicensing right (IP:RRG), or the full copyright (IP:CA). Some foundations do not require to receive any rights but rely on the project license to regulate intellectual property issues around the project. An example is the KDE e.V. (foundation), however, this is the more uncommon choice. (KDE offers a transfer but does not require it.) Most foundations ask contributors to sign a contributor agreement before they make their first contribution, which either provides the foundation with a relicensing right or directly signs over the copyright to the foundation.

- A relicensing rights grant asks a contributor to provide the foundation with the right to relicense the contributed software code. This is helpful should the foundation decide to change its license at a later point of time. It also provides the foundation control over the whole code base, because the foundation becomes the single and only holder of a complete relicensing right while each contributor holds rights only to their typically small piece.
- A copyright assignment asks a contributor to transfer all rights to the foundation, which then becomes the sole owner of the source code. This includes all the rights from the relicensing rights grant. In addition, it allows the foundation to act as the representative of the project, for example, in court. In particular, the Free Software Foundation requires a copyright assignment and declares its intent to enforce its intellectual property rights.

3.5   The Governance Model Category

The **Governance:Board Membership** of a foundation can be anything from democratic (GV:DB) on the one end through meritocratic (GV:MB) in between to autocratic (GV:AB) on the other end. Some foundations allow for elections of board members from the member base or even general public while others have a set board that answers only to itself. The Free Software Foundation and the Mozilla Foundation are examples of the latter, the Linux Foundation and the Apache Software Foundation are examples of the former.

The **Governance:Project Membership** can be anything from democratic (GV:DP) (elected by membership) through meritocratic (GV:MP) (earned status through continued project work) to autocratic (GV:AP) (appointed by board). This is particularly important for the project leadership. Most foundations, for example, the Apache Software Foundation and the Eclipse Foundation, support a meritocratic model in which project members earn their stripes before being elected into respective positions, but the other options also occur.

The **Governance:Natural Member Career** determines the career that a natural person, typically a developer, can have inside the foundation. The Apache Foundation provides the original model of this career [2]. The career design varies between foundation, but one can repeatedly find these three components [7]:

- The traditional open source career steps of increasing status are user, contributor, and committer (a.ka. maintainer) (GV:UDC). A user uses the software and helps others, a contributor makes contributions that have to pass review before they are accepted, and a committer reviews the work that contributors submit and can make contributions to the project that don't have to pass anyone else's review.
- Foundations make the project management level explicit (GV:PMC) that is tied to the committer role in traditional open source projects: Developers can become members of a project management committee (PMC). The PMC determines a project's road-map in the overall scope of the foundation. Thus, it manages the project's direction. A PMC member can become the leader of one or more PMCs.
- Finally, beyond project management, developers can become officers and board members of the foundation (GV:BRD), determining and contributing to its overall strategy and direction.

The **Governance:Juristic Member Level** determines the role that a juristic person can play within the foundation. Usually, the member level is closely aligned with the resources that a member provides, most notably financing (GV:FL) and development resources (GV:DL). The Eclipse foundation, for example, provides four types of corporate membership ("associate", "solution", "enterprise" and "strategic" members) while the TOPCASED foundation, whose software builds on the Eclipse platform, provides only one type of membership.

3.6   The Financing Model Category

The **Financing: (of the) Foundation** can be any or all of membership fees (F:MF), sponsorships (F:S), gifts and grants (F:GG), or revenues from a commercial subsidiary (F:FPS).

- Membership fees have the benefit of being predictable, while sponsorship may or may not happen. Sponsorship money may be tied to a particular project. Gifts and grants are also not predictable, however, for gifts and grants the foundation has to put in work and advertise or apply for it. These three are the most common forms of financing a foundation and most foundations rely on them.

- In addition, a foundation can finance itself through commercial subsidiaries. For example the Mozilla Foundation, with its for-profit subsidiary the Mozilla Corporation, funds itself through the income derived from products and services it sells for its open source software. In 2009, most of the Mozilla Foundation's $101M income came from its search related activities (the Firefox search box etc.) [3].

The foundation's income is usually spent on providing infrastructure services for the projects it is maintaining, for back office work, lawyers and legal work, and a (typically) small staff.

The **Financing: (of) Projects** may come directly from the foundation (F:PFF) or from the project participants (F:PMF), that is, the foundation members working on the project. For example, the Eclipse Foundation pays for (and maintains) all the infrastructure for its projects, while TOPCASED and GENIVI rely on their members to set-up and maintain the infrastructure on a per-project basis.

3.7   The Operations Model Category

The **Operations:Infrastructure** of a foundation's projects may be provided by the foundation itself (O:IFO) or by its members (O:IMO). This may be closely aligned with the financing of projects. The common choice is for the foundation to provide the infrastructure, as the Free Software Foundation, the Apache Software Foundation, the KDE e.V. and many others do. Sometimes, members perform these project services, as is the case with TOPCASED and GENIVI foundations.

The **Operations:Back Office** handles most of the back office work like maintaining a member database, collecting contributor agreements, and watching over proper processes. Much of this work may be performed by volunteers (O:BOV), but typically there are at least a few full or part-time employees of the foundation (O:BOE), paid for from the foundation's income.

4   Application of Model to Developer Foundations

4.1   Application Overview

A full confirmatory validation of the model has yet to be done. To demonstrate at least the usefulness of the model, we apply it to the nine foundations we used in the theory generation process. Tables 3 and 4 shows the result of this application.

4.2   Discussion of Application

The model fits the foundations well and no necessary changes to the model became apparent. This is not surprising, given that the model had been derived from these foundations. As described in Section 2, we took a multiple-step process, first deriving an initial model for six selected foundations, and then extending it by incorporating into the model what we learned from four more foundations. In a similar vein, if we were to apply it to more foundations, we might find more extensions to the model. We expect these possible modifications to be small and incremental.

Table 3. Application of Model to 9 Foundations, Part 1

Category	Attribute	Possible Values	Value Short Codes	Linux Foundation	Free Software Foundation	Apache Software Foundation	Eclipse Foundation	Mozilla Foundation	KDE e.V.	TOPCASED	GENIVI	OpenAPC
General	Purpose	• Public benefit	PB	-	PB	PB	-	PB	PB	-	-	-
		• Member benefit	MB	MB	-	-	MB	-	-	MB	MB	MB
	Incorporation	• Foundation	F	-	F	F	-	F	F	-	-	-
		• Consortium	C	C	-	-	C	-	-	C	C	C
Philosophy	Members	• Natural persons	NP	-	NP	NP	-	-	NP	-	-	-
		• Juristic persons	JP	JP	-	-	JP	-	JP	JP	JP	JP
	Open source stance	• Free software	FS	FS	FS	-	-	FS	FS	-	FS	-
		• Open source	OS	-	-	OS	OS	OS	-	OS	OS	OS
	Development model	• Open development	OD	OD	OD	OD	OD	OD	OD	OD	-	OD
		• Closed development	CD	-	-	-	-	-	-	-	CD	-
	Project license	• Reciprocal	RL	RL	RL	-	-	RL	RL	-	RL	-
		• Permissive	PL	-	-	PL	PL	PL	-	PL	PL	PL
Intellectual Property (IP)	Patent license grant	• No grant	NPG	-	-	-	-	-	-	-	-	-
		• Grant for use	UPG	-	-	-	UPG	-	-	UPG	-	UPG
		• Use + embedding	EPG	EPG	EPG	EPG	-	EPG	EPG	-	EPG	-
		• No IP required	NIP	-	-	-	-	NIP	NIP	-	-	-
	IP ownership	• Relicensing rights	RRG	RRG	-	RRG	RRG	-	-	RRG	RRG	RRG
		• Copyright assignment	CA	-	CA	-	-	-	-	-	-	-

Continued in Table 4

Table 4. Application of Model to 9 Foundations, Part 2

Category	Attribute	Possible Values	Value Short Codes	Linux Foundation	Free Software Foundation	Apache Software Foundation	Eclipse Foundation	Mozilla Foundation	KDE e.V.	TOPCASED	GENIVI	OpenAPC
Governance	Board membership	• Democratic	DB	-	-	-	-	-	DB	-	-	-
		• Meritocratic	MB	-	-	MB	-	-	-	-	-	-
		• Autocratic	AB	AB	AB	-	AB	AB	-	AB	AB	AB
	Project membership	• Democratic	DP	DP	-	-	-	-	DP	DP	DP	DP
		• Meritocratic	MP	-	-	MP	MP	MP	-	-	-	-
		• Autocratic	AP	-	AP	-	-	-	-	-	-	-
	Natural member career	• User/developer/committer	UDC	UDC	UDC	UDC	UDC	UDC	UDC	UDC	UDC	UDC
		• Project manager/leader	PMC	PMC	-	PMC	PMC	PMC	PMC	PMC	PMC	PMC
		• Board member	BRD	BRD	-	BRD	BRD	-	BRD	BRD	BRD	BRD
	Juristic member level	• Financing level	FL	FL	-	FL	FL	-	FL	-	-	-
		• Developer level	DL	DL	-	-	DL	-	-	DL	DL	DL
Financing	Foundation	• Membership fees	MF	MF	MF	-	MF	-	MF	MF	MF	MF
		• Sponsorship	S	-	-	S	S	-	S	-	-	-
		• Gifts and grants	GG	-	GG	GG	GG	GG	GG	-	-	-
		• For-profit subsidiary	FPS	-	-	-	-	FPS	-	-	-	-
	Projects	• Foundation	PFF	-	PFF	PFF	PFF	PFF	PFF	-	-	PFF
		• Members	PMF	PMF	-	-	-	-	-	PMF	PMF	-
Operations	Infrastructure	• Foundation	IFO	IFO	IFO	IFO	IFO	IFO	IFO	-	-	IFO
		• Members	IMO	IMO	-	-	-	-	-	IMO	IMO	-
	Back office	• Volunteers	BOV	-	-	BOV	-	-	BOV	-	-	-
		• Employees	BOE	BOE	BOE	BOE	BOE	BOE	BOE	BOE	BOE	BOE

5   Related Work

West and O'Mahoney investigate corporate sponsorship of open source communities, some of which are organized as foundations [12]. They call "participation architecture" what we call "foundation model". Their research, like ours, was qualitative in nature and based on interviews and supplementary materials review. West and O'Mahoney's Production category matches our Development Model category, their Governance category matches ours, except that we determined a separate Financing category, and their Intellectual Property category matches ours as well, except that ours involves Patent Handling. We became aware of this work only after performing our own, so we view similarities as additional validation of our work. West and O'Mahoney missed several categories like the more fine-grain member levels and careers that we determined. In general, we are providing more details with our possible values for attributes and the constraints between them.

Xia et al. distinguish between output and process benefits that consortium members achieve [13]. They take the view of a single company trying to gauge returns on participating in a consortium. Output benefits are derived from having a stake in the consortium's output. Process benefits take the form of social capital and learning that a company derives from participating. A survey shows these benefits and we expect the process benefits to apply to members of open source foundations as well.

Among the diversity of real consortia, open source foundations are closest to research and development (R&D) consortia. Aldrich et al. present a comparative study of R&D consortia in the U.S.A. and Japan [1]. They find that Japanese consortia all show similar structures and formalize long-standing inter-company relationships. In contrast, U.S.-based consortia show significant diversity in terms of organizational structure and processes and were more fluid than their Japanese counterparts. In contrast to these consortia, open source foundations tend to have an international perspective. Thus they tend to have little dependency on governmental support and despite necessary incorporation in a particular jurisdiction are more adjusted to international needs than their local and more traditional non-open-source counterparts.

6   Conclusions

This article presents a qualitative study of open source developer foundations. In a multiple-step process, it distills a model of the structure and governance of these foundations. The model takes the form of category, attribute, and possible-value triples that explain how to design such a foundation. To demonstrate the models usefulness, it is successfully applied to nine such foundations. The goal of this research is to provide to the leaders of community open source projects a guide for choosing an existing foundation or a blueprint for designing their own foundation.

Acknowledgments. We would like to thank the anonymous reviewers for their comments. We would also like to thank everyone who participated in the interviews. Finally, we would like to thank Wayne Beaton (Eclipse Foundation), Gervase Markham (Mozilla Foundation), Cornelius Schumacher (KDE e.V.) and Björn Schießle (Free Software Foundation Europe) for their help in improving this paper.

References

[1] Aldrich, H.E., Bolton, M.K., Baker, T., Sasaki, T.: Information Exchange and Governance Structures in U.S. and Japanese R&D Consortia: Institutional and Organizational Influences. IEEE Transactions on Engineering Management 45(3), 263 (1998)

[2] The Apache Software Foundation. How It Works, http://www.apache.org/
foundation/how-it-works.html (accessed December 25, 2011), http://
www.webcitation.org/64CSTesol

[3] Baker, M.: The State of Mozilla: Sustainability (November 18, 2010), http://www.
mozilla.org/foundation/annualreport/2009/sustainability.html
(accessed December 25, 2011), http://www.webcitation.org/64CSdMEdU

[4] Corbin, J., Strauss, A.: Qualitative Research. Sage Publications (2008)

[5] German, D., Di Penta, M., Davies, J.: Understanding and Auditing the Licensing of Open
Source Software Distributions. In: International Conference in Program Comprehension,
ICPC 2010 (2010)

[6] Open Source Initiative. Open Source Licenses, http://www.opensource.
org/licenses/index.html (accessed December 25, 2011), http://www.
webcitation.org/64CSEJk8G

[7] Riehle, D.: A New Developer Career (June 10, 2010), http://dirkriehle.com/
2010/06/10/linux-tag-keynote-slides-a-new-developer-career
(accessed December 25, 2011), http://www.webcitation.org/64CSLWhEV

[8] Riehle, D.: The Single-Vendor Commercial Open Source Business Model. Information
Systems and e-Business Management 10(1), 5–17 (2012)

[9] Riehle, D.: The Economic Case for Open Source Foundations. IEEE Computer 43(1),
86–90 (2010)

[10] Riehle, D.: The Economic Motivation of Open Source: Stakeholder Perspectives. IEEE
Computer 40(4), 25–32 (2007)

[11] Stallman, R.: Why Open Source Misses the Point (September 20, 2011), http://www.
gnu.org/philosophy/open-source-misses-the-point.html (accessed
December 25, 2011), http://www.webcitation.org/64CRzMBMq

[12] West, J., O'Mahoney, S.: The Role of Participation Architectures in Growing Sponsored
Open Source Communities. Industry and Innovation 15(2) (2008)

[13] Xia, M., Zhao, K., Mahoney, J.T.: Enhancing Value via Cooperation: Firms' Process
Benefits From Participation in a Consortium. UIUC College of Business Working Paper
08-0109 (2008)

Long-Term Sustainability of Open Source Software Communities beyond a Fork: A Case Study of LibreOffice

Jonas Gamalielsson and Björn Lundell

University of Skövde, Skövde, Sweden
{jonas.gamalielsson,bjorn.lundell}@his.se

Abstract. Many organisations have requirements for long-term sustainable software systems and associated communities. In this paper we consider long-term sustainability of Open Source software communities in Open Source projects involving a fork. There is currently a lack of studies in the literature that address how specific Open Source software communities are affected by a fork. We report from a case study aiming to investigate the developer community around the LibreOffice project, which is a fork from the OpenOffice.org project. The results strongly suggest a long-term sustainable community and that there are no signs of stagnation in the project 15 months after the fork. Our analysis provides details on the LibreOffice developer community and how it has evolved from the OpenOffice.org community with respect to project activity, long-term involvement of committers, and organisational influence over time. The findings from our analysis of the LibreOffice project make an important contribution towards a deeper understanding of challenges regarding long-term sustainability of Open Source software communities.

1 Introduction

Many organisations have requirements for long-term sustainable software systems and associated digital assets. Open Source software (OSS) has been identified as a strategy for implementing long-term sustainable software systems (Blondelle et al., 2012; Lundell et al., 2011; Müller, 2008). For any OSS project, the sustainability of its communities is fundamental to its long-term success. In this paper, we consider long-term sustainability of OSS communities in OSS projects involving a fork. In so doing, we undertake an investigation of how the LibreOffice (LO) project community has evolved from the OpenOffice.org (OO) project community with respect to project activity, long-term involvement of committers, and organisational influence over time.

Many companies need to preserve their systems and associated digital assets for more than 30 years (Lundell et al., 2011), and in some industrial sectors (such as avionics) even more than 70 years (Robert, 2006, 2007). In such usage scenarios "there will be problems if the commercial vendor of adopted proprietary software leaves the market" with increased risks for long-term availability of both software and digital

I. Hammouda et al. (Eds.): OSS 2012, IFIP AICT 378, pp. 29–47, 2012.

assets (Lundell et al., 2011). Similarly, for organisations in the public sector, many systems and digital assets need to be maintained for several decades, which cause organisations to vary concerning different types of lock-in and inability to provide long-term maintenance of critical systems and digital assets (Lundell, 2011). For this reason, sustainability of OSS communities has been identified as essential for long-term sustainability of OSS.

There are many different aspects of an OSS project that can affect community sustainability. Good project management practice includes to consider different incentives for contributing to OSS communities, which in turn may affect the future sustainability of communities (Bonaccorsi and Rossi, 2006). Earlier research has also suggested that an effective structure of governance is a basis for healthy and sustainable OSS communities (de Laat, 2007), and also that a community manager plays a key role for achieving this (Michlmayr, 2009). Further, the licensing of OSS may affect the community and it has been claimed that "fair licensing of all contributions adds a strong sense of confidence to the security of the community" (Bacon, 2009). It has also been claimed that the choice of an OSS license "can positively or negatively influence the growth of your community." (Engelfriet, 2010)

The issue of forking OSS projects has been an ongoing issue of debate amongst practitioners and researchers. It has been claimed that "Indeed, the cardinal sin of OSS, that of project forking (whereby a project is divided in two or more streams, each evolving the product in a different direction), is a strong community norm that acts against developer turnover on projects" (Ågerfalk et al., 2008), and it has been noted that few forks are successful (Ven and Maennert, 2008). It is therefore, perhaps, not surprising that it has been claimed that "there must be a strong reason for developers to consider switching to a competing project" (Wheeler, 2007). However, it has also been claimed that "forking has the capability of serving as an invisible hand of sustainability that helps open source projects to survive extreme events such as commercial acquisitions" (Nyman et al., 2011). Clearly, there is a need for increased knowledge about how OSS communities are affected by a fork.

The overarching goal of this study is to investigate how long-term sustainability of OSS communities is affected by a fork . We investigate this in the context of the LO project. The paper makes three principle contributions. Firstly, we establish a characterisation of project activity for the LO developer community before and after the fork from OO. In so doing, we specifically focus on contributions to the Software Configuration Management System (SCM). Secondly, we present findings regarding long-term involvement of contributors in the LO project. Thirdly, we present findings regarding the organisational influence in the LO project over time. Further, besides providing these three principle contributions, we also contribute approaches and metrics for analysing long-term sustainability of OSS communities (with or without forks) in OSS projects, and illustrate their use on the LO project.

There are a number of reasons which motivate a case study on the LO project. Firstly, LO is one of few OSS projects which have had an active community for more than 10 years (including the development in OO), with significant commercial interest. Secondly, there has been tensions within the OO project which finally led to the creation of the Document Foundation and the LO project (Byfield, 2010; documentfoundation.org, 2012). Thirdly, the project has reached a certain quality in that it has been adopted for professional use in a variety of private and public sector organisations (Lundell, 2011; Lundell and Gamalielsson, 2011). Therefore, its community is likely to attract a certain level of attention from organisations and individuals. Fourthly, previous studies of the parent project OO (Ven et al., 2007) and more recent studies of LO (Gamalielsson and Lundell, 2011) show that there is widespread deployment in many organisations in a number of countries. This in turn impose significant challenges from a geographically distributed user community. Further, previous results (Gamalielsson and Lundell, 2011) and anecdotal evidence from an official spokesperson for the LO project (Nouws, 2011) suggest significant activity in the LO community, which motivates more in-depth studies of the project.

In this paper we position our exploration of sustainability of OSS communities in the broader context of previous research on OSS communities (section 2). We then clarify our research approach (section 3), and report on our results (section 4). Thereafter, we analyse our results (section 5) followed by conclusions and discussion (section 6).

2   Background

In the context of OSS projects, it has been shown that "little research has been conducted on social processes related to conflict management and team maintenance" and that there are several open questions related to this, such as "How is team maintenance created and sustained over time?" (Crowston et al., 2012). Further, we note that there is a lack of reported insights on specific projects, and in particular a lack of research on OSS community involvement in projects involving a fork. One notable exception is a study on motivations for forking SourceForge.net hosted OSS projects (Nyman and Mikkonen, 2011). However, this study did not focus on community involvement over time.

Studies on the evolution of OSS projects over time do not always have a community focus and are not always targeted at specific projects. Examples include a study on the total growth rate of OSS projects (Deshpande and Riehle, 2008), and work on the evolution of social interactions for a large number of projects on SourceForge.net over time (Madey et al., 2004). Another example is a study on survival analysis of OSS projects involving the application of different metrics based on the duration of thousands of projects in the FLOSSMETRICS database (Samoladas et al., 2010). There are also studies which focus on the evolution of software over time for specific OSS projects but which do not consider the community aspect. An example is a study on the Linux kernel based on Lehman's laws of software evolution, which involved the application of code oriented metrics over time (Israeli and Feitelson, 2010). A similar approach was used in a case study on the evolution of Eclipse (Mens et al., 2008).

There are other studies that do have a focus on the evolution of communities for specific OSS projects, but do not address the effects of a fork. For example, case studies have been conducted on the Debian project involving quantitative investigations of evolution of maintainership and volunteer contributions over time (Robles et al., 2005; Michlmayr et al., 2007). Another study involved an investigation of developer community interaction over time for Apache webserver, GNOME and KDE using social network analysis (Lopez-Fernandez et al., 2006). A similar study involved the projects Evolution and Mono (Martinez-Romo et al., 2008). Case studies on the Nagios project (Gamalielsson et al., 2010), and TopCased & Papyrus (Gamalielsson et al., 2011) addressed community sustainability and evolution over time with a special focus on organisational influence. Other research partially focusing on community evolution are early case studies on the Linux kernel (Moon and Sproull, 2000), GNOME (German, 2003), Apache webserver (Mockus et al., 2002), and Mozilla (Mockus et al., 2002).

3   Research Approach

We undertook a case study of the LO project as our approach for investigating how long-term sustainability of OSS communities is affected by a fork.

First, to establish a characterisation of project activity for the LO developer community we undertook an analysis of release history, commits to the SCM and contributing committers over time. Second, to investigate long-term involvement of contributors we used different metrics that consider how long period of time committers have been active, recruitment of new committers over time, and to what extent committers contribute before and after the fork from OO. Third, to investigate organisational influence in the LO project over time we undertook an analysis of the use of different email affiliations in the SCM over time and in particular studied the difference in influence in connection with the fork from OO.

To investigate the sustainability of OSS communities, we adopt and extend approaches from earlier studies (Gamalielsson et al., 2011; Gamalielsson and Lundell, 2011) in order to analyse the contributions in terms of committed SCM artefacts of the OSS projects over time. The approaches used in this study for analysis of long-term involvement are the principal extensions to the approaches used in the earlier studies. The data for the LO project was collected from the LO website[1], where all listed Git subrepositories were used in the analysis. Git logs were extracted for the repositories and thereafter analysed using custom made scripts. More specifically, the date and committer email address for each commit was extracted and stored for subsequent analysis over time. The affiliation of a committer at the time of a commit was established by using the domain of the email address of the commit. We also used additional information regarding the affiliation of contributors[2] to further analyse the results on organisational influence. Further, a semi-automated approach involving manual inspection was used to associate email address aliases with the same actual committer.

4   Results

4.1   Project Activity

The combined version history of LO and OO is shown in table 1. It can be observed that there has been a continuous flow of new releases for more than 10 years. On 25

---

[1] http://www.libreoffice.org/developers-2/, accessed 3 March 2012
[2] http://cgit.freedesktop.org/libreoffice/contrib/gitdm-config/, accessed 3 March 2012

January 2011 the Document Foundation released its first stable version of LO, which constitutes a fork from the OO project (documentfoundation.org, 2012). Further, the version history is divided into 14 project intervals, where most intervals span between second-level releases. The start date of an interval is the date of the associated release, and the end date is the day before the next release in the table (except for the last interval where the end date is 2011-12-31). The intervals are used in the analysis of long-term involvement of contributors in section 4.2. Working towards major and second level releases demands a significant effort, and we therefore found it appropriate to report on long-term involvement at this level of abstraction.

Table 1. The combined version history of OpenOffice.org (OO) and LibreOffice (LO)

Releases	Date (YYYY-MM-DD)	Interval
OO Initial release	2001-10-01	I1
OO 1.0	2002-05-01	I2
OO 1.1	2003-09-02	I3
OO 2.0	2005-10-20	I4
OO 2.1	2006-12-12	I5
OO 2.2	2007-03-28	I6
OO 2.3	2007-09-17	I7
OO 2.4	2008-03-28	I8
OO 3.0	2008-10-13	I9
OO 3.1	2009-05-07	I10
OO 3.2	2010-02-11	I11
LO 3.3 B1	2010-09-28	I12
OO 3.3, LO 3.3	2011-01-25	I13
LO 3.4.0	2011-06-03	I14

The developer activity in LO is presented in Figure 1, which shows the number of commits for each month from September 2000 to December 2011. Our SCM analysis of the LO project includes the development in OO before the fork on 28 September 2010 (indicated with a vertical red line in Figure 1). We note that activity in the LO project varies, with distinct peaks in connection with the OO 2.0 (September 2005) and OO 2.4 (March 2008) releases (each peak with more than 50000 commits, which are not shown in the diagram for scaling reasons). Since October 2008 (with the release of OO 3.0) there have been 2700 commits each month on average.

Figure 2 illustrates the number of active committers during each month of the LO project. It can be observed that there is a large number of committers active early in the project, and that the activity decreases considerably shortly after the release of the first stable version of the software (OO 1.0) in May 2002. Further, the number of committers increases to a higher level after the release of OO 3.1 in May 2009. It can also be noticed that there is a significant peak in October 2010 in connection with the fork from OO (see vertical red line in Figure 2). In total, 665 unique committers (distributed over 1009 committer identifiers) have contributed to the LibreOffice Git repository from September 2000 until December 2011.

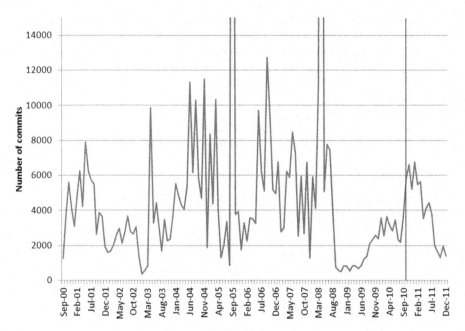

Fig. 1. Number of monthly commits for the LibreOffice project

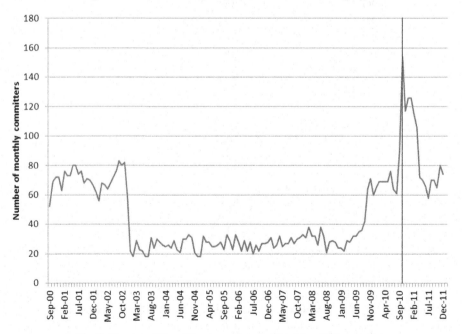

Fig. 2. Number of monthly committers for the LibreOffice project

4.2   Long-Term Involvement

Figure 3 provides an overall impression of the endurance and total activity of LO committers over time. The elapsed number of project intervals between the first and the most recent commit for each committer is shown. The committers are sorted in descending order from the bottom and upwards based on elapsed number of project intervals from the interval for the first commit until the interval for the most recent

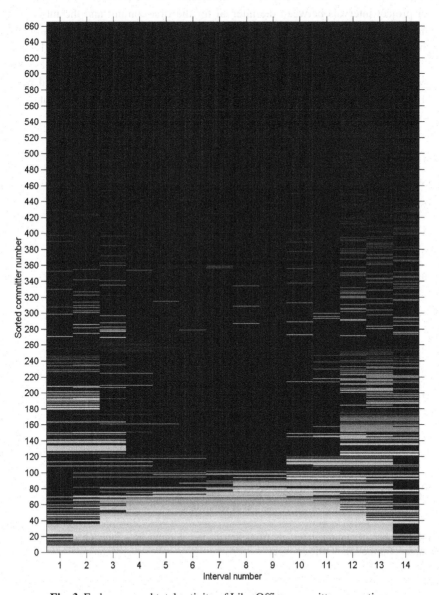

Fig. 3. Endurance and total activity of LibreOffice committers over time

commit. Committers with the same elapsed number of project intervals are secondarily sorted in descending order based on their total activity over all project intervals. For each combination of committer (along the Y-axis) and project interval (along the X-axis), the colour represents the total activity over all project months (dark blue represents low activity, whereas dark red represents high activity using a rainbow colour scale). The figure includes all committers who only provided a single commit, and for those the elapsed time is presented as one interval.

Figure 4 is based on the data visualised in Figure 3 and illustrates the elapsed number of project intervals between the interval for the first commit and the interval for the most recent commit as a function of proportion of committers. For example, the graph shows that 5% of the committers contribute over a period of at least 13 intervals. Further, 27% of the committers have contributed over a period of at least three intervals. Nine committers (1,4%) have committed over the longest observed period of 14 intervals. It can also be noted that 59% of the committers have contributed (one or several commits) during one single interval.

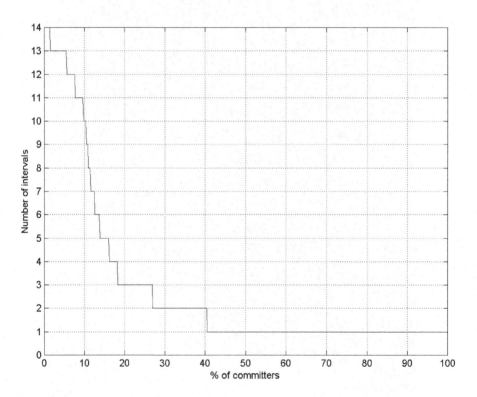

Fig. 4. Number of commit intervals from first to last commit as a function of proportion of committers for the LibreOffice project

Figure 5 shows the accumulated number of committers as a function of project interval. An observation is that 96 initial committers contribute during the first interval. Further, the growth rate in terms of new committers has varied during the project. There was for example a fast growth rate initially (during intervals 1-3), and also at the time of the fork and onwards (from interval 12). The other intervals are characterised by a slower growth in number of new committers.

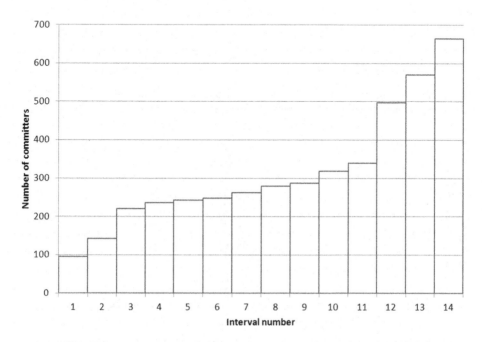

Fig. 5. Accumulated number of committers as a function of interval number

Figure 6 illustrates the involvement of committers over time in terms of number of active intervals. The left graph shows the number of active intervals as a function of proportion of committers only active before the fork (red trace), and length of the longest sequence of consecutive active intervals as a function of proportion of committers only active before the fork (blue trace). It can for example be observed that 38% of the committers contribute during at least two intervals and that 35% contribute during at least two consecutive intervals. Further, it can be noted that no committer is active during all 11 intervals before the fork. Similarly, the right graph illustrates the involvement of committers only active after the fork (using the same trace legend). For example, 23% of the committers contribute during at least two intervals and 20% contribute during at least two consecutive intervals.

Figure 7 is similar to Figure 6, and the left graph shows the number of active intervals as a function of proportion of committers active both before and after the fork (red trace), and length of the longest sequence of consecutive active intervals extending

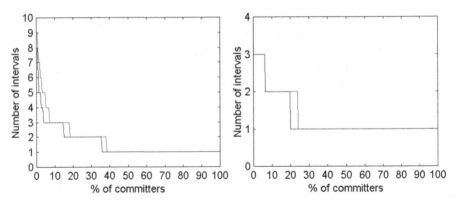

Fig. 6. Involvement of committers in terms of number of active intervals (left: committers active only before the fork, right: committers active only after the fork)

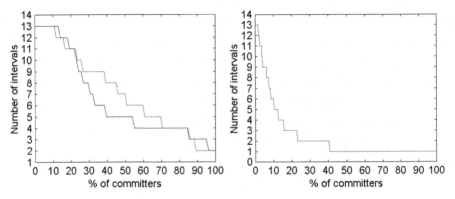

Fig. 7. Involvement of committers in terms of number of active intervals (left: committers active both before and after the fork, right: all committers)

upwards and downwards from the interval of the fork (blue trace). It can for example be observed that 38% of the committers contribute during at least nine intervals and that 38% contribute during at least six consecutive intervals The right graph illustrates the number of active intervals as a function of proportion of all committers. For example, 22% of all committers contribute during at least three intervals. One important observation from Figures 6 and 7 is that committers active both before and after the fork contribute during more intervals and during longer consecutive periods of intervals compared to committers who are only active either before or after the fork. This is a clear indication of endurance for contributors that are committed to the LO branch.

Figure 8 illustrates the proportion of commits as a function of proportion of committers. Specifically, the left graph shows the proportion of all commits during the project as a function of proportion of all committers (black trace), committers who contribute only before the fork (red trace), committers who contribute only after the fork (green trace), and committers who contribute both before and after the fork (blue trace). The total number of commits contributed by all 665 committers during the project is 587026, where 552620 (94%) of these commits are contributed by 102 committers (15% of all committers) that are active both before and after the fork. 20321 (3,5%) of the commits are contributed by 238 committers (36% of all committers) active only before the fork, and 14085 (2,5%) of the commits are contributed by 325 committers (49% of all committers) active only after the fork. From the graph it can for example be observed that 10% of all committers contribute 95% of all commits, and that 10% of committers that are active both before and after the fork contribute 80% of all commits. The same proportion of committers only contributing either before or after the fork contribute 2,4% and 1,9% of all commits, respectively. One important observation in the left graph of Figure 8 is that committers that are active both before and after the fork contribute the majority of the commits, which indicates that the most influential committers are committed to the LO branch. Further, committers only active either before or after the fork contribute a small proportion of the commits. One possible explanation for the limited influence of new committers since the fork is that only 15 months have passed after the fork. It should also be mentioned that a large proportion of all committers contribute few commits (18% only make a single commit, and 44% contribute 5 commits or less).

The right graph in Figure 8 is similar to the left graph, but shows the proportion of subgroup commits during the project as a function of proportion of committers. The subgroups are all committers (black trace), committers only contributing before the fork (red trace), committers only contributing after the fork (green trace), and committers contributing both before and after the fork (blue trace). It can for example be observed that for the set of commits for each committer subgroup, 10% of all committers contribute 95% of the commits (same as in left graph), and that 10% of committers that are active both before and after the fork contribute 85% of the commits. The same proportion of committers only contributing either before or after the fork contribute 69% and 80% of the subgroup commits, respectively. Hence, a relatively small proportion of committers contribute a major proportion of the commits within each committer subgroup.

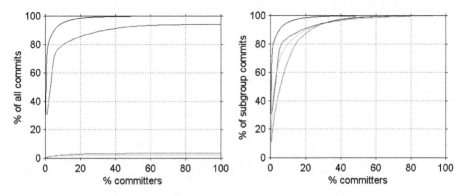

Fig. 8. Proportion of commits as a function of proportion of committers (left: for all commits, right: for commits in different committer subgroups)

4.3   Organisational Influence

The proportion of commits for the 10 most active affiliations over the time (from January 2007 to December 2011) in the LO project is shown in Figure 9 (like in Figure 1, the peak in April 2008 is not shown for scaling reasons). It can be observed that "openoffice" is dominating until August 2010, and that other affiliations break the dominance from September 2010 (the month of the fork) and onwards. It is also noted that "sun" is most active in the period from October 2009 to July 2010, and that "oracle" is most active from August 2010 to March 2011. Further observations are that "novell" and "suse" have been active for the entire four year period with an increased activity after the fork, and that "redhat" has become the major contributor ever since the fork.

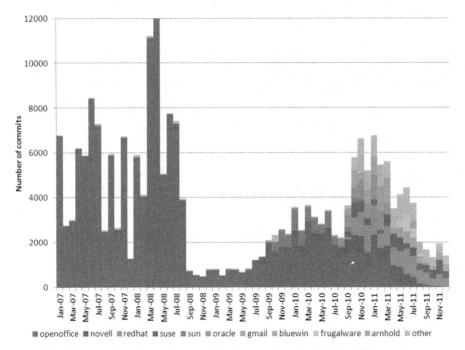

Fig. 9. Proportion of commits per affiliation over time for the LibreOffice project

Figure 10 illustrates the total affiliation commit influence for LO 15 months before and after the fork on 28 September 2010, and further emphasises the shift from "openoffice" domination to a more diversified developer community after the fork. This is especially evidenced by the increased proportion of "other" affiliations 15 months after the fork. The additional information[3] regarding the use of the

---

[3] http://cgit.freedesktop.org/libreoffice/contrib/gitdm-config/, accessed 3 March 2012

"openoffice" affiliation revealed that this affiliation is clearly dominantly used by committers employed by either Oracle or Sun. Further, we found that there were 148 different committers with 52 different affiliations contributing during the time period 15 months before the fork, whereas there were 424 different committers with 194 different affiliations contributing during the time period 15 months after the fork. In fact, there have been 377 different committers with 116 affiliations contributing from the start (September 2000) until the fork, which is less than the number of committers and affiliations contributing during 15 months after the fork. This together further strengthens the impression of a more diversified developer community after the fork.

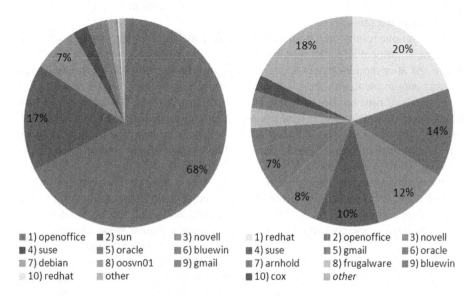

Fig. 10. Total affiliation commit influence (left pie: during 15 months before the fork, right pie: during 15 months after the fork) for the LibreOffice project

5   Analysis

From our results we make a number of observations related to our results on project activity. Firstly, there have been regular and frequent releases of stable versions of the software for a time period of more than ten years. Other examples of well known OSS projects with release histories extending over many years are Apache webserver[4] and the Linux kernel[5], which have had frequent releases since 1995 and 1991, respectively. We note that, as for the LO project, both these projects are governed by a

---

[4] http://httpd.apache.org/
[5] http://www.kernel.org/

foundation[6]. Secondly, despite a relatively limited time period (15 months) after the LO fork from OO, the transition and formation of the LO community seems to be successful. However, we acknowledge the short time period after the fork and that our early indications of a successful LO community after transition from OO need to be confirmed by an analysis over a longer time period at a later stage. As a comparison, a well-known fork with significant uptake and a long-term sustainable community is OpenBSD[7], which was forked from NetBSD in 1995 and still has an active developer community (Gmane.org, 2012). Thirdly, there has been substantial activity for more than ten years. Despite some variation between stable releases, our findings suggest a long-term trend towards a sustainable community as we have not observed any signs of a lasting decline in the community activity. As a comparison, there has been stable OSS community activity over many years in the aforementioned Apache webserver and Linux kernel projects.

Based on our results on long-term involvement we observe that a large proportion of the most influential committers have been involved for long periods of time both before and after the fork from OO, which indicates that the developer community has a strong commitment with the LO branch. A strong commitment of contributors over long periods of time has been observed earlier in a study on the Debian project where it was found that maintainers "tend to commit to the project for long periods of time" and that "the mean life of volunteers in the project is probably larger than in many software companies, which would have a clear impact on the maintenance of the software" (Robles et al., 2005).

Our results on organisational influence show that a number of committers representing different organisations provide substantial amounts of contributions to the project over a number of years. This may be considered a risk for the project in the long term unless new contributors join the project on a regular basis. However, this does not seem to be a significant risk for this project since our findings suggest that the community has successfully recruited new committers over time. Diversified developer communities with respect to affiliation have also been observed in earlier case studies on the Linux kernel project (Aaltonen and Jokinen, 2007), and on the Topcased and Papyrus projects (Gamalielsson et al., 2011).

Further, when considering OSS products in long-term maintenance scenarios for potential adoption, it is critical to understand and engage in communities related to the OSS project. For the base project analysed (OO), a governance structure has been established and the OO community is governed by its community council (openoffice.org, 2012). Similarly, the investigated branch after the fork (LO) has also established a governance structure referred to as the Document Foundation (documentfoundation.org, 2012). Despite such explicitly documented governance structures, project participants may decide to fork a project, which happened when the Document Foundation established the LO project as a fork from OO on 28 September 2010. In acknowledging a short time period after the fork (15 months), our results suggest that this fork may actually be successful. We note that our observation indicates that the

---

[6] The Apache Software Foundation (http://www.apache.org/) and the Linux Foundation (http://www.linuxfoundation.org/)

[7] http://www.openbsd.org/

LO project may be an exception to the norm since previous research claims that there has been "few successful forks in the past" (Ven and Mannaert, 2008).

The importance of engagement in OSS communities has been amplified by Shaikh and Cornford (2010) "Large companies understand that if they want to preserve a long term relationship with open source communities and harness the expertise and products they offer, then they must loosen up and relax, avoiding to much concern about their level of control.". Further, for the longevity of an OSS community, it is essential to be able to attract active contributors long-term. Our study shows that there is no single commercial company dominating the contributions to the LO project by the most influential contributors to the SCM. In fact, the LO community involves a large number of contributors from many different organisations, and the fork was not initiated by the organisation behind the base project. This is in contrast with a fork initiated by a company that controls the code base, something which occurred when Red Hat "forked their own codebase into Red Hat Enterprise Linux and Fedora Core Linux" (Gary et al., 2009).

There is a complex inter-relationship between community and company values which impacts on opportunities for long-term maintenance and support for OSS projects. In fact, for the investigated base project (OO) in this study, concerns for the long-term sustainability of its community have been raised (Noyes, 2010). In previous research, it has been claimed that companies "have valid concerns about the survival of and continued support for F/OSS products. The traditional telephone hotline and maintenance contract offer a comfort factor that a voluntary bulletin board—which is the main support for many F/OSS products—cannot provide." (Fitzgerald, 2004) On the contrary, practitioners in the embedded systems area experience that support from large OSS communities is "considered superior, compared to proprietary alternatives in some cases" (Lundell et al., 2011). Further, for the investigated OSS project, there are a number of companies offering support on a commercial basis, something which should be considered before potential adoption in addition to engagement in voluntary OSS communities.

To successfully master the art of establishing a long-term sustainable volunteer community is a huge challenge. As in all organisations, there are "times in every community when repetition, housekeeping, and conflict play a role in an otherwise enjoyable merry-go-round. When the community begins to see more bureaucracy and repetition than useful and enjoyable contributions, something is wrong." (Bacon, 2009) From our investigation in this study, our results indicate that the LO project seems to be successful in keeping old and recruiting new committers that contribute to the SCM over time. For software systems with long life-cycles, the success by which an OSS project manages to recruit new contributors to its community is critical for its long term sustainability. Hence, good practice with respect to governance of OSS projects is a fundamental challenge.

6   Conclusions and Discussion

In this paper we have reported from a case study on the LO project. From our analysis we make a number of observations which strongly suggest a long-term sustainable community, something which is a fundamental prerequisite for long-term maintenance of software systems and digital assets.

The findings from our analysis of the LO project make an important contribution towards a deeper understanding of challenges regarding long-term sustainability of OSS communities. In many usage scenarios, it is often the case that digital assets outlive the software systems that were used to generate them. For this reason, both software systems and the organisational structure in which such are developed, need to be maintained over very long life-cycles. It is therefore essential that there exist software systems with associated long-term sustainable communities, and our findings indicate that LO has a developer community that is sustainable in the long term.

For future work we intend to extend our study of the LO community to allow analysis over a longer time period after the fork from OO. In so doing, we plan to include data from the OO branch in our analysis. Such a study would also include an exploration of the relationships between different organisations governing the LO and the OO projects, and an exploration of how contributors are committed to the two different branches. Previous research has shown that the extent to which there is a commercial drive in OSS projects may impact on community values and contributor engagement (Lundell et al., 2010). To extend our analysis of the LO project we plan to undertake further investigations on developer experiences with respect to this issue in order to enrich our findings.

References

Behlendorf, B.: How Open Source Can Still Save the World. In: Boldyreff, C., Crowston, K., Lundell, B., Wasserman, A.I. (eds.) OSS 2009. IFIP AICT, vol. 299, pp. 2–2. Springer, Heidelberg (2009)

Aaltonen, T., Jokinen, J.: Influence in the Linux Kernel Community. In: Feller, et al. (eds.) Open Source Development, Adoption and Innovation, pp. 203–208. Springer, Berlin (2007)

Ågerfalk, P., Fitzgerald, B.: Outsourcing to an unknown workforce: Exploring opensourcing as a global sourcing strategy. MIS Quarterly 32(2), 385–410 (2008)

Bacon, J.: The Art of Community. O'Reilly, Sebastopol (2009)

Blondelle, G., Arberet, P., Rossignol, A., Lundell, B., Labezin, C., Berrendonner, R., Gaufillet, P., Faudou, R., Langlois, B., Maisonobe, L., Moro, P., Rodriguez, J., Puerta Peña, J.M., Bonnafous, E., Mueller, R.: Polarsys towards Long-Term Availability of Engineering Tools for Embedded Systems. In: Proceedings of the sixth European Conference on Embedded Real Time Software and Systems (ERTS 2012), Toulouse, France, February 1-2 (2012)

Bonaccorsi, A., Rossi, C.: Comparing Motivations of Individual Programmers and Firms to Take Part in the Open Source Movement: From Community to Business. Knowledge, Technology & Policy 18(4), 40–64 (2006)

Byfield, B.: The Cold War Between OpenOffice.org and LibreOffice. Linux magazine (October 22, 2010), http://www.linux-magazine.com/Online/Blogs/Off-the-Beat-Bruce-Byfield-s-Blog/The-Cold-War-Between-OpenOffice.org-and-LibreOffice (accessed March 3, 2012)

Crowston, K., Kangning, W., Howison, J., Wiggins, A.: Free/Libre open-source software development: What we know and what we do not know. ACM Computing Surveys 44(2), Article 7 (2012)

Deshpande, A., Riehle, D.: The Total Growth of Open Source. In: Russo, B., et al. (eds.) Open Source Development, Communities and Quality. IFIP, vol. 275, pp. 197–209. Springer, Boston (2008)

documentfoundation.org: The Document Foundation (2012),
    `http://www.documentfoundation.org/` (accessed March 3, 2012)

Engelfriet, A.: Choosing an Open Source License. IEEE Software 27(1), 48–49 (2010)

Fitzgerald, B.: A Critical Look at Open Source. IEEE Computer 37(7), 92–94 (2004)

Gamalielsson, J., Lundell, B., Lings, B.: The Nagios Community: An Extended Quantitative Analysis. In: Ågerfalk, P., Boldyreff, C., González-Barahona, J.M., Madey, G.R., Noll, J., et al. (eds.) OSS 2010. IFIP AICT, vol. 319, pp. 85–96. Springer, Heidelberg (2010)

Gamalielsson, J., Lundell, B.: Open Source communities for long-term maintenance of digital assets: what is offered for ODF & OOXML? In: Hammouda, I., Lundell, B. (eds.) Proceedings of SOS 2011: Towards Sustainable Open Source, Tampere University of Technology, Tampere, pp. 19–24 (2011) ISBN 978-952-15-2411-0, ISSN 1797-836X

Gamalielsson, J., Lundell, B., Mattsson, A.: Open Source Software for Model Driven Development: A Case Study. In: Hissam, S.A., Russo, B., de Mendonça Neto, M.G., Kon, F. (eds.) OSS 2011. IFIP AICT, vol. 365, pp. 348–367. Springer, Heidelberg (2011)

Gary, K., Koehnemann, H., Blakley, J., Groar, C., Mann, H., Kagain, A.: A Case Study: Open Source Community and the Commercial Enterprise. In: 2009 Sixth International Conference on Information Technology: New Generations, pp. 940–945. IEEE Computer Society, Los Alamitos (2009)

German, D.: The GNOME project: a case study of open source global software development. Journal of Software Process: Improvement and Practice 8(4), 201–215 (2003)

Gmane.org: Information about gmane.os.openbsd.cvs (2012), `http://dir.gmane.org/gmane.os.openbsd.cvs` (accessed March 3, 2012)

Israeli, A., Feitelson, D.G.: The Linux kernel as a case study in software evolution. Journal of Systems and Software 83(3), 485–501 (2010)

de Laat, P.: Governance of open source software: state of the art. Journal of Management and Governance 11(2), 165–177 (2007)

Lopez-Fernandez, L., Robles, G., Gonzalez-Barahona, J.M., Herraiz, I.: Applying Social Network Analysis Techniques to Community-driven Libre Software Projects. International Journal of Information Technology and Web Engineering 1(3), 27–48 (2006)

Lundell, B.: e-Governance in public sector ICT-procurement: what is shaping practice in Sweden? European Journal of ePractice 12(6) (2011), `http://www.epractice.eu/en/document/5290101`

Lundell, B., Gamalielsson, J.: Towards a Sustainable Swedish e-Government Practice: Observations from unlocking digital assets. In: Proceedings of the IFIP e-Government Conference 2011(EGOV 2011), Delft, The Netherlands, August 28-September 2 (2011)

Lundell, B., Lings, B., Lindqvist, E.: Open Source in Swedish companies: where are we? Information Systems Journal 20(6), 519–535 (2010)

Lundell, B., Lings, B., Syberfeldt, A.: Practitioner Perceptions of Open Source Software in the Embedded Systems Area. Journal of Systems and Software 84(9), 1540–1549 (2011)

Madey, G., Freeh, V., Tynan, R.: Modeling the F/OSS community: A quantitative investigation. In: Koch, S. (ed.) Free/Open Source Software Development, pp. 203–221. Idea Group Publishing, Hershey (2004)

Martinez-Romo, J., Robles, G., Ortuño-Perez, M., Gonzalez-Barahona, J.M.: Using Social Network Analysis Techniques to Study Collaboration between a FLOSS Community and a Company. In: Russo, B., et al. (eds.) Open Source Development, Communities and Quality. IFIP, vol. 275, pp. 171–186. Springer, Boston (2008)

Mens, T., Fernández-Ramil, J., Degrandsart, S.: The evolution of Eclipse. In: Proceedings of the 24th IEEE International Conference on Software Maintenance (ICSM 2008), pp. 386–395 (2008)

Michlmayr, M.: Community Management in Open Source Projects. The European Journal for the Informatics Professional X(3), 22–26 (2009)

Michlmayr, M., Robles, G., Gonzalez-Barahona, J.M.: Volunteers in Large Libre Software Projects: A Quantitative Analysis. In: Sowe, S.K., et al. (eds.) Emerging Free and Open Source Software Practices, pp. 1–24. IGI Publishing, Hershey (2007)

Mockus, A., Fielding, R.T., Herbsleb, J.D.: Two case studies of open source software development: Apache and Mozilla. ACM Transactions on Software Engineering and Methodology 11(3), 309–346 (2002)

Moon, Y.J., Sproull, L.: Essence of distributed work: The case of the Linux kernel. First Monday 5(11) (2000)

Müller, R.: Open Source – Value Creation and Consumption, Open Expo, Zürich (September 24-25, 2008), http://www.openexpo.ch/fileadmin/documents/2008Zuerich/Slides/35_Mueller.pdf (accessed March 3, 2012)

Nouws, C.: LibreOffice– the first year and looking forward! presented at ODF plugfest, Gouda, Netherlands (November 18, 2011), http://odfplugfest.org/2011-gouda/Nouws-LibreOffice.pdf (accessed March 3, 2012)

Noyes, K.: Don't Count on Oracle to Keep OpenOffice.org Alive, PC World (August 23, 2010), http://www.pcworld.com/printable/article/id,203910/printable.html

Nyman, L., Mikkonen, T.: To Fork or Not to Fork: Fork Motivations in SourceForge Projects. In: Hissam, S.A., Russo, B., de Mendonça Neto, M.G., Kon, F. (eds.) OSS 2011. IFIP AICT, vol. 365, pp. 259–268. Springer, Heidelberg (2011)

Nyman, L., Mikkonen, T., Lindman, J., Fougère, M.: Forking: the Invisible Hand of Sustainability in Open Source Software. In: Hammouda, I., Lundell, B. (eds.) Proceedings of SOS 2011: Towards Sustainable Open Source, pp. 1–5. Tampere University of Technology, Tampere (2011) ISBN 978-952-15-2411-0, ISSN 1797-836X

openoffice.org: Community Council (2012), http://wiki.services.openoffice.org/wiki/Community_Council (accessed March 3, 2012)

Robert, S.: On-board software development - The open-source way. In: IST/ARTEMIS Workshop, Helsinki, November 22 (2006)

Robert, S.: New trends and needs for Avionics Systems. In: ARTEMIS Conference, June 4-5, Berlin (2007)

Robles, G., Gonzalez-Barahona, J.M., Michlmayr, M.: Evolution of volunteer participation in libre software projects: evidence from Debian. In: Proceedings of the First International Conference on Open Source Systems, pp. 100–107 (2005)

Samoladas, I., Stamelos, I., Angelis, L.: Survival analysis on the duration of open source projects. Information and Software Technology 52(9), 902–922 (2010)

Shaikh, M., Cornford, T.: 'Letting go of Control' to Embrace Open Source: Implications for Company and Community. In: Proceedings of the 43rd Hawaii International Conference on System Sciences - 2010, pp. 1–10. IEEE Computer Society, Los Alamitos (2010)

Ven, K., Huysmans, P., Verelst, J.: The adoption of open source desktop software in a large public administration. In: Proceedings of the 13th Americas Conference on Information Systems (AMCIS 2007), Keystone, Colorado, August 9-12, pp. 9–12 (2007)

Ven, K., Mannaert, H.: Challenges and strategies in the use of Open Source Software by Independent Software Vendors. Information and Software Technology 50(9-10), 991–1002 (2008)

Wheeler, D.A.: Why Open Source Software / Free Software (OSS/FS, FLOSS, or FOSS)? Look at the Numbers (2007), http://www.dwheeler.com/oss_fs_why.html (revised April 16, 2007) (accessed March 3, 2012)

Step-by-Step Strategies and Case Studies for Embedded Software Companies to Adapt to the FOSS Ecosystem

Suhyun Kim, Jaehyun Yoo, and Myunghwa Lee

Software Engineering Lab, Software R&D Center, Samsung Electronics
416 Maetan-Dong, Yeongtong-Gu, Suwon, Gyeonggi-Do 443-742, Korea
{suhyun47.kim,sjh.yoo,mhlee}@samsung.com
https://opensource.samsung.com

Abstract. Due to the continuous expansion of the FOSS ecosystem and the introduction of high-quality FOSS, FOSS is increasingly used in consumer electronics (CE) such as smartphones, televisions, and cameras. As a result, manufacturers of CE products have developed a close relationship with the FOSS ecosystem. For CE product manufacturers, efficient adaptation to the FOSS ecosystem has become an essential component in their business operations. This paper will divide the activities of CE product manufacturers within the FOSS ecosystem into the following four levels: identification, adoption, compliance, and contribution. It will examine the main activities and obstacles that arise in each level. The paper will also present instances where companies have succeeded in overcoming these obstacles.

Keywords: FOSS, FOSS Ecosystem, Embedded Software.

1 Introduction

FOSS initially emerged from the free software movement in response to the tendency of companies to make software their proprietary property. A software freedom activist called Richard Stallman raised objections to AT&T's policy of hiding the UNIX source code. He pioneered the concept of copyleft and introduced the GPL (General Public License) [1], which contains copyleft philosophy, while launching the GNU project [2]. The success of GPL free/open source software (FOSS) such as GNU/Linux paved the way for numerous developers to join the FOSS ecosystem [3].

As a wide range of high quality FOSS applications was introduced, many companies increased their use of FOSS to keep up with the accelerated product development cycle. The use of FOSS allows the companies to reduce development period by building a product on top of an existing FOSS application. Companies' use of FOSS means that they participate in the FOSS ecosystem. Fig. 1 shows the process of companies' participation in the FOSS ecosystem.

Fig. 1. Steps for joining the FOSS Ecosystem

I. Hammouda et al. (Eds.): OSS 2012, IFIP AICT 378, pp. 48–60, 2012.

Most companies tend to jump from simply identifying and using FOSS to the compliance stage. Then they reach a phase in which they modify FOSS or contribute a code that they have developed to a FOSS project.

During the early stages of participation in the FOSS-ecosystem, a company focuses on complying with the clauses of FOSS licenses, such as disclosure of the source code and acknowledgment of its use of FOSS. However, to fulfill the objective of holding a leading share of the market, as in the case of Netscape's Mozilla project [4], or to efficiently adapt to the fast-evolving FOSS environment, embedded software companies use a local patch to quickly enter the FOSS contribution stage. This patch is used by a company to maintain its own internally developed source code without applying it to the mainline of its FOSS project and apply the patch whenever a new version of FOSS is used. For your reference, Fig. 2 shows that as the use of the Linux kernel continues to increase in embedded products, companies are also increasing their contribution of Linux kernel source code [5].

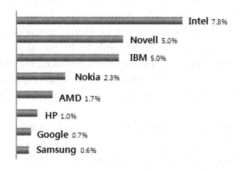

Fig. 2. Linux kernel contribution for embedded software companies

However, there are some obstacles that companies still need to overcome before participating in the FOSS ecosystem. This paper will divide a companies' participation process in the FOSS system into the following four levels: identification, adoption, compliance, and contribution. It will then examine the main activities and obstacles that arise within each level. Examples of overcoming these obstacles will be provided. Chapter 2 will introduce the requirements for identifying FOSS components. Chapter 3 will provide an overview of companies' activities to comply with FOSS licenses. Chapter 4 will explain the obstacles that arise in a company's contribution of FOSS. Lastly, Chapter 5 will analyze the trend of a new FOSS ecosystem that was developed in the wake of a new FOSS platform such as Android, and will introduce companies' reactions to it. Then it will draw a conclusion and propose aspects for further study.

2   Identification of FOSS Components

Most companies participate in the FOSS ecosystem through using FOSS. However, since there are no warranty clauses in commonly-used FOSS licenses, companies must identify and minimize the risks accompanying the use of FOSS.

In order to help select a FOSS that meets a company's requirements, many studies have been conducted to evaluate the quality of FOSS projects, such as FLOSSMetrics [6] and QualOSS [7], and to assess FOSS communities. In particular, the website ohloh.net offers a wide variety of information that allows users to access more concrete information on FOSS components, such as the number of developers and changes in the amount of source code lines for different periods of time, which can be viewed from a public repository [8].

In addition to assessing the FOSS quality and the maturity of FOSS communities provided by those studies, a company must look into the issue of copyrights/patent rights concerning FOSS. The dispute between Google and Oracle over the use of Java in Android, which is a FOSS-based operating system platform, puts a lot of pressure on Android-using manufacturers [9]. Although the FFmpeg project, which is a multimedia platform, endeavors to prevent problems involving hidden patents from emerging, it publicly maintains the FOSS philosophy-based position of no warranty. This means that if a company uses FFmpeg in its products, the company is required to pay patent royalties for all involved patents and to bear responsibility for all claims and suits filed over the neglect of paying such patent royalties [10]. This applies to all other FOSS projects.

Although there is a network called OIN [11] which shares a patent pool for open source projects and businesses to protect users from lawsuits, this kind of patent pool is rarely used in most OSS projects. Recently, lawsuits over patent rights or copyrights and court injunctions against sales have increased, but there is no "silver bullet." In this way, the use of FOSS always entails the risk of being embroiled in a lawsuit.

Some companies have established a system for examining various aspects of a newly-introduced OSS, including its patent or copyright, through the Open Source Review Board (OSRB) or others [12]. Nonetheless, such information is kept confidential within the company. Many companies do not have this kind of system and therefore, they are unable to fully examine the involvement of a third party's intellectual property in a newly-adopted OSS.

3   Compliance Activities

3.1   GPL Violation Enforcement Organizations

GPL violation enforcement organizations came about since an increasing number of companies did not comply with FOSS licenses, with many of them failing to disclose the source code for FOSS that they used. Among the most active organizations are Europe-based gpl-violations.org and US-based Software Freedom Conservancy

(SFC). Founded by Harald Welte, gpl-violations.org uses netfilter/iptable, msdosfs, and mtd which he copyrighted. It has filed claims against approximately 100 companies that have violated GPL licenses and won every single case [13]. As for SFC, of which Bradley Kuhn is an executive director, copyrighters of GPL-distributed Busybox gave the company the right to file lawsuits. SFC tracks down companies violating the GPL and take them to court.

In the case of gpl-violations.org, violators must simply comply with license clauses in order to settle the filed claims. However, SFC argues that in addition to complying with licenses, violators must also comply with all provisions of GPL if they intend to settle a legal issue involving them. When a claim is filed, it is generally processed privately between a GPL violation enforcement organization and the violating company, thereby preventing external exposure. However, when a lawsuit is filed in court, it attracts media attention regardless of the court's final ruling, thereby causing damage to the public image of the violating company. Table 1 shows the activities of violation enforcement organizations.

Table 1. GPL violation enforcement organizations

	gpl-violations.org	**Software Freedom Conservancy**
Member	Harald Welte	Bradley M. Kuhn
Area	Europe	USA
Copyright Software	netfilter/iptable, msdosfs, mtd	Busybox
GPL Enforcement	Claims (over 100)	Lawsuits (over 10)
Restoration	No need to obtain agreement with anyone. Compliance on particular GPL'ed software under ownership of gpl-violations.org	Need to obtain agreement with SFC. Compliance of all GPL'ed software which is contained in the product.

In addition to their independent investigation, GPL violation enforcement organizations also rely on information provided by external users to monitor companies' GPL violations. It also verifies whether or not GPL FOSS has been used by acquiring a binary of a program code contained in a product through a program called BAT (binary analysis tool). If it detects the use of the GPL-licensed FOSS, it investigates whether the company has taken appropriate measures, such as statements of the GPL or disclosure of the source code [14].

In addition to these monitoring activities, they raise companies' awareness of this issue by informing them of common violation cases and distribute related resources such as GPL Compliance Guide to help them to comply with provisions of GPL FOSS. Companies can use these guides to check whether or not they have violated the GPL [15][16][17].

3.2   Compliance Activities of Companies

When a company fails to comply with the provisions in the GPL and violates a copyright law, this usually occurs because departments for developing, testing, and distributing software have a poor understanding of FOSS licenses and there is no system in place to educate them. This section will introduce various company activities designed to prevent violation of the GPL.

Companies which place importance on compliance activities provide their employees with mandatory online courses to enhance their understanding of FOSS licenses [18]. The company studied in this paper (hereinafter referred to as the "subject company") offers mandatory online courses that explain the concept and clauses of FOSS licenses, as well as proper compliance with them as shown in Fig. 3. It also offers in-class courses to delve further into this subject.

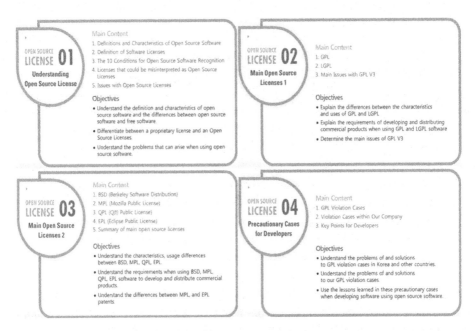

Fig. 3. Online courses on FOSS offered by the subject company

The following demonstrates how the subject company carries out activities related to FOSS compliance during the software development process. Fig. 4 shows the FOSS inspection process implemented by the companies studied.

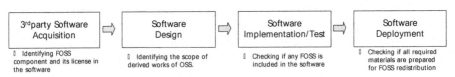

Fig. 4. FOSS inspection process of the subject company

In response to the issues introduced in Chapter 2 of this paper, the policy of checking FOSS licenses contained in software to determine whether the licenses can be used in products during the stage of adopting external software has been implemented. The subject company operates its own Open Source Advisory Board (OSAB) to handle these issues efficiently. Fig. 5 shows the composition of the OSAB. Through the OSAB, the studies and analyses of FOSS licenses and related case studies are shared and presented in written form, so that consistent OSS compliance policies can be implemented. In addition, an annual assessment is conducted to examine whether or not the verification process has been carried out in a proper manner by using a checklist similar to the Linux Foundation's Self-Assessment Compliance Checklist [19].

Fig. 5. The composition of OSAB for the adoption of software

It is very difficult to define the scope of GPL-derived materials [20]. In an attempt to deal with this problem, the subject company has been studying to assess the scope of GPL-derived materials during the design phase. By doing so, it prevents its core IP sector from being affected by FOSS licenses due to FOSS provisions on GPL derivative works as shown in Fig. 6.

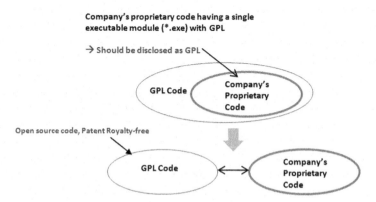

Fig. 6. Design stage reflecting the scope of GPL derivative works

During the implementation/testing phase, a code clone detection tool is used to check whether the source code includes FOSS, as shown in Fig. 7. If FOSS is detected in the source code during this process, the source code is disclosed, its use is indicated in the product manual, and the full text of the license is included in the source code during the distribution phase. This procedure has been established as an automatic system.

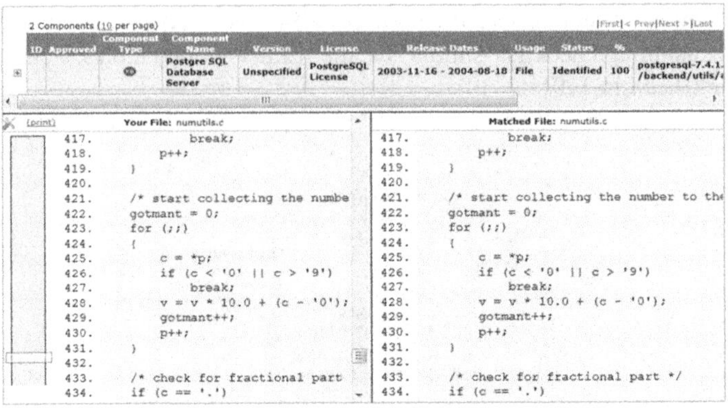

Fig. 7. Source code detection tool for FOSS

In the past, only a verification team checked the use of open sources. However, with their increasing use, the subject company has trained developers to check the use of open sources in the codes that they have developed, and to comply with clauses regarding open sources. It has also established an automated system/infrastructure to support this as shown in Fig. 8.

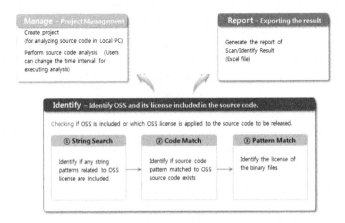

Fig. 8. FOSS self verification tool

During the distribution phase, as shown in Fig. 9, the subject company offers in writing to make FOSS source codes available on its website [21]. It also establishes a communication channel to respond to customers' inquiries on related subjects.

Fig. 9. A website offering source codes

4   Contribution Activities

According to basic FOSS philosophy, FOSS should continue to remain FOSS (copyleft) and knowledge should be shared so that it can be developed and become even more useful [22]. If a company merely carries out the activities introduced in Chapter 3, this constitutes nothing more than complying with the license provisions on FOSS continuously remaining FOSS. This does not mean that the company has participated in the ecosystem sought by FOSS, in which knowledge is shared with others and developed further [23]. When a company minimizes local patches and remains in sync with the fast-paced evolution of both FOSS and product development, this will benefit the company in the long term. When FOSS developers can develop source code from a company into more efficient source code, the FOSS ecosystem becomes beneficial to a greater number of users. Table 2 shows major companies' FOSS committers, as estimated by ohloh.net.

Table 2. FOSS committers (ohloh.net)

Company	Committers (estimated)	Communities (estimated)
Google	2,104	1,023 (Android)
Apple	266	Webkit
Intel	193	20 (Tizen)
Redhat	192	40 (Fedora)
HP	105	64 (Apache)
Nokia	84	28 (Symbian)

When a company undertakes such a contribution activity, it faces two major obstacles (other than the financial burdens resulting from the investment of resources in FOSS development). The first obstacle concerns the issue of protecting its IP. The second obstacle is the difficulty the company would face in becoming a FOSS project reviewer or committer, as well as possible conflict with other companies in light of the growing interest of companies in FOSS communities.

For example, in the case of the Android platform, which is released by Google under the Apache License [24], each Android maker offers its own version of Android, including unique user interface, by incorporating its own source code. Under the Apache License, however, companies usually do not provide source codes and do not apply them to the mainline of the Android Open Source Project. These files exist as local patches within companies. As a result, when Android platform source codes evolve, companies must keep up with the changes in local patches and reflect them in each of its models every single time. These local patches often contain patent applications or key technologies. Therefore, it is not easy to release source code as FOSS or make it public.

Another obstacle facing companies' contribution is an invisible wall that can block their entry into the domain. With the successful establishment of the FOSS philosophy and the increase of FOSS developers, companies try to use FOSS as part of their business strategy. In the case of WebKit, for example, a considerable number of developers who act as committers belong to Apple and Google. There is also a policy in place that requires a recommendation from existing committers or reviewers, as well as a set number of good commits. As long as this policy remains viable, it appears to be difficult for developers in competing companies to gain committer or reviewer status. Fig. 10 shows the committer ratio of companies for WebKit.

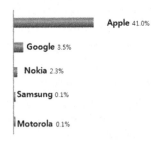

Fig. 10. Company's committer ratio for WebKit (ohloh.net)

In order to overcome these obstacles, the subject company plans to provide its developers with various incentives that would add momentum to their FOSS contributions. It also carries out a plan to train committers through support for major communities or support programs for university students.

5   New FOSS Ecosystem

This chapter will introduce the product-based FOSS ecosystem which evolved from component-based ecosystems.

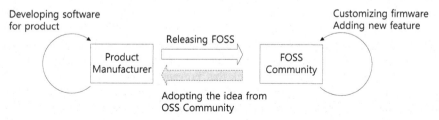

Fig. 11. Product-based FOSS ecosystem cycle

Recently, the scope of FOSS projects has expanded beyond the development of components such as Linux kernel, Webkit, and GStreamer to include platforms such as Android Open Source Project (AOSP) [25] and Tizen, which use FOSS components. In particular, companies are undertaking platform-level FOSS projects to expand potential business through the rapid dissemination of their platforms. Source codes are available on products that use open platforms. Unlike Windows Mobile, which is distributed by Microsoft, it is possible to modify them for each product. Therefore, companies are increasingly using platforms that correspond to their needs. Due to FOSS licenses, source codes of software in the products have been made available to the public. As a result, an increasing number of users have begun to develop desired functions based on these disclosed source codes. This has generated FOSS communities which continue to grow.

Table 3. Activities of FOSS communities related to certain products

Platform Upgrade	- GAOSP: firmware upgrade - GT-I9000 products: ICS upgrade
Performance Enhancements	- Project Voodoo: modification of file system / sound module [26] - Change of touch screen sensitivity
Usability Improvements	- Change of users' UI themes - CyanogenMod: development of the functions to revoke app permissions - Firmware and user data: development of backup/restore functions

Table 3 shows the activities of FOSS communities carried out on the basis of the source codes disclosed by the companies studied. Product-based activities of FOSS communities have much more impact than component-based FOSS projects, given that the former allow developers who purchase a product to upgrade and distribute software, which can then be used by the general public. These activities, which are designed to fit with users' needs, are continuously carried out in various fields. Product-based community activities can be divided into the following three categories: Platform Upgrade, Performance Enhancements, and Usability Improvements.

Sometimes, a project may be undertaken with insufficient knowledge of the principles of the dynamics of a product and its source codes. This can result in increased after-sale service costs for manufacturing companies. In an effort to prevent this, some companies charge after-sale service fees for products that contain binaries modified by users. Some also use a lock that prevents users from making changes. However, due to community protests, they are leaning toward providing an unlock code or software. Some companies are considering adopting backup/recovery solutions for products that have been affected by the user's modification of software.

Despite these problems, the growth of product-based FOSS communities has led to another FOSS ecosystem being established. Users' practical needs are reflected in the products resulting from these communities, and this is what companies may want to pay attention to. If a company proactively responds to users' needs in their product development, it can enhance customer satisfaction. Also, users may voluntarily upgrade software in outdated products for which a company can no longer provide technical support. The number of communities and the level of their maturity toward a certain product can even affect users' decisions to purchase a product. In light of this situation, companies should disclose their source codes to support communities' activities. The emergence of FOSS platforms has not only generated product-based FOSS, but also fueled its growth. This, in turn, has led companies to proactively participate in the ecosystem, thereby solidly establishing the product-based FOSS projects ecosystem.

6   Conclusion and Further Work

In this paper, a company's participation process in the more traditional component-based FOSS ecosystem was divided into four levels. The paper discussed activities and obstacles within each level and provided examples from companies that were studied. It also presented the new FOSS ecosystem which is formed from product-based FOSS communities, instead of component-based communities, following the emergence of FOSS platforms. There are still many difficulties looming ahead for companies that want to join FOSS communities, although the level of difficulty varies from one company to another. However, since participation in the FOSS ecosystem is inevitable, companies should continue to endeavor to resolve this issue. Above all, at a time when intellectual property rights are increasingly respected, companies should seek measures to minimize damages to their intellectual property rights during the distribution process of their source codes. They must also ensure that there are no intellectual property rights issues, including patent or copyright issues, when adopting FOSS.

In the future, we will continue to conduct research and activities to better adapt to the new FOSS ecosystem and to make better use of it. We are planning to monitor the activities of FOSS projects on a regular basis to discover the developer contribution field and to identify the needs of product users. In addition, we are planning to communicate with FOSS developers through the Open Source Release Center (OSRC) [27]. By proactively analyzing ideas and suggestions for improving products and then applying them, we seek to have more FOSS developers interested in our products. We also plan to make contributions to the FOSS ecosystem through various means of support for FOSS developers.

References

[1] GNU General Public License, http://www.gnu.org/copyleft/gpl.html
[2] Stallman, R.: The GNU Manifesto (1985),
    http://www.fsf.org/gnu/manifesto.html
[3] Goth, G.: Open Source Business Models: Ready for Prime Time. In: IEEE Software, pp. 98–100 (November/December 2005)
[4] Gonzalez-Barahona, J.M., Robles, G., Herraiz, I.: Impact of the creation of the mozilla foundation in the activity of developers. In: MSR, p. 28. IEEE Computer Society (2007)
[5] Corbet, J., Kroah-Hartman, G., McPherson, A.: Linux Kernel Development How Fast it is Going, Who is Doing It, What They are Doing, and Who is Sponsoring It
[6] Herraiz, I., Izquierdo-Cortazar, D., Rivas-Hernandez, F.: FLOSSMetrics: Free/Libre/Open Source Software Metrics. In: CSRM, pp. 281–284. IEEE Computer Society (2009)
[7] Deprez, J., Haaland, K., Kamseu, F.: QualOSS Methodology and QUALOSS assessment methods. In: QualOSS Project Deliverable 4.1 (2008)
[8] Allen, J., Collison, S., Luckey, R.: Ohloh Web Site API (2009), http://www.ohloh.net
[9] McLaughlin, L.: Inside the Software Patents Debate. In: IEEE Software, pp. 102–105 (2005)
[10] FFmpeg License and Legal Considerations (2011),
    http://ffmpeg.org/legal.html
[11] Open Invention Network, http://www.openinventionnetwork.com/
[12] Hewlett-Packard, FOSS Governance Fundamentals (January 2008)
[13] Welte, H.: About the gpl-violations.org?, http://www.gpl-violations.org/about.html#why
[14] Hemel, A., Kalleberg, K.T., Vermaas, R., Dolstra, E.: Finding Software License Violations through Binary Code Clone Detection. In: Proc. 8th Working Conference on Mining Software Repositories (MSR), Waikiki, Honolulu, HI, USA, pp. 63–72 (2011)
[15] Welte, H.: GPL Product Vendor FAQ (2004-2010), http://gpl-violations.org/faq/vendor-faq.html
[16] Hemel, A.: The GPL Compliance Engineering Guide (2008-2010), http://www.loohuis-consulting.nl/downloads/compliance-manual.pdf
[17] Schlesinger, D.: Working with Open Source: A Practical Guide. In: Interactions, ACM, pp. 35–37 (2007)
[18] Linux Foundation, LF488: Implementation and Management of Open Source Compliance

[19] Linux Foundation : Self-Assessment Compliance Checklist,
     http://www.linuxfoundation.org/programs/legal/compliance/se
     lf-assessment-checklist
[20] Meeker, H.J.: The Open source Alternative, Understanding Risks and Leveraging
     Opportunities CH14 The Border Dispute of GPLs. In: The Open Source Alternative.
     John Wiley & Sons, Inc. (2008)
[21] Samsung's Open Source Release Center, http://opensource.samsung.com
[22] Free Software Foundation: What is Copyleft?, http://www.gnu.org/copyleft/
[23] Raymond, E.S.: The Cathedral and the Bazaar. O'Reilly (1999)
[24] The Apache Software Foundation: Apache License, http://www.apache.org/
     licenses/
[25] Open Handset Alliance. Android Open Source Project,
     http://source.android.com
[26] Project Voodoo, http://project-voodoo.org/
[27] Samsung's Open Source Community site, https://opensource.samsung.com/
     community.do

Citizen Engineering: Evolving OSS Practices to Engineering Design and Analysis

Zhi Zhai, Tracy Kijewski-Correa, Ashan Kareem,
David Hachen, and Gregory Madey

University of Notre Dame, Notre Dame, IN-46556, USA
{zzhai,tkijewsk,akareem,dhachen,gmadey}@nd.edu

Abstract. Open Source Software (OSS) development has much in common with concepts such as crowdsourcing, citizen science, collective intelligence, human-based computation, and what we call "Citizen Engineering (CE)". We report on several pilot projects that apply these shared principles of OSS development to engineering activities beyond software engineering. CE models harness human computing power from open communities, which commonly consist of a cohort of geographically and/or institutionally scattered citizens - professionals or amateurs - to collaboratively solve real-world problems. In most cases, the problems targeted are challenging to computers, but manageable or trivial to human intelligence. In these systems, while humans play fundamental roles, whether they are project architects or problem solvers, the implementation of CE is greatly facilitated by the advance of information technology, particularly the Internet, considered as "creative mode of user interactivity, not merely a medium between messages and people" [10]. In this paper, we characterize existing citizen engineering practices into 6 major categories, followed by a discussion of 4 ongoing projects, aiming to provide new perspectives and insights for achieving successful CE project designs.

1 Introduction

Open Source Software (OSS) development is often researched for its novel approaches to software engineering. OSS is typically characterized by its openness, distributed and often voluntary participation, and end-user participation in the software engineering processes. It is observed that similar open, distributed, possibly voluntary and end-user based engineering activities are emerging under various labels, such as crowdsourcing, end-user participation in the design process, citizen science, collective intelligence, human-based computing, and what we call *Citizen Engineering*. Evolving information technologies provide unprecedented opportunities to solicit contributions from the public, i.e., citizens. Two popular examples are Wikipedia and YouTube, where regular citizens can freely contribute and evaluate contents as long as they abide by certain community rules. Advancing cyber-infrastructure, such as high speed networks, increasing computational capabilities, and high capacity databases, enables transformative

I. Hammouda et al. (Eds.): OSS 2012, IFIP AICT 378, pp. 61–77, 2012.
© IFIP International Federation for Information Processing 2012

platforms to diminish the barriers among geographically or institutionally dispersed users. People can easily channel their brainpower and "cognitive surplus" to accomplish meaningful work for a common good, largely in their spare time [25]. Characterizing the existing CE projects, we identify 6 major categories:

1. **Crowd Decisions**: Exemplified by the Reddit and Digg reader voting systems, by casting their votes, crowds have the capacity to collectively identify high quality products.
2. **Crowd Sumbission/Funding/Journalism**: Individuals in the crowd can make directed contributions, which could take the form of submitting a piece of content, chipping in a small amount of money, or reporting on what one has heard, witnessed, or interpreted. Together, pieces of contributions are channeled and possibly merged, and results are either fed back to serve community interests or stir up broader social attentions.
3. **Crowd Wisdom**: Networks of organized participants contribute their knowledge in specific areas, oftentimes leading to elaborate artifacts, e.g., the Mozilla web browser, considered as suitable alternatives for proprietary counterparts.
4. **Crowd Byproduct**: *Standalone* and *Piggyback* are the two major types[13]. In standalone systems, users contribute human-based computation as byproducts of major activities, e.g. Biogames [22]. Piggyback systems collect "user traces" generated out of other purposes to solve target problems [20]. For instance, in search engine optimization, Google records users' query history to prompt search keywords and suggests spell corrections later on.
5. **Micro Task**: Certain tasks can be divided into small units and assigned to online workers. Such small units of work usually require lower human skills, and their results are easy to merge. The online platforms, such as Amazon Mechanical Turk and Crowdflower, provide such services.
6. **Innovation Tournament**: Outside human resources can be harnessed via open challenges or competitions. If the ideas/inventions get adopted by the institutions seeking solutions, winners can be recognized by monetary rewards, non-monetary acclaims or both, e.g., the DARPA red-balloon competition [26].

Following the 6 categories above, we present 4 pilot CE projects in this paper, which come from a larger NSF funded study – *Open Sourcing the Design of Civil Infrastructure* [19]. These 4 pilot projects are: *Haiti Earthquake Photo Tagging* (Micro Task); *Smart Phone Infrastructure Monitoring* (Crowd Submissions); *OpenFOAM Simulation* (Crowd Wisdom), focused on citizen engineering requiring a high level of expertise; *Shelters For All* (Innovation Tournament). In Sections II-V, we discuss them in detail.

In addition to the 6 categories, we classify CE projects along 3 dimensions for a deeper understanding of CE implementation: 1) Contributor Motivation, 2) Human Skills Required - how tasks get fulfilled, and 3) Quality Evaluation - how results get evaluated. Fig. 1) shows how the 4 projects are positioned in this 3-dimensional feature space.

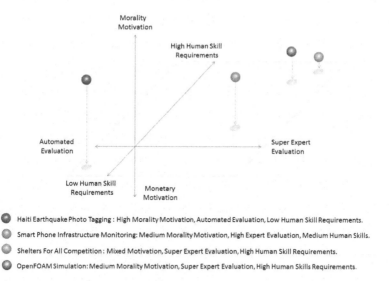

Haiti Earthquake Photo Tagging : High Morality Motivation, Automated Evaluation, Low Human Skill Requirements.

Smart Phone Infrastructure Monitoring: Medium Morality Motivation, High Expert Evaluation, Medium Human Skills.

Shelters For All Competition : Mixed Motivation, Super Expert Evaluation, High Human Skill Requirements.

OpenFOAM Simulation: Medium Morality Motivation, Super Expert Evaluation, High Human Skills Requirements.

Fig. 1. 3-Dimensional Classification of CE Projects: Motivation, Skill Level and Evaluation

2 Project I: Haiti Earthquake Photo Tagging

After the 2010 catastrophic Haitian earthquake, to help local residents rebuild their homeland, civil engineers from University of Notre Dame visited Haiti and took thousands of photos of impaired buildings, intending to classify common damage patterns, and thus to inform redesign and rebuilding efforts [23]. However, the volume of earthquake photos surpassed their capacity to process. To answer this call, a collaborative team of computer scientists, civil engineers, and sociologists built a CE platform, where crowds could be harnessed to fulfill photo classification tasks.

For this pilot project, students were recruited using announcements on mailing lists and school-wide posters, resulting in 242 students participating in the experiment as surrogates for citizen engineers. Their online activities were recorded in detail, including photo tagging classifications, the time spent tagging each photo, and login/logout timestamps.

Over 17 days, the crowd submitted 9318 photo classifications on 400 sample photos. The photo taggers came from a broad range of backgrounds – some of the participants were engineering and science majors, others were from finance, history or other humanities – and hence classifications were at times widely divergent. This heterogeneity mimics what is commonly observed in CE projects: highly diverse education levels of the users and variable quality of task fulfillment.

Positioning this project into the 3-dimension space: 1) contributors in the system were highly motivated by moral responsibilities, 2) the online crowds input their opinions about the images and collectively produced crowd consensus

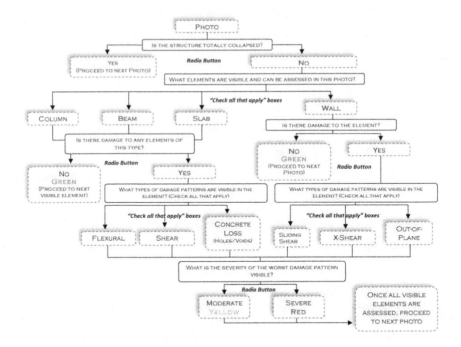

Fig. 2. Classification schema. As crowd went deeper along the tree, their answers diversified.

for organizers to consider, without expert evaluation involved, and 3) high-level civil engineering knowledge was not a prerequisite, since users could acquire required skills through tutorials provided by the platform.

2.1 Workflow Description [27]

Upon agreeing to terms and conditions on the front page, subjects were directed to a sign-up page, and asked to create their login credentials.

1. **Registration.** After subjects logged into the website, they saw a consent form with a brief description of the experiment: the task was to classify the types and serverity of earthquake damage depicted in 400 photos.
2. **Entry Survey.** The purpose of this questionnaire was to collect demographic and attitudinal data from the subjects.
3. **Tutorials.** The tutorial provides detailed information about how to properly classify the damage depicted in a photo, and by using hyper-links, subjects can return to this tutorial during their tagging process.
4. **Damage Classification.** To classify photos, subjects received a single, randomly chosen photo at a time, until they completed all 400 photos in the system or their allocated time period expired.

5. **Exit Survey.** At the end of a 7-day period, subjects were asked to complete a brief exit survey. The survey has questions like the motivation driving subjects to allocate time for voluntary work, the difficulty in classifying photos, the degree to which they found the task was interesting, etc.

2.2 Tagging Questions

As shown in Fig. 2, to classify a photo, subjects followed a 5-step damage assessment process. These steps are:

1. **Image Content.** Determine if an entire structure or only a part of the structure is visible in the image.
2. **Element Visibility.** Identify which elements (*beams, columns, slabs, walls*) of the building are visible and can be assessed.
3. **Damage Existence.** For each of these visible elements, determine if any of those elements are damaged.
4. **Damage Pattern.** For each of the elements identified as damaged, identify the damage pattern.
5. **Damage Severity.** For each of the elements identified as damaged, assess the severity of the damage (*Yellow* or *Red*).

Since there are at most 25 classification questions asked for each photo, maximumly, a user can earn 25 points from it. If the crowd consensus is that there is no damage on a certain element of the building, we do not further consider users' inputs about the damage pattern and severity of that building element. Compared to the similar image classification work conducted in [3], this workflow presents a comprehensive photo tagging schema with potential to generate new knowledge because of its depth.

Similar to Open Source Software development, when the end users are not developers themselves, the factors of human computer interaction (HCI) should be taken into consideration at early stage of development [17]. In this regard, we especially emphasized the web interface's friendliness and tutorials' clearness when developing the system.

3   Project II: Photo Sensing on Deteriorating Infrastructure

In United States, deteriorating infrastructure is in a worrying condition (See Fig. 3), and may lead to tragic disasters. In 2007, the busy I-35W Bridge in Minneapolis, MN, USA, collapsed during evening rush hour, claiming lives of 13 and injuring another 145, besides financial losses. In retrospect, this bridge had evidence of crumbling and corrosion before it collapsed. This may suggest that this type of accidents can be prevented if signs and traces indicating infrastructure deteriorating is timely reported to corresponding authorities.

Human sensing systems leverage a large number of volunteers to conduct mobile sensing, which can be a complement to traditional inspection procedures.

TABLE A ★ 2009 *Report Card for America's Infrastructure*	
Aviation	**D**
Bridges	**C**
Dams	**D**
Drinking Water	**D-**
Energy	**D+**
Hazardous Waste	**D**
Inland Waterways	**D-**
Levees	**D-**
Public Parks and Recreation	**C-**
Rail	**C-**
Roads	**D-**
Schools	**D**
Solid Waste	**C+**
Transit	**D**
Wastewater	**D-**
AMERICA'S INFRASTRUCTURE G.P.A.	**D**
ESTIMATED 5 YEAR INVESTMENT NEED	**$2.2 TRILLION**

NOTES Each category was evaluated on the basis of capacity, condition, funding, future need, operation and maintenance, public safety and resilience

A = Exceptional
B = Good
C = Mediocre
D = Poor
F = Failing

Fig. 3. Grades of American Infrastructure. Sources: American Society of Civil Engineers [1].

Given the increasing pervasiveness of 5.81 billion mobile phone subscribers [5], portable digital devices across the globe have evolved into a pervasive sensor platform, creating the possibility of organizing phone holders as human-based sensors [18]. This "human sensor network" [16][12], composed of digital devices and human subscribers, has demonstrated advantages compared to traditional sensor systems:

1. Hand-held digital devices, due to high penetration, have better coverage and flexibility. The resulting data, which are crumbling infrastructure photos in our case, provide significantly more informative insights.
2. New apps/add-ons/plug-ins can be timely installed and periodically updated by human users carrying the devices.

3. In a human-based system, each mobile device is associated with a phone holder, whose assistance could be leveraged to achieve complex functionality. For example, residents usually have intimate knowledge of patterns and anomalies in their communities and neighborhoods [11].

3.1   Components and Considerations

Inspired by previous practices [2][24][15], we piloted an infrastructure monitoring system. The workflow is shown in Fig. 4, and the following 9 components comprised the workflow:

1. ***User Recruitment.*** Citizen inspectors in this experiment were college juniors and sophomores. As their hometowns are widely spread across the country, collectively they have good coverage of the nationwide civil infrastructure.
2. ***User Education.*** Research in psychology shows that individuals motivated by goals that are both well-specified and challenging tend to have higher levels of effort and task performance than goals that are too easy or vague [21]. In design, we strive to provide a well-instructed and easy-to-follow tutorial.
3. ***Information Recording.*** Participants were encouraged to go outdoors and snap photos of problematic infrastructure, such as cracked structures, crumbling concrete, broken piers, and leaking tunnels. As photo-taking functionality is built in most digital devices, there is no need to develop new applications in this study.
4. ***Data Sending.*** Two options were provided for photo submission, as shown in Fig. 5:
   - If the user has any type of smart phones equipped with the geo-tagging function, s/he can email us photos directly or upload photos via web interface. Our software can automatically retrieve geo-coordinates from the submissions.
   - If the digital device cannot geo-tag the photo automatically, users can either input street address or use a movable marker to pinpoint the location on a Google Map embedded in the uploading page (See Fig. 6).
5. ***Data Collecting.*** A data repository hosts the web service, receiving data form the digital devices through different approaches. A MySQL database saves the metadata of each photo into database tables.
6. ***Data Processing.*** Data access was managed according to terms and conditions agreed by participants. The intricacy and importance of data security and privacy should be always emphasized [11]. This is a two-fold issue: (1) Privacy concerns: over time, timestamps on photo submissions, combined with geo-space information, provide traceable data about citizen inspectors' life patterns; (2)Homeland security: the weak points of the national infrastructure may become targets of potential terrorist attacks. In this regard,

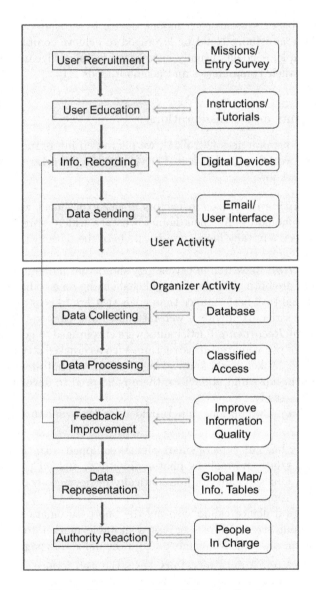

Fig. 4. Framework of Participatory Sensing

Fig. 5. Two Options for Photo Submission

the protection policy on our experimental portal was that any photos coming from an individual were only visible to that individual. The global map, where overall infrastructure photos were aggregated and presented, was only visible to project organizers, masked off from the public.

7. *Feedback and Improvement*
   If data was found missing, the user could revisit the venue and retrieve complement data, possibly from variable angles and different distances, thanks to the human intelligence associated with the digital device.

8. *Data Presentation*
   Aggregated data was visualized with color balloons on a global map, with each color balloon representing one damaged infrastructure photo, as shown in Fig. 7.

9. *Policy Influence*
   Relevant authorities can be reached and informed in the wake of possible disruptive development of inspected infrastructure, and the location and severity of deterioration can be further investigated to a finer resolution if necessary.

3.2   Result and Discussion

In a period of 12 days, we received 170 photos from 25 users, covering 30 cities/townships across 6 states in US. Most photos identified deteriorating infrastructure, with a large portion of submissions in fairly high quality (6 sample photos are shown in Fig. 8). This study provides a new perspective, where the CE approach can be leveraged to enhance human ability in the area of detecting infrastructure flaws, reducing financial resources, and more importantly saving lives.

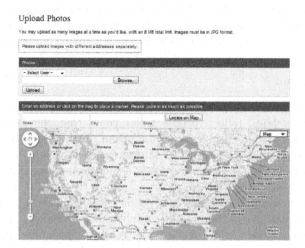

Fig. 6. Two Uploading Options: Street Fields Vs. Map Markers

Global Map

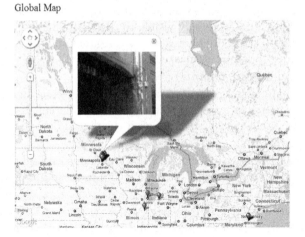

Fig. 7. Global Map: Data Representation and Visualization

4 Project III: Shelters for All Competition - Safe and Affordable Housing for the Developing World

When organizations encounter limited human resources to solve a challenging problem, they can pursue ideas outside the organization via open calls, namely innovation tournaments. Examples falling into this category include NetFlix Prize [8] for movie recommendations and IBM Innovation Jam [9] for sale improvement.

Enlightened by these successful experiments, we initiated a new innovation challenge, titled "Shelters For All Competition". By conducting this open competition, we aimed to achieve two goals (1) soliciting feasible designs of affordable housing in underdeveloped regions throughout the world; (2) assessing the pros and cons of the innovation tournament model in organizing crowdsourcing work.

4.1 Background

Fifteen of the twenty most populated cities in the world are currently located in developing countries, reflective of a wider trend that the majority of the world's population are increasingly hosted in urban zones. This results in densely populated, unstructured settlements or slums, the lack of safe drinking water, proper sanitation and other basic necessities in such landscapes, and other social issues.

Recognizing the need for housing innovations, this competition was designed to tap into the creativity of the public – individuals and teams – to design low-cost, safe housing to the world's urban poor. While adoption and sustainability by a target country or region is important, it is hoped that innovative solutions solicited from global community can have broader applications. To effectively

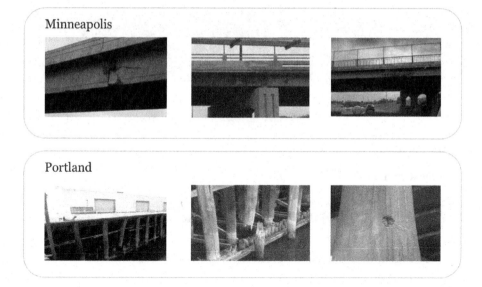

Minneapolis

Portland

Fig. 8. Sample Photos from User Submissions

meet the goals of improving living conditions of developing countries, desirable designs should have the following properties:

1. *Resiliency* to insure life-safety and protection against natural disasters and other environmental factors.
2. *Feasibility* to be practically implemented using locally available technologies, capabilities and materials.
3. *Sustainability* to be supported indefinitely using local resources (economic & natural), technologies & skills of the community, and can adapt to their evolving needs.
4. *Viability* to earn the support of most local stakeholders as culturally appropriate, so that ideas are not just accepted, but embraced and promoted.
5. *Scalability* to be applied elsewhere beyond the particular country or region used for solution development.

The welcome page of the competition platform is shown in Fig. 9, and competition prizes and awards are designed as:

1. *The grand prize* $10,000, granted to the best design among all submissions.
2. *Popular vote award* $1,000, awarded to the submission that obtains the highest score in peer reviews.
3. *Referral award* $600, distributed to the 3 individuals whose referrals result in the most submissions.

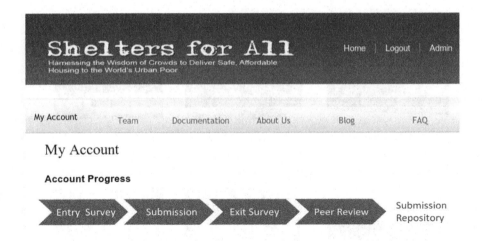

Fig. 9. User Interface of Shelters For All Competition Website

4.2 Results

By the time we closed the submissions site on Jan. 22, 2012, there were 99 valid solutions from 26 teams and 73 individuals. Most designs reflected participants' unique perspectives and considerations on tackling the challenge.

Similar to OSS projects, participants in this open competition are global citizens, with dramatically different working schedules and physical facilities. For them, the major connecting point and the information source are the project website. OSS experiences tell us that even a very short period of downtime on the server side would frustrate a certain number of participants. As such, as competition proceeded, we made particular emphasis on the system stability and scalability.

5 Project IV: Expert-Citizen Experiment - OpenFOAM Simulation

To design a successful Citizen Engineering system, an inevitable challenge is that the contributors, i.e., *Citizen Engineers* - professionals, researchers, students, and even the public at large - usually have a broad range of expertise and talents, since individuals are at various stages in their careers. Among them, there is a certain portion of well-trained professionals, who have received formal training and/or have years of practical experience. While many engineers are intrinsically motivated to provide voluntary service to society, for licensed engineers, Professional Development Hours (PDHs) are necessary to maintain licensure, and as such there may be pragmatic incentives for licensed engineers to engage in citizen engineering activities.

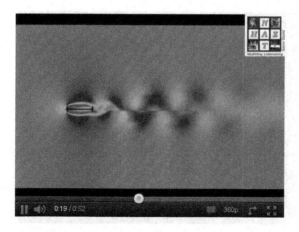

Fig. 10. Movie Tutorial For OpenFOAM Simulation

Such expert-citizens have unique goals and expectations that are different from average citizens, such as amateurs and hobbyists in traditional citizen science projects. To leverage the expertise of skilled citizens, we need to develop new principles and guidelines to achieve successful designs. These new guidelines may be different from the strategies of fulfilling tasks that require less experience.

Inspired by previous research on leveraging "citizen expert groups" to achieve common social scientific goals [14][7], we identify the following 3 challenges that are unique to expert citizen engineering projects.

1. *Task Complexity.* In expert citizen projects, tasks usually demand high human intelligence and skill level. For example, experts can be solicited to provide insightful, informative and/or authoritative judgments.
2. *Recruitment Difficulty.* Due to the complexity inherent in tasks, available human resources are limited and membership eligibility is rather selective compared to traditional crowdsourcing tasks.
3. *Resource Requirement.* Complicated tasks may require sophisticated analysis tools and high performance computational resources [6]. For example, some analysis and design methods, such as nonlinear finite element analyses of complex structures, can easily over stress in-house computational capabilities of many firms and laboratories.

These challenges motivate us to investigate more effective engineering designs that can leverage expertise and experience afforded by highly skilled citizen engineers [28]. In this pilot project, highly skilled experts were invited to use a computational fluid dynamics (CFD) tool to analyze channel flow movements.

5.1 OpenFOAM Package

On the web platform, the primary simulation suite we provided is the OpenFOAM (Open Field Operation and Manipulation) Toolbox developed by OpenCFD Ltd

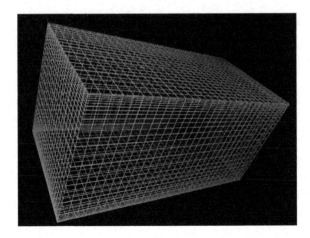

Fig. 11. Mesh Visualization of the Channel Flow. This screenshot is from one student's report.

[4]. The toolbox is an OSS package, licensed under the GNU General Public License (GPL). OpenFOAM's ability to simulate complex turbulence, and its openness to user customization and extension make itself one of most popular CFD simulation tools. It has been widely used by practitioners worldwide, and validated and verified intensively [4]. Moreover, conveniently, OpenFOAM has an embedded meshing utility, which helps expert-citizens better present their results.

5.2 Experiment Procedures

The expert engineers in this pilot came from a graduate-level class – CE 80200 Wind Engineering – offered by the Department of Civil Engineering and Geological Sciences at Notre Dame. This senior graduate-level course covers primary design considerations under a variety of wind types. Topics include the analysis of structural response due to wind loading, modeling of wind-induced forces, and principles of resilient design under high wind loads. 9 graduate students and visiting scholars enrolled in the class; all had extensive formal training in civil engineering, equipped with knowledge of both civil engineering and OpenFOAM software.

5.3 Workflow

First, users were presented with a question set, in which questions were designed to test users' basic understanding of lecture materials. After the questions, users were taken to the main interface, Fig. 10, where they could receive the work assignment, review the previous documents, login to run the simulation platform and submit their results in the end. A sample mesh generation is shown in Fig. 11.

5.4 Post-experiment Interview

After the experiment was complete, we interviewed subjects who had first-hand experience about the platform. Most concerns were centered around the robustness of the simulation platform. When users were asked this question, "Please describe the difficulties you had using the simulation platform?", here are some representative responses:

- *"The performance, error handling and reliability of the computing services could be improved."*
- *"Sometimes, I cannot proceed with my simulation because of the high traffic on the platform."*

It is implied by users' concerns that when our web site has provided basic functionalities, expert citizens especially emphasize the reliability and stability of the system that can facilitate them to navigate through complicated tasks. In this regard, the retention of expert citizens to a large degree depends on the satisfaction of their high expectations on user experience. "Being usable and being likable are two different goals" [29]. Easiness and smoothness plays a more primary role for professional users than it does for average users.

6 Discussions and Future Work

In this paper, we introduced 6 general categories of CE practices: Crowd Decisions, Crowd Submissions/Funding/Journalism, Crowd Wisdom, Crowd Byproduct, Micro Task, and Innovation Tournament. OSS development can be a form of crowd wisdom, where loosely connected online software engineers make large or small contributions over time, and the quality of the collective artifacts gradually get improved. Likewise, end users of OSS make contributions to the development through their feature requests, bug reports, and Q&A on the project forums. We can apply the same approaches/principles proved successful in OSS development to other engineering domains. The 4 pilot projects presented in the previous sections attempt to generalize these rules beyond the OSS domain.

As always, more research problems emerged than were answered. For example, in Micro Task, what is the optimal number of users to work on the same task in order to secure a quality result? How should we rate and group online users based on their performance? In Crowd Wisdom, how can we efficiently divide the task into units and aggregate crowds' inputs later on, when the tasks are interdependent? How can we automate the verification and evaluation process? In Innovation Tournament, how can a competition be more appealing to those users with strong expertise and professional background? Higher monetary prize or stronger moral motivation in recognition? Appropriately answering these questions will help the future research and development of CE systems, more effectively leveraging the "wisdom of the crowd".

Acknowledgment. The research presented in this paper was supported in part by an award from the National Science Foundation, under Grant No. CBET-0941565. Any opinions, findings, and conclusions or recommendations expressed in this material are those of the author(s) and do not necessarily reflect the views of the National Science Foundation. The authors would also like to thank Zack Kertcher, Peter Sempolinski, Douglas Thain, Ellen Childs, Daniel Wei for valuable contributions.

References

1. American Society of Civil Engineers (ASCE). Report Card for America's Infrastructure (2009)
2. CENS, http://research.cens.ucla.edu/ (retrieved August 2011)
3. ImageCat, http://www.imagecatinc.com/ (retrieved August 2011)
4. OpenFOAM, http://www.openfoam.com/features/index.php (retrieved July 2011)
5. Global mobile cellular subscriptions, http://www.itu.int/ITU-D/ict/statistics/ (retrieved March 2012)
6. OSDCI, http://www.ne.edu/~opence/ (retrieved March 2012)
7. Ahlheim, M., Ekasingh, B., Frör, O., Kitchaincharoen, J., Neef, A., Sangkapitux, C., Sinphurmsukskul, N.: Using citizen expert groups in environmental valuation - Lessons from a CVM study in Northern Thailand. Technical Report 283/2007, Department of Economics, University of Hohenheim, Germany (2007)
8. Bennett, J., Lanning, S.: The Netflix prize. In: KDD Cup and Workshop in Conjunction with KDD (2007)
9. Bjelland, O.M., Chapman Wood, R.: An inside view of IBM's Innovation Jam. MIT Sloan Management Review 50(1), 32–40 (2008)
10. Brabham, D.C.: Crowdsourcing as a model for problem solving: An introduction and cases. Convergence 14(1), 75 (2008)
11. Burke, J., Estrin, D., Hansen, M., Praker, A., Ramanathan, N., Reddy, S., Srivastava, M.: Participatory sensing. In: ACM Sensys World Sensor Web Workshop, Boulder, CO, USA (October 2006)
12. Campbell, A.T., Eisenman, S.B., Lane, N.D., Miluzzo, E., Peterson, R.A., Lu, H., Zheng, X., Musolesi, M., Fodor, K., Ahn, G.-S.: The rise of people-centric sensing. IEEE Internet Computing 12, 12–21 (2008)
13. Doan, A., Ramakrishnan, R., Halevy, A.Y.: Crowdsourcing systems on the worldwide web. Communications of ACM 54(4) (April 2011)
14. Fischer, F.: Citizen participation and the democratization of policy expertise: From theoretical inquiry to practical cases. Policy Sciences 26, 165–187 (1993)
15. Goldman, J., Shilton, K., Burke, J., Estrin, D., Hansen, M., Ramanathan, N., Reddy, S., Samanta, V., Srivastava, M., West, R.: Participatory Sensing: A citizen-powered approach to illuminating the patterns that shape our world. Foresight & Governance Project, White Paper (2009)
16. Goodchild, M.: Citizens as sensors: the world of volunteered geography. Geo Journal 69(4), 211–221 (2007)
17. Hedberg, H., Iivari, N.: Integrating HCI Specialists into Open Source Software Development Projects. In: Boldyreff, C., Crowston, K., Lundell, B., Wasserman, A.I. (eds.) OSS 2009. IFIP AICT, vol. 299, pp. 251–263. Springer, Heidelberg (2009)

18. Kansal, A., Goraczko, M., Zhao, F.: Building a sensor network of mobile phones. In: Proceedings of the 6th International Conference on Information Processing in Sensor Networks, IPSN 2007, pp. 547–548. ACM, Cambridge (2007)
19. Kijewski-Correa, T., et al.: Open sourcing the design of civil infrastructure (OSD-CI): A paradigm shift. In: Proceedings of Structures Congress, Las Vegas, NV, USA (April 2011)
20. Kittur, A., Chi, H., Suh, B.: Crowdsourcing user studies with mechanical turk. In: Proceedings of CHI 2008, pp. 453–456. ACM Press (2008)
21. Locke, E.A., Latham, G.P.: A theory of goal setting and task performance. Prentice-Hall, Englewood Cliffs (1990)
22. Mavandadi, S., Dimitrov, S., Feng, S., Yu, F., Sikora, U., Yaglidere, O., Padmanabhan, S., Nielsen, K., Ozcan, A.: Distributed medical image analysis and diagnosis through crowd-sourced games: A malaria case study. PLoS ONE 7(5), e37245 (2012)
23. Mix, D., Kijewski-Correa, T., Taflanidis, A.A.: Assessment of residential housing in Leogane, Haiti after the January 2010 earthquake and identification of needs for rebuilding. In: Earthquake Spectra (October 2011)
24. Reddy, S., Mun, M., Burke, D.E.J., Hansen, M., Srivastava, M.: Using mobile phones to determine transportation modes. ACM Transactions on Sensor Networks 6(2) (February 2010)
25. Shirky, C.: Cognitive Surplus: Creativity and Generosity in a Connected Age. Allen Lane (2010)
26. Tang, J.C., Cebrian, M., Giacobe, N.A., Kim, H.-W., Kim, T., Wickert, D.B.: Reflecting on the DARPA Red Balloon Challenge. Communications of the ACM 54(4), 78–85 (2011)
27. Zhai, Z., Hachen, D., Kijewski-Correa, T., Shen, F., Madey, G.: Citizen engineering: Methods for "crowd sourcing" highly trustworthy results. In: Proceedings of the Forty-fifth Hawaii International Conference on System Science (HICSS-45), Maui, HI, USA, January 4-7 (2012)
28. Zhai, Z., Sempolinski, P., Thain, D., Madey, G.R., Wei, D., Kareem, A.: Expert-citizen engineering: "crowdsourcing" skilled citizens. In: DASC, pp. 879–886. IEEE (2011)
29. Zhang, P., von Dran, G.M.: Satisfiers and dissatisfiers: A two-factor model for website design and evaluation. Journal of the American Society for Information Science 51(14), 1253–1268 (2000)

Gender Differences in Early Free and Open Source Software Joining Process

Victor Kuechler, Claire Gilbertson, and Carlos Jensen

School of Electrical Engineering and Computer Science
Oregon State University, Corvallis, OR, USA
kuechlej@onid.orst.edu, claire.gilbertson@gmail.com,
cjensen@eecs.oregonstate.edu

Abstract. With the growth of free and open source software (FOSS) and the adoption of FOSS solutions in business and everyday life, it is important that projects serve their growingly diverse user base. The sustainability of FOSS projects relies on a constant influx of new contributors. Several large demographic surveys found that FOSS communities are very homogenous, dominated by young men, similar to the bias existing in the rest of the IT workforce. Building on previous research, we examine mailing list subscriptions and posting statistics of female FOSS participants. New participants often experience their first interaction on a FOSS project's mailing list. We explored six FOSS projects – Buildroot, Busybox, Jaws, Parrot, uClibc, and Yum. We found a declining rate of female participation from the 8.27% of subscribers, to 6.63% of posters, and finally the often reported code contributor rate of 1.5%. We found a disproportionate attrition rate among women along every step of the FOSS joining process.

Keywords: joining process, diversity, mailing lists.

1 Introduction

Although a similar percentage of men and women receive bachelor's degrees today [19], there is a significant difference in the percentage for computer science and engineering. Only 25% of IT workers are women [20], and women earn around 18% of IT-related bachelor's degrees [28]. A smaller percentage of women actively participate in FOSS, less than 2% [7, 9, 14, 18, 24]. Why do so few women participate in FOSS, and what can attribute to these differences?

FOSS projects need to attract and maintain active users. The volunteer nature of FOSS and the general lack of financial incentives to participate lead to high turnover, and the need for a continuous influx of developers [29]. The transition from user to contributor begins on a mailing list. Mailing lists are at the heart of all communication and discussion in FOSS projects, and therefore at the heart of all FOSS projects. Its archival nature also preserves past, present and future design and implementation decisions, as well as the project's evolving culture.

Joining a FOSS project often begins with lurking or silently observing the community by subscribing to its mailing list. Since the majority of communication occurs on

I. Hammouda et al. (Eds.): OSS 2012, IFIP AICT 378, pp. 78–93, 2012.
© IFIP International Federation for Information Processing 2012

mailing lists, we need to understand how this first step affects newcomers' motivations and future behavior.

A previous study found that almost 80% of newbies received a positive reply to their first post, and those who received a timely response were more likely to continue participating [11]. This study also found that messages from men and women were treated similarly in terms of tone, helpfulness, and likelihood of replies, yet significantly fewer women posted (2.68%). The study did not address the time users lurked on mailing lists before posting, which may be an influential factor.

Building on previous research, we examined subscriber logs and data for six FOSS projects: Buildroot, Busybox, Jaws, Parrot, uClibc, and Yum. We examined the differences between posters and non-posters to determine the attrition rate of women at different stages of the joining process. More specifically we sought to examine the following research questions:

RQ1:   Once subscribed to a FOSS mailing list, are women as likely to participate (post) as men?

RQ2:   Do women participate (post) with the same frequency as males?

RQ3:   Do women lurk longer than men before posting?

RQ4:   Do men and women participate (subscribe) for equal amounts of time?

The paper is structured as follows: First we review work related to FOSS communities and project joining. Next, we describe our methodology for collecting and analyzing data. In section 4 we describe our results. In section 5 we discuss our research questions. We finish by reviewing our data and presenting our conclusion.

2   Related Work

The influence of FOSS has grown over the last decades and shows that FOSS software can be more reliable and perform better than proprietary software [27]. FOSS encompasses a great variety in projects, from the highly technical Linux Kernel, supporting operating systems like Ubuntu, Fedora and Debian, to end-user applications like Android, Wikipedia, and business solutions like Open Office and the GIMP.

FOSS is a volunteer-driven development paradigm that brings together developers and contributors from around the world. Only 30% of developers are paid [7, 14] and what motivates contributors can be both intrinsic and extrinsic [5, 14]; a majority of FOSS developer surveys find that contributors are motivated by the opportunity to improve their programming skills [7, 14, 24]. Working on FOSS allows users of any age, education, or experience level to gain valuable skills. One study shows that a significant number of people "wished to improve software products for other developers," [9] and another finds that 77% of respondents thought giving back to the community is very important [14]. A passionate user may also start their own project because he or she has an unaddressed interest or need that could be met by a FOSS solution [22]. FOSS projects are also expanding to address humanitarian needs, which attract a different kind of developer [1].

Surveys of FOSS developer demographics, although outdated, show that FOSS communities are 98% male [7, 9, 14, 18, 24] with an average age of 27 [7, 9, 14, 24].

On average, FOSS developers are highly educated with 30% having at least a bachelor's degree and 10.6% a graduate degree. Most contributions are from Western Europe and the United States. Many FOSS communities have taken steps to address inequalities by starting different programs aimed at recruiting and retaining underrepresented groups. While some projects acknowledge the importance of different types of diversity, most focus on recruiting and retaining female contributors.

There are several text-based forms of communication used in FOSS projects to maintain project awareness. Internet Relay Chat (IRC) is used for real-time communication. Asynchronous communication in the form of blogs, wikis, forums, and bug-tracking systems archive project discussions, documentation and project news. These channels tend to augment mailing lists, the primary medium used for interaction in FOSS communities [10]. This tool allows everyone to participate asynchronously, keep up-to-date with new developments, bounce ideas back and forth, and encourage discussions about the project. Gutwin et al. not that "there is a strong culture of 'making it public' [in FOSS] where developers are willing to answer questions, discuss their plans, report on their actions, and argue design details, all on the mailing list" [10].

Several studies focus on mailing list activity and its influence on future participation. Lampe and Johnston examine the Slashdot community over a one-month period and found that more than 55% of newcomers made only one comment and those that received no feedback were less likely to continue to comment [15]. Krogh et al. studied Freenet's developer list for one year and find that of successful joiners, over three-quarters started a new thread, and that the 10% of participants who never received replies dropped out [13].

Jensen et al. focus on new users instead of developers [11]. They observe the first posts made by new users and how existing members greeted them. After examining the newbie's tone, nationality, and gender they find that newbies received equally prompt replies, but flaming or aggressive replies were not uncommon. They also argue that because this behavior is public it could have far-reaching effects: "Thus, while OSS participants were generally polite to newbies, it is possible that newbie expectations and perceptions of politeness could be colored by how the regulars engage with each other" [11]. In other words, lurkers may be pushed away based solely on observed negative behavior on mailing lists.

Mailing lists keep an exact record of public discussions. "Mailing lists allow people to find out who the experts are, simply by initiating a discussion: because the messages go to the entire group, the 'right people' will identify themselves by joining the conversation." [10]. This makes mailing lists a great source of information, and subscription logs let us see not only who uses the list, but also who is lurking to test the waters.

FOSS communities are hierarchical in nature and the Onion Model in Figure 1, developed by Ye and Kishida [29], shows a very simplistic hierarchy of roles in FOSS communities. Newcomers often begin at the outer layers as passive users who may have subscribed to a mailing list or IRC channel. It is difficult to understand lurker behavior, in part due to the difficulty determining who is a lurker.

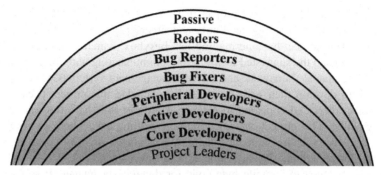

Fig. 1. Onion Model of FLOSS joining process [29]

Nonnecke and Preece examined lurking as a transitional phase needed in order for users to feel comfortable contributing to a technical discussion. They find that the transition could last anywhere from weeks to months, but they did not examine the effects of gender on this process [21]. Other studies, mostly of discussion forums and mailing lists, show lurkers make up from 50% [21, 25] to 90% [12, 16] of an online community. Lurking is recommended to newcomers in FOSS communities as a method to learn the current state of the project, who to talk to, what channels of communication to use, and project culture.

3 Methodology

3.1 Data Collection

The Oregon State University Open Source Lab (OSL) hosts over 150 projects and "distribute software to millions of users globally" [2]. The OSL acted as agents in gaining access to mailing list data and user subscription logs, with projects' consent. We selected active projects with many users and high traffic.

We also asked numerous other communities (not hosted at the OSL) for access to their data, with mixed results; some communities were willing to share their data but did neither use mailing lists nor keep subscription logs. Some were wary about sharing user's information, seeing potential privacy issues. Without a complete set of message files and corresponding logs, we could not use these projects for comparison.

The data we collected was all from mature, highly technical projects. These data sets spanned at least 500 days and have between 73 and 944 subscribers per mailing list.

3.1.1 Project Descriptions

We used data from six FOSS projects: Buildroot, Busybox, Jaws, uClibc, Yum and Parrot. From these we selected eleven mailing lists: Buildroot, Busybox, Jaws, Jaws-announces, Jaws-bugs, Jaws-commits, Jaws-developers, Jaws-general, uClibc, Yum, Yum-devel, and Parrot. Table 1 shows the time coverage of each mailing list.

Buildroot is a technical project that helps users install Linux on embedded systems [6]. Buildroot has one mailing list and a very active community that communicates about commits, questions, bug reports, and patches.

Busybox is a highly technical project that merges numerous UNIX utilities commonly found in GNU fileutils, shellutils and others [2], specifically for embedded systems [3]. This project has one mailing list, busybox, which is the main source of communication and the suggested medium for communicating with the community.

Jaws is a technical framework and content management system (CMS) that encourages users to develop their own modules. We included this project because it was smaller than others and appeared to cater to a broader user base (anyone with web authoring skills). This project contained multiple mailing lists, which we combined to more effectively compare with the others. We analyzed at Jaws, Jaws-announces, Jaws-bugs, Jaws-commits, Jaws-developers, and Jaws-general.

Parrot is designed to compile byte code for dynamic languages. Parrot's website directs users to the parrot-dev mailing list for development and discussion. Other documentation sends new users to parrot-users, which is practically unused [26].

uClibc or the "microcontroller C library" [4] is a smaller alternative to the GNU C Library, and almost all applications supported by glibc are compatible. uClibc has two mailing lists–one for discussion and development (uClibc) and another for source commits (uClibc-cvs), which was dedicated to different files for bug patches and other code changes. We chose to examine the list for discussion and development since this is where new users are most likely to interact with the community.

Yum or "yellowdog updater modified" is a package management system that provided tools to automate software installation, upgrading, configuring and uninstallation [30]. Yum works with RPM-based Linux distributions. This project had four mailing lists: rpm-metadata, yum, yum-commits, and yum-devel. We chose to examine yum-devel and yum since these mailing lists were more active and included a variety of users, including newcomers. The commits list mostly included code modifications and updates with few questions or other communication. The rpm-metadata list was not available at the time.

Table 1. Time period of each mailing list subscription log per project

Projects		# of subs	Start	End	Days
Buildroot		944	11/20/08	10/12/10	691
Busybox		695	11/20/08	05/18/10	544
Jaws	**Announces**	73	11/12/07	11/02/10	1085
	Bugs		11/02/07	08/30/10	1063
	Developers		11/12/07	10/07/10	1059
	General		11/12/07	11/02/07	1086
	Commits		11/12/07	11/03/10	1087
Parrot		698	07/30/08	05/16/10	989
uClibc		428	12/04/08	05/18/10	529
Yum		360	09/26/08	05/13/10	594
Yum-devel		112	09/26/08	05/18/10	599
All lists (mean)		3310	N/A		~600

3.2   Data Parsing

Using documentation from QMAIL [17], we created a Java program to parse the MBOX files and subscription logs to extract the following data (when available):

- Email address
- First name
- Last name
- Subscribe date (if any)
- Unsubscribe date (if any)
- Time on mailing list (Unsubscribe – Subscribe date)
- Number of posts
- Gender
- Date of first post

- Time spent on the list before first post (First post – subscribe date)
- Last Post
- Frequency of posts [(Last - First Post) / (number of Posts)]
- List (used when combining data from multiple lists)

The program iterated over users in the subscription logs for each MBOX file and counted the number of posts made by that person. When the users signed up for the list they could choose to add a first and/or last name in addition to the required email address. We used this information to determine the gender of the subscriber. When available we parsed this information from the logs. When this was not available, we attempted to extract a name from the email address. We used pattern matching to find possible names using the following patterns:

First.last@...
First_last@...
First-last@...

If these schemes did not offer a match, we added the entire *username* portion of the email to the *first name* field.

We recorded users' mailing list subscribe and unsubscribe dates; some users subscribed and unsubscribed multiple times. In these cases, we treated the first subscription as the join date and the last un-subscription as the unsubscribe date. Some users did not have a subscription or unsubscribe date in the logs. Since we only had data for approximately two years for each list, some long-time subscribers did not join or leave during that time period. For these we assigned a join and leave date based on their earliest and latest activity. For this study, we focused on newcomer behavior and lurking, so these experienced subscribers were less of an interest. We calculated the total hours spent on the list for each subscriber.

For each user, we counted how many posts, if any, he or she contributed. We did not thread the posts or group them in any way; each post whether a reply or a new topic was counted. For each poster, we recorded the date of their first and last post. From these data points, we determined the amount of time they lurked before posting and their posting frequency.

Using data from the U.S. Census, we matched names to lists of the most common female and male names. We identified 666 users using this process. Some common names are used for both women and men, for instance Alex, Robin, or Morgan. In these cases, we looked at the frequency of use for each gender for each name. If there was a disproportionate use in one gender, we assigned all users with that name to that gender. For example, Alex is ranked as the 63rd most common name for males in the United States, and 990th for females. Therefore, all Alex's were assumed to be male. In cases where the rankings were close, we put the user in an "unknown" category.

Next, we manually filtered obvious "non-names" such as thepirate@yahoo.com and identified possible names that did not make it on the list of common U.S. names, or names that did not follow the aforementioned patterns. These names were then shown to other researchers and international students via a web application. These "reviewers" could assign a gender, mark the email address as "not a name," label it as an "unknown" for ambiguous names, or skip the name. We asked reviewers to only assign a sex where they were 100% certain. In the end, we identified 1594 users as either male or female, and were left with 975 unidentified users. Grouping unknown and "not a name" together, 41.66% of subscribers were unidentifiable. While this is unfortunate, we believe this represents a good effort and the users identified were a significant and representative sample of the overall community.

Within this dataset were many extreme values; many users contributed little, and a few users contributed a lot. To normalize the data we arranged the users in each mailing list by the number of posts. If we found a jump of more than an order of magnitude between a user and the next highest contributor, we set this as a cutoff point and excluded the user from our set. We did this to prevent a handful of very frequent posters skewing our statistics. Table 2 shows the number of users excluded from each mailing list.

In addition to treating each list separately, we combined all in order to compare data across FOSS mailing lists. As some of the projects are commonly used jointly (Busybox, Buildroot, and uClibc) and projects have multiple lists (e.g., Yum and Yum-devel) it is possible that users were counted multiple times in these comparisons.

Table 2. Number of outliers excluded from each data set

Project	Buildroot	Busybox	Jaws	Parrot	uClibc	Yum	Yum-devel	All Lists
Male	0	0	2	0	0	0	0	2
Female	1	0	0	1	1	0	0	3
Unknown	0	0	2	0	0	4	4	10
Total	1	0	4	1	1	4	4	15

4   Results

This section explores our finding and relates them to our research questions. First, we begin by looking at the gender of the subscribers. Secondly, we examine the time subscribers spend lurking before their first post. Next, we present the posting frequency by gender of subscribers and lastly, inspect the amount of time users subscribe to the mailing lists.

4.1 R1: Gender of Subscribers and Posters

Given that women participate at a disproportionately low rate, even by IT standards, can we determine how early in the FOSS joining process these differences emerge? We know from the work of Jensen et al. that by the time a user posts, only 3% of posters are women [11].

In order to answer this question, we counted the number of women and men who subscribed to each mailing list; we found 1769 men and 162 women. 91.73% of all subscribers were male and 8.27% were female. This was more than a 50% decrease when compared to the 20% rate of women in IT, but still much higher than the population of women who contributed code to FOSS projects. Table 3 shows a breakdown of our findings.

Table 3. Number of men, women, and unknown subscribed to each mailing list

Project	Buildroot	Busybox	Jaws	Parrot	uClibc	Yum	Yum-devel
Male	556	423	48	289	218	177	58
Female	52	29	3	27	30	17	4
Unknown	336	243	22	382	180	166	50
Total	944	695	73	698	428	360	112

Are women as likely to participate (post) as men once subscribed? Table 4 contains an overview of the data. The percentage of female posters ranged from 0 to 10.58% of the total number of subscribers, with an average of 6.63%. This was a statistically significant decrease from the expected value of 8.37% of subscribers ($\chi 2 = 5.30$, p= 0.0213). 110, or 67.90% of women never post after joining a mailing list. In comparison, 1065, or 59.30 % of men never posted after they joined a mailing list.

Table 4. Number of men, women, and unknown posters to each mailing list

Project	Buildroot	Busybox	Jaws	Parrot	uClibc	Yum	Yum-devel	All Lists
Male	254	208	9	58	93	80	29	731
Female	21	8	0	4	11	6	2	52
Unknown	157	115	1	47	83	73	23	499
Total	432	331	10	109	187	159	54	1282

4.2 Posting Frequency

Do women post as frequently as men on these lists? In order to determine the number of hours between posts, we examined the time between a user's first and last post and divided this number by the number of posts for that particular user, see Equation 1. We looked at 563 users who posted at least twice. Table 5 shows the average posting frequency for each list, and for the combined data set.

Table 5. Average posting frequency of men, women, and unknown per mailing list

Lists	Male (hours/post)	Female (hours/post)	Unknown (hours/post	Δ M-F	Average (hours/post)
Buildroot	289.96	304.29	320.73	-14.32	301.03
Busybox	326.31	246.67	321.74	79.64	322.76
Jaws	168.67	N/A	N/A	N/A	168.67
Parrot	525.33	527.50	490.61	-2.17	512.47
uClibc	393.24	409.63	825.59	-16.39	565.80
Yum	399.26	115.20	749.36	284.06	541.60
Yum-devel	202.10	133.00	722.53	69.10	419.83
All combined	341.70	306.90	495.17	34.81	395.91

$$\frac{1}{n} \left[\sum_{user=1}^{user=n} \frac{(Last\ Post_{user} - First\ Post_{user})Hours}{Number\ of\ Posts_{user}} \right] \quad (1)$$

Equation. 1. Equation used to calculate the average number of hours between posts

The majority of our lists (excluding Jaws and Yum) showed that men and women posted equally as often. Statistically we did not find any significant difference between men and women here. We broke separated this set of data into more categories by looking at users who posted at least once, more than once, more than twice, etc.

We also observed that as we look at the "stickiness" of the community, which is measured by continued participation on the mailing list, the participation of women decreased. Women make up about 6% of posters who submitted between 1 and 3 posts, about 4% of those who submitted between 4 and 8 times, about 2% of those who submitted 9 or 10 times, and 1% submitted more than 10 times. It is interesting to see a near linear trend in the data. Statistical tests show that the proportion of women posters decreased over time ($\chi 2 = 30.346$, p= 0.0107). This shows that over time women posted less often, which demonstrates that somewhere along the line women are discouraged from continued participation.

4.3   Lurking Habits

The time spent observing a group before contributing is a formative experience that can encourage or discourage users. In most cases, women lurk less than men (note, no female posters were found in the Jaws data set and so it was excluded from the study). The Parrot mailing list turned out to be an extreme outlier; women lurked 2,235.00 hours, which was more than 50% longer than men who lurked 1,406.47 hours. The data from this Parrot (for both men and women) was an extreme outlier, with averages more than 2 standard deviations from that of the other lists. Parrot was therefore excluded from the analysis. A t-test analysis of the two populations (excluding Jaws and Parrot) showed no statistically significant differences in the mean lurking times (p-value=1.72).

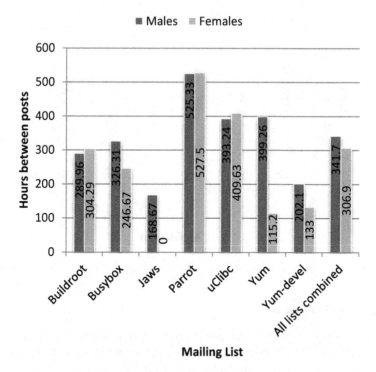

Fig. 2. Posting frequency by hours between posts

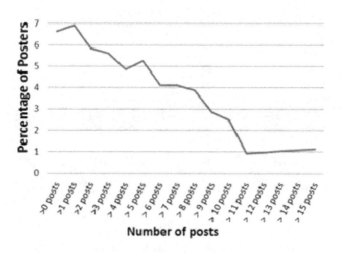

Fig. 3. Posting frequency by hours between posts

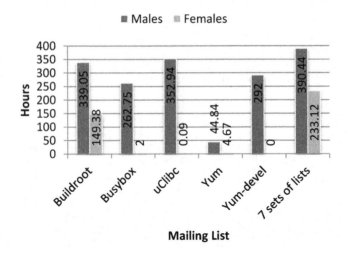

Fig. 4. Posting frequency by hours between posts

4.4   Subscription Length

Do men and women participate (stay subscribed) for similar lengths of time? Interestingly, women and men subscribed for a similar length of time (except in Yum-devel and Parrot), and there were no statistically significant differences.

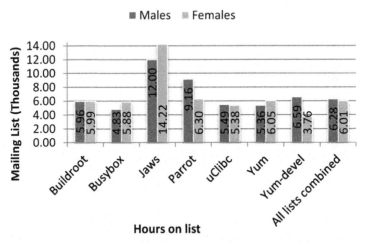

Fig. 5. Subscription length by hours on list

5   Discussion

Jensen et al. [11] found that about 3% of posters in their sample were women. However they focused on a variety of attributes, and gender was not the primary focus. As a consequence, their data had a much larger number of unknown participants, which may have skewed their data. We spent more time manually identifying users as male, female or unknown. We believe our results are in line with other studies that found between 1.5% and 2% of code-contributors are female [7, 9, 14, 18, 24]. We know that the FOSS joining process is complex and the commitment time needed to move into a developer role often excludes newbies with family or social commitments, something that may disproportionately affect women.

Building upon the findings in Jensen et al. [11], we found that 8.39% of the FOSS mailing list subscribers were women. This was significantly lower than the 20% of women in IT. In fact, we discovered an attrition rate throughout the joining and lurking process. Figure 6 shows the decreasing participation of women in FOSS communities.

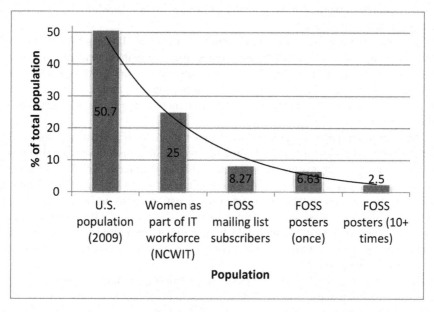

Fig. 6. Women in IT and FOSS

Where and why do gender differences emerge? Joining a mailing list is the first step and location in the FOSS joining process that we can collect data. There are however, other non-documented steps: exploring a project's website, scanning documentation, downloading source code, chatting on IRC, or exploring forums, messages boards or wikis. This leaves a variety of interactions prior to, or in parallel with, the mailing lists that may also influence women to turn away from FOSS projects. Of those who subscribe to a mailing list, 67.90% of women and 59.30% of men never post, and in our sample only 6.63% of posters were identifiable as women. We found that the number of women sequentially decreases to just over 1% as the number of posts grow to 10, which is in the range of what has been found by other studies.

Over the last ten years, there has been a push to increase the amount of contributor diversity in FOSS. FOSS projects like Dreamwidth have also appeared and managed to attract a 75% female contributor base [23]. However, from our data we cannot see that these efforts are having a strong global effect. More data is needed to determine this however, since the last major FOSS developer survey was performed in 2006 [18].

On average, men posted every 341.70 hours and women 306.90 hours. This shows us that although there is a high attrition rate among women, they are not being excluded from the FOSS conversation. That is not to say there are not many situations in FOSS where women have felt uncomfortable, excluded or specifically targeted in a demeaning way [8]. However, if all women were being forced away, we would expect women to post less frequently than males. What is interesting is that along every step of the joining process, we lose a disproportionate number of women. However, given the small sample of women and our choice of projects, it is difficult to draw statistical conclusions about the causes.

The all subscription logs varied in duration. In particular, Jaws and Parrot covered about 1,000 days, and we found that, on average, users from these two lists subscribed longer than users on other mailing lists, which covered less than 700 days. On nearly all of the lists, women subscribed for slightly less time than males, however we did not find any statistically significant correlation between gender and duration of subscription.

After examining posting statistics, we found that the only statistically significant differences between men and women were the average number of posts and the number of women who kept posting declined more sharply than men. We did not examine the type of messages posted, and it is possible that many users were not interested in joining the project, but rather asked one-time questions. It is unclear why women would be more likely to fall into this category than men. Adding a message-type category to this line of investigation would be beneficial. In addition, the projects we chose are highly technical and therefore comparing them with less technical projects may yield other results.

What drives women away from FOSS in disproportionate numbers? After disproving a number of hypotheses, we are left with two likely factors: women are driven by different sets of motivations and cost-benefit tradeoffs than men or, the social dynamics in projects are more unappealing or hostile to women. As documented by Jensen et al. [11] this may not be blatant or intentional, but the kind of public flaming and aggression documented could be enough to distort participation among a small minority, such as women who may already be hesitant about how they will be received. This does not apply to all women and all projects, since there are many examples of individual success.

Most importantly, what our study shows is that this problem is likely not technical, because most women drop out of FOSS early in their project membership. Efforts to address diversity in FOSS should therefore focus on the first social experiences through programs such as mentorships and making sure novices find the help and support they need.

In the future it would be interesting to evaluate consumer or corporate-oriented projects hosted from a variety of locations. This study used data from very technical projects, which were all hosted in the same location. Also these projects had a similar number of users contributing, and incorporating smaller and larger projects may yield different and possible more representative results. A system to categorize posts from newbies might add insight about a user's intention to join a FOSS community or otherwise.

6   Limitations

This study used data from very technical projects of similar size, all hosted in the same location (osuosl.org). Our results may have been different if we had sampled less technical, or smaller or larger projects. Lastly, naming conventions, and the subjective nature of matching name and gender could have introduced errors. We did, however, ask reviewers to only assign a gender if they were 100% certain. Studies have shown that women are more likely to try to obscure their gender online, so our analysis may have been skewed.

7   Conclusions

Understanding the reasons behind the gender struggle in FOSS will lead to policies and strategies that encourage greater diversity in FOSS communities. As more companies adopt FOSS software, and FOSS projects diversify to serve a broader population, supporting community infrastructure will be a vital in addressing the issues related to the lack of women in FOSS.

We studied eleven mailing lists and corresponding subscription logs from six FOSS projects, with a combined 3,310 users, of which 1,769 were males, 162 females and 1,379 unknown. We found 8.39% of subscribers were women, which is less than half of the expected 20% population of women in IT. Only 6.63% of posters were women, and the only significant difference we found, in terms of behaviors of men and women, was the average number of posts. Another important finding was the proportion of women who made frequent posts. The percentage of women who posted at least 10 times decreased to about 1%.

On average, males lurked slightly longer (390.44 hours) than females (233.12 hours) before posting to the mailing list for the first time. Also, males subscribed about 270 hours longer than women (less than 5% difference). However, we did not find any statistically significant values in these averages.

Acknowledgements. Thanks are due to the HCI group at Oregon State University, OSU's Open Source Lab, and the project leaders of Buildroot, Busybox, Jaws, Parrot, uClibc, and Yum, for their willingness to participate in this study.

References

1. About Us. The Humanitarian FOSS Project, http://www.hfoss.org/index. php/about-us
2. About OSUOSL. OSUOSL, http://osuosl.org/about-osuosl
3. Andersen, E.: BusyBox, http://busybox.net
4. Andersen, E.: UClibc, http://uclibc.org
5. Bitzer, J., Schrettl, W., Schroder, P.: Intrinsic Motivation in Open Source Software Development. Journal of Comparative Economics 35(1), 160–169 (2007)
6. Buildroot, http://buildroot.uclibc.org/
7. David, P., Waterman, A., Arora, S.: The Free/Libre/Open Source Software Survey for 2003. Stanford University (2003), http://www.stanford.edu/group/ floss-us/
8. Fisher, A., Margolis, J.: Unlocking the Clubhouse: the Carnegie Mellon Experience. In: Proc. SIGCSE Bulletin, vol. 34, pp. 79–83 (2002)
9. Ghosh, R.A., Glott, R., Krieger, B., Robles, G.: Free/Libre and Open Source Software: Survey and Study, Part 4: Survey of Developers (June 2002), http://www. flossproject.org/report/
10. Gutwin, C., Penner, R., Schneider, K.: Group Awareness in Distributed Software Development. In: Proc. CSCS 2004, pp. 72–88. ACM Press (2004)
11. Jensen, C., King, S., Kuechler, V.: Joining Free/Open Source Software Communities: An Analysis of Newbies' First Interactions on Project Mailing Lists. In: Proc. of HICSS 2011, pp. 1–10 (2011)
12. Katz, J.: Luring the Lurkers (1998), http://news.slashdot.org/story/98/ 12/28/1745252/Luring-the-Lurkers
13. Krogh, G., Spaeth, S., Lakhani, K.: Community, joining, and specialization in open source software innovation: a case study. Research Policy 32(7), 1217–1241 (2003)
14. Lakhani, K.R., Wolf, R.G.: The Boston Consulting Group Hacker Survey (2002), http://ftp3.au.freebsd.org/pub/linux.conf.au/2003/papers/Hem os/Hemos.pdf
15. Lampe, C., Johnston, E.: Follow the (Slash) dot: Effects of Feedback on New Members in an Online Community. In: Proc. of the 2005 Int. Conf. on Supporting Group Work, pp. 11–20 (2005)
16. Mason, B.: Issues in virtual ethnography. In: Proc. of Ethnographic Studies in Real and Virtual Environments: Inhabited Information Spaces and Connected Communities, pp. 61–69 (1999)
17. MBOX Documentation. Qmail Mirror Selection (1998), http://www.qmail.org/ man/man5/mbox.html
18. Nafus, D., Leach, J., Krieger, B.: Deliverable D16: Gender: Integrated Report of Findings. Free/Libre/Open Source Software: Policy Support, http://www.flosspols.org/
19. U.S. Department of Education, National Center for Education Statistics. The Condition of Education 2011. NCES, Table A-26-2 (2011), http://nces.ed.gov/fastfacts/ display.asp?id=72

20. About: Fact Sheet. National Center for Women and Information Technology, http://www.ncwit.org/about.factsheet.html
21. Nonnecke, B., Preece, J.: Lurker Demographics: Counting the Silent. In: CHI 2000, pp. 73–80. ACM Press (2000)
22. Raymond, E.S.: The Cathedral & the Bazaar: Musings on Linux and Open Source by an Accidental Revolutionary. O'Reilly, Beijing (1999)
23. Robert, K.: Standing out in a Crowd. Keynote Presentation. In: OSCON 2002, Dreamwidth (2002), http://www.oscon.com/oscon2009/public/schedule/detail/10173
24. Robles, G., Scheider, H., Tretkowski, I., Webers, N.: Who Is Doing It? A research on Libre Software developers (2001), http://widi.berlios.de/paper/study.html
25. Soroka, V., Jacovi, M., Ur, S.: We can see you: a study of the community's invisible people through ReachOut. In: Huysman, M., Wenger, E., Wulf, V. (eds.) Proc. of Int. Conf. on Communities and Technologies, pp. 65–79. Kluwer Academic Publishers (2003)
26. Users & Documentation. Parrot VM. Web (August 21, 2011), http://parrot.org/dev/docs/user
27. Wheeler, D.: Why Open Source Software/Free Software (OSS/FS, FOSS, or FLOSS)? Look at the Numbers! (April 16, 2007), http://www.dwheeler.com/oss_fs_why.html
28. Women, Minorities, and Persons with Disabilities in Science and Engineering. U.S. National Science Foundation (2011), http://www.nsf.gov/statistics/wmpd/
29. Ye, Y., Kishida, K.: Toward an Understanding of the Motivation Open Source Software Developers. In: Proc. ICSE 2003, pp. 419–429 (2003)
30. Yum Package Manager, http://yum.baseurl.org/

Emerging Hackerspaces – Peer-Production Generation

Jarkko Moilanen

University of Tampere, School of Information Sciences, Kalevantie 4,
33014 Tampereen Yliopisto, Finland
jarkko.moilanen@uta.fi

Abstract. This paper describes a peer-production movement, the hackerspace movement, its members and values. The emergence of hackerspaces, fablabs and makerspaces is changing how hacker communities and other like-minded communities function. Thus, an understanding of the nature of hackerspaces helps in detailing the features of contemporary peer-production. Building on previous work on 'fabbing', two different sets of results are presented: (1) empirical observations from a longitudinal study of hackerspace participants; and (2) a theoretical description of hacker generations as a larger context in which peer-production can be located. With regard to (1), research data has been collected through prolonged observation of hackerspace communities and two surveys.

Keywords: hackerspace, makerspace, fablab, community, open source, motivation, survey, fabbing, peer-production, movement, sustainability.

1   Introduction and Motivation

Hackers form a global community, which consists of multiple micro-communities [2]. The autonomous micro-communities are constantly on the move; evolving, mixing, forking, hibernating and dying. The hacker community exists both in the real and the virtual worlds, although the latter is often emphasized. The diversity and autonomy of hacker communities can be described through the different type of activities that hackers participate in. For example some hackers are more prone to do network related hacking while others might be more interested in social hacking. In the broadest sense hackers see the society as a system which can be hacked. Not all hackers are interested in the same set of technologies or programming languages. Some might be more interested in phones, hardware, games or biohacking.

Over the past years hackers around the world, mostly in Europe and North America, have begun to move hacker networks and communities out of the virtual into the real world. They have begun to form hackerspaces, hacker communities which have both virtual and real world bodies. The history of hackerspaces begins already in the 1990's. Farr [5] has defined three development waves in hackerspace history. During the early 1990's "[t]he First Wave showed us that hackers could build

I. Hammouda et al. (Eds.): OSS 2012, IFIP AICT 378, pp. 94–111, 2012.

spaces" [5]. Examples of hackerspaces of the 90's are L0pht, New Hack City (Boston and San Francisco), the Walnut Factory and the Hasty Pastry. The second wave occurred during the late 1990's and European hackers (especially in Germany and Austria) began building spaces. The second wave also initiated early theoretical discussions about the development of hackerspaces. The second wave was about "proving Hackers could be perfectly open about their work, organize officially, gain recognition from the government and respect from the public by living and applying the Hacker ethic in their efforts" [5]. The third wave started after the turn of millennium. The amount of active hackerspaces in 2010 was 254 [15] and currently there are over 500 active hackerspaces around the world[1] and a few hundred under construction.

This proliferation of hackerspaces can be seen as a significant change in hacking and the formation of hacker communities. Hackers are setting up new kind of communities, with features unknown in earlier hacker communities. Since the hackerspace movement is relatively new, a simple and compact definition of "hackerspace" is still missing even among the persons who are involved in the movement. Different hacker communities use different names: fablab, techshop, 100k garage, sharing platform, open source hardware and so on. The variety of names for the new 'do-it-yourself' communities expresses the variety and diversity of the movement, which might be best described as a "digital revolution in fabrication [... which] will allow perfect macroscopic objects to be made out of imperfect microscopic components" [7]. Scientific attempts to clarify the differences of various 'do-it-yourself' hacking communities are still rare. A shared understanding of how to use the different descriptions and names of the movement is still missing, but some attempts toward a consensus exist.

2   Methodology and Research Questions

The hackerspace community has gone through several discussions about what a hackerspace is. Consensus has not been reached, but the discussions have brought up some criteria for what being a hackerspace means. Firstly, a hackerspace is owned and run by its members in a spirit of equality. Secondly, it is not for profit and open to the outside world on a (semi)regular basis. Thirdly, people there share tools, equipment and ideas without discrimination. Fourthly, it has a strong emphasis on technology and invention. Fifthly, it has a shared space (or is in the process of acquiring a space) as a center of the community. Finally, it has a strong spirit of invention and science, based on trial, error, and freely sharing information.[2]

The five criteria have been tested by conducting a yearly survey of hackerspace communities. So far, the survey has been conducted twice, in July 2010 and June 2011. In addition to questions on the criteria, the survey contains questions which aim to provide more information about the values, interests and motivations of members

---

[1] Number is based on hackerspace list given in http://hackerspaces.org/wiki/ List_of_ Hacker_Spaces which is maintained by the community.
[2] Naturally, not all members of all hackerspaces agree on the above criteria.

of different hackerspaces around the world. The overall research setting contains elements of social anthropology and ethnographic methods such as observation. The author has been an active member of the hackerspace community both locally and internationally since 2009. The information gathered by living and working as a part the community is used in directing and conducting the research.

The research was inspired by discussions that have been going on through the hackerspaces mailing list (http://hackerspaces.org/wiki/Communication) for ages. The discussions have included several questions such as "What is a hackerspace? How can it be defined? Should some of the spaces listed in hackerspaces.org be removed or not? If so, based on what criteria?" The result has been almost always the same. Hackerspaces can and should not be defined rigidly, because that would create artificial boundaries and that is not a part of hacker culture or values. Discussions have involved business aspects, too. Some hackerspaces are more oriented toward business than others. It has been debated whether so called commercial hackerspaces should be seen as hackerspaces or not. Consequently, an interesting research question is the attitude towards donations (money, devices, equipment) coming from companies. Does the desire to be independent rule company donations out? What about governmental support? Is that more acceptable? Thus, questions on funding were added to the initial set of questions, that can be grouped under four headings: 1) What kind of hackers/people participate in hackerspaces? 2) What is the motivation to participate and 3) what do people do in hackerspaces? Additionally, 4) What is the bigger context of hackerspaces?

The latest survey was launched on June 16th, 2011 and was closed on June 30th, giving two weeks time to participate. A message about the research and a link to the online survey was posted to hackerspace discussion list (http://lists.hackerspaces.org/ mailman/listinfo/discuss), the diybio list (http://groups.google.com/group/diybio/ topics) and some other minor hacker oriented lists. The survey was not advertised in social media in order to avoid biased participants. If twitter or other social media would have been used in launching the survey, some non-hackers would have most likely taken the part. A reminder was posted a few days before closing.

The longitudinal survey discussed in this paper continues 2012 as P2P Foundation project, which can be found from http://surveys.peerproduction.net. All information collected with surveys will be anonymized and open sourced under Commons license.

3   Results

The survey in 2011 seems to confirm most of the results found in 2010. No dramatic changes were found. (A comparison of the basic numbers from both surveys is presented in table 1.) Two hundred and fifty (250) participants (25 females, 223 males, 2 'no answer'; mean age = 31 years, range: 13-62 years) from 87 hacker communities in 19 countries took part in the study; in 2010 there number of participants was 201. The majority of the respondents were from active hackerspaces (90,4%). Similarly, the most of the respondents were members in only one hackerspace (90,8%). About 48% of the participants lived in Northern America, 39% in Europe, over 9% in Australia and 3,6% in Southern America. One participant was from Asia (China). None of the participants were from Africa. Compared to the stats of the survey in 2010, the percentage of European respondents dropped by nearly 9%, and hackers from Australia found the survey this year (8,7% up). The low amount of Asian respondents might be partly explained by limitations in access to web content (for example in China).

Table 1. General view of 2010 and 2011 survey statistics

Basic statistics	2010	2011	Change
Participants	201	250	49
Men	185	223	38
Women	12	25	13
Mean age	30	31	1
Age range	15 – 53	13 – 62	-
Amount of different communities	72	87	15
Geographical distribution	2010	2011	Change
From Northern America	48,0%	48,0%	0,0%
From Southern America	0,0%	3,6%	3,6%
From Europe	47,5%	38,6%	-8,7%
From Asia	4,0%	0,4%	-3,6%
From Australia	0,5%	9,2%	8,7%
Amount of different countries	20	19	-1

3.1   Members – Age, Gender and Education

The gender and age distributions of hackerspace community members follow the results found in FLOSS related surveys [1,14]. In 2010, the typical member was a 26-29 years old male (94%) with college level or higher education. In 2011, the typical member is a 27-31 (35%) years old male (90%) with college level or higher education (64%). It must be noted that even though 90% of respondents were male, this does not necessarily imply that the same applies to hackerspaces in general.

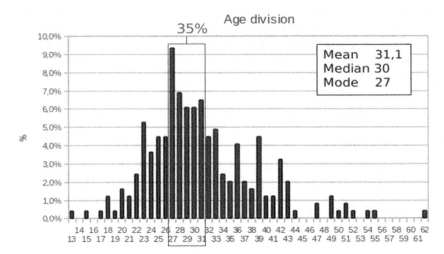

Fig. 1. Age division 2011

When respondents are grouped by age, gender does not vary much (see Fig. 2). In both genders, 26 – 35 year old members are the majority (women 58%, men 52%). The minors (under 18 years old) are rare and only men.

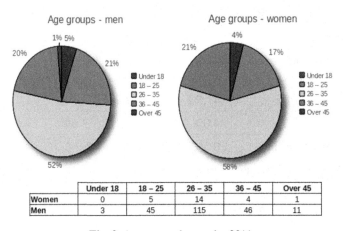

	Under 18	18 – 25	26 – 35	36 – 45	Over 45
Women	0	5	14	4	1
Men	3	45	115	46	11

Fig. 2. Age groups by gender 2011

With regard to education, the only significant change between 2010 and 2011 is the increase in the amount of hackers with a Master's Degree. In 2010 it was 14% and this year it was over 20%. (Detailed comparison in table 2.)

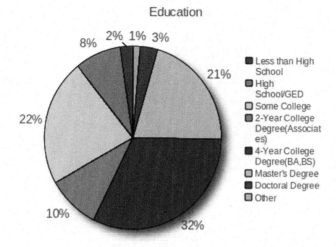

Fig. 3. Respondents' education in 2011

Table 2. Respondents education 2011 and 2010

Education level	Percentage 2011	Percentage 2010
Less than high school	3%	3%
High School/GED	8%	6%
Some College	22%	27%
2-Year College Degree (Associates)	10%	9%
4-Year College Degree (BA,BS)	32%	32%
Masters Degree	21%	14%
Doctoral Degree	3%	5%
Other	1%	5%

3.2   Members – Membership

Based on the survey results, most hackers are members of just one community (nearly 91%). Compared to the results in 2010, memberships in two communities has dropped by nearly 7%. The trend seems to be that respondents are members in fewer hackerspace communities. This can be seen when comparing multi-community membership counts in 2010 and 2011 (see Fig. 4).

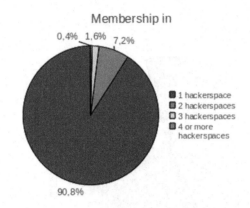

	2011	2010	Change
1 hackerspace	90,8%	84,7%	6,10%
2 hackerspaces	7,2%	13,9%	-6,70%
3 hackerspaces	1,6%	1,0%	0,60%
4 or more hackerspaces	0,4%	0,5%	-0,10%

Fig. 4. Hackerspace membership 2010 and 2011

This might suggest that hackers have found their 'home' and are more engaged and committed to one local hacker community. This could be partly explained with the disappearance of some hackerspaces, causing membership concentration to strong and active hackerspaces. However, at this point this is just speculation and can't be confirmed from the data. Another possibility is that simply the raised participant count in 2011 has caused the change.

3.3   Members – Interests

Members interests were inquired about in one question: "In general my interest with the hackerspace is MOSTLY about ...". Respondents were given list of predefined groups of interest areas such as software hacking, networks and building objects. Respondents were informed to choose max. 3 options, but some selected all.

In the 2011 survey one new option was added: in 2010 the social aspects of hacking communities were not present on the list. Since then the need for that option has become clear. The term 'social aspects' refers to events and meeting people – the term was clarified to respondents in parenthesis. Respondents were also given an opportunity to choose 'Other' and give some sort of clarification. Figure 5 presents a comparison chart.

In the 2011 survey, the top three interests are building objects (82%), social aspects (67%) and software hacking (65%). Compared to 2010, both mobile hacking and game development dropped. Of course, adding the new option 'social aspects' might have partly caused the change.

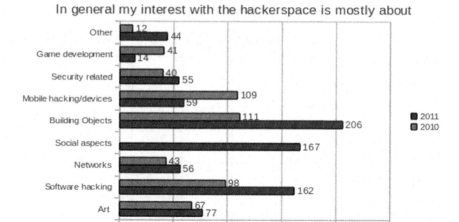

Note! People may have selected more than one option (max 3 options)

Fig. 5. Interests in 2010 and 2011 in comparison

Nevertheless, it seems to be clear that hacker communities are about building things. Option 'other' included several topics and areas as identified by the respondents. To mention just a few: learning, biohacking, biology, biotech, energy, diybio, robotics, 3D printing, chemistry, science & math, foundry work, fabrication techniques not available at home, podcasting, fibre-crafts and chemistry & physics. Among the above topics, the term 'Learning' appeared several times, which suggests that learning in general is important for participants. Also robotics and biology related hacking were mentioned several times. This suggests that hackers are getting more and more active in DIYbio (referring to communities focusing on biology), a fact that has also caught the attention of the press [see for example 4, 13, 17].

3.4   Members – Motivation

The participants were asked to tell how significant different reasons for contributing in hackerspaces are. The question included eight claims and options were presented using a five-point Likert scale (see Table 3).

Altruism, community commitment, meeting other hackers in real world and having fun seem to be the most important factors of motivation. About 80% (last year 77%) of the participants seem to be contributing to community without expecting something in return. About 75% feel that commitment to community is one of the most important sources of motivation. For nearly all (95%) meeting other hackers and hacker-minded people and having fun (98%) are the most important reasons to participate in hackerspace activity. In other words, the social factor of peer production communities seems to be the key element.

Table 3. Motivation for taking part in hackerspaces – 2011

	Strongly agree	Agree	Do not know/does not matter	Disagree	Strongly disagree
participate for the fun	69%	29%	2%	0%	0%
want to help people, without getting something in return	34%	46%	16%	3%	1%
participate because you re committed to the community	34%	41%	21%	4%	1%
want to help people and expect to get something in return	5%	24%	**44%**	20%	7%
participate to build up a reputation	10%	44%	26%	15%	5%
participate because need software/hardware improvements	12%	**36%**	**30%**	16%	6%
participate to earn money with it	1%	7%	27%	26%	39%
to meet (in real world) other hackers/hacker-minded people	70%	25%	3%	2%	0%

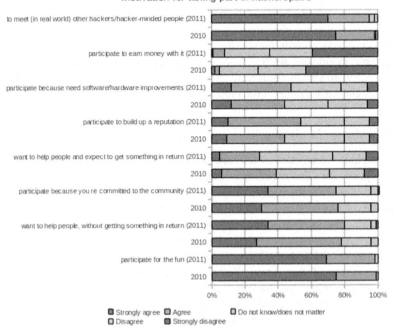

Motivation for taking part in hackerspace

Fig. 6. Member motivations in 2010 and 2011 in comparison

When compared to results in 2010, no major changes can be found (Fig. 6). Attitude towards earning money and reputation building have become slightly less negative.

3.5   Members – Time Spent on Hackerspace Related Activities

Survey participants were asked to tell how much time they spend on hackerspace related activities in a week. The answers were given in free text format, not as predefined options (which could have been better). The responses were grouped into 2-hour periods and a few answers were dropped away: it seems highly unbelievable (and even impossible) that someone would use 300 hours or more on hackerspace activities in a week.

Roughly, the respondents use the same amount of time as in 2010 (2011: 10,6 hours and 2010: 9,7 hours). The histogram in Fig. 7 seems to suggest some changes. In 2010, two options – 4-6 hours and 10-12 hours – were most common, while other amounts were less popular. In 2011, the distribution is more even. It seems that respondents use either a little time (2-4 hours) or a lot of time (18 hours or more) in hackerspace related activities. The values in the middle got lesser hits. This might suggest that there are two groupings: 'the mass' (a few hours) and enthusiasts (high amount of hours).

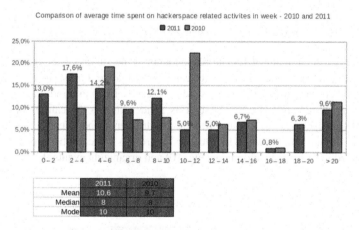

Fig. 7. Time spent on hackerspace related activities per week - 2010 and 2011

3.6   Members – Activity

The respondents participate in community related activities for about 10 hours per week. What kind of things do they do? The answer to this question was sought by asking: "In general my projects in the hackerspace are about ..." which was followed with 7 predefined Likert scale options. The given options were: Software development / hacking, Hardware development / hacking, Website/Web-app development, Management (financial or otherwise), Organize events/nights/sessions etc., Administrative tasks (email lists, servers, etc.) and Mobile device related hacking.

Results (see Fig. 8) suggest that hackerspace members are mostly involved in projects related to software development (over 55%) and hardware development (over 65%). The least popular project contents are Mobile device related hacking (6%) and Organizing events (less than 10%).

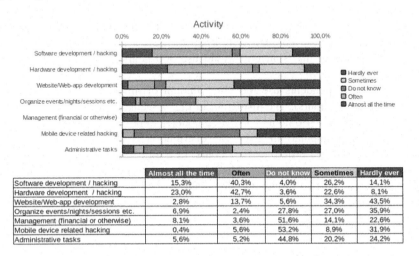

	Almost all the time	Often	Do not know	Sometimes	Hardly ever
Software development / hacking	15,3%	40,3%	4,0%	26,2%	14,1%
Hardware development / hacking	23,0%	42,7%	3,6%	22,6%	8,1%
Website/Web-app development	2,8%	13,7%	5,6%	34,3%	43,5%
Organize events/nights/sessions etc.	6,9%	2,4%	27,8%	27,0%	35,9%
Management (financial or otherwise)	8,1%	3,6%	51,6%	14,1%	22,6%
Mobile device related hacking	0,4%	5,6%	53,2%	8,9%	31,9%
Administrative tasks	5,6%	5,2%	44,8%	20,2%	24,2%

Fig. 8. In general my projects in the hackerspace are about ..." (2011)

Even though the amount of female respondents in the surveys was rather low, some cross tabulation using gender as one factor can be informative. I must stress that gender is not the issue here; it is used just for the sake of research. Keep in mind that hacker ethics does not want to use bogus criteria (such as gender, age or education) in evaluating people. The intention was to find out if there are differences between the genders; what men like to do and what women like to do. The results indicate that women are more often involved in website development (Fig. 10) and organizing events (Fig. 9).

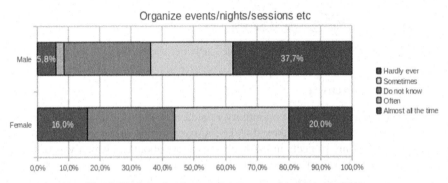

Fig. 9. Participation in organizing events by gender in 2011

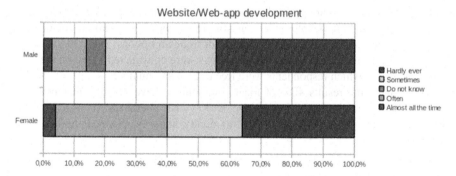

Fig. 10. Doing website related development by gender in 2011

Men are more prone to software and hardware hacking. Women have strong interest in software development and a little less in hardware related projects. Mobile device hacking was not popular among respondents and it is dominated by men. Both genders are equally disinterested in management and administrative tasks.

3.7   Community – Amount of Members

A few of the questions in the surveys were about the local communities in which the respondents were members. For instance, respondents were asked to give estimated amount of members in their local community. This does not correlate directly to reality, since some respondents might be less aware of the status of their community.

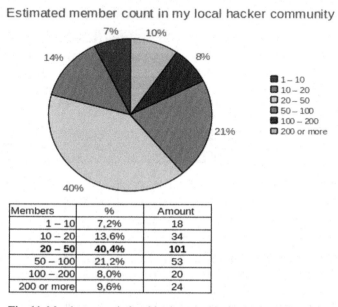

Members	%	Amount
1 – 10	7,2%	18
10 – 20	13,6%	34
20 – 50	**40,4%**	**101**
50 – 100	21,2%	53
100 – 200	8,0%	20
200 or more	9,6%	24

Fig. 11. Member count in local hacker community (estimated) in 2011

In other words, answers are probably mostly given by 'gut-feeling'. Furthermore, it is somewhat unclear how people understand the term "member", who is included and who is not. The question included predefined drop-down options: 1-10, 10-20, 20-50, 50-100, 100-200 and 200 or more. These options were constructed based on the 2010 survey results, in which respondents were free to give any number.

According to the results 40% of local communities have 20 – 50 members (see Fig. 11). The second most common size is 50 – 100 members. It must be noted that these figures include all kind of community statuses: planned, building and active.

3.8   Community – Funding

The topic of funding was added to the survey in 2011. Discussions related to sources of funding have been constantly on the agenda inside hackerspace communities and therefore attitudes towards different funding sources are interesting. The survey participants were given a list with the following possible funding sources (with Likert scale options): company donations (money), company donations (devices, equipment, etc.), membership fees, governmental sources (aid from different programs which help building and maintaining volunteer activities) and donations from individuals (money or other resources).

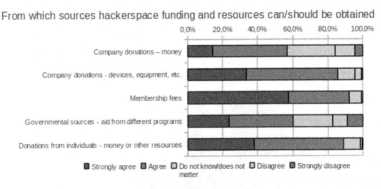

	Strongly agree	Agree	Do not know/does not matter	Disagree	Strongly disagree
Company donations – money	14,4%	42,4%	27,2%	11,6%	4,4%
Company donations - devices, equipment, etc.	33,6%	52,0%	10,0%	3,6%	0,8%
Membership fees	57,6%	34,8%	6,8%	0,8%	0,0%
Governmental sources - aid from different programs	23,6%	36,4%	22,8%	8,4%	8,8%
Donations from individuals - money or other resources	38,0%	50,8%	9,6%	1,2%	0,4%

Fig. 12. Opinion about sources for hackerspace funding and resources

The results (Fig. 12.) suggest that company donations (money) are less disagreeable than governmental support, but only slightly. Membership fees seem to be the most approved source of funding. Device and other equipment donations from companies and all sorts of donations from individuals gained a lot of support. It must be noted that in some cases, if company donations are accepted, they must be without strings attached. The policy is required in order to maintain community independence from external forces. Nevertheless, it is clear that money or other kind of support in any form coming from individuals is preferred over company or governmental sources.

4   Discussion and Conclusions

According to the survey results the typical hackerspace member is a 27-31 (35%) years old male (90%) with college level or higher education, committed to one hackerspace; he uses in average ca. 10 hours per week in hackerspace related projects, which are commonly software or hardware related. Altruism, community commitment, meeting other hackers in the real world and having fun seem to be the most important factors of motivation. Compared to the motivation models discussed in research on open source development [for example 3], hackerspace communities have a strong 'social motivation factor'. The members in the communities have a high interest towards meeting other hacker-minded people in real life. Most communities aim to have a physical space that functions as a community center. They are also known to arrange a lot of real life activities which are often related to learning, education and of course having fun. Having fun is one of the most important motivation factors and having fun is a fundamental part of social life.

Women seem to have found peer-production communities (hackerspaces, makerspaces, fablabs, diybio, etc.). Peer-production communities are still 'man caves', but the amount of women in hacking seems to be rising at least through the hackerspace movement. The emergence of biohacking was also visible in the survey.

Hackerspaces can be seen as hacker versions of 'third places' as defined by Oldenburg [19]. According to Oldenburg 'third places' refer to social settings or surroundings separate from the 'first place' (home and other similar settings) and 'second place' (workplace) [19]. The third places are 'anchors' of community life that facilitate and foster broader, more creative interaction. These places serve as focal points of community life which has eroded due to commercial chains and unifunctional zoning policy [19]). Third places are needed to reconnect to each other and strengthen community ties. To become a successful third place, a place must be locally owned, independent and small-scale and be based on steady-state business [19]. Furthermore, the places should be highly accessible, within walking distance, free or cheap and involve regularity. When these criteria are compared to the characteristics of hackerspaces, the similarities become obvious.

All hacker and other computer related groups or clubs can not be called hackerspaces. Some groups or places that look like hackerspaces don't even want to be labeled as such. Some hackerspaces avoid using the word itself in the group's name or in the descriptions of the group. Reasons for avoiding the word vary, but the most common is related to the uncertainty of how 'others' will react to any description that includes or refers to the word 'hacker'. This fear of the opinions of others is an example of how communities are shaped, defined and identified also by people that are not members of the communities. The identity is not carved in stone, but constantly evolving. Yet some features can be listed even though the features are not universally agreed upon in the community. The reason for some level of diaspora may lie in the desire not to define hackerspaces rigidly, which in turn is derived from the values of hacker ethic.

Since a shared understanding of how to name the 'fabbing' movement is still missing (not the least in the academic context) and in order to put the movement in a larger context, I suggest that it could be seen as a continuum to the different hacker generations mentioned above. As discussed above, 'fabbing' is bigger than just hackerspaces and therefore I have labeled this new hacker generation as 'peer-production' (see Fig. 13.) in order to include the different forms described by Troxler [26].

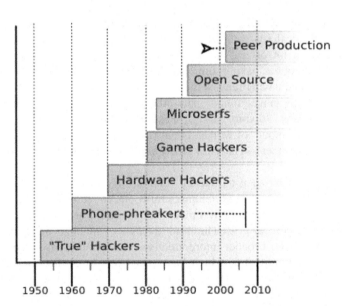

Fig. 13. Suggested view of hacker generations. Source: Modified from Taylor [24], peer-production added by the author. Beginning of peerproduction generation is debatable. Hackerspaces emerged in small scale around 1995, but breakthrough happened around 2001-2002 and after that other forms of peer-production emerged. Phone-phreakers generation as a movement ends at 2006 because last "phreakable" MF-signalled N2 carrier was replaced with a T1 carrier.

While the above mentioned hacker generations are acknowledged by some scholars (see for example 23 - 24] the descriptions provided so far are missing the latest development, namely peer-production.

The description of peer-production movement as a hacker generation needs more research and thought. Nevertheless, hackerspaces as instances of peer-production have a clear identity and constitute a large, growing and global movement. Hackerspaces and previous hacker generations share some values such as altruism and believe in hacker ethic. As the survey results indicate, hackerspace members are if not obsessed then at least focused to hardware hacking, which was fundamental part of 'hardware hacking' generation. Peer-production generations adapts that obsession and extends it with social aspects. Peer-production generation overlaps with the Open Source generation as well. Both value sharing, collaborative work, openness and transparency. Open source has become part of the main stream in software development. Companies have become part of the open source communities, started to form ecosystems and the border between working hours and contribution has become fuzzy. Hackerspace communities have chosen the other way. They want to stay as independent as possible from external forces such as companies and governments. This might indicate that freedom is more valued than resources. Valuing freedom over resources and restraining external (often business related) influences, does not exclude creating new business. Some of the fundamental parts of 3D printing device development (such as RepRap and Ultimaker) have started from peer-production communities.

Yet, hackerspaces are different kind of communities compared to communities formed by previous hacker generations at least in two aspects. Firstly, hackerspaces focus on social aspects in virtual and physical world. Hackerspace communities organize events, which are about having fun and learning. Examples of virtual events are monthly organized hackathons[3], in which people gather together to solve technical problems to create something new in collaboration. Physical world events are often educational in nature focusing on different technical issues and skills such as programming languages, soldering skills, 3D printing and biohacking. Furthermore, these events are often open to public. That indicates will to educate 'others', those who are not yet members of the community. Reasons for this free-time based education might be to lure in more members and share the gained knowledge and skills. Secondly, they aim to build and maintain physical spaces which function as community centers. Hackerspaces and alike have taken a significant role in how hackers and hacker-minded people organize themselves and activities.

References

1. Aalbers, M.: Motivation for participation in an open source community (2004), http://download.org/documentation/bc2004/Martine_Aalbers/res ults-summary (accessed June 12, 2010)

---

3   See more http://en.wikipedia.org/wiki/Hackathon

2. Barber, R.: Hackers profiled - who are they and what are their motivations? Computer Fraud & Security (2), 14–17 (2001) ISSN 1361-3723, doi:10.1016/S1361-3723(01)02017-6

3. Bonaccorsi, A., Rossi, C.: Comparing motivations of individual programmers and firms to take part in the open source movement: From community to business. Knowledge, Technology & Policy 18(4), 40–64 (2006)

4. Bloom, J.: The geneticist in the garage (2009), http://www.guardian.co.uk/technology/2009/mar/19/biohacking-genetics-research (retrieved June 9, 2011)

5. Farr, N.: Respect the Past, Examine the Present, Build the Future (2009), http://blog.hackerspaces.org/2009/08/25/Respect-the-Past-Examine-the-Present-Build-the-Future (retrieved October 27, 2011)

6. Flowers, S.: Harnessing the hackers: The emergence and exploitation of outlaw innovation. Research Policy 37(2), 177–193 (2008)

7. Gershenfeld, N.: Fab: the coming revolution on your desktop - from personal computers to personal fabrication. Basic Books (2007)

8. Gollin, M.: Theft or innovation? Nature 463(7284), 1022–1023 (2010)

9. Lakhani, K., Wolf, R.: Why hackers do what they do: Understanding Motivation Effort in Free. Open Source Software Projects (2005)

10. Lakhani, K., Von Hippel, E.: How open source software works. Research Policy 32(6), 923–943 (2003)

11. Levy, S.: Hackers: Heroes of the computer revolution. Anchor Press/Doubleday Garden City, NY (1984)

12. Lin, Y.: Hacker culture and the FLOSS innovation. In: Handbook of Research on Open Source Software: Technological, Economic, and Social Perspectives, p. 34 (2007)

13. Mackey, P.: DIY Bio: A Growing Movement Takes on Aging (2010), http://hplusmagazine.com/2010/01/22/diy-bio-growing-movement-takes-aging (retrieved July 6, 2011)

14. Mikkonen, T., Vadén, T., Vainio, N.: The Protestant ethic strikes back: Open source developers and the ethic of capitalism. First Monday 12(2), 1–12 (2007)

15. Moilanen, J.: Hackerspaces, members and involvement, survey study (2010), http://blog.ossoil.com/2010/07/19/hackerspaces-members-and-involvement-survey-study (retrieved July 6, 2011)

16. Moilanen, J.: Over 500 active hackerspaces (2011), http://blog.ossoil.com/2011/09/23/over-500-active-hackerspaces (retrieved July 6, 2011)

17. Mosher, D.: DIY Biotech Hacker Space Opens in NYC (2010), http://www.wired.com/wiredscience/2010/12/genspace-diy-science-laboratory (retrieved June 9, 2011)

18. Oldenburg, R.: The great good place: Cafes, coffee shops, bookstores, bars, hair salons, and other hangouts at the heart of a community. Da Capo Press (1999)

19. Oldenburg, R.: Celebrating the third place: inspiring stories about the "great good places" at the heart of our communities. Da Capo Press (2001)

20. Raymond, E.: The cathedral and the bazaar: musings on Linux and open source by an accidental revolutionary. O'Reilly & Associates, Inc., Sebastopol (2001)

21. Rosenbaum, R.: Secrets of the little blue box, copy of original article (1971), http://www.lospadres.info/thorg/lbb.html (retrieved June 12, 2010)

22. Sauer, R.: Why develop open-source software? The role of non-pecuniary benefits, monetary rewards, and open-source licence type. Oxford Review of Economic Policy 23(4), 605 (2007)

23. Sterling, B.: The hacker crackdown (2002), `http://www.mit.edu/hacker/hacker.html` (retrieved July 18, 2010)
24. Taylor, P.: From hackers to hacktivists: speed bumps on the global superhighway? New Media & Society 7(5), 625 (2005)
25. Torvalds, L., Diamond, D.: Just for fun: The story of an accidental revolutionary. Harper Paperbacks (2002)
26. Troxler, P.: Commons-based peer-production of physical goods - is there room for a hybrid innovation ecology? (2010), `http://wikis.fu-berlin.de/download/attachments/59080767/Troxler-Paper.pdf` (retrieved October 15, 2010)

Exploring the Barriers and Enablers to the Use of Open Educational Resources by University Academics in Africa

Tanya Percy and Jean-Paul Van Belle

Department of Information Systems, University of Cape Town
Private Bag, 7701 Rondebosch, South Africa
TBPercy@gmail.com, Jean-Paul.VanBelle@uct.ac.za

Abstract. Considerable effort has gone into Open Educational Resource (OER) initiatives in the past decade. These initiatives have created free, high quality educational resources for everyone and anyone to use. However, these open and free resources appear to remain largely unused by university academics on the educationally resource-poor African continent. The objectives of the research study are to explore the inhibitors and enablers are experienced by academics that use OER, and what barriers prevent academics from using OER. The sample consists of academics from East, West and Southern Africa. Information was gathered by means of a survey questionnaire. A modified version of the Unified Theory of Acceptance and Use of Technology model was used to identify the influence of certain factors on a user's intention to adopt OER. Some of the key findings indicate that Performance Expectancy and Effort Expectancy have a positive effect on a user's Behavioural Intention to use OER, and the latter has a strong influence on the Actual Use of OER. Facilitating Conditions do not have a statistically significant impact. Additionally, significant differences were found in the barriers which users and potential users of OER have identified as either limiting their current use of OER, or negatively affecting their intention to use OER. These barriers include discovery, relevance, context and individual resources. Addressing these factors could lead to a more widespread adoption of Open Educational Resources in Africa and, consequently, more pervasive and higher quality educational opportunities.

1   Introduction

Education is seen as a basic human right which is central to the sustainable development of countries. However, this right is dependent on the relevant infrastructure being in place (Geith & Vignare, 2008). This could include anything from content repositories to bandwidth to the removal of any barriers which prevent accessibility to educational resources.

The open education movement has been identified as a possible enabler of the educational shift from a teacher-centric model, where the educator is seen as the dispenser of knowledge, to a competency, learner-centred educational model (Geser, 2007). Making Open Educational Resources (OER) more accessible could reduce the

I. Hammouda et al. (Eds.): OSS 2012, IFIP AICT 378, pp. 112–128, 2012.

social inequalities which exist in developing countries (Mora, Hassin, Pullin & Muegge, 2008). It could provide a means of bypassing the educational barriers of economy, demographics and geography (Petrides, Nguyen, Jimes, & Karaglani, 2008), correcting the imbalance which exists in the quality of education between developed and developing countries (Mora et al., 2008).

Considerable effort has gone into Open Educational Resource initiatives in the past decade. These initiatives have created free, high quality educational resources for everyone and anyone to use. However, even though these resources are open and free, it is not evident that these resources are being used by university academics on the relatively resource-poor African continent. This research study explores this question from an African academic's viewpoint. The objectives of the research study are to explore what barriers and enablers academics who use OER have experienced, and what barriers prevent academics from consuming OER.

2   Literature Review

2.1   What Are Open Educational Resources (OER)?

The term "Open Educational Resources" (OER) was first described at a UNESCO forum in 2002 as "the open provision of educational resources, enabled by information and communication technologies, for consultation, use and adaptation by a community of users for non-commercial purposes" (Friesen, 2009, p.1). Perhaps a more descriptive definition is: "digitized educational resources that are freely available for use by educators and learners, without an accompanying need to pay royalties or license fees. The digitized resources may be shared via the Internet or using media such as disk-drives. OER are usually, not exclusively, licensed using a Creative Commons license. Both the original owners of the material and the subsequent users need to clearly understand the terms of these contracts to appreciate the ways in which the materials may be remixed and shared." (West & Victor, 2011, p.9). The latter definition highlights the key attributes of Open Educational Resources:

Educational resources should be in a digitized form. This indicates that educational resources should be made available on the internet or via another form of digitized media so that material is easier to distribute and reuse with the least cost. This is supported by the Organization for Economic Co-operation and Development (OECD), as their definition of OER is "digitised materials offered freely and openly to educators, students and self-learners to use and reuse for teaching, learning and research" (Mora et al., 2008 , p.1). Additionally, the tools which are used to support open educational initiatives must be open source in nature, where the source code is available for use (Geser, 2007).

Educational resources should be free and open to use. This allows users to collaborate, improve upon and share educational content and make the content more freely available and open to a global community (Petrides et al., 2008) under a licensing agreement, namely the creative commons license.

Educational resources should be easily remixed and shared. OER content can be applicable to one user but not applicable to another (Koohang & Harman, 2007). It is important that the content may be edited and versioned to the needs of the educator, learner or institution. West and Victor (2011) define Open Educational Resources as digitized educational material which can be edited and expanded for other uses. Figure 1 illustrates the range of resources that are typically included under OER.

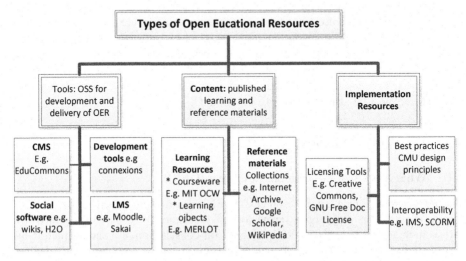

Fig. 1. Types of Open Educational Resources (Margulies, 2005)

2.2   Benefits of Using OER

Many advantages for using Open Educational Resources have been identified (D'Antoni, 2009). Educators have the option to download information as a supplement to the educators' coursework, and the ability to version and localize the content for their own use (Gourley & Lane, 2009). Through the localizing of existing content, they can save time as copyright concerns would have already been resolved, and they do not need to produce content from scratch (Geser, 2007). Educators can be exposed to what colleagues are doing, and through observing others teaching practices, their own teaching can be improved (Hilton & Wiley, 2010). Additionally, educators can provide their own comments on the educational material, by giving insight on how the content can be improved, and the lessons learnt through their sharing of the information (Geser, 2007).

It is through the use of Open Educational Resources that educators are encouraged to share materials and their ideas with other educators (Gourley & Lane, 2009). Through this sharing of educational resources, which is core to academic values, educators encourage the development and support of new knowledge societies and, through such initiatives, the educators' reputation may be improved (D'Antoni, 2009). In a broader context, OER aims to make the best ideas available to those who want to use them and, additionally, empowers individuals to make use of alternative education avenues beyond those provided by the traditional education system (D'Antoni, 2009) e.g. e-learning and Open CourseWare [OCW] repositories.

2.3   Enablers and Barriers to the Use of OER

The main enablers and barriers identified in the literature can be grouped under the following themes: technology; copyright; politics and culture; communities of practice; quality; and discovery, context and relevance.

2.3.1 Technology

As OER are digital by nature, they require that the basic Information and Communication Technology (ICT) infrastructure be in place in order to enable access to the localization and adoption of OER content.   However, since basic ICT infrastructure often does not exist in developing countries (Stacey, 2007), technological barriers, such as the lack of access to modern computers and the internet, still prove to be barriers to the use of OER. Less than 10% of the population in South Africa has access to the internet; this figure is still lower in countries like Kenya, Nigeria and Tanzania (Wilson, 2008). Bandwidth is another issue (Stacey, 2007).

By making OER content available through web-based interfaces, technology has assisted in bypassing the barrier of interoperability and in making OER more accessible (Atkins et al., 2007).   Their lack of skills in the technology inhibited educators from using the OER portal due to the amount of time it would take to learn the technology before content could be produced or edited (Petrides et al., 2008). Where users had experience in producing and editing content on the technology platform, the level of use and reuse was high. To achieve this, however, educators need to be trained in the creation, use and reuse of learning materials (Panke, 2011). Comment facilities on open content portals assisted users in producing or editing content (Petrides et al., 2008), as it was not completely new and daunting.

2.3.2 Copyright

Educators were concerned that copyright claims may be laid against them for the use or reuse of material where the author of the material had not granted the necessary permissions (Davis, et al., 2010). To counter these copyright concerns, a licensing system called the Creative Commons (CC) was established by Larry Lessig and others in 2001(Wiley & Gurrell, 2009). The CC licensing framework allows individuals and organizations to publish their work (West & Victor, 2011) under different types of Intellectual Property licenses (Kozinska et al., 2010). Additional flexibility of the framework allows authors to customize the license according to their requirements (Geith & Vignare, 2008). Thus when potential users see the Creative Commons license, which changed the "all rights reserved" to "some rights reserved open licensing" (Gourley & Lane, 2009, p.58), they know that the educational content is open and freely available for use (West & Victor, 2011).

However, the use of Creative Commons licensing is subject to some debate, especially the "commercial" and "non-commercial" license options (Joyce, 2007; Bissell, 2009). Additionally, licensing can become a point of confusion where content is mixed from different sources. If one content source is registered under the non-commercial ShareAlike license and the other under the attribution ShareAlike license, a derivative of the original material cannot be used as the original licenses are incompatible (Wiley & Gurrell, 2009).

2.3.3 Politics and Culture

The right to education is currently more of an attainable goal in the developed, wealthier countries, whose aim is more on secondary education than it is in the poorer developing countries, whose aim is mainly primary education (Kozinska et al., 2010). Political, social and economic factors influence accessibility to information and communication technologies (ICT) (Mora et al., 2008).

Developing countries have additional barriers which exist, to a lesser extent, in developed countries. Of the open education content produced by developed countries, a large amount is in English and is based on Western Culture. This in itself could pose a large barrier to the adoption and use of open content in non-English speaking developing countries which may have fewer resources for translating materials (Mora et al., 2008). However, as the OER movement gains momentum and more organizations join the fray, the amount of OER content which has been translated has increased (Geith & Vignare, 2008). Although potential cultural issues have also been mentioned (Mora et al., 2008), no actual supporting evidence has been provided for this barrier.

2.3.4 Community of Practice

The concept of "build it and they will come" (Hatakka, 2009, p.1) does not apply to open educational initiatives. In order for individuals to use Open Educational Resources, they have to feel part of the process and experience a sense of belonging (Windle, Wharrad, McCormick, Laverty, & Taylor, 2010). This can be achieved through communities of practice.

There appears to be a correlation between the author group size and reuse of OER initiatives (Petrides et al., 2008). The size of an author group, and resultant collaboration between authors, increases the chance of reuse of OER initiatives (Petrides et al., 2008). These author groups can also be referred to as communities of practice.

Communities of practice can be seen as vehicles to improving the scalability of OER, as the members share a common interest or goal, in producing and sharing knowledge. The members have the freedom to join or leave the community, and to provide a mixed bag of different skills and experiences which, when combined, can create scalable OER (Koohang & Harman, 2007).

A good example of a community of practice is the OpenCourseWare consortium which, by creating "a broad and deep body of open educational content using a shared model" (Friesen, 2009, p.10), provided institutions with the facility to apply the MIT model to their own courses. Wikipedia is another example where the Wikipedia community has assisted in improving the overall quality of content, through collaboration and redevelopment of content (Petrides et al., 2008). The Hewlett Foundation, a funding body for OER initiatives, is focusing on a community building model which will provide incentives to all the stakeholders, and will encourage a "culture of contribution" (Atkins et al., 2007, p.3).

2.3.5 Quality

With the increase in the amount of OER content being shared, quality and quality assurance have been raised as major concerns (Kozinska et al., 2010). The term "quality" in itself is an issue, as quality can also be associated with the context within which it is used, and a sense of quality can only be gained once an individual forms a relationship with the material (Wiley & Gurrell, 2009). Iiyoshi and Kumar (2008) support this by saying that, in order to be able to evaluate the quality of content, it needs to be understood by whom the information will be used, how it will be used and when it will be used. For example, if a resource is written in Spanish but used by an individual who speaks Chinese, then the content would not be seen as high-quality material for that individual.

OER is open and free, which makes it more easily available to individuals to use; however, the term "free" is often incorrectly associated with poor quality (Panke, 2011). The Open Source Software movement was originally seen in the same light. When the concept of "free software" originally arose, questions were raised about its quality (Wiley & Gurrell, 2009). However, free and open software (FOSS) products have seen great successes, the openness associated with this software movement, has only increased the quality of the product.

2.3.6 Discovery, Relevance and Context

Finding resources on the World-Wide Web can be difficult due to the enormous amount of content available (Panke, 2011), and due to the lack of useful metadata. OER metadata is important in providing detail around the resource. For example, if an educator is searching for a video on a particular topic, but the video has to be viewed in order to decide its relevance, the educator would soon give up, as to review the entire video to determine its relevance would take too long (Wenk, 2010).

Contextual information is also important in order for the educator to decide resource relevance. For example, what was the feedback from learners who used this information, and was the quality of the content deemed to be of a high standard (Davis, et al., 2010)?

Some initiatives have been started to assist in overcoming these issues. For instance, the Commonwealth of Learning (COL) has provided a Google search called the Commonwealth of Learning's Knowledge Finder (Open Educational Resource, 2005) which can be used on any website to assist with the search for relevant OER material (Panke, 2011). This tool can be found at http://www.col.org/resources/knowServices/Pages/kf.asp.

West and Victor (2011) identified that often the educational material is based on outdated educational design principles, and to update the material will burden the already overtaxed lecturers. When educators try to use the online learning content for their lectures, there may be issues if the content is not organized into smaller more manageable modules which can easily be mixed and combined to form learning content which matches that of the institution's course curriculum (Johnstone, 2005).

3   Research Methodology

Currently there is very little research around the use of Open Educational Resources by the academic community specifically within an African context. Additionally, the focus of most OER research is still on the development and publication of OER repositories and on establishing policies around the creation and use of OER material (Andrade, 2011). By contrast, this research aims to identify the actual level of use of OER by academics in Africa, and to explain the factors which influence an academic's individual use of Open Educational Resources. The researchers adopted a positivist research philosophy.

3.1   Research Model

Through the critical literature review, the Unified Theory of Acceptance and Use of Technology (UTAUT) model was determined to be applicable to this research. The UTAUT model was developed through the analyses of elements across eight models (Venkatesh, Morris, Davis & Davis, 2003). There are four core independent constructs or determinants of intention and use: Performance Expectancy, Effort Expectancy, Social Influence and Facilitating Conditions (Venkatesh et al., 2003). These four constructs have been used along with two additional constructs: Attitude toward Using Technology and Information Quality. Although these constructs have traditionally not had much influence on behavioural intention to adopt various types of information technologies (Venkatesh et al., 2003), the researchers thought it prudent to include them given the nature of the research question (quality was identified as an important attribute of educational resources) and the resource constraints faced by African academics (and students).

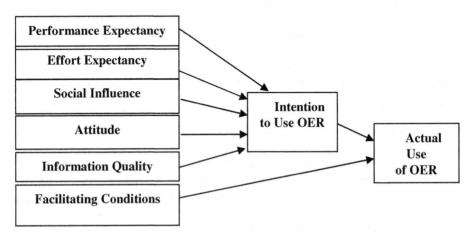

Fig. 2. Amended research model based on UTAUT with two additional constructs

The independent variables are described in table 1 below.

Table 1. Explanation of the independent variables used in the research model

Construct	Code	Description
Performance Expectancy	PE	How much the academic believes that OER will assist them in performing better in their job.
Effort Expectancy	EE	How easy it is to access and use OER.
Social Influence	SI	The extent to which academics are affected by people within their circle of influence e.g. colleagues or friends.
Facilitating Conditions	FC	The extent to which an academic believes that there are adequate resources i.e. technical infrastructure to support their use of OER.
Attitude towards technology	A	The overall reaction to using OER.
Information Quality	Q	The extent to which believes that the quality of the content of the OER is sufficiently high for use in their courses.

3.2 Research Design

The target population includes academics in higher education institutions in Africa. The original population group was divided into the following strata: region, institution type and faculty. The regional strata were restricted to the English speaking regions of the African continent, namely South, East and West Africa. Within each of these regions higher educational institutions were identified and, to ensure that the barriers and enablers were adequately researched, the faculty strata covered both global and local content. The disciplines of Information Systems, Science and Mathematics were selected to ensure that the population group included areas where content can be used globally, as there is not much differentiation between local and global curricula. From a localized content perspective, the disciplines of Social Sciences and Humanities were incorporated into the research.

The actual sampling approach was convenience sampling, as it was identified that the responses would not be essentially or critically different across the different stratification dimensions, and there was "little variation in the population group" (Saunders et.al, 2009, p.41). The site used to gather information was the University Directory Worldwide (http://www.university-directory.eu/index.html) website, which provided a breakdown of universities by country. Some countries were omitted due to political tensions at the time of the survey or because insufficient academic contact data was publicly available.

Given the large geographic spread of the population of African academics, a survey was deemed to be the most appropriate data collection method. Apart from the demographic section, the questionnaire used the same items from previous surveys, as these were considered to be valid and reliable.

A total of 693 surveys were emailed to academics. 11 participants opted out of the survey, and 53 emails were undelivered. The total number of responses which could have been received was 629. The total number of participants who started the survey was 96. Although most completed the demographic questions, only 68 respondents completed the entire questionnaire. Of those who responded but did not complete the survey, the following reasons were provided: *"I [...] am absolutely flooded at the moment"; "it has been very hectic for me", "I had problem with internet access."*

4   Data Analysis

The quantitative data has been analysed using quantitative analysis techniques including graphs and statistics. The analysis has assisted in exploring the data, and has identified trends and relationships within the data.

4.1   Sample Demographics

Respondents were well spread between the English-speaking African regions West Africa (27%), East Africa (28%) and Southern Africa (41%). There were also three respondents indicating that they were from North (2) or Central Africa (1).

Respondents were predominantly male with males accounting for 75% of the final data sample. However, this is representative of the target population of African academics since it corresponds quite closely with the original mailing list where the percentage of males varied from 87% (West Africa) to 72% (Southern Africa). Most respondents were in their thirties (35%) or forties (32%). Encouragingly, there were also quite a few young academic respondents (18% in their twenties) but only 10 (15%) of the academics older than 50. Almost one third (32.4%) had 5 years or less of lecturing experience with a further 31% from 6-10 years. Only 15% had more than 20 years' experience.

There was also a good spread among faculties or disciplines: 29% were in information technology, 25% in the social sciences, 16% in science, 13% in the humanities, 12% in mathematics and only 4% from engineering. The majority of the respondents held the position of lecturer (53%) or senior lecturer (19%) while only 17% fell into a professorial category.

4.2   Descriptive Analysis and Implications

Firstly, the number of respondents which are users and non-users of OER was examined. The option in the questionnaire included a scale of use, from yes to some extent to a great extent. For the descriptive analysis, a breakdown of both the scale and the overall yes/no response will be analysed for completeness. Table 2 shows that the majority of the respondents are users of OER. However, this is unlikely to be representative of the larger academic population in Africa due to response bias: academics that are using OER can be assumed to be much more inclined to respond to the survey than the non-users.

Table 2. Use of OER by survey respondents

	Frequency	Proportion
No, not at all	15	20.0%
Yes, to a limited extent	31	41.3%
Yes, to some extent	21	28.0%
Yes, to a great extent	8	10.7%
Total	75	100.0%

Also of interest is what type of Open Educational Resources the sample population is accessing the most. As identified in Figure 3, lecture notes and presentations are the most widely used OER.

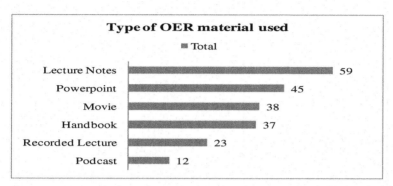

Fig. 3. Type of OER material used by respondents

4.3   UTAUT Model

This section tests the modified Unified Theory of Acceptance and Use of Technology (UTAUT) model regarding the factors which influence the Behavioural Intention to use (BI) and the actual Use Behaviour (UB) of Open Educational Resources.

4.3.1   Validity and Reliability Tests

The first step before performing any tests to support the UTAUT model is to ensure that the data used to support the model is both valid and reliable. In order to confirm this, a factor analysis and Cronbach Alpha test was performed on the data. The factor analysis is used to produce a matrix of the data, and assists in identifying correlations in the data which in turn are grouped into factors (Cairns, Oshlyansky & Thimbleby (2007). This factor analysis has identified what questions have strong loadings to each other.

The initial factor analysis consisted of 6 factors, with a loading factor of .6 which is acceptable in the exploratory nature of this research study. However, the test items related to the constructs of attitude and information quality did not load clearly on distinct factors in the factor analysis tests and thus the model was reduced to the original UTAUT independent constructs, namely Performance Expectancy (PE), Effort Expectancy (EE), Social Influence (SI) and Facilitating Conditions (FC). Table 3 shows the factor loadings for the final model. Not all test items loaded fully on the remaining constructs and those were also removed for further analysis.

Since multiple item constructs were used, it is important to test the reliability of the constructs (Hong, Im & Kang, 2010). The common test for this is the Cronbach alpha test. The Cronbach's Alpha coefficients were high, ranging from 0.766 (UB) to 0.894 (EE), except for the Facilitating Conditions (FC) construct which had a Cronbach α score of .678. However, this was considered acceptable given the small sample size.

Table 3. Factor loadings for final test items on the four factors

Variable	Factor Loadings (Varimax normalized) (2_stats_dat Extraction: Principal components (Marked loadings are >.600000)			
	Factor 1	Factor 2	Factor 3	Factor 4
Q11-AddValueWork	0.653724	0.252669	0.145020	0.386150
Q12-SupplementInfo	0.748003	0.105167	-0.158091	-0.197293
Q13-EnhanceTeaching	0.813590	0.003901	0.088276	-0.069086
Q14-StudentBenefit	0.689388	-0.123261	0.061129	0.164467
Q15-EnhanceEffectiveness	0.833967	-0.136840	0.152946	0.199629
Q16-EasierToDoJob	0.694027	-0.018325	0.223319	0.200278
Q19-IncreaseQualityTeaching	0.766278	-0.267031	0.037528	0.191982
Q20-ImproveQualityWork	0.674451	-0.027562	0.316588	0.301214
Q41-OERGoodIdea	0.688746	0.281148	-0.202692	0.117587
Q42-LectureInteresting	0.724533	0.053511	0.169815	0.309113
Q22-FormatApplicable	0.309082	0.276301	-0.181066	0.763372
Q23-EditMixMaterial	0.280280	0.262609	-0.097467	0.822505
Q40-FearCriticism	0.070532	-0.082305	0.906259	-0.079742
Q47-FearQuestions	-0.057728	0.517517	-0.549841	-0.333532
Q39-PeopleFaculty	0.224372	0.229541	0.824894	-0.192585
Q33-HaveResources	-0.043127	0.782036	-0.099084	0.009957
Q34-QuickEasyDownload	0.097639	0.667427	0.098947	0.305174
Q35-KnowledgeToFindUse	-0.124497	0.750801	0.097745	0.315708
Expl.Var	5.602239	2.356478	2.177901	2.143630
Prp.Totl	0.311236	0.130915	0.120995	0.119091

4.3.2 Data Analysis and Implications

The UTAUT model is used to analyze the direct determinants of a user's intention to use a technology and their usage behaviour (Venkatesh, Morris, Davis & Davis, 2003).

To support the UTAUT model, the independent variables of Performance Expectancy (PE), Effort Expectancy (EE) and Social Influence (SI) were analysed to identify if they had a positive or negative effect on the dependent variable Behavioural Intention (BI). Additionally, the independent variable Facilitating Conditions (FC) was analysed to identify if there was a positive or negative correlation between FC and Usage Behaviour (UB).

The most important relationships of the UTAUT model are those relationships between the independent constructs of PE and EE, to the use intention (Hong, Im & Kang, 2010). It needs to be noted that the scores for each construct were weighted prior to any data analysis.

Performance Expectancy was used to determine how much an individual believed that a certain technology would assist them in performing better in their job. 87.9% of the responses to the questions concerning Performance Expectancy gave a rating of agree somewhat to strongly agree. This implies that OER adds both value and quality to academics' teaching, thereby improving their overall job performance. The correlation between PE and BI was statistically significant ($p < 0.05$).

The questions for the EE construct are focused on what the population perceived as the expected effort required in using OER. If the effort required in adopting a technology is high, then the chances of those individuals adopting the relevant technology will be low, and vice versa. 55% of the participants agreed that OER is easy to format and mix, 24% were undecided and, of the remainder, 10.59% disagree. Even though the majority agreed that they expected there wouldl be little expected effort required to adopt OER, large portions of the population were undecided or disagreed with the questions. Detailed analysis indicates that it is the non-users who were undecided about the amount of effort required to use OER, as 46% of them selected the undecided option. This could be indicative of their lack of experience and or exposure to OER, and to their resultant uncertainty about how much effort would be required to adopt OER. There is a statistically significant correlation between EE and BI ($p < 0.05$).

The Social Influence construct focused on the influence which other individuals had on the participant's intention to use OER. The two questions which make up this construct are on faculty members' influence and on the fear of criticism from others if the participant used OER. The majority of the participants disagreed with these questions, indicating that academics are not influenced to any great extent by others. Additionally, the Pearson correlation coefficient between SI and BI is too low to be significantly significant. Out of the four constructs of PE, EE, SI and FC, SI has the least impact on an individual's intention to use OER.

The facilitating conditions construct identifies whether participants have access to resources or have the knowledge to use or find OER. As per the UTAUT model, it is identified that facilitation conditions influence the Use Behaviour of an individual but not the individual's intention to use OER. However, in this research study, Facilitating Conditions were positively and statistically significantly correlated to both an individual's Behavioural Intention and their Use Behaviour towards OER.

The Behavioural Intention construct focuses on the user's intention to use OER, and is a dependent construct in our model. The responses for these test items (Table 4) confirm the "use" responses shown earlier (Table 2).

Table 4. Behavioural intention to use OER

	Agree strong-ly	Agree	Agree some-what	Un-decided	Disagree some-what	Dis-agree	Dis-agree strongly
OER fits the way I work	10%	35%	29%	18%	3%	1%	3%
Will use OER in future	21%	44%	24%	10%	1%	0%	0%
Will use OER in next 2 years	10%	41%	24%	15%	3%	3%	4%
Would join OER community	7%	32%	25%	21%	1%	9%	4%

Use behaviour was measured by 7 test items. A statistically significant and positive correlation exists between Behavioural Intention (BI) and Use Behaviour (UB). A multiple regression test was done in order to estimate the strength of relationships between the dependent and independent constructs.

The multiple regression analysis (Table5) for the dependent variable BI shows an overall R^2 score of 0.53. This indicates that 53 % of the variance in the Behavioural Intention to adopt OER is explained by the three constructs Performance Expectancy, Social Influence and Effort Expectancy. However, SI is not a significant predictor ($p = 0.171$) when the other two significant variables are taken into account.

Table 5. Multiple regression summary for Behavioural Intention to Use OER

	b*	Std.Err.	b	Std.Err.	t(64)	p-value
Intercept			0.0980	0.1138	0.8604	0.3928
Performance Expectancy (PE)	0.5060	0.1015	1.2302	0.2468	4.9853	0.0000*
Social Influence (SI)	0.1249	0.0903	0.0475	0.0343	1.3836	0.1713
Effort Expectancy (EE)	0.3018	0.0989	0.1215	0.0398	3.0527	0.0033*
R^2=0.5280; Adjusted R^2=0.5059; F(3,64)=23.866; p<0.00000; Std.Err of estimate: 0.1778

Table 6. Multiple regression summary for Use Behaviour of OER

	b*	Std.Err.	b	Std.Err.	t(64)	p-value
Intercept			0.1360	0.0415	3.2763	0.0047*
Behavioural Intention (BI)	0.7315	0.0959	0.3659	0.0480	7.6300	0.0000*
Facilitating Conditions	-0.0400	0.0959	-0.0146	0.0350	-0.1475	0.6777
R^2=0.7153; Adjusted R^2=0.5117; F(2,65)=34.052; p<0.00000; Std.Err of estimate: 0.0897

For the dependent variable UB, the overall R^2 score was 0.51 (Table 6). This indicates that 51% of the variance in UB can be explained. However, the direct impact of Facilitating Conditions is not statistically significant when BI's contribution is taken into account. Figure 4 shows the overall correlations between the independent and dependent constructs using the Beta coefficients from the multiple regression tests.

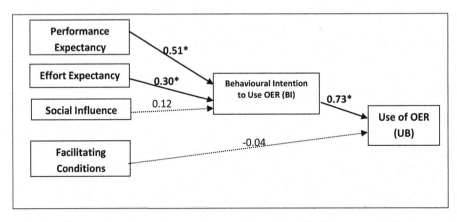

Fig. 4. Correlations between model constructs (* = significant at p<0.05)

4.4   Perceived Barriers to the Adoption of OER

In a manner, this reduces the final validated model back to the original parsimonious Technology Acceptance Model, where Performance Expectancy can be seen to represent Perceived Usefulness, and Effort Expectancy as a proxy for Ease of Use.

The second objective of this research was to analyze the perceived barriers to the use of OER. Respondents were requested to select multiple options which they perceived to be barriers to using Open Educational Resources. The resultant selected barriers from the survey questionnaire were grouped into the six main themes identified earlier in the literature review. Where the data did not fit into the predetermined groupings, a new barrier grouping was created.

The cumulative score per barrier grouping was calculated to identify the highest perceived barriers to the use of OER by academics (figure 5).

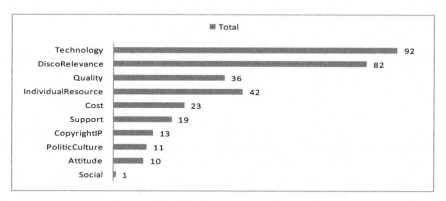

Fig. 5. Perceived barriers to the adoption of OER

The two most crucial barriers appear to be the technological barrier – as previously identified by Stacey (2007) – and the difficulties experienced in discovering OER and assessing their relevance and context. Also important are the lack of individual resources (time and personal skills) and the perceived quality of OER.

The barriers were also compared between users and non-users of OER, to identify whether the overall barriers experienced by users and non-users are the same. A Chi-square analysis confirmed that there were statistically significant differences between the two groups of academics ($p = 0.0028$). The main contributor to the significant difference was the lack of individual resources (which was rated as the most critical barrier for the non-users), although users rated the difficulty in discovering and assessing their relevance/context also significantly higher than the non-users.

Note that, although the political and cultural barrier was not identified as being significant in this research, there were perhaps insufficient questions around what political or cultural barriers the academic population could experience within an African context. Future research should look at this barrier on its own within the academic OER context, in order to identify whether the political and cultural barriers effect the adoption of OER within Africa as compared to developed countries. Additionally, local legal and organisational circumstances may have constrained academics from adopting OER, e.g. where they cannot change the curriculum.

5   Conclusion

The research has identified that academics' attitudes towards OER is positive as the majority of the respondents agree that OER can add value to their work as an academic. Interestingly, only two of the UTAUT model influencing variables were found to exert significant influence on the academics' intention to adopt OER: the Performance Expectancy i.e. the degree to which OER are expected to add value to their work, and Effort Expectancy, the amount of work they expect to have to do to obtain and use OER. In effect, these findings reduce the model to the original, more parsimonious Technology Acceptance Model which was the foundation of the UTAUT model, where (Perceived) Usability and Usefulness were hypothesized to be the key drivers of Behavioural Intention. However, these two variables explained more than half of the variance in Behavioural Intention to Use OERs, and the latter also explained over half the variance in OER Use Behaviour.

Another aim of this research study was to identify the main barriers to the use of Open Educational Resources by academics within Africa. The main barriers identified are those of technology, discovery, relevance, quality and individual resources.

The key barrier experienced by the respondents is that of technology i.e. lack of access to computers, lack of internet access and/or poor bandwidth. Although these issues have been identified in prior research, the confirmation of these findings adds more urgency to the need to find solutions to the poor technological infrastructure which exists in developing countries.

A more unexpected finding is that OER users rated the difficulty of both discovering what Open Educational Resources are available to use and determining their relevance to their environmental context or subject area as equally critical barriers. Interestingly, the expected barrier of Western context or bias, considering most of the published OER material originates from developed countries, was not seen as a significant barrier.

5.1   Recommendations

One of the questions in the survey questionnaire was for academics to comment on what would encourage them to use OER. Some of the underlying themes were communication, advertising, training and awareness.

The recommendation to the OER community is to market and advertise OER to the African academic community. It will improve academics' awareness of what is available and what benefits can be gained through using OER. This may address the key barrier of discovery, relevance and context, since, even though there have been improvements in the search facilities and repositories of OER content, these changes have not been communicated effectively to the greater African academic community.

From a skills perspective, academics believe that gaining access to and using OER is complicated, and that individuals need to be trained in the necessary skills required to use OER. Although this point does have some merit for individuals without a basic level of computer literacy, there needs to be better communication around which OER repositories exist and the ease with which Open Educational Resources can be accessed.

5.2   Future Research

The sample was fairly small and there is a strong suspected response bias towards respondents that are familiar with and have used OER. A larger scale and more systematic survey would be more representative of the African academic community. In particular, future research should attempt to include academics from the Arabic and French-language North and West African regions. OER research in other developing countries could compare both the model fit and barriers and possibly highlight those factors that are more uniquely African.

Future research could also examine the barriers to OER adoption in more detail. A larger sample is likely to reveal additional significant influencing factors beyond Effort and Performance Expectancy.

In particular, the barriers of culture and politics were not investigated to a great enough extent in this research. In order to determine whether politics and culture (or other factors) have a significant impact on an individual's adoption and use of OER, a qualitative study could be completed for academics within Africa, in order for the underlying feelings and attitudes towards culture and politics to be understood.

References

Andrade, A., Ehlers, U., Caine, A., Carneiro, R., Conole, G., Kairamo, A., et al.: Beyond OER: Shifting Focus to Open Educational Practices. Open Education Quality Initiative (2011)

Atkins, D.E., Brown, J.S., Hammond, A.L.: Resources (OER) Movement: Achievements, Challenges, and New Opportunities (2007)

Bissell, A.N.: Permission granted: open licensing for educational resources. Open Learning 24(1), 97–106 (2009)

Carson, S.: The unwalled garden: Growth of the OpenCourseWare consortium, 2001–2008. Open Learning 24(1), 23–29 (2009)

D'Antoni, S.: Open Educational Resources: reviewing initiatives and issues. Open Learning 24(1), 3–10 (2009)

Davis, H.C., Carr, L., Hey, J.M., Howard, Y., Millard, D., Morris, D., et al.: Bootstrapping a Culture of Sharing to Facilitate Open Educational Resources. IEEE Transactions on Learning Technologies 3(2), 96–108 (2010)

De Liddo, A.: From open content to open thinking. In: World Conference on Educational Multimedia, Hypermedia and Telecommunications (Ed-Media 2010), Toronto, Canada (2010)

Downes, S.: Models for Sustainable Open Educational Resources. Interdisciplinary Journal of Knowledge and Learning Objects 3, 29–44 (2007)

Dulle, F.W., Minishi-Majanja, M.: The suitability of the UTAUT model in open access adoption studies. Information Development 27(1), 32–45 (2011)

Friesen, N.: Open Educational Resources: New Possibilities for Change and Sustainability. International Review of Research in Open and Distance Learning 10(5), 1–13 (2009)

García-Peñalvo, F.J., Figuerola, C.G., Merlo, J.A.: Open knowledge: challenges and facts. Online Information Review 34(4), 520–539 (2010)

Geith, C., Vignare, K.: Access to education with online learning and open educational resources: Can they close the gap? Journal of Asynchronous Learning Networks 12(1), 1–22 (2008)

Geser, G.: Open Educational Practices and Resources. EduMedia Group, Salzburg (2012)

Gourley, B., Lane, A.: Re-invigorating openness at The Open University: the role of Open Educational Resources. Open Learning: The Journal of Open, Distance and e-Learning 24(1), 57–65 (2009)

Hatakka, M.: Build it and they will come? Inhibiting factors for reuse of open content in developing countries. The Electronic Journal on Information Systems in Developing Countries 37(5), 1–16 (2009)

Hilton, J., Wiley, D.A.: The Creation and Use of Open Educational Resources in Christian Higher Education. Christian Higher Education 9(1), 49–59 (2010)

Hýlen, J.: Giving Knowledge for Free: The Emergence of Open Educational Resources. OECD-CERI, Paris (2007)

Johnstone, S.: Open Educational Resources Serve the World. Educause Quarterly 3, 15–18 (2005)

Kanwar, A., Kodhandaramana, B., Umar, A.: Toward Sustainable Open Education Resources: A Perspective From the Global South. American Journal of Distance Education 24(2), 65–80 (2010)

Koohang, A., Harman, K.: Advancing Sustainability of Open Educational Resources. Issues in Informing Science and Information Technology 4, 535–543 (2007)

Kozinska, K., Kursun, E., Wilson, T., McAndrew, P., Scanlon, E., Jones, A.: Are open educational resources the future of e-learning? In: 3rd International Future-Learning Conference: Innovations in Learning for the Future. The Open University, Instanbul (2010)

Mora, M., Hassin, K., Pullin, A., Muegge, S.: Open Educational resources and the evolving value chain of education in developing countries. In: IEEE International Symposium on Technology and Society, June 26-28, pp. 1–10 (2008)

Panke, S.: An Expert Survey on the Barriers and Enablers of Open Educational Practices (2011), http://elearningeuropa.info

West, P.G., Victor, L.: Background and action paper on OER (2011), http://www.paulwest.org/public/Background_and_action_paper_on_OER.pdf

OSS Integration Issues and Community Support: An Integrator Perspective

Claudia Ayala[1], Daniela S. Cruzes[2], Anh Duc Nguyen[2], Reidar Conradi[2]
Xavier Franch[1], Martin Höst[3], and Muhammad Ali Babar[4]

[1] Universitat Politècnica de Catalunya
{cayala,franch}@essi.upc.edu
[2] Norwegian University of Science and Technology
{dcruzes,anhn,conradi}@idi.ntnu.no
[3] Lund University, Sweden
martin.host@cs.lth.se
[4] IT University of Copenhagen, Copenhagen, Denmark
malibaba@itu.dk

Abstract. The reuse and integration of Open Source Software (OSS) components provided by OSS communities is becoming an economical and strategic need for today's organizations. The integration of OSS components provides many benefits, but also risks and challenges. One of the most important risks is the lack of effective and timely OSS community support for dealing with possible integration problems. For gaining an understanding of the common problems that organizations face when integrating OSS components, and the role played by OSS communities, we performed an exploratory study on 25 OSS integration projects from different European organizations. The results show that the main way of reducing integration problems was the use of OSS components from well-established communities; therefore very few integration problems were identified. In most of the cases these problems were successfully solved with the support from the OSS community and/or colleagues. In addition, contrary to the common belief that understanding code from someone else is a hard and undesirable task, some integrators consider OSS code even more understandable than their own code.

1 Introduction

The free availability of Open Source Software (OSS) has over the last decade had a significant impact, not only on the software IT industry, but also on software-intensive organizations. OSS is significantly influencing the ways these organizations develop, acquire, use, and commercialize software [1], and actual evidence shows that organizations are clearly becoming a very important part of the OSS communities

In particular, the integration of OSS components is one of the most popular ways of adopting OSS [2]. It involves including OSS components into other software products or systems and this again may involve modifying, extending, or wrapping the OSS components.

I. Hammouda et al. (Eds.): OSS 2012, IFIP AICT 378, pp. 129–143, 2012.

OSS integration might have many benefits, such as significantly lower (purchasing) costs, availability of high quality products, adherence to open standards and vendor independence [1]. However, it also implies several challenges. On the one hand, we may mention that OSS components do not always satisfy all the requirements. In certain cases, some "glue code" or modifications are required to make OSS components work together. This however creates a customized version of the OSS component. The integrator (i.e., the person(s) in charge of integrating OSS component(s) into the software system) is then faced with the issue of maintaining this derived version, and must decide how to handle these extensions and modifications. As a result, each organization that modifies OSS components and incorporates them in its own applications is faced with the issue of whether to contribute or not to the OSS community [3], [4]. On the other hand, some studies emphasize that high-quality OSS components rely heavily on having a large, sustainable community to develop code rapidly, debug code effectively, and build new features [5]. Thus, the organizations that integrate OSS components into their systems represent a potential base of contributing members needed to sustain the OSS communities [6].

It is therefore vital to provide evidence that help OSS communities to envisage strategies to improve potential integration issues; as well as organizations to meet some practical challenges related to OSS integration. In this context, the goal for this study is therefore gaining an understanding of the common problems that organizations face when integrating OSS components, and the role that the OSS communities play in such integration processes. Thus, we conducted an empirical study on European organizations from Norway, Spain, Sweden and Denmark. It consisted on semi-structured interviews with 25 integrators from different organizations that represented 25 different integration projects. Based on their answers, we were able to draw some observations. We report our main findings in this paper.

The rest of the paper is organized as follows: Section 2 provides an overview of existing evidence on OSS integration and companies' participation. Section 3 provides details of the empirical study. Section 4 summarizes the most relevant observations from the interviews. Section 5 discusses the results. Threats to validity are presented in Section 6, while Section 7 summarizes the conclusions and future work.

2   Background and Related Work

Recent systematic reviews reveal that integration is one of the most popular strategies of adopting OSS [2], [4].

The company-community relationships have been explored in works as [7], [8], [9]. In [7], the authors identify three types of organization-community relationships:

- Symbiotic: Both the community and the organization benefit from the relationship.
- Commensalistic: The organization benefits from the relationship but the community is not affected.

- Parasitic: The organization benefits from the relationship but at the same time it damages the community.

Several barriers to contribute back to the community have been also investigated as for instance by Ven and Mannaert [10] that found that deciding not to contribute can also be risky as one may be forced to maintain a parallel copy of the product.

Furthermore, Stol and Ali Babar in [4] did a systematic synthesis of the reported challenges of integrating OSS and ended up with a comprehensive list of challenges related to OSS integration. Even though there is a considerable body of research on the challenges of integrating OSS components in the development of software products [2], [4], the majority of these works refer to success stories derived from single case studies or experience reports that provide very limited information about the real industrial landscape of companies integrating OSS components. Moreover, the role that OSS communities play on supporting integrators to solve their integration problems has not been further explored.

Therefore, our overall objective is gaining an understanding of the common problems that organizations face when integrating OSS components, and the role that the OSS communities play in such integration processes.

3   Survey on OSS Integration Issues and Community Support

Our overall objective has been broken down into two research questions that are at their turn broken down into more concrete sub research questions.

On the one hand, RQ1 was aimed to inquiry on potential integration issues. RQ1.1 is focused on inquiring the most common integration problems. Furthermore, the literature has pointed out the underestimation of integration effort and inefficient debugging as problematic areas that require further investigation [20]; therefore, we stated RQ1.2 and RQ1.3 respectively. Finally, as a previous study [13] reported that getting OSS components information seems to become a continuous monitoring activity rather than being on a project demand basis, we stated RQ1.4 to understand how integrators monitor OSS communities.

On the other hand, as pointed out in the previous section, company-community relationships have been reported before (e.g., [7-9]), however, there are no sufficiently deep studies to further understand what kind of assistance and/or contributions are mostly requested/provided by integrators, and which means are used to do so. Therefore, RQ2.1, RQ2.2, and RQ2.3 were stated.

RQ1: How Do Integrators Deal with Integration Issues?
RQ1.1-What are the most relevant integration problems?
RQ1.2-How are integration/testing costs estimated?
RQ1.3-What are the differences on locating/fixing bespoke software bugs vs. OSS related bugs?
RQ1.4-How are OSS communities being followed up?

RQ2: To what Extent Integrators Interact with/Contribute to the Community?
RQ2.1-What kind of help do integrators request from the OSS community?
RQ2.2-What kind of contributions do integrators provide to the OSS community?
RQ2.3-Which means are used to interact with the OSS community?

3.1   Research Method

Interviews, observation and analysis of documents are some of the most common data collection methods. However, a stated in [12], qualitative (approached by interviews) and quantitative (approached by questionnaires) surveys are the two most relevant types of studies for component-based software engineering investigation. Thus, as the nature of our research questions was clearly exploratory, we decided to carry out the study using a qualitative research approach based on semi-structured interviews to collect data directly from software-intensive organizations that integrate OSS in software product development. Semi-structured interviews allowed us to have certain flexibility to further explore what was going on in the area.

Participants. Participating organizations were chosen from our direct or indirect industrial collaboration network. They include organizations with different sizes and in different application domains. 69 organizations were invited to participate by phone call and email. Some of the contacts were not eligible for participating due to several reasons, such as lack of integration of OSS components in the projects, or privacy of the OSS adoption strategy. We ended up with 25 integrators from different organizations that represented 25 different projects. Table 1 shows some details of the organizations and the analyzed projects.

The Instrument. The interview guide was carefully designed following the guidelines stated in [11] and previous experience performing international surveys from several members of the team [12], [13], [14, [15]. The survey was designed as a 5-section survey, with both closed and open questions. The closed questions were used to solicit information about the respondent and project context. The open questions were used to gather information on integration issues and community relationship. The survey also included an introductory section concerning relevant terminology and background in order to offer a common understanding to all participants. In this paper we report our finding related to the relationship among integrators and communities (other results from the study have been also reported in [16]). In general, the guide mostly focused on a single software development project with at least one release of the corresponding software product, and with integration of one or more OSS components. If the respondents had experience with several such projects, they were asked to choose the most familiar one.

Data Collection Procedure: The interview guide was sent to all participants some days before the interview meeting. In this way, they could be prepared for the interview. The participants were asked to fill in the first two parts of the survey and give back to us beforehand. The next three parts of the survey were asked directly to the participant during the interview. Interviews were mainly performed in the mother tongue of the respondents (some exceptions occurred in Norway, where the interviews were performed in English) and when possible face-to-face in their working place or by phone, by one to three researchers of the team. Interviews lasted around 40 to 75 minutes each and were recorded for subsequent analysis.

Table 1. Some details of the organizations and projects studied

Id	# Employees	Application Domain	Project Staff	Staff with experience in OSS integration	Some OSS used	% OSS of the system	Total effort (person/ months)
A	170	Defense (communications)	20-25	30%	JBPM, Jetty, Spring, LogBack, Maven	90%	>2000
B	1	ICT Industry	4	50%	Impact, LPng	10%	480
C	3	ICT Industry	2	100%	SolR, Xapian, Twisted: NLTK.	80%	12
D	350	Embedded systems	18	25%	Linux Kernel, MD5 Checksum	-	-
E	500	Oil and gas industry	2	50%	PDfLib, OpenPyExcel	77%	18
F	-	Public sector	200	60%	Flex Framework, Batch part of Spring	75%	-
G	230	Bank	4	100%	WideShot, CryptoPP, ParseXs	10%	36
H	190	Public sector	20	100%	JBoss, OpenSummer, USD	66%	1000
I	6	Finance	1.5	66%	Python, Soap and Django	90%	3
J	4	Public sector (Education)	3	100%	SunGridEngine, Cluster FS, Linux Debian, Ganglia	90%	30
K	100	Private services (entertainment, sales)	3	100%	Apache, MySQL, PHP, FFTP tools	5%	7.5
L		Public sector	5	100%	Mantis, Ant, Apache	80-90%	72
M	150	Public sector (Education)	6	100%	Jasper Reports, DOJO, Apache, Quark	25%	157
N	30	ICT	7	14%	Jenkins, Cucumber, Mercurial	10%	84
O	15	ICT	3	100%	Joomla	50%	56
P	5	Public sector	2.5	67%	Zope and Plone	99%	6
Q	14	ICT	3	100%	Varnish, Engine egg	80%	9
R	500	ICT	25	80%	Jasper Reports, Junit, Jmeter, MediaWiki, OpenCSV	30%	900
S	2	Public sector	2	100%	RXTX, MySQL, Palcom	60%	36
T	>1000	ICT	250	50%	OSS platform	50%	1000
U	11	Energy	2	100%	Speed -Typo3CMS, FPDF, Apache, Stability	40%	20
V	2500	ICT	4	100%	Mongo DB	100%	8
W	4	Whole-sale, retail and entertainment	10	50%	Apache, MySQL, PHP Suite,	100%	24
X	1	Public sector (Education)	1	100%	Sbuntu Enterpise Cloud (UEC) & Eucalyptus, NappIt, pfSense, FreeBSD	100%	6
Y	7	Medical	1	0	Zope, Plone, Apache, Mysql, Ubuntu	100%	3

(-) respondent did not answer or asked to keep this information confidential.

Data Analysis: Interviews were prepared for analysis by the manual transcription of audio records to text documents (the transcripts vary from 13 to 21 pages in size). When needed, a summary of each interview was translated to English so that the whole research team could assess and discuss the data. We analyzed the filled-in questions and transcripts using a qualitative approach that consisted on the assessment of the interview documents by two different researchers and the subsequent generation of categories by grouping sentences or phrases that described the same idea, action or property [11]. We tried to be exhaustive with the categories in order to include as much detail provided by the respondents as possible.

4   Results

This section presents the results of the study. They are grouped in 2 subsections according to the research questions introduced above, when possible, we use tables to illustrate the resulting categories.

4.1   RQ1: How Do Integrators Deal with Integration Issues?

RQ1.1- What Are the Most Relevant Integration Problems?

Twenty out of 25 respondents did not mention any relevant integration problem in the project they based their answers on. Some of them commented: *"We use components that are like standards and with a big community behind, so it is hard that you are the first one that experiences a problem"* (K); *"In this case, we were lucky. The documentation was complete and updated"* (P).

Only five respondents mentioned that they experienced some kind of integration problem. Two of them said that they dropped and changed the OSS component to solve the problem. One emphasizes: *"[The potential problems] depend on getting the right component"* (X). Two respondents agreed that the problem was solved by learning how other people proceeded in similar cases: *"It was a problem related to incompatibility among versions. But, we solve it by searching in Google and finding people that have explained their solution for it"* (O); *"Yes, we had some problems, but they were already reported by someone else in the forum, so we just learn some tricks to solve it"* (R). One respondent stated that the problem came from the lack of documentation *"We struggle a little with data formats, because sometimes the documentation was incomplete"* (V).

RQ1.2 How Are Integration/Testing Costs Estimated?

On the question about integration/testing costs, sixteen out of 25 respondents agreed that integration costs were estimated based on the experience of the development team. One respondent said: *"There is a kind of guessing in this. We ask the development team and with their experience they come with numbers and we put a bill on it"* (U). In addition, there were some mixed views on how costly the OSS integration was. One respondent for example thought the cost was low: *"It is difficult to say, but in any cases it would be less than developing the component yourself. For the small component, the integration cost is very low anyway because they have a nicer interface..."* (G). But another respondent said: *"There is normally a lot of costs involved with testing and integration. Lots of money is involved from exchanging part to integrating part. Integration sometimes involves competition with closed systems or exchange with other systems"* (Y).

Three respondents pointed out that they used piloting as a way to estimate costs of integration. In these cases the pilot took from one to two months. Two respondents answered that the estimation was part of the preliminary study of the candidate components. In two interviews, respondents said that their organizations had a marketing department responsible for the estimation costs, so the respondents did not know details about such estimation. One respondent stated that their estimation was driven by a testing tool *"We used a testing tool. Integration and testing was around 20% of the whole development"* (Q). Finally, another integrator stated that they used specific templates for the estimation (T). Table 2 summarizes the obtained categories.

Table 2. Categories of Integration Costs Estimation

Count	Categories
16	Experience-Based
3	Did a pilot
2	In-house marketing department
2	Preliminary study of the candidate components and their integration problems
1	Testing tools
1	Templates

RQ1.3 What Are the Differences on Locating/Fixing Bespoke Software Bugs vs. OSS Related Bugs?

We inquired about the differences among bespoke vs. OSS bugs' locating/fixing process. Nine respondents stated that they do not try to locate bugs in the OSS components. One of them commented: *"the components we used are like standards. Everything has been proven several times and it is well documented, so we did not find bugs"* (K). Nine respondents emphasize that there was no difference on how they located/fixed the bugs. At this respect, one respondent said: *"in my experience, most open source libraries and components are well written and the author usually put pride in putting out something that is well commented and nice formatting, and usually it is quite easy to navigate around so; actually, the process is a bit similar"* (E). On the other hand, two respondents said that the main difference resides on the fact that it is harder to look at someone else's code. *"We run code. If it does not work, we isolate the faulty areas. Then we get to know whether it is in own code or OSS code. It is usually in our own code. It rarely happens that OSS component has errors and they are cumbersome to resolve as we don't know that code"*(U). One striking answer was on one respondent stating *"It is harder to find bugs in our own code. In the OSS components we didn't have the same amount of bugs than those bugs from us, because they were pretty much stable components. We didn't have to do any formal testing in these OSS components"* (F). One respondent stated that an external company was subcontracted to fix those bugs related to the OSS component that were not trivial *"When there is a problem that is trivial or small, we try to fix it by our self. When the problem is something different from standard Linux libraries, we have a company to fix. It is a consultant that deals with third party libraries, mismatches..."* (D). Finally, 3 respondents did not answer to this question. Table 3 summarizes the resulting categories.

Table 3. Differences Among Bespoke Software Bugs vs. OSS Bugs

Count	Categories
9	Do not try to locate OSS bugs
9	No difference with locating bespoke software bugs
3	No answer
2	It is harder to look at someone else code
1	Subcontract a company to fix OSS components bugs.
1	It is harder to find bugs in own code

RQ1.4 How Are OSS Communities Being Followed Up?

Fifteen respondents answered that they did not have someone following up with the OSS project. Some of their comments are: *"No, only if there is a problem we go to the community"* (J); *"We don't have anyone watching the update stuff...We don't usually update the OSS component. For instance, now we chose the JBPM version 4.4. We wait sometime until someone realizes that there is a new version, but we don't watch the community"* (A).

Eight respondents stated that there was a responsible for OSS component issues. In seven of these eight cases, such a person was a colleague in the organization. One of them commented *"Yes, there is a community coordinator who is the one that is the face of a community, and hence he/she follows the trends in this community."* One respondent stated that instead of having a dedicated person inside the organization, they subcontracted a company to select the OSS components and support them in any integration issue (D).

Finally, two respondents did not answer this question.

4.2 RQ2: To What Extent Integrators Interact With/Contribute to the OSS Community?

RQ2.1 What Kind of Help Do Integrators Request From the OSS Community?

The analysis of the interviewees' responses regarding the support from the community shows that thirteen respondents did not explicitly request help from the OSS community. Instead, they just used what it was already available on the community portal or managed to solve doubts by consulting their colleagues or using

Google. *"We did not make any contact extending the normal use of community forums and discussion boards. Most of our issues could be handled by information already available in the community portal"* (F).

Ten respondents stated that for some specific aspects, they requested community help and were satisfied with the obtained support: *"In a couple of technical aspects, we asked for opinions about what it was the better way to proceed"* (P); *"[There is] usually a very quick response"* (E).

One respondent stated that they started requesting help and became involved in the community so now they are active co-providers: *"We were the ones that uploaded this part of the OSS, so we were the ones that better knew such part"* (Q). Finally, one respondent stated that asked for help but did not get it (X).

RQ2.2 What Kind of Contributions Do Integrators Provide to the Community?

We asked the respondents what kind of contributions they provided to the community. We consolidated their answers as shown in Table 4.

On the one hand, twelve respondents stated that they had reported bugs, but only nine of them eventually contributed by fixing them. Some of their motivations were: *"bug fixing is something we would sent back definitely because we are very interested to give it into the main branch so we don't have to fix it every time we do an update"*(H); *"It is so much easier to get the bug fixed if you submit the fix of course. And with the open source project you can do that"*(C).

On the other hand, twelve respondents stated that they mostly take advantage of the community without contributing: *"we have not done anything. We just used the components"* (N); *"We do not dedicate a budget to OSS bugs notification nor contribution activities"* (L). In addition, 4 respondents stated that they became co-providers of the community by contributing back some OSS components.

Finally, five respondents emphasize that they participate in organizations or activities to promote the OSS culture as for instance *"We are founding members of Open source foundation"* (U), or *"We presented our resulting system in Workshops and Seminars to show how integrating OSS components can work"* (J).

Table 4. Results of integrators' contribution to the OSS community

Answer	Own bug reports	Bug fixes with code	Become co-providers	Promoting the OSS culture
YES	12	9	4	5
NO	12	15	19	9
Unknown/no answer	1	1	1	10

RQ2.3 Which Means Are Used to Interact With the OSS Community?

Nineteen respondents mentioned that they use to different extent bulletin boards, forums, email lists and the bug tracking system from the community project. Forums and bulletin boards were mentioned the most. However, there were six extreme cases were the respondents did not need any kind of direct interaction with the community:

"No cooperation with community. We just downloaded the software" (V). *"We did not need to communicate with the community as the components we used were very well documented"* (K);*"We don't need direct contact with open source projects. We use the product because we have so much competence, either in the team or friend-to-friend. So, we don't need to communicate with the community directly"* (A); *"We mostly read the documentation and things published in the OSS community, but did not collaborate directly. Furthermore, in cases when problems appeared, we used Google to find related hits or portals like StackOverFlow"* (M).

5   Discussion of Main Findings

In this section we discuss the obtained results and establish whenever possible links to the findings of previous studies.

For most of the analyzed projects, integrators did not mention any relevant problem. Although this was an interesting observation, (as integration problems have been highlighted as one of the main concerns of organizations that integrate third-party components [20]), it is important to understand these results in the context of the analyzed projects. In fact, in the analyzed projects, integrators tried to minimize potential integration problems by selecting OSS components that fulfilled an adequate level of documentation/information and/or ensuring that they would have enough (own or subcontracted) expertise to solve the potential problems. Thus, it can be observed from Table 1 that the OSS components used by most of the respondents refer to OSS projects with great activity and vitality. In addition, some of these OSS components have become de facto standards.

It is worth to mention that although some works have claimed that much of the literature does not reflect the huge diversity in OSS initiatives and projects, focusing instead on large, well-established communities. In our case, even if we did not have control over the projects selected by the organizations, we ended up mostly analyzing projects that integrated OSS components from well-established communities as organizations actually use these kinds of components. Thus, we agreed with Choi et al [18] that demonstrated that the mature status of well-known OSS projects likely attracts users given their greater activity and vitality. However this pathway is unavailable for most of the OSS projects and those newly initiated projects that struggle to attract users and contributors [19]. This also confirms the importance of studies that help OSS communities -especially those newly initiated projects that need to attract users- to envisage strategies for attracting integrators.

Regarding the way bugs were processed, we found, on the one hand, that nine out of 25 respondents do not even try to locate bugs on OSS components; instead, they rely on the expected functionality. On the other hand, other nine respondents emphasized that it was not difference on the way they fixed bugs in their own code instead of fixing bugs from OSS components, mainly because the OSS code was understandable and well commented. In addition, one also said that OSS code is even more understandable than their own code. Most of them also claimed that finding bugs in OSS was not usual. In addition, it was interesting to see that 8 organizations have a responsible of the community trends. This seems to show the importance that the OSS communities are gaining in the organizations.

Regarding costs estimation, we found that most integrators did not further estimate integration costs; instead, they just made an informal approach based on their experience. So, it seems that the claim from Li et al [20] about the relevance of estimating the time that the component(s) integration takes, do not hold in most of our analyzed projects.

Furthermore, in most of the analyzed projects, integrators managed to deal with their integration problems by themselves, without requesting specific help to the community. They mostly used information/documentation already available in the community portal or asked their colleagues for help. In line with this observation, our results also show that forums and bulleting boards from OSS communities were typically used in a passive way (i.e., integrators navigated through documentation and previous posts more than actively participate by adding new posts or content).

It is worth to highlight that the perception of the integrators about the support received from the community was good. 24 out of 25 said that they managed to solve the potential integration problems by using the information available in the portal or requesting help to the community with usually a quick response. Only one case stated that he/she did not receive the expected help.

Regarding the integrator's contribution, our results show that most integrators had limited interaction/contribution to the communities. This confirms the observations from [21-24] that emphasize that most organizations seem to have rather limited contributions to the OSS communities. Furthermore, although our results show that the most frequent way to contribute was by providing bug reports without code, the number of integrators that also submitted the code for fixing the bug was also high. This seems to confirm the claim from [25] and [26] regarding that the number of organizations contributing to OSS seems to be increasing. In addition, other ways of contributing that have been usually overlooked by previous research are related to activities to promote the OSS culture by for instance funding OSS initiatives or sharing the knowledge with colleagues.

Regarding the involvement of the approached organizations in terms of the company-community relationships described by Dahlander and Magnusson [7], [8] (see section 2), our results show that almost all studied organizations seemed to have a commensalistic relationship with the community (i.e., the organization just benefits from the community). It was interesting to see that 4 out of 25 organizations have become active members of the community as co-providers of some specific parts of the OSS project, thus establishing a symbiotic relationship.

Furthermore, a common motivation for those that contributed to the community seemed to be to make sure that modifications to the component's code were maintained, while a common inhibitor to contribute in those organizations that did not contribute was that their budget did not include time neither resources to participate in the communities. These factors have been also mentioned by Ven and Mannaert [10]. In addition, most integrators that did not contribute to the communities also mentioned that they try to use the component as is (i.e., without modifications). This agrees with the results stated by Li et al. [20] that showed evidence that the source code of OSS components is seldom modified, or Höst et al. [27] that in a focus group meeting found that practitioners based on their experience do not recommend adapting OSS components that are included in products. However, if they need to adapt them, the recommendation is to do this through "glue code".

6   Limitations of the Study

This study was performed by means of a rigorous planning and the establishment of protocols for data collection and data analysis. This was especially important as the research involved several researchers and participants from different countries. In addition, the interview guide was carefully designed and piloted to improve its understandability. As a result, some changes in the interviews were done to enhance the elicitation process. Some vocabulary was defined at the beginning of the interview guide to homogenize concepts.

Some relevant decisions were taken for approaching a further understanding of the project contexts. One of these was to focus most of the questions of the interview guide on a single product development project so we could further inquire and analyze specific contexts of the projects. This enhanced the value of our analysis and observations. In addition, we sent the interview guide in advance to the respondents so that they could be informed of the kind of questions to be asked. As a result, when performing the study, we rarely experienced respondents having difficulty remembering project details. Furthermore, we explained to the respondents that our study was not focused on analyzing "wrong practices" but on knowing "how integration is done in industrial practice". In several cases we experienced that the interviewer(s) shall skip some questions given time restrictions of the respondent; therefore, some questions results did not cover all participants. Despite this, the results obtained for these questions were valuable as most of the respondents provide their answers. With respect to the data analysis strategy, recording all interviews (and later on transcribing them) contributed to a better understanding and assessment of the data gathered. The generated categories were analyzed, discussed and reviewed by all researchers of the team to ensure their accuracy, understanding and agreement.

Regarding external validity, we addressed several topics in our study. Some of the most relevant ones are listed. First, the companies in this study were selected by a strategy combining convenience and maximum variation sampling from 4 different countries (Spain, Norway, Denmark and Sweden). Second, we had no control over the projects chosen by the respondents. Nevertheless, most of the resulting projects from the participating companies did not cover domains such as real time or life critical requirements neither development for product lines. We are aware that these factors may have an impact on integration, and so we highlight that our findings should not be taken as assertions but also as potential hypotheses that need to be further validated. Thus, we emphasize that our results should not be generalized and might be interpreted with caution, keeping in mind the context from the participating organizations.

7   Conclusions

We have described the main findings from an exploratory study based on semi-structured interviews to integrators from organizations that integrate OSS components in their software products. The study aimed to explore the problems that organizations face when integrating OSS components, and the role that the OSS communities play in such integration processes.

The reported results might be valuable for researchers, organizations and OSS communities that may use the provided evidence to more clearly understand the real OSS integration problems that integrators face and properly align their efforts for facing them.

On the one hand, researchers may get an overview of the state of the practice, identify new research questions, and position and align their own work. On the other hand, organizations may use the provided evidence to understand how other companies integrate OSS and leverage their own integration strategy identifying the practical challenges they might face when doing so. Finally, OSS communities can be informed of the perception of integrators regarding support and to envisage improvements for fostering the collaboration of integrators with the community; this is especially useful for newly initiated OSS communities that usually struggle to attract contributors.

That is, researchers might need to establish new agendas or check potential hypothesis generated by our results. Practitioners might have to adjust processes or methodologies. And OSS communities might have to crate special integration groups or improve integration documentation.

Acknowledgments. We thank all people that participated in piloting an early version of the interview guide and the interview participants who took time from their workdays to participate in our interviews.

This work has been partly supported by the Spanish project TIN2010-19130-C02-01, and the Industrial Excellence Center EASE - Embedded Applications Software Engineering, (http://ease.cs.lth.se).

Jyoti Nandrajog contributed to the interview part of this study in Denmark.

References

1. Ayala, C.P., Cruzes, D., Hauge, Ø., Conradi, R.: Five Facts on the Adoption of Open Source Software. IEEE Software, 95–99 (March-April 2011)
2. Hauge, Ø., Ayala, C.P., Conradi, R.: Adoption of Open Source Software in Software-Intensive Organizations - A Systematic Literature Review. Information & Software Technology 52(11), 1133–1154 (2010)
3. Bac, C., Berger, O., Deborde, V., Hamet, B.: Why and how to contribute to libre software when you integrate them into an in-house application? In: Proceedings of the First International Conference on Open Source Systems, pp. 113–118 (2005)

4. Stol, K., Ali Babar, M.: Challenges in using open source software in product development: a review of the literature. In: Proceedings of the 3rd Workshop on Emerging Trends in FLOSS Research and Development, pp. 17–22. ACM, Cape Town (2010), doi:10.1145/1833272.1833276
5. Aberdour, M.: Achieving Quality in Open Source Software. IEEE Software, 58–64 (January-February 2007)
6. Nakakoji, K., Yamamoto, Y., Nishinaka, Y., Kishida, K., Ye, Y.: Evolution Patterns of Open-Source Software Systems and Communities. In: Proc. International Workshop Principles of Software Evolution, pp. 76–85. ACM Press (2002)
7. Dahlander, L., Magnusson, M.G.: Relationships between open source software companies and communities: observations from Nordic firms. Research Policy 34(4), 481–493 (2005), doi:10.1016/j.respol.2005.02.003
8. Dahlander, L., Magnusson, M.G.: How do firms make use of open source communities? Long Range Planning 41(6), 629–649 (2008), doi:10.1016/j.lrp.2008.09.003
9. Capra, E., Francalanci, C., Merlo, F., Rossi Lamastra, C.: A Survey on Firms' Participation in Open Source Community Projects. In: Boldyreff, C., Crowston, K., Lundell, B., Wasserman, A.I. (eds.) OSS 2009. IFIP AICT, vol. 299, pp. 225–236. Springer, Heidelberg (2009)
10. Ven, K., Mannaert, H.: Challenges and strategies in the use of open source software by independent software vendors. Information and Software Technology 50(9-10), 991–1002 (2008), doi:10.1016/j.infsof.2007.09.001
11. Oates, B.J.: Researching Information Systems and Computing. Sage Publications, London (2006)
12. Conradi, R., Li, J., Slyngstad, O.P.N., Kampenes, V.B., Bunse, C., Morisio, M., Torchiano, M.: Reflections on Conducting an International Survey on Software Engineering. In: Proceedings of the International Symposium on Empirical Software Engineering (ISESE 2005), pp. 214–223. IEEE CS Press (2005)
13. Ayala, C., Hauge, Ø., Conradi, R., Franch, X., Li, J.: Selection of Third Party Software in Off-The-Shelf-Based Software Development - An Interview Study with Industrial Practitioners. The Journal of Systems & Software 84, 620–637 (2011)
14. Denger, C., Feldmann, R.L., Höst, M., Lindholm, C., Shull, F.: A Snapshot of the State of Practice in Software Development for Medical Devices. In: Short paper at First International Symposium on Empirical Software Engineering and Measurement, Madrid, Spain, September 20-21 (2007)
15. Babar, A.M., Gorton, I.: Software Architecture Review: The State of Practice. IEEE Computer 42(7), 26–32 (2009)
16. Nguyen, D.A., Cruzes, D., Conradi, R., Höst, M., Franch, X., Ayala, C.P.: Collaborative Resolution of Requirements Mismatches When Adopting Open Source Components. In: Regnell, B., Damian, D. (eds.) REFSQ 2011. LNCS, vol. 7195, pp. 77–93. Springer, Heidelberg (2012), doi:10.1007/978-3-642-28714-5_7
17. Sandelowski, M., Barroso, J.: Handbook for Synthesizing Qualitative Research. Springer (2007)
18. Choi, N., Chengalur-Smith, I., Whitmore, A.: Managing First Impressions of New Open Source Software Projects. IEEE Software, 73–77 (November-December 2010)
19. Capiluppi, A., Lago, P., Morisio, M.: Evidences in the Evolution of OS Projects through Changelog Analyses. In: Proc. 3rd IEEE Workshop Open Source Software Eng (WOSSE 2003). ICSE, pp. 10–24 (2003)

20. Li, J., Conradi, R., Slyngstad, O.P.N., Torchiano, M., Morisio, M., Bunse, C.: A State-of-the-Practice Survey of Risk Management in Development with Off-the-Shelf Software Components. IEEE Transactions on Software Engineering 34(2), 271–286 (2008)
21. Bonaccorsi, A., Rossi, C.: Comparing motivations of individual programmers and firms to take part in the open source movement: from community to business. Knowledge, Technology, and Policy 18(4), 40–64 (2006), doi:10.1007/s12130-006-1003-9
22. Chen, W., Li, J., Ma, J., Conradi, R., Ji, J., Liu, C.: An Empirical Study on Software Development with Open Source Components in the Chinese Software Industry. Software Process: Improvement and Practice 13(1), 89–100 (2008)
23. Glance, D.G., Kerr, J., Reid, A.: Factors affecting the use of open source software in tertiary education institutions. First Monday 9(2)
24. Hauge, Ø., Sørensen, C.-F., Conradi, R.: Adoption of Open Source in the Software Industry. In: Russo, et al. (eds.) Proceedings of the 4th IFIP Working Group 2.13 International Conferences on Open Source Software (OSS 2008) – Open Source Development Communities and Quality. IFIP AICT, vol. 275, pp. 211–222. Springer, Heidelberg (2008)
25. Robles, G., Dueñas, S., González-Barahona, J.M.: Corporate involvement of libre software: study of presence in debian code over time. In: Feller, et al. [29], pp. 121–132, doi:10.1007/978-0-387-72486-7_10
26. Aaltonen, T., Jokinen, J.: Influence in the Linux kernel community. In: Feller, et al. [29], pp. 203–208, doi:10.1007/978-0-387-72486-7_16
27. Höst, M., Oručević-Alagić, A., Runeson, P.: Usage of Open Source in Commercial Software Product Development – Findings from a Focus Group Meeting. In: Caivano, D., Oivo, M., Baldassarre, M.T., Visaggio, G. (eds.) PROFES 2011. LNCS, vol. 6759, pp. 143–155. Springer, Heidelberg (2011)
28. Robson, C.: Real World Research: A Resource for Social Scientists and Practitioner-researchers, 2nd edn. Blackwell Publishers Inc. (2002)
29. Feller, J., Fitzgerald, B., Scacchi, W., Sillitti, A. (eds.): Proceedings of the 3rd IFIP Working Group 2.13 International Conference on Open Source Software (OSS 2007) – Open Source Development, Adoption and Innovation. IFIP AICT, vol. 234. Springer, Heidelberg (2007)

Designing Secure Systems Based on Open Architectures with Open Source and Closed Source Components

Walt Scacchi and Thomas A. Alspaugh

Institute for Software Research
University of California, Irvine
Irvine, CA 92697-3455 USA
wscacchi@ics.uci.edu, http://www.ics.uci.edu/~wscacchi
thomas.alspaugh@acm.org, http://www.thomasalspaugh.org/

Summary. The development and evolution of secure open architecture systems has received insufficient consideration. Such systems are composed of both open source and closed software software components subject to different security requirements in an architecture in which evolution can occur by evolving existing components, replacing them, or refactoring their interfaces, interconnections and configuration. But this may result in possible security requirements conflicts and organizational liability for failure to fulfill security obligations. We are developing an approach for understanding and modeling software security requirements as *security licenses*, as well as for analyzing conflicts among groups of such licenses in realistic system contexts and for guiding the acquisition, integration, or development of systems with open source components in such an environment. Consequently, this paper reports on our efforts to extend our existing approach to specifying and analyzing software Intellectual Property (IP) licenses to now address software security licenses that can be associated with secure OA systems.

1 Introduction

A growing number of enterprises are adopting a strategy in which a software-intensive system is developed with an open architecture (OA) [19,2,5,21], whose components may be open source software (OSS) or closed source with open application programming interfaces (APIs). Such systems evolve not only through the evolution of their individual components, but also through replacement of one component by another, possibly from a different producer or under a different copyright license. With this approach, the system development organization becomes an integrator of components largely produced elsewhere that are interconnected through middleware or open APIs as necessary to achieve the desired result.

An OA development process arises in a software ecosystem in which the integrator is influenced from one direction by the goals, interfaces, license choices, and release cycles of the component producers, and in another direction by the

I. Hammouda et al. (Eds.): OSS 2012, IFIP AICT 378, pp. 144–159, 2012.

needs of its consumers. As a result the software components are reused more widely, and the resulting OA systems can achieve reuse benefits such as reduced costs, increased reliability, and potentially increased agility in evolving to meet changing needs. An emerging challenge is to realize the benefits of this approach when the individual components are subject to different security requirements.

We have been able to address an analogous problem of how to specify and analyze the Intellectual Property (IP) rights and obligations of the licenses of software components [2,3,5,6]. Our efforts now focus on the challenge of how to specify and analyze software components and composed system security rights and obligations using a new information structure we call a security license. Alternative renderings for a security license are beyond the scope of this paper, but at this point, we believe it is appropriate to develop candidate security policy expressions that can be incorporated into security licenses. Further, we seek to articulate security license terms and conditions in ways that can be easily formalized and readily applied to large-scale OA systems, as well as be automatically analyzed or tested in ways we have already demonstrated [5,6]. This is another goal of our research here.

Next, the challenge of specifying secure software systems composed from secure or insecure components is inevitably entwined with the software ecosystems that arise for OA systems. An example software ecosystem producing and

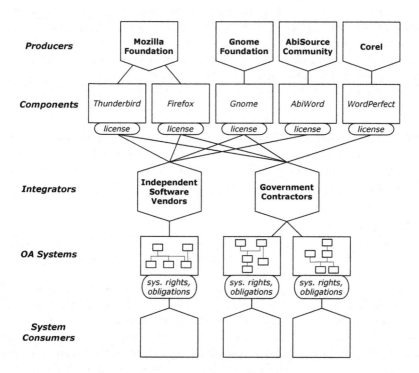

Fig. 1. A sample software ecosystem in which secure OA systems may be developed

integrating software components subject to different security practices is portrayed in Fig. 1. We find that an OA software ecosystem involves not only organizations and individuals producing and consuming components, and supply paths from producer to consumer; but also:

- the OA of the system(s) in question, and how best to secure it,
- the open interfaces provided by the components, and how to specify component security requirements that are enforceable or satisfiable at the interface level,
- the evolution of related components, and how to assess that evolution in terms of how overall system security rights and obligations may change, and
- the rights and obligations resulting from the security licenses under which various components are released, and that propagate from producers to consumers.

In order to most effectively use an OA approach in developing and evolving a system, it is essential to consider its OA ecosystem. An OA system draws on components from proprietary closed source software vendors and open source software projects. Its architecture is bounded and facilitated by the relevant ecosystem of producers, from which the initial components are chosen. The choice of a specific OA begins with a specialized software ecosystem involving components that meet (or can be encapsulated or "wrapped" to meet) the open interfaces used in the architecture. We do not claim this is the best or the only way to reuse components or produce secure OA systems, but it is an ever more widespread way. In this paper we build on previous work on heterogeneously-licensed systems [14,21,2] by examining the role of security licenses for components included within OA software ecosystems.

In the remainder of this paper, we survey some related work (Section 2), define and examine characteristics of open architectures with or without secure software elements (Section 3), define and examine characteristics for how secure OA systems evolve (Section 4), introduce a structure for security licenses (Section 5), outline security license architectures (Section 6), and sketch our approach for security license analysis (Section 7). We then close with our conclusions (Section 8).

2   Related Work

Software systems, whether operating as standalone components, applications, or elements within large system compositions, are continuously being subjected to security attacks. These attacks seek to slip through software vulnerabilities known to the attackers but perhaps not to the software component producers, system integrators or consumers. These attacks often seek to access, manipulate, or remotely affect for nefarious purposes the data values or control signals that a component or composed system processes, or seek to congest or over-saturate networked services. Recent high profile security attacks such as Stuxnet [10] reveal that security attacks may be very well planned and employ a bundle of attack vectors and social engineering tactics in order for the attack to reach strategic systems that are mostly isolated and walled off from public computer networks. The Stuxnet attack entered through software system interfaces at either the component, application subsystem, or base operating system level (e.g., via removable thumb drive storage devices), and their goal was to go outside or beneath their entry context. Furthermore, as the Stuxnet attack involved the use of corrupted certificates of trust from approved authorities as false credentials that allowed corrupt evolutionary system updates to go forward, it seems clear that additional preventions are needed that are external to, and prior to, their installation and run-time deployment. In our case, that means we need to specify and analyze software security requirements and evolutionary update capabilities at architectural design-time and system integration build-time, and then reconcile those with the run-time system composition. It also highlights the need to maintain the design-time, build-time, and run-time system compositions in repositories remote from system installations, and then cross-check and independently verify them prior to run-time deployment in a high security system context.

As already noted, both software intellectual property licenses and security licenses represent a collection of rights and obligations for what can or cannot be done with a licensed software component. Licenses thus denote non-functional requirements that apply to a software systems or system components as intellectual property (IP) or security requirements (i.e., capabilities) during their development and deployment. But rights and obligations are not limited to concerns or constraints applicable only to software as IP. Instead, they can be written in ways that stipulate non-functional requirements of different kinds. Consider, for example, that desired or necessary software system security properties can also be expressed as rights and obligations addressing system confidentiality, integrity, accountability, availability, and assurance [8,9]. It is often the case that developing robust specifications for non-functional software system security properties in natural language produces specifications that are ambiguous, misleading, inconsistent across system components, and lacking sufficient details [22]. Using a semantic model to formally specify the rights and obligations required for a software system or component to be secure [8,9,22] means that it may be possible to develop both a "security architecture" notation and model specification that associates given security rights and obligations across a software system, or system of systems. Similarly, it suggests the possibility of developing computational tools or interactive architecture development environments that can be used to specify, model, and analyze a software system's security architecture at different times in its development — design-time, build-time, and run-time. The approach we have been developing for the past few years for modeling and analyzing software system IP license architectures for OA systems [3,5,6,21], may therefore be extendable to also being able to address OA systems with heterogeneous "software security license" rights and obligations. Furthermore, the idea of common or reusable software security licenses may be analogous to the reusable security requirements templates proposed by Firesmith [12]. But such an extension of the semantic software license modeling, meta-modeling, and computational analysis tools to also support software system security can be recognized as a next stage of our research studies.

3   Secure Open Architecture Composition

Open architecture (OA) software is a customization technique introduced by Oreizy [19] and further expanded [2,5,6,21] that enables third parties to modify a software system through its explicitly modeled architecture, evolving the system by replacing its components. Increasingly more software-intensive systems are developed using an OA strategy, not only with open source software (OSS) components but also proprietary components with open APIs. These components may or may not have their own security requirements that must be satisfied during their build-time integration or run-time deployment, such as registering the software component for automatic update and installation of new software versions that patch recently discovered security vulnerabilities or prevent invocation of known exploits. Using this approach can lower development costs and increase reliability and function, as well as adaptively evolve software security [21]. Composing a system with heterogeneously secured components, however, increases the likelihood of conflicts, liabilities, and no-rights stemming from incompatible security requirements. Thus, in our work we define a secure OA system as a software system consisting of components that are either open source or proprietary with open API, whose overall system rights at a minimum allow its use and redistribution, in full or in part, such that they do not introduce new security vulnerabilities at the system architectural level.

It may appear that using a system architecture that incorporate secure OSS and proprietary components, and uses open APIs, will result in a secure OA system. But not all such architectures will produce a secure OA, since the (possibly empty) set of available security license rights for an OA system depends on: (a) how and why secure or insecure components and open APIs are located within the system architecture, (b) how components and open APIs are implemented, embedded, or interconnected, and (c) the degree to which the IP and security licenses of different OSS components encumber all or part of a software system's architecture into which they are integrated [21,1].

The following kinds of software elements appearing in common software architectures can affect whether the resulting overall composed systems are open or closed, as well as compliant with specified security policies (rights and obligations propagated from components to the overall system) [7].

Software source code components — These can be either (a) standalone programs, (b) libraries, frameworks, or middleware, (c) inter-application script code such as shell scripts, (d) intra-application script code, as for creating Rich Internet Applications using domain-specific languages such as XUL for the Firefox Web browser [11] or "mashups" [18], or (e) similar script code that can either install and invoke externally developed plug-in software components, or invoke external application (helper) components. In each case the source code is available and if the component is compiled it can be rebuilt. Each may have its own distinct IP/security requirements.

Executable components — These components are in binary form, and the source code may not be open for access, review, modification, or possible redistribution [20]. If proprietary, they often cannot be redistributed, and so such components will be present in the design- and run-time architectures but not in the distribution-time architecture.

Software services — An appropriate software service can replace a source code or executable component.

Application programming interfaces/APIs — Availability of externally visible and accessible APIs is the minimum requirement for an "open system" [17].

Software connectors — Software whose intended purpose is to provide a standard or reusable way of communication through common interfaces, e.g. High Level Architecture [16], CORBA, MS .NET, Enterprise Java Beans, and GNU Lesser General Public License (LGPL) libraries. Connectors can also limit the propagation of IP license obligations, mandate the propagation of license obligations (e.g. via use of a license like the Affero GPL), or provide additional security capabilities.

Methods of connection — These include linking as part of a configured subsystem, dynamic linking, and client-server connections. Methods of connection affect license obligation propagation, with different methods affecting different licenses.

Configured system or subsystem architectures — These are software systems that are used as atomic components of a larger system, and whose internal architecture may comprise components with different licenses, affecting the overall system license and its security requirements. To minimize license interaction, a configured system or sub-architecture may be surrounded by what we term a license firewall, namely a layer of dynamic links, client-server connections, license shims, or other connectors that block the propagation of specific obligations.

Fig. 2 shows a high-level run-time view of a composed OA system whose reference architectural design in Fig. 3 includes all the kinds of software elements listed above. This reference architecture has been instantiated in a build-time configuration in Fig. 4 that in turn could be realized in alternative run-time configurations in Figs. 5, 6, and 7 with different security capabilities (policies) and overall system security schemes. The configured systems consist of software components such as a Mozilla Web browser, Gnome Evolution email client, and AbiWord word processor (similar to MS Word), all running on a RedHat Fedora Linux operating system accessing file, print, and other remote networked servers such as an Apache Web server. Components are interconnected through a set of software connectors that bridge the interfaces of components and combine the provided functionality into the system's services. However, note that the software architecture does not pre-determine how security capabilities will be assigned and distributed across different variants of the run-time composition.

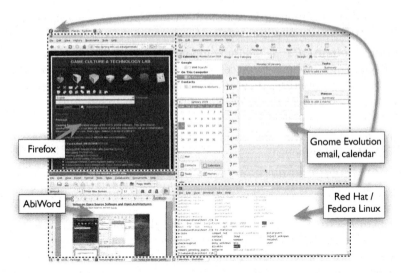

Fig. 2. An example composite OA system potentially subject to different IP and security licenses

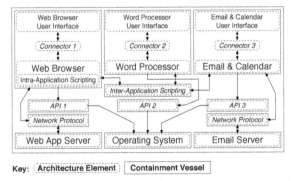

Fig. 3. The design-time architecture of the system in Fig. 2 that specifies a required security containment vessel (domain) scheme

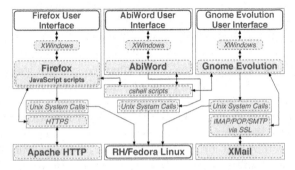

Fig. 4. A secure build-time architecture describing the version running in Fig. 2 with a specified security containment vessel scheme

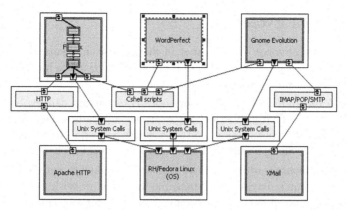

Fig. 5. Instantiated build-time OA system with maximum security architecture of Fig. 4 via individual security containment vessels (domains) for each system element

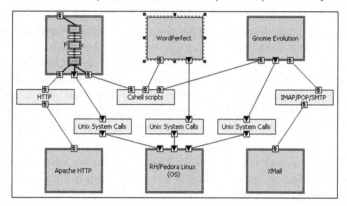

Fig. 6. Instantiated build-time OA system of Fig. 4 but with a minimum security architecture via a single overall security containment vessel (domain) for the complete system using a common software hypervisor

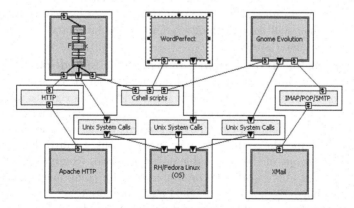

Fig. 7. Instantiated build-time OA system of Fig. 4 but with a mixed security architecture via security containment vessels for some groupings of elements

4   OA System Evolution

An OA system can evolve by a number of distinct mechanisms, some of which are common to all systems but others of which are a result of heterogeneous IP and security licenses in a single system.

By component evolution — One or more components can evolve, altering the overall system's characteristics (for example, upgrading and replacing the Firefox Web browser from version 3.5 to 3.6 which may update existing software functionality while also patching recent security vulnerabilities).

By component replacement — One or more components may be replaced by others with different behaviors but the same interface, or with a different interface and the addition of shim code to make it match (for example, replacing the GPL'd AbiWord word processor with either Open Office or MS Word, perhaps depending on which is considered less vulnerable to security attack).

By architecture evolution — The OA can evolve, using the same components but in a different configuration, altering the system's characteristics. For example, as discussed in Section 3, changing the configuration in which a component is connected can change how its IP or security license affects the rights and obligations for the overall system. This could arise when replacing email and word processing applications with web services like Google Mail and Google Docs, which we might judge to be more secure since the Google services (operating in a cloud environment) may be less easily accessed or penetrated by a security attack.

By component license evolution — The license under which a component is available may change, as for example when the license for the Mozilla core components was changed from the Mozilla Public License (MPL) to the current Mozilla Disjunctive Tri-License; or the component may be made available under a new version of the same license, as for example when the GNU General Public License (GPL) version 3 was released. Similarly, the security license for a component may be changed by its producers, or the security license for a composed system changed by its integrators, in order to prevent or deter recently discovered security vulnerabilities or exploits before an evolutionary version update (or patch) can be made available.

By a change to the desired rights or acceptable obligations — The OA system's integrator or consumers may desire additional IP or security license rights (for example the right to sublicense in addition to the right to distribute), or no longer desire specific rights; or the set of license obligations they find acceptable may change. In either case the OA system evolves, whether by changing components, evolving the architecture, or other means, to provide the desired rights within the scope of the acceptable obligations. For example, they may no longer be willing or able to provide the source code for components with known vulnerabilities that have not been patched and eliminated.

The interdependence of integrators and producers results in a co-evolution of software within an OA ecosystem. Closely-coupled components from different producers must evolve in parallel in order for each to provide its services, as evolution in one will typically require a matching evolution in the other. Producers may manage their evolution with a loose coordination among releases, for example as between the Gnome and Mozilla organizations. Each release of a producer component creates a tension through the ecosystem relationships with consumers and their releases of OA systems using those components, as integrators accommodate the choices of available, supported components with their own goals and needs. As discussed in our previous work [3,4,6], license rights and obligations are manifested at each component's interface, then mediated through the system's OA to entail the rights and corresponding obligations for the system as a whole. As a result, integrators must frequently re-evaluate an OA system's IP/security rights and obligations. In contrast to homogeneously-licensed systems, license change across versions is a characteristic of OA ecosystems, and architects of OA systems require tool support for managing the ongoing licensing changes [3,4,5,6].

We propose that such support must have several characteristics.

– It must rest on a license structure of rights and obligations (Section 5), focusing on obligations that are enactable and testable.
– It must take account of the distinctions between the design-time, build-time, and distribution-time architectures (Sections 3, 5, and 6) and the rights and obligations that come into play for each of them.
– It must distinguish the architectural constructs significant for software licenses, and embody their effects on rights and obligations (Section 3).
– It must define license architectures (Section 6).
– It must provide an automated environment for creating and managing license architectures. We have developed a prototype that manages an IP license architecture as a view of its system architecture [2,3,5,6].
– Finally, it must automate calculations on system rights and obligations so that they may be done easily and frequently, whenever any of the factors affecting rights and obligations may have changed (Section 7).

5   Security Licenses

Licenses typically impose obligations that must be met in order for the licensee to realize the assigned rights. Common IP/copyright license obligations include the obligation to publish at no cost any source code you modify (MPL) or the obligation to publish all source code included at build-time or statically linked (GPL). The obligations may conflict, as when a GPL'd component's obligation to publish source code of other components is combined with a proprietary component's license prohibition of publishing its source code. In this case, no rights may be available for the system as a whole, not even the right of use, because the two obligations cannot simultaneously be met and thus neither component can be used as part of the system. Security capabilities can similarly be expressed and bound to the data values and control signals that are visible in component interfaces, or through component connectors.

Some typical security rights and obligations might be:

- The right to read data in containment vessel T.
- The right to replace specified component C with some other component.
- The right to add or update specified component D in a specified configuration.
- The right to add, update, or remove security mechanism M.
- The obligation for a specific component to have been vetted for the capability to read and update data in containment vessel T.
- The obligation for a user to verify his/her authority to access containment vessel T, by password or other specified authentication process.

The basic relationship between software IP/security license rights and obligations can be summarized as follows: if the specified obligations are met, then the corresponding rights are granted. For example, if you publish your modified source code and sub-licensed derived works under MPL, then you get all the MPL rights for both the original and the modified code. Similarly, software security requirements are specified as security obligations that when met, allow designated users or other software programs to access, modify, and redistribute data and control information to designated repositories or remote services. However, license details are complex, subtle, and difficult to comprehend and track—it is easy to become confused or make mistakes. The challenge is multiplied when dealing with configured system architectures that compose a large number of components with heterogeneous IP/security licenses, so that need for legal counsel or expert security review begins to seem inevitable [20,13].

We have developed an approach for expressing software licenses of different types (intellectual property and security requirements) that is more formal and less ambiguous than natural language, and that allows us to calculate and identify conflicts arising from the rights and obligations of two or more component's licenses. Our approach is based on Hohfeld's classic group of eight fundamental jural relations [15], of which we use right, duty, no-right, and privilege. We start with a tuple <actor, operation, action, object> for expressing a right or obligation. The actor is the "licensee" for all the licenses we have examined. The operation is one of the following: "may", "must", "must not", or "need not", with "may" and "need not" expressing rights and "must" and "must not" expressing obligations. The action is a verb or verb phrase describing what may, must, must not, or need not be done, with the object completing the description. A license may be expressed as a set of rights, with each right associated with zero or more obligations that must be fulfilled in order to enjoy that right. Fig. 8 shows the meta-model with which we express licenses.

Designers of secure systems have developed a number heuristics to guide architectural design in order to satisfy overall system security requirements, while avoiding conflicts among interacting security mechanisms or defenses. However, even using design heuristics (and there are many), keeping track of security rights and obligations across components that are interconnected in complex OAs quickly becomes too cumbersome. Automated support is needed to manage

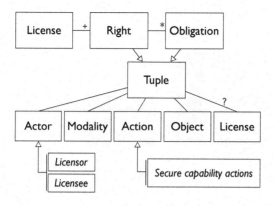

Fig. 8. Security license meta-model

the complexity of multi-component system compositions where different security requirements must be addressed through different security capabilities.

6   Security License Architectures

Our security license model forms a basis for effective reasoning about licenses in the context of actual systems, and calculating the resulting rights and obligations. In order to do so, we need a certain amount of information about the system's configuration at design-time, build-time, and run-time deployment. The needed information comprises the license architecture, an abstraction of the system architecture:

1. the set of components of the system (for example, see Fig. 2) for the current system configuration, as well as subsequently for system evolution update versions (as seen in Fig. 9);
2. the relation mapping each component to its security requirements (specified and analyzed at design-time, as exemplified in Fig. 3) or capabilities (specified and analyzed at build-time in Fig. 4 and run-time across alternatives shown in Fig. 5, 6, and 7);
3. the connections between components and the security requirements or capabilities of each connector passing data or control signals to/from it; and
4. possibly other information, needed to detect or prevent IP and security requirements conflicts, which is as yet undetermined.

With this information and definitions of the licenses involved, it should possible to automatically calculate rights and obligations for individual components or for the entire system, as well as guide/assess system design and evolution, using an automated environment of the kind that we have previously demonstrated [2,3,5,6].

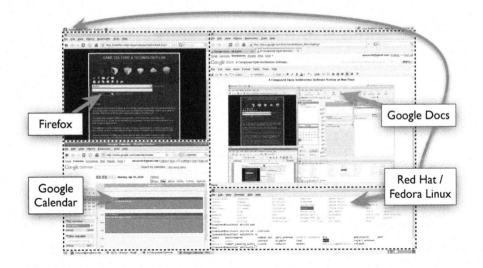

Fig. 9. A second instantiation at run-time (Firefox, Google Docs and Calendar operating within different Firefox run-time sessions, Fedora) of the OA system in Fig. 3 as an evolutionary alternative system version, which in turn implies or requires an alternative security containment scheme

7   Security License Analysis

Given a specification of a software system's architecture, we can associate security license attributes with the system's components, connectors, and sub-system architectures, resulting in a license architecture for the system, and calculate the security rights and obligations for the system's configuration. Due to the complexity of license architecture analysis, and the need to re-analyze every time a component evolves, a component's security license changes, a component is substituted, or the system architecture changes, OA integrators really need an automated license architecture analysis environment. We have developed a prototype of such an environment for analogous calculations for software copyright licenses [2,3,4,5,6], and are extending this approach to analyze security licenses. But here we identify two types of analysis that are representative of those our approach supports.

7.1   Security Obligation Conflicts

A security obligation can conflict with another obligation, can negate a related right for the same or nearby components, or require a right that is not available. For instance, consider two components C and D with the following security obligations:

(**O1**) *The obligation for component C to block access to containment vessel T by any other component.*

(**O2**) *The obligation for some component connected to component D to grant it access to data in containment vessel T.*

Obligations O1 and O2 cannot be simultaneously satisfied under any conditions.

Suppose C is replaced with component C' connected to D and having the following obligation:

(**O3**) *The obligation for component C' to have been successfully vetted for the capability to grant access to data in containment vessel T.*

If C' has not been vetted, then O3 is not satisfied; by extension, neither is O2, even though O1 is no longer in force.

Consider the following security right:

(**R1**) *The right to grant access to data in containment vessel T.*

Even if C' was successfully vetted, it requires that R1 be available to it in order to fulfil O2. If R1 is unavailable, then O2 cannot be satisfied.

These kinds of conflicts must be taken into consideration in different ways at different development times:

- at design time, ensuring that R1 can be available and that it will be possible to vet C';
- at build time, ensuring that the specific implementation of C' has been vetted successfully; and
- possibly at run time as well, confirming that C' is certified to have been vetted, or (if C' is dynamically connected at run time) vetting C' before trusting the current connection to it.

The absence of such conflicts does not mean, of course, that the system is secure. But the presence of conflicts reliably indicates it is not secure.

7.2   Rights and Obligations Calculations

The rights available for the entire system (the right to read and update data in containment vessel T, the right to replace components with other components, the right to update component security licenses, etc.) are calculated as the intersection of the sets of security rights available for each component of the system. If a conflict is found involving the obligations and rights of interacting components, it is possible for the system architect to consider an alternative scheme, e.g. using one or more connectors along the paths between the components that act as a security firewall. This means that the architecture and the automated environment together can determine what OA design best meets the problem at hand with available software components. Components with conflicting security licenses do not need to be arbitrarily excluded, but instead may expand the range of possible architectural alternatives if the architect seeks such flexibility and choice.

8   Conclusion

This paper introduces the concept and initial scheme for systematically specifying and analyzing the security requirements for complex open architecture systems. We argue that such requirements should be expressed as operational capabilities that can be collected and sequenced within a new information structure we call a security license. Such a license expresses security in terms of capabilities that provide users or programs obligations and rights for how they may access data or control information, as well as how the may update or evolve system elements. These security license rights and obligations thus play a key role in how and why an OA system evolves in its ecosystem of software component producers, system integrators and consumers.

We note that changes to the license obligations and rights, whether for control of intellectual property or software security, across versions of components is a characteristic of OA systems whose components are subject to different security requirements or other license restrictions. A structure for modeling software licenses and automated support for calculating its rights and obligations in the context of its ecosystem are needed in order to manage an OA system's evolution.

We have outlined an approach for achieving these and sketched how they further the goal of reusing components in developing software-intensive systems. Much more work remains to be done, but we believe this approach turns a vexing problem into one for which workable, as well as robust formal, solutions can be obtained.

Acknowledgments. This research is supported by grants #N00244-10-1-077 and #N00244-12-1-0004 from the Acquisition Research Program at the Naval Postgraduate School, and by grant #0808783 from the U.S. National Science Foundation. No review, approval, or endorsement implied.

References

1. Alspaugh, T.A., Antón, A.I.: Scenario support for effective requirements. Information and Software Technology 50(3), 198–220 (2008)
2. Alspaugh, T.A., Asuncion, H.U., Scacchi, W.: Analyzing software licenses in open architecture software systems. In: 2nd International Workshop on Emerging Trends in FLOSS Research and Development (FLOSS), pp. 1–4 (May 2009)
3. Alspaugh, T.A., Asuncion, H.U., Scacchi, W.: Intellectual property rights requirements for heterogeneously-licensed systems. In: 17th IEEE International Requirements Engineering Conference (RE 2009), pp. 24–33 (2009)
4. Alspaugh, T.A., Asuncion, H.U., Scacchi, W.: Presenting software license conflicts through argumentation. In: 23rd International Conference on Software Engineering and Knowledge Engineering (SEKE 2011), pp. 509–514 (July 2011)
5. Alspaugh, T.A., Asuncion, H.U., Scacchi, W.: The challenge of heterogeneously licensed systems in open architecture software ecosystems. In: Jansen, S., Cusumano, M., Brinkkemper, S. (eds.) Software Ecosystems: Analyzing and Managing Business Networks in the Software Industry (to appear, 2012)

6. Alspaugh, T.A., Scacchi, W., Asuncion, H.U.: Software licenses in context: The challenge of heterogeneously-licensed systems. Journal of the Association for Information Systems 11(11), 730–755 (2010)
7. Bass, L., Clements, P., Kazman, R.: Software Architecture in Practice. Addison-Wesley Longman Publishing Co., Inc., Boston (2003)
8. Breaux, T.D., Anton, A.I.: Analyzing goal semantics for rights, permissions, and obligations. In: 13th IEEE International Requirements Engineering Conference (RE 2005), pp. 177–188 (2005)
9. Breaux, T.D., Anton, A.I.: Analyzing regulatory rules for privacy and security requirements. IEEE Transactions on Software Engineering 34(1), 5–20 (2008)
10. Falliere, N., Murchu, L.O., Chien, E.: W32.Stuxnet dossier. Technical report, Symantec (October 2010), http://www.symantec.com/content/en/us/enterprise/media/security_response/whitepapers/w32_stuxnet_dossier.pdf
11. Feldt, K.: Programming Firefox: Building Rich Internet Applications with XUL. O'Reilly Media, Inc. (2007)
12. Firesmith, D.: Specifying reusable security requirements. Journal of Object Technology 3(1), 61–75 (2004)
13. Fontana, R., Kuhn, B.M., Moglen, E., Norwood, M., Ravicher, D.B., Sandler, K., Vasile, J., Williamson, A.: A legal issues primer for open source and free software projects. Technical report, Software Freedom Law Center (March 2008)
14. German, D.M., Hassan, A.E.: License integration patterns: Addressing license mismatches in component-based development. In: 28th International Conference on Software Engineering (ICSE 2009), pp. 188–198 (May 2009)
15. Hohfeld, W.N.: Some fundamental legal conceptions as applied in judicial reasoning. Yale Law Journal 23(1), 16–59 (1913)
16. Kuhl, F., Weatherly, R., Dahmann, J.: Creating computer simulation systems: an introduction to the high level architecture. Prentice-Hall (1999)
17. Meyers, B.C., Oberndorf, P.: Managing Software Acquisition: Open Systems and COTS Products. Addison-Wesley Professional (2001)
18. Nelson, L., Churchill, E.F.: Repurposing: Techniques for reuse and integration of interactive systems. In: International Conference on Information Reuse and Integration (IRI-08), p. 490 (2006)
19. Oreizy, P.: Open Architecture Software: A Flexible Approach to Decentralized Software Evolution. PhD thesis, University of California, Irvine (2000)
20. Rosen, L.: Open Source Licensing: Software Freedom and Intellectual Property Law. Prentice Hall (2005)
21. Scacchi, W., Alspaugh, T.A.: Emerging issues in the acquisition of open source software within the U.S. Department of Defense. In: 5th Annual Acquisition Research Symposium, pp. 230–214 (May 2008)
22. Yau, S.S., Chen, Z.: A Framework for Specifying and Managing Security Requirements in Collaborative Systems. In: Yang, L.T., Jin, H., Ma, J., Ungerer, T. (eds.) ATC 2006. LNCS, vol. 4158, pp. 500–510. Springer, Heidelberg (2006)

Using Multiple Case Studies to Analyse Open Source Software Business Sustainability in Sub-Saharan Africa

Sulayman K. Sowe[1] and Maurice McNaughton[2]

[1] United Nations University Institute of Advanced Studies (UNU-IAS)
1-1-1 Minato Mirai, Yokohama, 220-8502, Japan
sowe@ias.unu.edu
[2] Mona School of Business
University of the West Indies, Mona
maurice.mcnaughton@uwimona.edu.jm

Abstract. Amidst the debate about what sort of technology is appropriate for achieving sustainable development, Free and Open Source Software (FOSS) offers some solutions to today's technology problems for many developing countries. However, there is a paucity of empirical evidence to help us understand the potentials FOSS technologies have for small businesses in Sub-Saharan Africa. This research utilizes nine case studies data from seven African countries to find out how entrepreneurs are leveraging FOSS to help them create sustainable business based on openness. The findings show increasing awareness of the business potential of FOSS, and a business model incorporating both FOSS and proprietary software is needed to run a sustainable IT business in these countries. However, the lack of skilled FOSS developer base, the absence of appropriate policies, and poor payment habits by clients are just some of the factors affecting businesses. Other problems encountered, possible solutions to those problems and lessons to be learnt from each case study are also discussed. The research offers entrepreneurs, ICT practitioners, and policy makers the platform to understand the *Why* and *How* FOSS technologies are impacting the traditional way of doing business in Sub-Saharan Africa.

1   Introduction

The plethora of Free and Open Source Software (FOSS) applications available throughout the internet in projects and forges are not only having huge socioeconomic impact in many sectors in many different parts of the world, but are continuously redefining the way businesses (small and big) operate. The past few years have witnessed growing research interest in FOSS and its adoption and utilization in the business sector [16, 22, 28]. However, research results (e.g. [29, 30]) posit that in most businesses, FOSS solutions will not operate in isolation but will exist side by side with their commercial counterparts. In fact, [33] has conceptualized the *"AIM Postulate"*,

I. Hammouda et al. (Eds.): OSS 2012, IFIP AICT 378, pp. 160–177, 2012.
© IFIP International Federation for Information Processing 2012

which advocates an emerging business posture towards software co-existence by moving away from (Fear, Uncertainty and Doubt/Distrust) FUD to collaborative ecosystems. The AIM postulate is grounded in the empirical observation of an emerging trend where businesses are more inclined to determine: "Where in my business operation do I need FOSS?" "How best can I leverage FOSS projects and communities to support my business?" According to AIM, software co-existence is all about

   i. Applying best practices (closed or open) to software process, products, and services.
   ii. Integrating with existing knowledge, experience, IT infrastructure, and
   iii. Maximizing business value and organizational learning opportunities.

However, in many companies top level management still expressed some concerns towards full-scale FOSS adoption or the integration of FOSS technologies as a key business strategy [14]. Some of the concerns are associated with the difficulty of finding the right staff and developing the competencies necessary to work with FOSS [19]. Software support [27,9], quality [34], security, and the ability to integrate FOSS with existing infrastructure are also major concerns for many FOSS entrepreneurs.

The trend in the adoption and utilization of FOSS has remained, to a large extent, a phenomenon for the developed economies. For example, a series of case studies conducted by [25] shows that many regional municipalities in Europe are using FOSS. The Gartner study [12] reported that 85% (N=274) of enterprises in Asia Pacific, Europe and North America are using FOSS. Furthermore, the study projected that, by 2012, at least 80% of all commercial software solutions will include substantive FOSS components. These findings are consistent with similar studies carried out by Actuate [1, 2], using data obtained from surveys conducted with about 1,000 businesses in North America, UK, Germany and France. In general, the economic impact of FOSS for Europe and the rest of the developed world are well documented in the FLOSS Impact report [13]. Research evidence on the adoption and utilization of FOSS in business environments tends to concentrate on big businesses from North America, Europe [1, 2], China [2], and Australia [14]. Furthermore, FOSS business models adopted by Europe SMEs have extensively been discussed by [8].

1.1 Research Contribution and Questions

According to the FOSSDeva survey [10], many people (65.91%) strongly agree that FOSS is the way forward for developing countries; 51.14% see FOSS as a means to stimulate indigenous software industries, create local jobs, and lower technology acquisition costs. Over 60% believe that governments FOSS policy can help the spread and adoption of FOSS. Furthermore, [39] conducted an empirical study to investigate the main facilitators and inhibitors of FOSS adoption in the Tunisian software business sector. In another study, [40] discussed the perceptions, attitudes, and barriers to FOSS adoption and diffusion patterns in Jamaican SMEs. While, [21] discussed how the Chinese software industry can leverage the FOSS movement for its own development. Although these studies focus on FOSS adoption and diffusion in

SMEs in developing countries, there exist diminutive research literature on FOSS business activities that can help us understand how small- and medium-sized enterprises (SMEs) in Sub-Saharan African are leveraging FOSS to either start their business ventures or enhance their existing business practices. The contribution of this research to the FOSS body of knowledge aims to fill this gap in the literature by offering answers to the following research question:

How are small businesses in Sub-Saharan Africa leveraging benefits inherent in FOSS to create sustainable businesses?

By addressing this question the research hopes to offer insight into other questions which may arise, such as

   (i) how are Africa SMEs leveraging FOSS to support their business practices?
   (ii) what are the FOSS business benefits for SMEs?
   (iii) what problems or difficulties do they encounter and what are the possible solutions to those problems?
   (iv) what lessons can we learn about the unique way of doing FOSS business in this part of Africa?

An empirical analysis of case studies data obtained from nine ICT-based SMEs from Uganda, Ethiopia, South Africa, Kenya, Tanzania, Nigeria, and Mozambique is used to show how the SMEs in these countries are leveraging benefits inherent in FOSS to create sustainable businesses. Business benefits include low business start-up and technology acquisition costs [21, 39, 40], free access to source code and software, low total cost of ownership (TCO), availability of community support, and ability to customize the software to meet local business needs. A case study research strategy or approach advanced by [37] is used to gather the information needed to profile the companies, analyse their revenue generation models, capture their motivation for engaging in FOSS business, and list down some lessons that can be learnt from the way the companies operate.

This kind of research is important in a number of ways: increase our understanding of the FOSS business landscape in Sub-Saharan Africa, provide business opportunities by helping African entrepreneurs understand how to leverage the benefits inherent in FOSS, find possible ways of integrating FOSS into the African research and development agenda, provide guidelines for regional FOSS cooperation projects, integrate FOSS education into existing engineering curricular, and increase FOSS awareness on the continent. It is also hoped that this kind of research may act as an eye-opener for ICT businesses already investing or planning to do business in this region of the world. Furthermore, the findings from these case studies may provide guidelines for policymakers in the region to implement a "new" kind of ICT governance framework based on openness.

The rest of the paper is organized as follows. Section two presents background and related work on the impact and socioeconomic status of FOSS in the global and African context. The research methodology, presented in section three, demonstrates the use of a case study approach to investigate FOSS business sustainability. This is followed by section four where we present our analysis and discussion of the case studies results, as well as the validity threats and future work. Concluding remarks are presented in section five.

2   Background and Related Work

A multitude of interrelated factors are contributing to the upward trend in global adoption and utilization of FOSS. Some of these factors include: global acceptance that FOSS can stand at par and, even in some instances, perform better than its commercial proprietary counterparts [5, 15]; continued improvement in the quality of FOSS [34]; an alternative Bazaar style of developing software [26, 31]. The Bazaar as opposed to the Cathedral style of developing FOSS [26] harnesses diverse talents of globally distributed teams of software developers who, for the most part, freely volunteer their time and efforts to develop and maintain the software. The development model promises faster and cost effective software development cycle. Compared to proprietary software, FOSS is also said to have lower total cost of ownership. Entrepreneurs have hybrid business models opportunities [24, 8], customers are free from vendor lock-ins, users have greater learning and knowledge sharing prospects [32], and regions or countries can support technology independence [7, 20, 23] by adopting and encouraging the use of FOSS.

The economic impact of FOSS is highlighted by many studies. For example, the IDC study [11] predicts that FOSS will grow at a 22.4% rate to reach US$8.1 billion by 2013. The growth rate is mainly due to increased enterprise adoption from major firms such as IBM [30, 5], or Hewlett Packard. The study also found out that hybrid business models are taking more permanence in modern software business. That is, many proprietary software businesses or vendors are also involved in the development, deployment, support and maintenance, and even consultancy of FOSS solutions. These findings are consistent with a study carried out with U.S. companies and government institutions' usage of FOSS [36]. The authors found out that, motivated by reduce IT costs, faster systems delivery, and making systems more secure, 87% of the companies (N = 512) surveyed are using FOSS, and bigger companies with at least US$50 million annual revenue are more likely to use FOSS than smaller companies. This trend is in sharp contrast with what is observed in Europe, where small firms are the lead adopters of FOSS [17].

Thus, it can be argued that FOSS is really in vogue; the technology is having a real impact and redefining the software industry. There is gradual shift in focus from protecting software knowledge to maximizing gain from FOSS development, use, and distribution. As the FOSS development paradigm grants "free" access to the source code, software companies are not obligated to pay software licenses fees. If a company has staff with the technical knowledge, they can download and compile the source code, customize the software to suit the company's customer's needs, or even localize the software to suit a particular business market. However, if a company is not endowed with such technical savvies, it can leverage assistance available 24/7 in forums and mailing list or contract a vendor or a developer to carry out the modifications needed by the customer. Notwithstanding the availability of these community support options, it is more likely that the typical small business will be constrained by limited ICT literacy, and the lack of the business analytic skills, and absorptive capacity to effectively identify and deploy appropriate FOSS solutions to support their business. Hence intermediaries will play a crucial role in the adoption of complex ICT applications by SMEs, and strategically placed community intermediaries within local and regional and national business ecosystems will be essential to the effective adoption and diffusion of FOSS by SMEs [43] This provides new business models for ICT services SMEs in developing countries, where FOSS becomes both a compelling alternative to propriety software and an option to help them support a sustainable business. Another compelling reason, argued [40] is that the FOSS domain offers an increasingly mature portfolio of business applications that represents viable alternative solutions to meet customers' expectations.

Furthermore, FOSS can, arguably, bring about new business opportunities for small businesses in developing countries [7, 27, 28, 35]. For established SMEs, FOSS enables them to move from product-based to service-based (software hosting, support, consulting, training, integration, or customization) activities [39]. Generally, FOSS is increasingly being recognized by many governments, regional municipalities, and businesses as the means by which developing countries can expand their use of ICTs without the need for huge capital expenditure.

3   Research Methodology

The methodology employed in this research aims to investigate FOSS business sustainability in the African context. The methodology employs case studies to find out how and why FOSS is being used by ICT-based SMEs to support and sustain their business ventures. The reason for choosing case studies as research instruments is grounded on Yin's [37] argument that a case study design should be considered when "the focus of the study is to answer how and why questions" and when the researcher wants to "cover contextual conditions" which are believed to be relevant to the phenomenon under study. Thus, a case study approach is considered appropriate technique for this research since it can add value [4] and contribute to the body of knowledge by helping researchers and practitioners in the domain to better understand FOSS business sustainability in Sub-Saharan Africa. The methodology employed in this research is schematically shown in figure 1, with the key steps marked in circles and are numbered from 1-7.

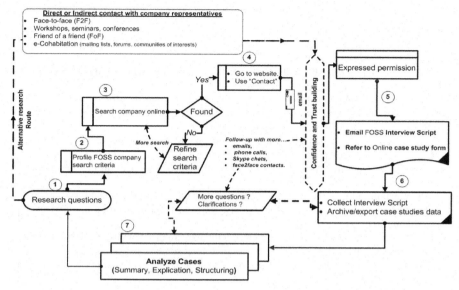

Fig. 1. Case Studies Methodology to Study FOSS Business Sustainability

In the first instance, an FOSS Interview Script, shown in **box 1**,was developed and used to collect the case studies data from the SMEs. The script consists of a set of case study research questions (Step 1), which are grouped into three main areas; Company profile, motivation for engaging in FOSS business, revenue generation or company's main source of income, and an experience report section. The script, which also has an online version, concludes with a case study feedback section where subjects as asked to indicate (Yes/No) whether they would like to receive further information about the case study they submitted and would like to be contacted for further clarification.

Box 1: FOSS Interview Script for African ICT-based companies

Case Study Code:...
(e.g. SA01 meaning the 1st case study from South Africa, country prefix SA)

Company profile:
  Q1. Name/email of contact person: ......
  Q2. Country of residence: ......
  Q3. Name of the city/town where the company is located: ......
  Q4. Registered full name and acronym of the company: ......
  Q5. Company's web presence (if any) : ......
  Q6. When was the company established? ......
  Q7. How many people are employed in this company? ......

Motivation for engaging in FOSS business:
  Q1. Please describe your motivation for using Open Source in your business

......

Revenue generation or source of income:
Q1. Which services (e.g. ICT Training, Web Hosting, Software Development, Consultancy, etc.) are you offering? ......
Q2. If you are offering "FOSS/IT Outsourcing" as a service. Which of the following describes your outsourcing strategy? ......
    a)   Offshore outsourcing (e.g. to other countries outside Africa)
    b)   Onshore outsourcing (e.g. to other countries within Africa)
    c)   Both offshore and onshore outsourcing
Q3. Which service in Q1 is generating more income for your company? ......
Q4. What is your company's annual turnover (in USD)? ......
Q5. Who are your most prolific customers and the types of services they request most? ......
Q6. What are some of the strategies you use to market your products and services?
Q7. What are some of the difficulties, if any, you face in getting paid for the services you offer? ......
Q8. Please describe whether you are developing new products or customizing existing FOSS solutions (bespoke software) to fit your customers' needs? ......
Q9. Are you localizing (translating into local languages) some of your products? ......

Experience Report:

Q1. Looking at other companies (in and outside your country) who may be offering similar services as you do, what would you say works well for your company? ......
Q2. What is your advice for someone starting FOSS business in Africa in general and your country in particular? ......
Q3. Please describe three key problems you have encountered in running this kind of business and your solutions to those problems? ......
Q4. What are some of your business plans which will ensure the viability and sustainability of the business in the long run? ......

Case studies feedback:
Would you like to receive frequent updates about the status of the Case Study information you supplied (Yes/No)?

Subsequently, case study participants were given a choice to record their case study using either the Interview Script (emailed to them as attachment) or by completing the case study form online (Step 5). With the former choice, participants were asked if one week is sufficient to collect the FOSS interview script responses (Step 6). After five days, a reminder was sent asking if the interviewee is on course and will be able to submit responses. In some cases the responses collected generated more questions or more clarifications on some of the responses given was needed. Where this was the case, the interviewee was contacted again (using emails, phone calls, and Skype chats) and asked to provide more clarification before analyzing the case studies (Step 7).

Qualitative content analysis was used to describe each case study. Content analysis can be defined as "the study of recorded human communications" [3]. As a process, content analysis is the transformation of raw text data into a standardized, orderly form. In analyzing the case studies, three aspects of content analysis proposed by [18] were adopted:

- *Summary*: in summarizing the responses received from the case studies, attempts were made to preserve the essential content but still trying to capture the main ideas submitted by the interviewees.
- *Explication*: this process of re-examination and reading between the lines involves explaining, clarifying and annotating the responses supplied via the FOSS interview script or online case study form.
- *Structuring*: responses received from the companies follow the designed pattern of the FOSS Interview Script. The main aim of the structuring process is to filter out a structure from the responses provided and apply that structure in the analysis of the case studies. The outcome of the structuring process is what is used to profile each case study, as shown in table 3.

The methodology also shows an alternative research route. This "direct or indirect contact with company representatives" can act as a possible means of recruiting more case studies and bypassing the online search paths in Steps 2 - 4. This can take many forms; such as meeting company representatives face-to-face in workshops, seminars, conferences or through a friend of a friend, through participation in mailing lists, forums, social media where company representatives may be subscribed to; a phenomenon referred to in this research as "e-cohabitation".

3.1   Case Studies Data

Table 1 shows the major characteristics of the case studies, including the case study code, the geographical distribution of the companies studied, the year founded, and the staff strength of each company as of January 2012. As shown, the companies are relatively young and have been in existence, on the average, for 7.66 years. Furthermore, considering the European Commission's definition of SMEs [41], which considered a company to be an SME in terms of the number of employees and either turnover or balance sheet total, we can conclude that most or seven of the companies studied are *micro-* (ET01, KE01, NG01, SA02, SA03, TZ01, UG01). These SMEs have ten or less employees and are considered as the main forces in economic growth and job creation, not only in developed economies, but also in emerging economies or economies in transition [40]. MZ01 and SA01 can be described as *small-* since they have employees numbering more than ten and less than fifty employees. However, since this research was not able to register either the turnover or balance sheet totals of the companies, the term enterprise may be most appropriate to use to refer to the companies as entities engaged in an economic activity. They are, in effect characterized as "self-employed, family firms, partnerships and associations regularly engaged in an economic activity" [41].

Table 1. Major Characteristics of the Case Studies

Case study code	Country	Company Name	Year founded	No. of staff
ET01	Ethiopia	Amest Santim Systems	2005	5
KE01	Kenya	OpenWorld	2004	7
MZ01	Mozambique	SENFOSS	2006	12
NG01	Nigeria	Future Software Resources	2008	5
SA01	South Africa	GIS Global Image	2000	17
SA02	South Africa	Ntinga Information Systems	2007	1
SA03	South Africa	Linux Holding	2003	1
TZ01	Tanzania	Zalongwa Technologies	2006	8
UG01	Uganda	Linux Solution	2000	10

4   Results and Discussions

Table 2 shows the FOSS related business activities captured for each of the case studies. It is interesting to note that all the enterprises are engaged in developing and customizing FOSS solutions as part of their business activity. However, a conversation with the director of SA01 revealed that by FOSS development, most of the enterprises mean customizing the GUI and adding functionalities. Thus, it was not clear as to whether the enterprises are actually coding or developing FOSS solutions or just customizing existing FOSS. This might explain why in all the case studies, we have "Yes" for both software development and software customization. Nevertheless, this underscores one of the key, often understated attributes of FOSS, which is the considerable degree of flexibility and adaptability relative to proprietary software, which makes it possible to customize ICT solutions to fit business needs and operating processes of smaller organisations. All the enterprises are also involved in providing FOSS maintenance and support. With the exception of SA02, all the enterprises employ 'mixed' business activities involving both FOSS and proprietary software. For example, SA02 provides both FOSS and proprietary Geographical Information Systems (GIS) software solutions and services in the areas of system design and implementation, GIS consulting services such as Information Management Policies and GIS strategies. One explanation for this general trend is because, as noted in SA03 and KE01, clients request services on both FOSS and proprietary software. Most customers are just interested in whatever solution they can use to accomplish their objectives (UG01). This finding is in support of the AIM postulate [33] discussed earlier, which highlighted the increasing integration and co-existence in mainstream business computing ecosystems. There is also great consistency across the business cases relating to FOSS consultancy services, and the development and hosting of web services such as websites. Training is the only service that exhibited significant variation with half the respondents offering training services.

Table 2. FOSS Business Activities Captured

Case study code	Company Name	FOSS Business Activities Captured						
		Dev	Cus	Con	Tra	MaS	Web	Mix
ET01	Amest Santim Systems	Y	Y	Y	N	Y	Y	Y
KE01	OpenWorld	Y	Y	Y	Y	Y	Y	Y
MZ01	SENFOSS	Y	Y	Y	Y	Y	Y	Y
NG01	Future Software Resources	N	Y	Y	N	Y	Y	Y
SA01	GIS Global Image	Y	Y	Y	Y	Y	Y	Y
SA02	Ntinga Information Systems	Y	Y	Y	N	Y	Y	N
SA03	Linux Holding	Y	Y	Y	Y	Y	Y	Y
TZ01	Zalongwa Technologies	Y	Y	N	N	Y	Y	Y
UG01	Linux Solution	Y	Y	Y	Y	Y	N	Y

Dev. = Software development, **Cus.** = Customization, **Con.** = Consultancy, **Tra.** = Training, **MaS** = Maintenance and Support, **Web** = Web base service development and hosting, **Mix** = both FOSS and proprietary software, **Y** = Yes, **N** = No

Results of the qualitative content analysis of the case studies are summarized in table 3. In the summary each SME or enterprise is profiled according to FOSS business motivation, services offered and method of revenue generation, problems the company encounters in doing FOSS business and possible solutions, and lessons learnt about the unique way the company does business.

Some consistent themes and patterns of business practice were identified in the case responses. As distinct from the early years of the FOSS revolution, advocacy is a much less prevalent business motivation. Only one case [UG01] mentioned "encouraging FOSS adoption" as a motivation. Otherwise the range of business motivations were all anchored on the perceived value proposition of FOSS, including:

a)   the use of FOSS as a low-cost tool in software/web development;
b)   providing customizable FOSS business solutions; and
c)   Using FOSS expertise as a service differentiator.

As reflected earlier in Table 2, there is a degree of consistency in the business models based on FOSS, with almost all of the cases offering a similar portfolio of services i.e. Consultancy, Software development & Customization, Software Maintenance and Support, Web based service development and hosting, and generally supporting mixed computing environments with both FOSS and proprietary software. The business models resonate with the OSS2.0 archetypes suggested by [44] which suggested the emergence of small service centric software companies that thrive by providing training, technical support, and consultancy for local organizations that deploy open source products

Problems encountered, specific to FOSS, also fell generally into two categories;

a)   managing and changing client perceptions of FOSS as a legitimate business computing solution; and
b)   acquiring and maintaining the requisite level of resident FOSS expertise.

Table 3. Profile of the Case Studies

Case study code	FOSS Business Motivation	Services and revenue generation	Problems encountered and possible solutions	Lessons learnt
ET01	Not "re-inventing the wheel" - tools the founders needed for software and website development are freely available	Software development and web hosting (domain name registration), networking, maintenance, consulting, outsourcing, technical support.	- Lack of skill labour or getting staff who are experts in GNU/Linux and FOSS - Building a client base who are comfortable with FOSS / - Train your staff locally and make sure they stay with the company after training. Make them feel as if they are part of the company and decision making process.	- Boldly participate in public bids for projects. - Make products and services affordable by reducing costs. - Involve customer in FOSS customization
KE01	- Use and customize freely available FOSS solutions. - Keep costs down. - Interact with a larger software developer and user communities. - Use the latest, cutting-edge, technologies to satisfy customers' needs.	Consultancy, Training, Product development and Support.	- Building a client base who trust FOSS solutions. - Getting necessary registration and company documents - Hiring employees with experience in FOSS / - Educate customers about FOSS capabilities. - Go to the customer instead of waiting for customers to come to you	Trying the untested, and always be ready to do things differently in terms of responding to client requests.
MZ01	- To carve out a niche in the ICT market. - Turn FOSS experience into profitable business activity to earn a living.	- FOSS training, consultancy, application development, server (mail and web) installation and maintenance with key ministries, banks, and telecoms.	-Expansion in the region because of language barrier (all our activities are conducted in Portuguese). - Prompt payment from our major customers, especially government ministries. / - We're gradually developing and customizing applications in English and French to help us reach other markets in Africa. -mostly take bank loans to cover some operational costs.	-Language is an essential business enable. It can be a plus because CENFOSS in MZ01 is the only Portuguese company in the Eastern Africa region, but it can also be disadvantageous because MZ01 finds it difficult to expand beyond Mozambique.
NG01	- Keep costs at a minimum by reusing FOSS components and outsourcing essential development activities. - Reduce the main start-up costs by using FOSS to building and market websites.	- Web site design and hosting, software customization, consultancy.	- Company registration procedures. - Finding skilled work force that is willing to work for a low salary. / Outsource most of their work to India	- Try and test software in-house before deploying it to customers - Research on various types of software that do the same thing. - Engage and understand the FOSS project whose software you are customizing, distributing, or localizing. - Have an individual with vast experience and a good track record in participating in FOSS projects and communities.

Table 3. (*continued*)

Case study code	FOSS Business Motivation	Services and revenue generation	Problems encountered and possible solutions	Lessons learnt
SA01	- Access to software being developed and maintained by a larger developer community. - Lower software development and maintenance costs.	- Both FOSS and proprietary GIS software solutions - GIS systems design and implementation, training. - Sales and support of flagship product (Papyrus Spatial), Consultancy.	- Difficult to retain staff who know and are experience in FOSS development and how to deal with communities. - Working with Gov. depts. and implementing GIS solutions based on FOSS	- Organize free software installation demos/ training sessions in schools and colleges. Company lunches / dinners for potential customers	- Educating the client in what the FOSS is all about. - Building a strong personal and business profile and networks online using social media. - Participate in FOSS forums and mailing lists.
SA02	-Awareness and experience that there is huge potentials for FOSS business in South Africa. -High demand of FOSS professionals and people are becoming increasingly frustrated with security issues of proprietary software.	Mainly from distributing (installing and configuring) FOSS applications such as GNU/Linux servers (web and mail) and providing maintenance and upgrade services.	-coping with demands for services, especially on the server side. - getting paid on time	-have a schedule and follow a plan. -don't continue working for customers who don't pay but be flexible	A sustainable business is one where there is flexibility. Hard work and learn as much as possible about FOSS and clients.
SA03	- Put interest and experience in FOSS into business use. - Transfer their curriculum development and teaching experience into FOSS - Utilize freely available FOSS training materials for business purpose while contributing to FOSS communities and projects.	FOSS training (80% of company's revenue) as a major business. Marketing for other FOSS companies, hosting GNU/Linux servers and developing and selling websites.	- Making people (customers) understand that even though FOSS is "free", people still need to pay for services and training. -Poor payment habits from clients	- establish a firm policy on getting paid before delivering services or before students register and complete their courses. -get a good and well experience account. -educate your customers.	- Part of business is to enjoy what you do and you are passionate about. - A proper strategic plan (3-5yrs) in place which has the capacity to expand and accommodate unexpected changes in market conditions. - Look at what your potential competitors are doing and learn from them. Think of what sort of services the market needs. -Be knowledgeable in the industry you are going to do business in and know the laws and policies governing business in the country.

Table 3. (*continued*)

Case study code	FOSS Business Motivation	Services and revenue generation	Problems encountered and possible solutions	Lessons learnt
TZ01	- Distinguish the company from other established proprietary IT companies. - Ease software development by adopting ready and mature FOSS. -Less cost in terms of money and time. - benefit and learn from large community of developers and users -Sustain the company's flagship FOSS product (SARIS).	- Web site development, web-based programming using PHP, database solution, e-business solutions, custom Internet web applications development, and readymade web site packages for small sites. - Selling FOSS products, hosting websites for customers, maintenance and other services.	- Getting company start-up capital - Financing new projects or business initiatives, - Managing and retaining staff - Poor payment habits of clients	Employ a finance officer acts as the revenue "Collector" - Partner investment - Hire university students as interns and train them as future staff for your company. - On-the-job training of young programmers, website designers, database administrators.
UG01	- Encouraging FOSS adoption - Prove FOSS has business potentials - Carve out a niche in the market	- Technical support, consultancy, software deployment, IT hardware sales/supply. - Mixture of FOSS and proprietary. - Customizing of existing FOSS solutions than developing new ones.	- Start-up capital, financing new projects. - Procuring proprietary software from abroad. - Retaining competent staff - Poor payment habits by clients and Qualifying for government contracts.	Avoid specializing in only one service sector or product. - Start as a small and gradually grow. - Preference for private sector clients. - Strictly enforced payment terms

With increased FOSS adoption and use by SMEs within local, regional and national business ecosystems the latter challenge of maintaining the requisite level of resident, highly technical FOSS expertise is likely to manifest as a recurrent problem for service providers. This identifies a critical role for strategically placed community intermediaries as suggested by [45] that can provide aggregated technical services that are important to clusters of SMEs to facilitate the adoption of complex ICT applications. These challenges also suggest opportunities for Policy interventions at the state or national level that will endorse and encourage the legitimacy and use of FOSS, as a means of stimulating the indigenous software industry, creating local jobs and entrepreneurial opportunities.

4.1   Validity Threats

While this research may have provided some insight into the business potential for ICT-based enterprises in Sub-Saharan Africa, we have only introduced nine case studies from seven out of possible fifty-four African countries. Given the increasing prominence of FOSS on the continent, we posit that there are many more enterprises leveraging FOSS for business purpose. There might even be variations in FOSS business practices by enterprises within the same country or region. Furthermore, since our case studies are just from English speaking Africa, language may even be a factor that can bias our sample. Thus, there is danger in generalizing the results presented here to the entire African FOSS business ecosystem. However, as [42] found out in their study of the Apache web server, the analysis of sometimes few cases or even a single case can provide important insights and ground for future research in this area. Therefore, we hope that the methodology and analytical framework provided in this paper can form the groundwork for further research work to investigate FOSS business sustainability and innovation in Sub-Saharan Africa.

4.2   Future Work

The research presented in this paper has opened avenues for future work which may provide supplementary information to help researchers further understand FOSS business sustainability and innovation in Sub-Saharan Africa. As a follow-up to this research an online "FOSS Case Studies for African ICT Companies[1]" is being launched to provide more case studies for this kind of research. More case studies data will help ICT4D, entrepreneurs, and Information Systems researchers better understand the trend in FOSS business innovation activities over time and the factors influencing them.

5   Conclusion

This research presented and discussed how small businesses in Sub-Saharan Africa are leveraging the benefits inherent in FOSS to create sustainable businesses. The

---

[1] http://servnet.ias.unu.edu/limesurvey/index.php?sid=67749&
lang=en, Last accessed, May 15, 2012.

literature review highlighted the global trend, economic impact, and sustainability aspects of FOSS and how all these factors come into play to provide unique technology opportunities for Sub-Saharan Africa. A methodology was presented to show that a case study research approach can be a possible means of investigating how ICT businesses are using and benefiting from FOSS. In the analysis, each case study was presented showing the profile, FOSS business motivation, and the services offered. Problems encountered and solutions adopted in operating a mix FOSS-proprietary software business in the particular country, as well as lessons to be learnt from the way the companies do business was also presented.

The case studies showed that FOSS provides an alternative business model option for ICT firms in Sub-Saharan Africa. However, operating solely on FOSS solutions and services is not a sustainable business option. Rather, companies operate a form of quasi-business; taking advantage of the low cost and ability opportunities to customize FOSS solutions, and at the same time selling and doing maintenance of proprietary software. Furthermore, the companies' main motivation for engaging in FOSS business is driven by reduction in the cost of software development and deployment. For most of the companies, the software they needed to start a business (e.g. building websites, deploying and maintain a learning management system) was readily available as FOSS. This helped them avoid problems, such as purchasing and paying high licenses cost, associated with associated with starting a business with proprietary software.

The qualitative nature of the study, provides insights into the emerging FOSS business models in sub-Saharan Africa, problems encountered by businesses and lessons to be learnt from the case studies individually and collectively. It provides a basis for replication in other developing contexts, as well more extensive quantitative studies, based on the trends and factors highlighted. In conclusion, similar to the advice given to China's software industry by [21], this research ascertains that there is substantial evidence from these case studies to suggest that Africa should focus on its domestic software market as a starting point and develop a more comprehensive strategy for the long term. The study highlights opportunities for Policy interventions that can help to stimulate the growth and development of entrepreneurs and existing businesses that base their business model on FOSS. Such interventions could seek to endorse the legitimacy of FOSS, and demonstrate by example through Government's own adoption and use of FOSS. Such initiatives could help to deflect the level of uncertainty or distrust that may continue to persist among prospective FOSS business clients and could also help to stimulate greater investment in FOSS training and expertise in the sector, two of the challenges cited by respondents in the case study.

Acknowledgment. The first author wishes acknowledge the Japan Society for the Promotion of Science (JSPS) for funding this research under the Grant-in-Aid number: P10807. The authors wish to extend sincere gratitude and thanks to the companies for providing the case studies data. We are greatly indebted to the three anonymous reviewers for their constructive comments and suggestions which helped us improve the quality of the original manuscript submission.

References

[1] Actuate. Open Source Enters the Mainstream. The Acutate Annual Open Source Survey (2008), http://www.actuate.com/company/news/press-release/?articleid=13847 (accessed, Monday, August 16, 2010)

[2] Actuate. The 2009 Actuate Annual Open Source Survey (2009), http://www.actuate.com (accessed, Thursday, August 19, 2010)

[3] Babbie, E.: The practice of social research, 9th edn. Belmont, Wadsworth (2001)

[4] Pamela, B., Susan, J.: Qualitative Case Study Methodology: Study Design and Implementation for Novice researchers. The Qualitative Report 13(4), 544–559 (2008)

[5] Pfaff, B., David, K.: Society and open source. Why open source software is better for society than proprietary closed source software (1998), http://benpfaff.org/writings/anp/oss-is-better.html (accessed, Thursday, August 19, 2010)

[6] Peter, C., Steven, F., Steve, G., David, S.: A history of IBM's open-source involvement and strategy. IBM Systems Journal 44(2), 249–257 (2005)

[7] CATIA. Catalysing Access to ICTs in Africa (CATIA) programme, Free/open source software (FOSS) policy in Africa: A toolkit for policy-makers and practitioners, bridges. org and the Collaboration on International ICT Policy for East and Southern Africa (CIPESA) (2005)

[8] Carlo, D.: FLOSS Guide for SMEs (2009), http://guide.flossmetrics.org/index.php/3._Basic_FLOSS_adoption_models (accessed, Thursday, August 19, 2010)

[9] Dice and The Linux Foundation. 2012 Linux Jobs Report (February 16, 2012)

[10] FOSSDeva. FOSS for Sustainable Development in Africa (FOSSDeva) Survey (2011), http://servnet.ias.unu.edu/limesurvey/index.php?sid=86668&lang=en (valid until August 31, 2012)

[11] Michael, F.: Worldwide Open Software Forecast. International Data Corporation (IDC), document Nr. 219260 (2009)

[12] Gartner Inc., User Survey Analysis: Open-Source Software, Worldwide (2008), http://www.gartner.com/DisplayDocument?ref=g_search&id=757916&subref=simplesearch (accessed March 10, 2009)

[13] Ghosh, R.: Economic Impact of FLOSS on Innovation and Competitiveness of the EU ICT Sector (2006), http://ec.europa.eu/enterprise/sectors/ict/files/2006-11-20-flossimpact_en.pdf (accessed, Tuesday, August 17, 2010)

[14] Goode, S.: Something for nothing: management rejection of open source software in Australia's top firms. Information and Management 42(5), 669–681 (2005)

[15] Gross, M.: Productive Anarchy? Networks of Open Source Software Development, Forum: Qualitative Social Research 8(1) (2007), http://www.qualitative-research.net/index.php/fqs/article/view/225 (retrieved September 4, 2010)

[16] Gurbani, V.K., Garvert, A., Herbsleb, J.D.: A case study of a corporate open source development model. In: Proceedings of the 28th International Conference on Software Engineering, Shanghai, China, pp. 472–481 (2006)

[17] i2010, Preparing Europe's digital future. i2020 Mid-Term Review, A European Information Society for growth and employment. COM (2008) 199, SEC (2008) 470, vol. (1-3), http://ec.europe.eu/i2010 (accessed, Thursday, August 19, 2010)

[18] Kohlbacher, F.: The Use of Qualitative Content Analysis in Case Study Research. Forum: Qualitative Social Research 7(1), 1–23 (2006)

[19] Morgan, L., Finnegan, P.: Open Innovation in Secondary Software Firms: An Exploration of Managers' Perceptions of Open Source Software. The Database for Advances in Information Systems 41(1), 76–95 (2010)

[20] Dwomoh-Tweneboah, M.: Information Technology for Africa. In: iBiz2008 Workshop for Net Business Ethics, Honolulu, USA, February 10-11 (2008)

[21] Li, M., Lin, Z., Xia, M.: Leveraging the Open Source Software Movement for Development of China's Software Industry. Information Technologies and International Development 2(2), 45–63 (2004)

[22] Morgan, L., Finnegan, P.: Open innovation in secondary software firms: an exploration of managers' perceptions of open source software. SIGMIS Database 41(1), 76–95 (2010)

[23] Jabu, M., Elmarie, B.: An investigation into the implementation of open source software within the SA government: an emerging expansion model. In: SAICSIT 2008: Proceedings of the 2008 Annual Research Conference of the South African Institute of Computer Scientists and Information Technologists on IT Research in Developing Countries, pp, pp. 148–158 (2008)

[24] Munga, N., Fogwill, T., Williams, Q.: The Adoption of Open Source Software in Business Models: A Red Hat and IBM Case study. In: SAICSIT 2009, pp. 112–121 (2009)

[25] OSOR (n.d) The Open Source Observatory and Repository for European public administrations, https://joinup.ec.europa.eu/page/osor.eu (accessed, Thursday, March 1, 2012)

[26] Raymond, E.S.: The Cathedral and the Bazaar. In: Musings on Linux and Open Source by an Accidental Revolutionary, O'Reilly & Associates, Inc., USA (2001)

[27] van Reijswoud, V., de Jager, A.: Free and Open Source Software for Development: exploring expectations, achievements and future. Polimentrica Published Book, Italy (2008)

[28] Watson, R.T., et al.: The Business of Open Source: Tracking the changing competitive conditions of the software industry. Communication of the ACM 51(4), 41–46 (2008)

[29] Ajila, S., Wu, D.: Empirical study of the effects of open source adoption on software development economics. Journal of Systems and Software 80(9), 1517–1529 (2007)

[30] Samuelson, P.: IBM's pragmatic embrace of open source. Commun. ACM. 49(10), 21–25 (2006)

[31] Sowe, S.K., Stamelos, I., Samoladas, I. (eds.): Emerging Free and Open Source Software Practices. IDEA Group Publishing, Hershey (2008)

[32] Sowe, S.K., Ioannis, S., Angelis, L.: Understanding Knowledge Sharing Activities in Free/Open Source Software Projects: An Empirical Study. Journal of Systems and Software 81(3), 431–446 (2008)

[33] Sowe, S.K.: Free and Open Source Software in Business: Implications for Policy Efficiency. In: International Conference of the Open Source Software Business Information Group (OSSBIG 2011), Vienna, Austria, May 31 (2011b)

[34] Stamelos, I., Angelis, L., Oikonomou, A., Bleris, G.L.: Code quality analysis in open source software development. Information Systems Journal 12, 43–60 (2002)

[35] UNCTAD. Free and Open-Source: Implications for ICT Policy and Development. Chapter 4, E-Commerce and Development Report. UNCTAD/SIDTE/ECB/2003/1 (2003)

[36] Stephen, W., Gynn, D., von Rotz, B.: The Growth of Open Source Software in Organizations. Publication Report. Optaros Inc. (2005)

[37] Yin, R.K.: Case Study Research, 3rd edn. Sage, Thousand Oaks (2003)

[38] Chapter 7: Open Source Software Adoption Best Practices: Myths, Realities, Processes and Economic Growth
[39] Imed, H.: Open Source Ecosystem in Tunisia: An Empirical Study. In: Sowe, S.K., Parayial, G., Sunami, A. (eds.) Free and Open Source Software and Technology for Sustainable Development, ch. 9, pp. 153–170. UNU-Press (2012)
[40] Maurice, M., Sherly, T., Evan, D.: Adoption and Diffusion patterns of FOSS in Jamaican SMEs: A Study of Perceptions, Attitudes and Barriers. In: Sowe, S.K., Parayial, G., Sunami, A. (eds.) Free and Open Source Software and Technology for Sustainable Development, ch. 10, pp. 171–185. UNU-Press (2012)
[41] European Commission (2003/361/EC). THE New SME Definition. User Guide and Model Declaration. Official Journal of the European Union L 124, 36 (May 20, 2003)
[42] Mockus, A., Fielding, R., Herbsleb, J.A.: Two case studies of open source software development: Apache and Mozilla. ACM Transactions on Software Engineering and Methodology 11(3), 1–38 (2002)
[43] Brown, D., Lockett, N.: Potential of critical e-applications for engaging SMEs in e-business: A provider perspective. Journal of Information Systems 13(1), 21–34 (2004)
[44] Fitzgerald, B.: The Transformation of Open Source. Software. MIS Quarterly 30(3), 587–598 (2006)
[45] Brown, D., Lockett, N.: Potential of critical e-applications for engaging SMEs in e-business: a provider perspective. Journal of Information Systems 13(1), 21–34 (2004)

Exploring the Role of Commercial Stakeholders in Open Source Software Evolution

Andrea Capiluppi[1], Klaas-Jan Stol[2], and Cornelia Boldyreff[3]

[1] Brunel University, United Kingdom
[2] Lero—The Irish Software Engineering Research Centre
University of Limerick, Ireland
[3] University of East London, United Kingdom
`andrea.capiluppi@brunel.ac.uk`, `klaas-jan.stol@lero.ie`,
`c.boldyreff@uel.ac.uk`

Abstract. It has been lately established that a major success or failure factor of an OSS project is whether or not it involves a commercial company, or more extremely, when a project is managed by a commercial software corporation. As documented recently, the success of the Eclipse project can be largely attributed to IBM's project management, since the upper part of the developer hierarchy is dominated by its staff. This paper reports on the study of the evolution of three different Open Source (OSS) projects — the Eclipse and jEdit IDEs and the Moodle e-learning system — looking at whether they have benefited from the contribution of commercial companies. With the involvement of commercial companies, it is found that OSS projects achieve sustained productivity, increasing amounts of output produced and intake of new developers. It is also found that individual and commercial contributions show similar stages: developer intake, learning effect, sustained contributions and, finally, abandonment of the project. This preliminary evidence suggests that a major success factor for OSS is the involvement of a commercial company, or more radically, when project management is in hands of a commercial entity.

1 Introduction

Governance and control in Open Source Software (OSS) has been dramatically changing [30]. The *traditional* volunteer-based OSS project model is now being accompanied by *sponsored* OSS, where commercial stakeholders provide effort beyond voluntary programmers. It has been argued that OSS projects have become increasingly hybrid with respect to this type of contributing stakeholders [12].

Since their inception in the early 1980s, OSS projects were mostly volunteer-based (or *Traditional OSS*, right end of Figure 1), heavily relying on personal efforts and non-monetary recognition, and reportedly suffering from communication and coordination problems [14].

Nowadays, so-called *Sponsored OSS* projects have also been documented as more similar to *Closed Source* systems (as in far left of Figure 1). They could be industry-led OSS projects, where a commercial stakeholder plays a major role in the development and decision making, as in the case of the Eclipse project by IBM [25,24,19,33]. They

I. Hammouda et al. (Eds.): OSS 2012, IFIP AICT 378, pp. 178–200, 2012.

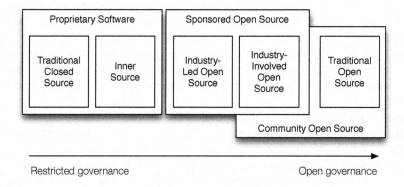

Fig. 1. Continuum of governance in software projects: proprietary software (left) to Open Source Software (right)

can also be *industry-involved* OSS projects when they are driven by an OSS community, but often have one or several companies or institutions (e.g., universities) among their stakeholders, as in the case of the Moodle Content Management System (CMS) [8].

Both the *industry-led* and *industry-involved* scenarios introduce new challenges to OSS projects: the first is based on one (or a small subset of) critical stakeholder(s), which could eventually halt the project if they decide to abandon it[1]. In the case of Eclipse, for example, IBM staff have been identified as the top contributors, with only a few external developers working on the core system [36]. For *Community* OSS, especially in the case of large and complex OSS systems, there is a need of proper incentives for different types of stakeholders, with complementary expertise and requirements, in particular when their contributions are relevant to a system's core functionality.

This paper aims to explore these three scenarios and to study whether the involvement of commercial companies can help sustaining the evolution of OSS projects. To that end, the paper presents different analyses of the evolution of a *commercial* and a *traditional* OSS systems (Eclipse and jEdit), sharing the same application domain, and one *community* OSS project (Moodle).

By exploring the type of activities performed by commercial stakeholders, and by comparing the results achieved by similar OSS projects (sharing the same application domain, but with different involvement of stakeholders), this paper explores a research area that only recently started to be covered in the literature [28,27,31].

1.1 Terminology

Existing literature typically distinguishes between *community-managed* (also called *autonomous* [32]) and *sponsored* communities. However, current terminology for this has some issues. For instance, OSS projects that are led by firms are referred to as *commercial OSS*, whereas an OSS project that involves commercial stakeholders (companies),

---

[1] This happened with Netscape Navigator (then Mozilla) when Netscape Communications Corporation (NCC) released it as open source, but without further evolving it.

but is led by an OSS community (consisting of "traditional" community members) is referred to as *Community OSS*. We argue that both terms are not precisely defined and need further refinement. Commercial OSS suggests that profit is made from the OSS project. The term "Community OSS" does not clearly distinguish projects that involve companies from "traditional" OSS projects (that do not involve companies). Therefore, in this paper we propose the following new terminology for the various models of involvement:

Traditional OSS projects are those projects in which no companies are involved.

Industry-involved OSS projects are projects in which commercial firms are involved as contributors, but the project is still managed by the "community".

Industry-led OSS projects are projects that are led by a commercial firms. The wider community can contribute (as with any OSS project), but since a company has control over the project, it defines the evolution strategy.

Together, industry-involved and industry-led projects are **Sponsored** OSS projects, whereas industry-involved and traditional projects are both forms of **Community** projects (see Figure 1) as they are led by a community (as opposed to a company).

1.2 Structure of This Paper

The remainder of this paper is structured as follows: Section 2 presents the goals, questions and metrics of the study. Section 3 presents the research design. Sections 4 and 5 presents the Eclipse and jEdit case studies, respectively. Section 6 focuses on the Moodle system as an example of an industry-involved OSS system, and explores the relevance of the commercial stakeholders, and how they differ from individual developers. Section 7 discusses the results followed by conclusions in Section 8.

2   Background and Related Work

This section provides a brief overview of relevant background and related studies. Most reports on participation of firms in OSS projects present results from large-scale surveys.

Bonaccorsi and Rossi studied contributions to OSS projects by commercial firms. They conducted a large-scale survey among 146 Italian companies that provide software solutions and services based on Open Source Software [6]. One of the findings was that approximately 20 per cent of companies were coordinating an OSS project. Furthermore, almost half of the companies (46.2%) had never joined an OSS project. It is important to note that these results were published in 2004, and that these numbers may have changed significantly over the last eight years; we suggest that a replication of this study would be a valuable contribution.

Bonaccorsi and Rossi have further studied (using data from the same survey) motivations of firms to contribute to OSS projects [7,29].

Bonaccorsi et al. [5] have investigated whether and how firms contribute to OSS projects. Their study investigated which activities firms undertake in OSS projects, as well as whether the presence of firms affect the evolution of OSS projects. To address these questions, Bonaccorsi et al. conducted a survey of 300 OSS projects hosted on

SourceForge.net. They found that almost one in three of the studied projects had one or more firms involved. In a survey of 1,302 OSS projects by Capra et al. [13], similar results were found, namely that firms were involved in 31% of the projects. Different types of involvement were identified: (1) project coordination, (2) collaboration in code development, and (3) provision of code. Capra et al. [13] made a slightly different classification of participation models: the *Management model* (for project coordination), the *Support model* (sponsoring through financial or logistic support) and the *Coding model* (contributing code, bug fixes, customization, etc.). In most cases, it was found that the firms founded the OSS project, but in some cases firms took over by replacing a project's coordinator.

Aaltonen and Jokinen [1] studied the influence in the Linux kernel community and found that firms have a large impact in the project's development.

Martinez-Romo et al. [22] have studied collaboration between an OSS community and a company. They conducted case studies of two OSS projects: Evolution and Mono.

Companies can sponsor OSS projects in different ways. Berdou [4] investigated the dynamics of cooperation in community-led projects that involve paid contributors, and proposed a framework to understand this relationship.

Dahlander and Magnusson [15] proposed a typology consisting of *symbiotic* (win-win), *commensalistic* (firm gains, community indifferent) and *parasitic* (firm gains, community loses) approaches to characterize firm–community relationships. These relationships only apply in community-led projects.

The last decade of research in OSS has well established the relationship between firms and OSS projects. This relationship has been shown to have a direct effect on a project's sustainability. However, what kind of effects this relationship has on a project's evolution has not been studied. Therefore, we set out to explore this by means of a comparative case study. The next section outlines the research design.

3   Research Design

This section presents the research design of the empirical study following the *Goal-Question-Metric* (GQM) approach [3].

3.1   Goal

The long term objective of this research is to understand whether there are (and there likely will be) differences in the maintenance and evolution activities of OSS projects as long as commercial stakeholders join or drive the development.

3.2   Questions

This paper addresses the following research questions:

1. Are there differences in the evolution of similar-scoped OSS applications, as long as one (or more) commercial stakeholders play a major role in the development?
2. When considering projects in the same application domain, are different "categories" achieving different results or patterns of maintenance?

3. From an effort perspective, do commercial stakeholders behave similarly to individual developers?

3.3 Method and Metrics

Given the exploratory nature of this topic, we decided to perform an exploratory multiple case study. Since this topic has not been studied in depth, this multiple case study can be considered as a *revelatory* case study [37]. Rather than seeking to make generalizations with respect to the influence of commercial stakeholders in OSS evolution, we have aimed at exploring this phenomenon with the purpose to identify more precise hypotheses that can be studied in more depth and with different research methods (e.g., surveys).

The choice of the studied projects was grounded in the fact that they are appropriate examples of the three types of involvement models mentioned earlier, and was also supported by the fact that the first author was familiar with these projects through previous studies [8,9,35] as well as ongoing (as of yet unpublished) studies.

Our study is a quantitative analysis of the studied projects, for which two types of metrics are used: *code* metrics and *effort* metrics. These are discussed below.

Code Metrics Given the available (public) releases, a set of data was extracted from the studied projects: two systems (Eclipse and jEdit) are implemented mostly in Java, while Moodle is implemented in PHP, and partially relying on OO features, evidenced by a visible number of PHP classes. The terminology and associated definitions for these metrics are extracted from related and well-known past studies, for example, the definition of *common* and *control* coupling ([2,21,16]).

- **Methods** (or functions in PHP): the lowest level of granularity of the present analysis. Within this attribute, the union of the sets of OO methods, interfaces, constructors and abstract methods was extracted.
- **Classes**: as containers of methods, the number of classes composing the systems has been extracted. Differently from past studies [25], *anonymous* and *inner* classes [20] were also considered as part of the analysed systems.
- **Size**: the growth in size was evaluated in number of SLOCs (physical lines of code), number of methods, classes and packages.
- **Coupling**: this is the union of all the *dependencies* and *method calls* (*i.e.*, the common and control coupling) of all source files as extracted through Doxygen[2]. The three aggregations introduced above (methods, classes and packages) were considered for the same level of granularity (the *method-to-method*, *class-to-class* and the *package-to-package* couplings). A strong coupling link between package A and B is found when many elements within A call elements of package B.
- **Complexity**: the complexity was evaluated at the method level. Each method's complexity was evaluated via its McCabe index [23].

---

[2] http://www.doxygen.nl, supporting both the Java and PHP languages.

Effort Metrics A second set of data was extracted based on the availability of CMS servers: this data source represents a regular, highly parsable set of atomic transactions (i.e., 'commits') which details the actions that developers (i.e., 'committers') perform on the code composing the system. Two metrics were extracted:

- **Effort**: the effort of developers was evaluated by counting the number of unique (or *distinct*, in a SQL-like terminology) developers in a month.
- **Output metrics**: the work produced was evaluated by counting the monthly creations of, or modifications to, classes or packages. Several modifications to the same file were also filtered with the SQL *distinct* clause, in order to observe how many different entities were modified in a month[3].

4   Industry-Led Open Source Project: Eclipse IDE

The Eclipse project has attracted a vast amount of attention by researchers and practitioners, in part due to the availability of its source code, and the openness of its development process. Among the recent publications, several have been focused on the "architectural layer" of this system [34,19], extracting the relevant information from special-purposed XML files used to describe Eclipse's features and extensions (*i.e.*, plugins) implementing them, in this way representing some sort of "module architecture view" [18].

As recently reported, the growth of the major releases in Eclipse follows a linearly growing trend [24], when studying the evolution of its lines of code, number of files and classes. The study on Eclipse's meta-data indicated that, over all releases, the size of the architecture has increased more than sevenfold (from 35 to 271 *plugins*) [34].

The present study is instead performed at the method level, and on two release streams (*trunk* and *milestones*). Regarding Eclipse, 26 releases composing the stream of "major" and "minor" releases of Eclipse (from 1.0 to 3.5.1) and some 30 additional releases tagged as "milestones" (M) or "release candidates" (RC), were considered in this study, spanning some 8 years of evolution. For each release, we performed an analysis of the source code with the Doxygen tool. This latter analysis lasted a few hours for the early releases, but it required more than one day of parsing for the latest available releases, mostly due to the explosion in size of the project (490,000 SLOCs found in the 1.0 release of Eclipse, up to more than 3 million SLOCs found in the 3.6 releases[4]). Overall, it required more than one month to perform the analysis on the whole batch of Eclipse releases.

The remainder of this section presents the results of the analysis of Eclipse. Subsection 4.1 presents the results of the evolution of the size of Eclipse. Subsection 4.2 presents the evolution of Eclipse's complexity.

---

[3] In specific cases, specific committer IDs were excluded, when it was clear that they are responsible for automatic, uninteresting, commits; it was also excluded from this metric any activity concerning the 'Attic' CMS location (which denotes deleted source material).

[4] Statistics were collected with SLOCCount, http://www.dwheeler.com/sloccount/

4.1 Results – Eclipse Size

This study considered the "main" releases (3.0, 3.1, etc.), and the "milestone" releases (e.g., 3.2M1, 3.2M2, etc.) and "release candidates" (e.g., 3.3RC1, 3.3RC2, etc.) release streams of the Eclipse project. The overall growth is almost fivefold, while it is also evident from Figure 2 that the main stream of releases has a stepwise growth, the steps being the major releases[5].

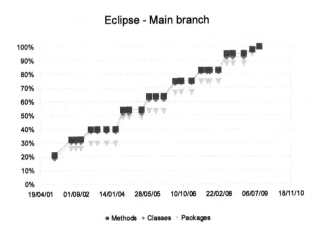

Fig. 2. Growth in the "main" branch of Eclipse

Major releases of Eclipse are regularly devoted to new features, while milestone and release candidates releases are devoted to maintaining existing ones (Figure 3). The milestones stream has a more linear path: plotting the number of methods against the "build date" of the relative release, a linear fit is found with an appropriate goodness of fit ($R^2 = 0.98$). The step-wise growth for the main release stream, and the linear trend for the milestones release also reflect what was found when studying the evolution of Eclipse at a larger granularity level, i.e. its plugins [34].

4.2 Results – Eclipse Complexity

The study at the method level shows a distribution of the McCabe cyclomatic indexes which is constant along the two streams of releases (main and milestones) of Eclipse. This is visible when assigning the cyclomatic complexity of each method (cc_i) in the four following clusters:

1. $cc_i < 5$
2. $5 \leq cc_i < 10$
3. $10 \leq cc_i < 15$
4. $cc_i \geq 15$

---

[5] The overall size growth has been normalized to 1 for easing the reading of the graph.

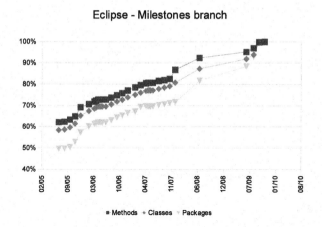

Fig. 3. Growth and maintenance patterns in the "milestones" branch of Eclipse

Figure 4 shows the relative evolution of the fourth cluster, and reveals a quasi-constant evolutionary trend (for reason of clarity, the other trends are not displayed, although they follow a similar evolutionary pattern). The amount of highly complex methods ($cc > 15$, [23]) present in the system never reaches the 2% of the overall system. As reported in other works, this shows a profound difference from other traditional Open Source projects, where this ratio (for C and C++ projects) has been observed at around 10% of the system [10].

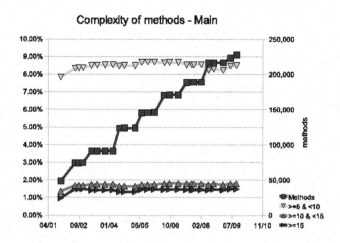

Fig. 4. Patterns of highly complex methods (McCabe index > 15) in the main branch of Eclipse

4.3 Results – Eclipse Coupling

The number of couplings (i.e., unique method calls) has been counted for each of the two streams of releases. The set of added, deleted and kept couplings has been evaluated between two subsequent releases in each stream, and plotted in Figure 5. As shown, these findings confirm previous ones [34] regarding Eclipse's maintenance patterns: in the main stream, a large amount of modifications to its existing connections is made between minor and major releases, reaching more than 60% of new couplings added during the transition between the subsequent versions 2.1.3 and 3.0.

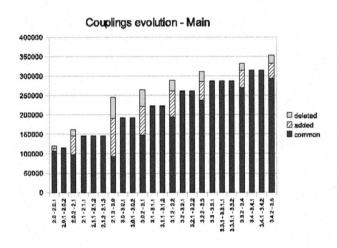

Fig. 5. Distribution of coupling in the main branch of Eclipse

On the other hand, the Milestones stream (Figure 6) confirms a recurring pattern, where the milestones show a great deal of added and removed couplings, whereas the Release Candidates (RC's) show a much lower activity in the same activity of coupling restructurings (the amount of shared couplings between two subsequent releases is not shown for clarity purposes).

4.4 Results – Eclipse Cohesion

The cohesion of classes or packages was measured by counting the number of elements connected with other internal elements, and then cumulated for all the classes or packages. Figure 7 shows the evolution of cohesion at the package level, and it confirms the observations achieved when evaluating the highly complex methods (Figure 4). Although there is a vast increase in the number of methods and classes, most of the connections are confined within the same package, keeping the cohesion constant throughout the life-cycle until the latest observed release. This measurement is also found higher in the earliest releases (some 73%), and declining sharply until release 3.0, where it stabilizes to some 69 − 70% for the last 6 years.

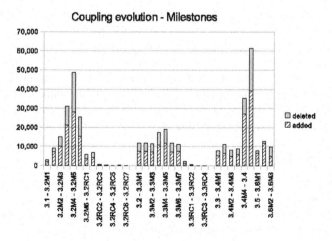

Fig. 6. Distribution of coupling in the milestones branch of Eclipse

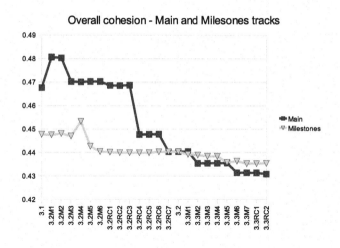

Fig. 7. Patterns of cohesion of the two branches of Eclipse

5   Traditional Open Source Project: jEdit

Given the results from the above study, a *community-driven* OSS project (i.e., where no commercial company is "sponsoring" the development [12]) was studied in a similar way to evaluate and compare in some way the quantitative results of Eclipse. Although not exactly implementing all the features within Eclipse, the jEdit project also aims to be a fully-fledged IDE, benefiting from a large number of add-ons and plugins, independently developed and pluggable in the core system. Though any two software systems are always different to some degree, this study was not performed for the purpose of comparing features, but for the sake of observing whether the patterns observed in a very large and articulated project are similarly found in a much smaller project, and whether good practices should be inferred in any direction.

Similarly to the Eclipse project, the 14 releases available of jEdit were therefore collected on the largest OSS portal (*i.e.*, SourceForge), from 3.0 to 4.3.1 (earlier releases do not provide the source code). Being a much smaller project, collecting the information via Doxygen was much quicker, both at the beginning of the sequence (57 kSLOCs, jEdit-3.0) and at the end (190 kSLOCs, jEdit-4.3.1). The 14 considered releases are the ones made available to the community, and span some 10 years of development.

5.1   Results – jEdit Size

The second system also shows a linear growth, with an adequate goodness of fit ($R^2 = 0.97$), albeit with a lower slope than what found in Eclipse, as to summarise a slower linear growth in Figure 8. A similar linear trend is found in the evolution of methods, classes and packages. The most evident difference with the evolution of Eclipse is the pace of the public releases in jEdit: between releases 4.2 and 4.3 some 5 years passed, although the jEdit configuration management system contains information on the ongoing activity by developers.

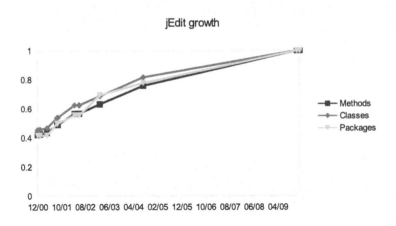

Fig. 8. Evolution of size in jEdit

5.2   Results – jEdit Complexity

Regarding jEdit, the evolution of the complexity at the methods' level brings an interesting insight: for this project, it was found that more than 25% of the methods are constantly over a threshold of high complexity, at any time of jEdit's evolution. This complexity pattern has been observed also in other OSS systems [10]. Large and complex methods are typically a deterrent to the understandability and maintainability of a software system, and a vast refactoring of these methods has been achieved in the last two public releases, as visible in the graph, where a significant drop of highly complex methods is achieved even in the presence of a net increase in the number of methods.

5.3   Results – jEdit Coupling

The maintenance patterns of jEdit present a more discontinuous profile, with changes between major releases typically presenting large additions of new couplings (see Figure 9, bottom), and minor releases where less of such modifications were made. More importantly, the maintenance of couplings appears not to be planned, where the largest modifications (between 4.2 and 4.3) appear after a long hiatus of five years, and represent a full restructuring of the underlying code architecture, with added and deleted couplings representing three-times and twice as many couplings as the maintained ones, respectively.

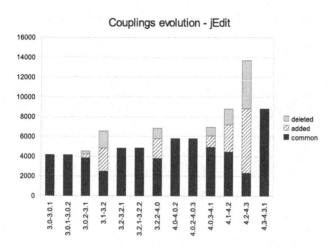

Fig. 9. Coupling in jEdit

6   Industry-involved OSS Project: Moodle

As per the definition of an *industry-involved* OSS project, Moodle's development is primarily centered around the OSS community, but various other actors have interest in its development. A number of organizations across the world are directly contributing to the development of Moodle by way of funding or contributing their expertise, and have been defined as "Moodle partners".

Similarly to the other two case studies, we extracted the size, complexity and cohesion of the PHP code contained in the publicly available releases[6]: overall we studied some 90 releases of this project. By checking on the official website, it can be observed that Moodle was evolved in one single stream of release until version 1.7: from 1.8 onwards, several branches have been evolved at the same time (e.g., 1.7.x, 1.8.x, 1.9.x etc). For each of these branches we kept the results on size, coupling and complexity separated from the other branches.

---

[6] A list of the releases (with the relative releasing date) since 2002 is available at http://docs.moodle.org/dev/Releases

6.1   Results – Moodle Size

As observed in Eclipse, the evolution of Moodle resembles a step-like pattern (see Figure 10), where the major releases consist of the addition of a large number of files, classes and functions, and the minor releases show smaller additions in all the measured metrics. From release 1.8 onwards, all the various branches maintain the same pattern as well, albeit the growth is intertwined in time with all the other branches (Figures 11 middle and bottom): during the interim releases between minor (e.g., 1.8) and development (e.g., 1.8.1) releases, the growth in number of functions, classes and source files is minimal, while the step-wise growth pattern is observed between minor releases (e.g., between 1.8 and 1.9). Therefore, for this system the increase in size has changed the approach to development, requiring the project to define and maintain various branches at the same time.

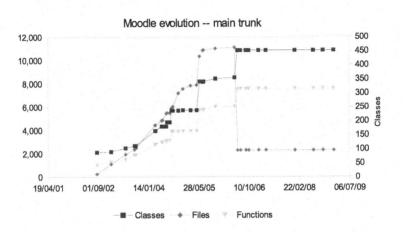

Fig. 10. Growth of size in the main branch of Moodle (up to release 1.7)

6.2   Results – Moodle Complexity

Since Moodle is written in the PHP programming language, which is based on procedural and object-oriented constructs, we evaluated the complexity of the functions contained in the source code. This was plotted per release, as above, and the percentage of highly complex functions tracked throughout. The summary in Figure 12 shows how the excessive complexity (i.e., the sum of functions whose McCabe cyclomatic index is > 15, and depicted in the continuous line) has been kept under control even though the system constantly increases the number of its functions (depicted as a continuous line in the same figure). What is quite evident is also the major refactoring that was undertaken between releases 1.x and 2.x. In the latter, a larger number of functions were introduced, in a step-wise growth, while parallel work was done to reduce the amount of complexity in existing and new functions, with a step-wise descent of highly complex functions.

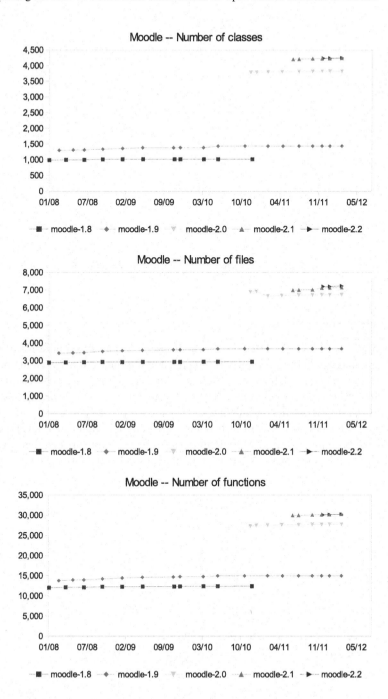

Fig. 11. Growth of size in the parallel branches of Moodle (after release 1.7)

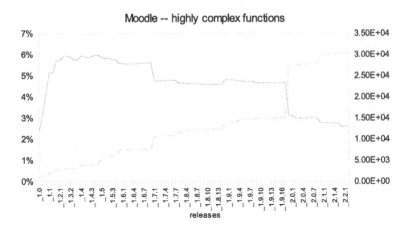

Fig. 12. Evolution of complexity in Moodle (continuous line) and overall increase in number of functions (dashed)

6.3   Results – Moodle Coupling

The functions composing the releases of Moodle were also analysed in terms of their connections, and which of the connections were added or removed between major and minor releases, and between branches. As done for the previous cases, the releases were analysed by the Doxygen engine, extracting all the links between low level entities, that were later lifted to file-to-file dependencies.

As reported for the size growth, it becomes clear that the minor and development releases have become central in Moodle to perform several adjustments, that trail off in proximity of the next release, similarly to what is found in the Eclipse environment

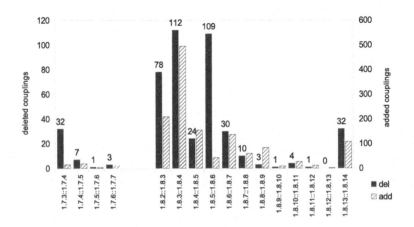

Fig. 13. Added and removed couplings in Moodle (branches 1.7.x and 1.8.x)

(see Figure 13, displaying the 1.7.x and 1.8.x branches of releases). This has evolved in Moodle: the earlier branches (e.g., Moodle-1.1.x or Moodle-1.2.x) did not display long sequences of development (e.g., only Moodle-1.1 and Moodle-1.1.1 have been released within the Moodle-1.1.x branch). With more recent releases, the pattern observed in Eclipse is also visible in Moodle, with longer sequences of development releases (14 development releases in Moodle-1.8.x, 17 in Moodle-1.9.x), in which fewer and fewer couplings are added and removed, until the release is being discontinued and not supported further.

7   Discussion

The two cases of Moodle and jEdit show that similar issues are faced by the developers: even if companies are involved in development of the Moodle project, they do not *drive* the development, as for Eclipse. Given it is taken for granted that industry-led OSS projects do not have an issue of long-term sustainability, industry-involved and traditional OSS projects need to address the issue of how to attract and maintain the existing contributors in the development loop. In the following subsections, we analyse how effectively developers and contributors are attracted and maintained within the two projects, and whether lessons learned can be drawn in both cases.

7.1   Contributions on the Periphery

In both the Moodle and jEdit projects, the "core" of the system is separated from the "plugins" or "contributors" section. We assume that contributing to the "core" of a project is more time-consuming, and requires more skills, than contributing to the "modules" or the "plugins" sections[7]. Therefore we investigated whether a sustained intake of contributors is achieved in Moodle and jEdit, or whether these projects face an issue in this respect.

Moodle – Two main directories are found in the CMS server: the core 'Moodle' directory (which makes for the public releases, that we consider as "core"), and the 'contrib' folder, organized in 'plugins', 'patches' and 'tools' (but not wrapped in the official releases). As visible in Figure 14 (left), the evolution of the core Moodle system follows the typical pattern of an early (or 'cathedral' [26]) OSS project: few contributors are visible in the first months (mostly the main Moodle developer), with few other contributors being active in a discontinuous way. A further, sustained period is also visible, where the number of active developers follows a growing trend with peaks of over 30 developers a month contributing, and revealing a 'bazaar' phase [11]. The main issue that is visible in the Moodle "core" system is revealed at around 3/4 of its life-cycle, where the number of active developers start to decline. From the point of view of the sustainability, we posit that this could represent a serious issue in the long-term evolution of this system.

---

[7] This is because writing plugins or additional modules, where the system is modular, should be possible without modifying other files, but just using the system's APIs.

On the other hand, the activity of Moodle has been devoted more and more to the 'contrib' folder, rather than in the 'core': this reflects a more and more distributed participation to the Moodle development, and a low barrier to entry, albeit not all the contributed modules are selected for inclusion in the publicly available releases. The overall distribution of changes throughout the Moodle evolution proceeds on a linear trend ($R^2 = 0.78$): in recent months, the inflection of productivity in the "core" Moodle has been balanced by the late growth of contributions to the other parts. That reflects a more and more distributed participation to the Moodle development, and a low barrier to entry, but several of the proposed modules have not been selected for inclusion in the main Moodle system.

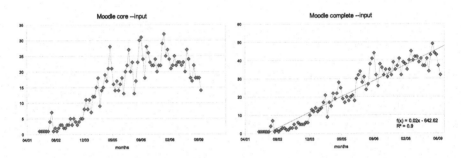

Fig. 14. Active monthly contributors in the "core" (left) and in the overall Moodle project (right)

jEdit – The main difference between jEdit and Moodle in the intake of developers is visible in Figure 15 (below): albeit the 'core' (or 'trunk') is separated from the 'plugins', few contributors were added in the latter, following a cyclic development pattern overall. Differently from Moodle, the intake of contributors does not follow a linear pattern: the presence of developers in the "core" declines at around $3/4$ of the life-cycle, and so does the number of contributors working on the periphery of the system. This makes jEdit even more brittle to sustainability issues, specifically around the intake of new developers.

7.2 Three-Layered Contributions

The study of Moodle as an industry-involved OSS project resulted in an in-depth analysis of the types of contributors who actively produce code for the system. Interesting insights were discovered when studying each developer's actual contribution to the code: in a first attempt to categorize the intake, the contributions, and the developers leaving the project, three categories are clearly distinguishable, not based on the amount of effort inputed in the system, but purely on the length of the activity of each developer:

1. **Sporadic** developers: this refers to the extremely low presence of certain contributors in the development. Within Moodle, 60 developers have been active for just one month; other 70 developers have been active between 2 and 6 (not necessarily consecutive) months.

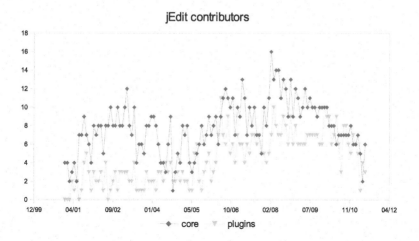

Fig. 15. Active monthly contributors in the "core" and in the "plugins" parts of jEdit

2. **Seasonal** developers: as reported recently [28], most OSS projects benefit seasonal developers, i.e., those developers who are active for a short period of time (we are not referring to 'recurring' or 'returning' developers).
3. **Stable** developers: those developers showing a sustained involvement (say, more than 24 months for the Moodle system). Both seasonal and stable developers can be part of the top 20% developing most of the system, as in the definition of 'generation of OSS developers' given in the past [5].

Some of the Moodle partners have been found acting as *seasonal* developers; the *Catalyst* partner[8] has so far provided a large number of modifications to the core Moodle, by deploying several developers who became active contributors within the community. The profile of the contributed outputs is visible in Figure 16 (bottom), and can be defined as a 'seasonal' effort pattern, meaning a large contribution on a very specific time interval, and lower levels of effort before and after it. Comparing this curve to a selection of seasonal Moodle individual developers (Figure 16, top), a similar pattern is visible: an initial period of low commit rates, followed by a peak were a high level of contributions is observed, finally a leveling-off.

7.3 Limitations of This Study

We are aware of a few limitations of this study, which we discuss below. Yin [37] lists four types of threats to validity, namely, *construct*, *internal* and *external* validity, and *reliability*.

Construct Validity. Construct validity is concerned with *establishing correct operational measures for the concepts that are studied* [37]. In this study, construct validity

---

[8] http://www.catalyst.net.nz/

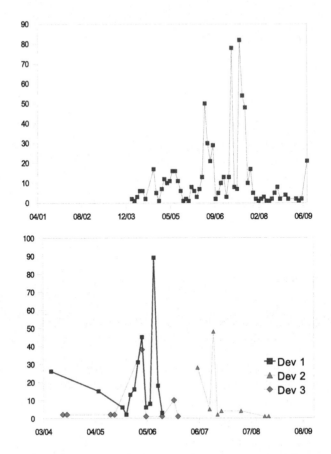

Fig. 16. Output produced by one of the partners (Catalyst, top), as compared to seasonal developers in Moodle

relates to the measures we have used to collect and analyze the data, namely, code metrics such as size, coupling and complexity, and effort metrics such as number of developers and number of modifications made. We argue that these are well established metrics that appropriately represent the concepts being studied.

Internal Validity. Internal validity is concerned with establishing a causal relationship. In our study, the relationship that we have explored is between the nature of the stakeholders (i.e., commercial versus non-commercial) and the evolution of OSS. The results of this exploratory study suggest that there is, in fact, an influence from the presence of commercial stakeholders. However, changes in evolutionary patterns may not be due to the involvement of commercial stakeholders. Further research is needed to establish the nature of this relationship in more detail.

External Validity. External validity is concerned with the extent to which findings of a study can be generalized to other settings. A common critique of the case study methodology is that findings cannot be generalized. However, the purpose of conducting case study research is not to look for *statistical* generalizability, such as aimed for in large-scale quantitative surveys, but rather to seek *theoretical* generalization [37]. In other words, in this paper we have started to explore a theory relating to the influence of commercial stakeholders on the evolution of OSS. We like to emphasize that our study is of *exploratory* nature, and as such serves the purpose of exploring our initial ideas and defining more focused hypotheses for further research.

Reliability. Reliability of a study refers to the degree to which a study can be repeated and attaining the same results. One strategy to increase a study's reliability is to establish an audit trail [17]. Our audit trail consists of the extracted data as well as spreadsheets that contain the analysis.

8 Conclusions and Future Work

The terminology around the OSS phenomenon has been radically changing in the past few years. This research has studied how commercial stakeholders can have an influence on the evolution and maintenance of OSS systems. Eclipse has been studied as an *industry-led* OSS system, since it is backed by the IBM corporation; the Java IDE jEdit was selected as an exemplar of a *traditional* OSS system; while Moodle was chosen as an exemplar of *industry-involved* system, built mostly by the OSS community, although several commercial stakeholders have write-access to it. The public releases of each system, and their configuration management systems (CMS), were jointly analyzed, to determine the best type of information to draw results from.

The study of the releases allowed us to focus on the main points along the evolution of the studied systems. The industry-led OSS system presents several "best practices" of software engineering: low complexity of units, continuous evolution and regular maintenance cycles. The traditional OSS system, in the same application domain, achieves very different results: 1 in 4 units are too complex, discontinuous evolution, and the maintenance is not regularly achieved. Finally, the industry-involved system shows more and more regular patterns of evolution, increasing control of complexity and alignment of its maintenance cycles to multi-branch, large software systems with parallel maintained releases.

On the other hand, the study of the CMSs allowed the effort of the contributors to be tracked along the life-cycle of these systems, with the specific objective of determining issues in the sustainability of OSS systems. Analysing the industry-led project, we posit that it does not present (yet) issues of sustainability, as it is backed by a large corporation. The industry-involved project shows that the amount of active developers and the output produced follow an increasing, linear trend. Factors for these trends were found in the increasing number of contributions and plug-ins, and the presence of commercial partners driving the evolution, that act exactly as typical developers, joining in the projects, producing contributions, and then leaving. As observed, and different from

Eclipse, the studied commercial stakeholder in Moodle is a *seasonal* contributor, after some time trailing off and leaving the project.

The study of the effort in the traditional system shows instead that, even with a sustained number of releases, jEdit has fewer and fewer developers in both the "core" system as well as in the periphery, showing more issues of sustainability than the other two cases.

What these findings demonstrate could have a profound impact on what is considered as "Open Source" development and raises the following questions:

- Is the presence of commercial stakeholders a necessary condition to achieve sustained evolution?
- Are "traditional" OSS projects eventually destined to trail off and be abandoned?
- Is the lack of adherence to basic software engineering principles an obstacle to OSS development?

These are fundamental questions to be answered by further research studies in order to understand how the OSS phenomenon will change in the future.

Acknowledgments. The authors wish to thank Dr Fernández-Ramil for his extensive comments on an earlier draft of this paper. We thank the two anonymous reviewers who provided constructive feedback on this paper. This work was supported, in part, by Science Foundation Ireland grant 10/CE/I1855 to Lero—The Irish Software Engineering Research Centre (www.lero.ie).

References

1. Aaltonen, T., Jokinen, J.: Influence in the linux kernel community. In: Feller, J., Fitzgerald, B., Scacchi, W., Sillitti, A. (eds.) Open Source Development, Adoption and Innovation. IFIP, vol. 234, pp. 203–208. Springer, Heidelberg (2007)
2. Arisholm, E., Briand, L.C., Foyen, A.: Dynamic coupling measurement for object-oriented software. IEEE Transactions on Software Engineering 30(8), 491–506 (2004)
3. Basili, V.R., Caldiera, G., Rombach, D.H.: The goal question metric approach. In: Encyclopedia of Software Engineering, pp. 528–532. John Wiley & Sons (1994)
4. Berdou, E.: Insiders and outsiders: paid contributors and the dynamics of cooperation in community led f/os projects. In: Damiani, E., Fitzgerald, B., Scacchi, W., Scotto, M., Succi, G. (eds.) Open Source Systems 2006. IFIP, vol. 203, pp. 201–208. Springer, Heidelberg (2006)
5. Bonaccorsi, A., Lorenzi, D., Merito, M., Rossi, C.: Business firms' engagement in community projects. empirical evidence and further developments of the research. In: Proc. First International Workshop on Emerging Trends in FLOSS Research and Development. IEEE Computer Society, Washington, DC (2007)
6. Bonaccorsi, A., Rossi, C.: Contributing to os projects. a comparison between individual and firms. In: Proc. 4th Workshop on Open Source Software Engineering (WOSSE), pp. 18–22 (2004)
7. Bonaccorsi, A., Rossi, C.: Intrinsic motivations and profit-oriented firms. do firms practise what they preach? In: Proc. First International Conference on Open Source Systems, pp. 241–245 (2005)

8. Capiluppi, A., Baravalle, A., Heap, N.W.: Engaging without Over-Powering: A Case Study of a FLOSS Project. In: Ågerfalk, P., Boldyreff, C., González-Barahona, J.M., Madey, G.R., Noll, J. (eds.) OSS 2010. IFIP AICT, vol. 319, pp. 29–41. Springer, Heidelberg (2010)
9. Capiluppi, A., Baravalle, A., Heap, N.W.: From "community" to "commercial" floss – the case of moodle. In: Proc. Third Workshop on Emerging Trends in Free/Libre/Open Source Software Research and Development, pp. 11–16. ACM (2010)
10. Capiluppi, A., Fernández-Ramil, J.: Studying the evolution of open source systems at different levels of granularity: Two case studies. In: Proc. 7th International Workshop on Principles of Software Evolution (IWPSE), pp. 113–118. IEEE Computer Society, Washington, DC (2004)
11. Capiluppi, A., Michlmayr, M.: From the cathedral to the bazaar: An empirical study of the lifecycle of volunteer community projects. In: Feller, J., Fitzgerald, B., Scacchi, W., Silitti, A. (eds.) Open Source Development, Adoption and Innovation. IFIP, vol. 234, pp. 31–44. Springer, Heidelberg (2007)
12. Capra, E., Francalanci, C., Merlo, F.: An empirical study on the relationship between software design quality, development effort and governance in open source projects. IEEE Transactions on Software Engineering 34(6), 765–782 (2008)
13. Capra, E., Francalanci, C., Merlo, F., Rossi Lamastra, C.: A Survey on Firms' Participation in Open Source Community Projects. In: Boldyreff, C., Crowston, K., Lundell, B., Wasserman, A.I. (eds.) OSS 2009. IFIP AICT, vol. 299, pp. 225–236. Springer, Heidelberg (2009)
14. Crowston, K., Wei, K., Howison, J., Wiggins, A.: Free/libre open-source software development: What we know and what we do not know. ACM Computing Surveys 44(2) (2012)
15. Dahlander, L., Magnusson, M.G.: Relationships between open source software companies and communities: Observations from nordic firms. Research Policy 34(4), 481–493 (2005)
16. Fenton, N.E., Pfleeger, S.L.: Software metrics: a practical and rigorous approach. Thomson (1996)
17. Guba, E.: Criteria for assessing the trustworthiness of naturalistic inquiries. Educational Communication and Technology 29(2), 75–91 (1981)
18. Hofmeister, C., Nord, R., Soni, D.: Applied Software Architecture: A Practical Guide for Software Designers. Addison-Wesley Professional (2000)
19. Hou, D.: Studying the evolution of the Eclipse Java editor. In: ECLIPSE 2007: Proc. OOPSLA Workshop on Eclipse Technology Exchange, pp. 65–69. ACM, New York (2007)
20. Igarashi, A., Pierce, B.C.: On inner classes. Information and Computation 177(1), 56–89 (2002)
21. Li, W., Henry, S.: Object-oriented metrics that predict maintainability. The Journal of Systems and Software 23(2), 111–122 (1993)
22. Martinez-Romo, J., Robles, G., González-Barahona, J.M., Ortuño-Perez, M.: Using social network analysis techniques to study collaboration between a floss community and a company. In: Russo, B., Damiani, E., Scott Hissam, B.L., Succi, G. (eds.) Open Source Development, Communities and Quality, pp. 171–186. Springer, Heidelberg (2008)
23. McCabe, T.J., Butler, C.W.: Design complexity measurement and testing. Communications of the ACM, 1415–1425 (December 1989)
24. Mens, T., Fernández-Ramil, J., Degrandsart, S.: The evolution of Eclipse. In: Proc. 24th International Conference on Software Maintenance (ICSM), pp. 386–395 (October 2008)
25. Merlo, E., Antoniol, G., Di Penta, M., Rollo, V.F.: Linear complexity object-oriented similarity for clone detection and software evolution analyses. In: Proc. 20th IEEE International Conference on Software Maintenance (ICSM), pp. 412–416. IEEE Computer Society, Washington, DC (2004)
26. Raymond, E.S.: The Cathedral and the Bazaar. O'Reilly & Associates, Inc., Sebastopol (1999)

27. Robles, G., Dueñas, S., González-Barahona, J.M.: Corporate involvement of libre software: Study of presence in debian code over time. In: Feller, J., Fitzgerald, B., Scacchi, W., Sillitti, A. (eds.) Open Source Development, Adoption and Innovation, pp. 121–132. Springer, Heidelberg (2007)
28. Robles, G., Gonzalez-Barahona, J.M., Herraiz, I.: Evolution of the core team of developers in libre software projects. In: Proc. 6th IEEE International Working Conference on Mining Software Repositories (MSR), pp. 167–170 (2009)
29. Rossi, C., Bonaccorsi, A.: Why profit-oriented companies enter the os field?: intrinsic vs. extrinsic incentives. In: Proc. 5th Workshop on Open Source Software Engineering (WOSSE). ACM, New York (2005)
30. Santos Jr, C.D., Kuk, G., Kon, F., Suguiura, R.: The inextricable role of organizational sponsorship for open source sustainability. In: Proc. 2nd Workshop Towards Sustainable Open Source (2011)
31. Schaarschmidt, M., von Kortzflieisch, H.F.: Divide et impera! the role of firms in large open source software consortia. In: Proc. 15th Americas Conference on Information Systems, AMCIS (2009)
32. Shibuya, B., Tamai, T.: Understanding the process of participating in open source communities. In: Proc. 2nd Workshop on Emerging Trends in Free/Libre/Open Source Software Research and Development (2009)
33. Wermelinger, M., Yu, Y.: Analyzing the evolution of eclipse plugins. In: Proc. International Working Conference on Mining Software Repositories (MSR), pp. 133–136. ACM, New York (2008)
34. Wermelinger, M., Yu, Y., Lozano, A.: Design principles in architectural evolution: a case study. In: Proc. 24th International Conference on Software Maintenance (ICSM), pp. 396–405 (2008)
35. Wermelinger, M., Yu, Y., Lozano, A., Capiluppi, A.: Assessing architectural evolution: a case study. International Journal of Empirical Software Engineering, 623–666 (2011)
36. Wermelinger, M., Yu, Y., Strohmaier, M.: Using formal concept analysis to construct and visualise hierarchies of socio-technical relations. In: Proc. 31st International Conference on Software Engineering (ICSE), Companion Volume, pp. 327–330. IEEE (2009)
37. Yin, R.K.: Case Study Research: Design and Methods, 3rd edn. SAGE Publications (2003)

Exploring the Role of Outside Organizations in Free / Open Source Software Projects

Darren Forrest, Carlos Jensen, Nitin Mohan, and Jennifer Davidson

School of EECS, Oregon State University, Corvallis OR 97331, USA
{forresda,jenseca,mohanni,davidsje}@eecs.orst.edu

Abstract. Free/Open Source Software (FOSS) projects have a reputation for being grass-roots efforts driven by individual contributors volunteering their time and effort. While this may be true for a majority of smaller projects, it is not always the case for large projects. As projects grow in size, importance and complexity, many come to depend on corporations, universities, NGO's and governments, for support and contributions, either financially or through seconded staff. As outside organizations get involved in projects, how does this affect their governance, transparency and direction? To study this question we gathered bug reports and commit logs for GCC and the Linux Kernel. We found that outside organizations contribute a majority of code but rarely participate in bug triaging. Therefore their code does not necessarily address the needs of others and may distort governance and direction. We conclude that projects should examine their dependence on outside organizations.

Keywords: Governance, Contributor affiliation, Participation metrics, Community sustainability.

1 Introduction

Free/Open Source Software (FOSS) development is a key part of our modern IT infrastructure, responsible for the running of core Internet and server infrastructure. The governance and management of FOSS projects is therefore an essential concern for the continued growth and evolution of the Internet.

FOSS development differs from "traditional" closed-source software in a number of fundamental aspects. One important aspect is that it is not only possible for anyone to view and use FOSS code, but that projects depend on an open participation model where anyone can contribute, and where the best ideas win. This FOSS development ideology is a key strength, as it enables a large and diverse group of developers to pool resources to develop software benefiting everyone.

The culture surrounding FOSS projects can differ substantially, and studies have been done documenting these cultures [16]. In general FOSS projects are seen as meritocracies, where an individual contributors' worth and influence is based upon the quantity and quality of their past contributions to the community. Because of this, despite the fact that FOSS participation is driven by altruism and collaboration [3],

I. Hammouda et al. (Eds.): OSS 2012, IFIP AICT 378, pp. 201–215, 2012.
© IFIP International Federation for Information Processing 2012

there is inherent tension and competition within projects. "Because Apache is a meritocracy, even though all mailing list subscribers can express an opinion by voting, their action may be ignored unless they are recognized as serious contributors" [14].

This inherent competition may be part of the reason why many of FOSS projects are seen as hostile to those trying to join. In a meritocracy, increasing the number of participants means increased competition for resources, or in this case attention and influence. It may therefore be in contributors' interest to erect barriers to ensure fewer people join. Even if one adopts a more benign view of humanity, developers in a meritocracy that primarily rewards code contributions (as is the case with most FOSS projects) are unlikely to "waste" their time writing documentation or mentoring newcomers, as these activities are not rewarded. These factors may in part account for the perceived elitism of some long time FOSS contributors, which can manifest itself in hostility and flaming of newcomers [2, 10].

Another common perception is that FOSS projects are predominantly driven by volunteer efforts. While this was true in the early days, and is still likely true for many smaller projects, studies have shown that a growing number of FOSS developers receive some form of compensation for participation [8]. This compensation can take a number of forms, including release time from other work or monetary or resource donations to fund the work of core project members. This is especially common in larger and more important projects [11].

To a certain extent, compensation is a necessary response to the increased needs of large and important projects. While smaller projects can afford to adopt a more ad-hoc work and leadership model, larger and more crucial projects require more oversight and leadership, something that is difficult to provide with volunteer effort. The fact that an increasing number of FOSS developers are making a living through these projects is a sign of a healthy eco-system. These economic incentives can change the dynamics of FOSS projects. Regardless of whether paid developers are in a leadership position initially, they will tend to drift toward such position because of the meritocracy system. They will be able to dedicate more time to the project, and thus gain more influence.

The distributed organization of FOSS projects and ability for anyone to modify the source code is at the core of what makes FOSS successful. This freedom has to be balanced against the needs of the community, which necessitates cooperation and coordination. The responsibility for managing FOSS projects is in the hands of project maintainers. These individuals manage the code; they are responsible for choosing which contributions to incorporate into a release, and who has the ability to submit code. Because of these powers, they have a measure of control over the direction and participation of the project above and beyond any planning or leadership activities [19, 24].

Control of the code, and thus the direction of a FOSS project, is important. A project may end up alienating, or neglecting the needs of a subset of their users if these are not represented in the project. This is a very real problem. The code-base of the Linux Kernel for instance has ballooned [25] as hardware manufacturers add support for high-performance hardware. While the rapid growth of the code-base may be of only minor concern to those running large data-centers, it can be a serious concern for those wishing to run Linux on minimal hardware.

Despite the importance of code, this is not the only way to contribute to projects. People contribute through bug reporting, documentation, mailing list discussions, mentorship, or governance. It is therefore important to track and understand how participation in these different activities contributes to the health of projects, and the influence different organizations exert through these activities. However, most FOSS projects and researchers focus on only one participation metric. This may lead to a distorted view of what is taking place within their community.

This knowledge is not just important to the projects themselves, but to potential FOSS adopters or developers. Understanding who is supporting and influencing the project is crucial to making better decisions about whether this is a project worth investing in. Having broad support is important; an indicator of the potential and sustainability of a project. The recent and highly public fork of the OpenOffice project should serve as an example of the risks that can be manifest if the direction of a project differs from the desires of the community. The Linux Foundation recognizes the importance of such information in risk analysis and issues a yearly report on its contributor base [15]. Our research may enhance the risk analysis that businesses and other organizations must do by examining the importance of complimentary metrics.

In this exploratory work, we perform a preliminary analysis comparing different metrics tracking participation and influence in projects, whether businesses and other organizations are biased in their participation. To this end we focused on two research questions:

RQ1: Does bug reporting correlate with code contributions for large organizations?

RQ2: Is there evidence of participation bias, and if so in what direction do organizations tend to lean?

It is important to note that the purpose of our study is not to malign the sponsorship or participation of corporations or governments in FOSS, but to show how these may skew the dynamics of a FOSS project. This influence may not be negative; having professional developers on-board can make a project more successful. However, it is important to be aware of what impact sponsorship can have, and manage the influence that these may have.

In the next section of this paper we review related work. We then discuss our methodology and follow with our key findings, and describe their implications for the future study of FOSS communities and their governance. Given that this is an exploratory study, we follow up with a discussion of the limitations of the study, and important future work. Finally, we wrap up with our conclusions.

2   Related Work

There is a growing body of work examining the development practices and governance of FOSS projects [4, 11, 12, 24]. One finding is that FOSS community structure is incredibly diverse. Where one organization might have a well-defined structure of who is doing what, others may operate on a much more ad-hoc fashion.

A number of studies of FOSS communities have relied on bug reporting and code commit records. Ko and Chilana used bug reports to look at how power users impacted the bug reporting process. This can be an especially powerful approach when combined with linguistic analysis of bug reports [12, 13]. Sandusky and Gasser studied bug reports from the Mozilla project to investigate negotiations between reporters and developers [23]. Gall et al studied the evolution of FOSS projects using concurrent versions system (CVS) data for the PACS project [6]. German also used CVS data to study software evolution, but focused on visualization of the development process [7].

To the best of our knowledge no one has used an exhaustive set of project metrics to study FOSS participation. Bug reports, code commits and mailing lists have been used together to explore feature tracking [5], knowledge reuse [17], and the development process [20]. Antoniol et al. sought to connect bug reports with code repository information to allow for easier searching [1]. Each of these combined data from different sources, but did not examine the affiliations of the participants.

Nearest to our work is a series of surveys of FOSS developers and projects (although somewhat dated) [8, 9, 18, 22]. These surveys covered a myriad of topics from demographics to ideology, methodology, and motivations of contributors. Most telling from these studies and further verified by [11] was the employment status of FOSS developers. According to [8], more than 50 percent of contributors are somehow compensated for FOSS development. Jensen found this to be especially true of core developers [11]. Nguyen et al. found that whether bug reporters are paid or voluntary has an effect on the time taken to resolve an issue for some projects [21]. They also found that developers paid to work on FOSS projects were able to resolve more issues because of the increased amount of time those developers had for work on the project.

Most developers work on more than one FOSS project and development is dominated by a few core developers. More than 60% of FOSS participants work on two or more projects [9]. The Orbiten Free Software Survey covered 12,706 developers in 3,149 projects and found that the top 10% of respondents contributed more than 70% of the code. The top ten authors alone contributed almost 20% of all code [8]. This distribution coupled with the meritocracy model suggests that a small number of contributors have very heavy influence over the direction of projects.

According to Bonaccorsi and Rossi, individuals and firms have different motivations for participating in FOSS projects [3]. Firms' motivations for contributing centered on the economic and technological, while individuals were driven by social and personal reasons. Ye and Kishida found that a desire to learn is one of the core motivations for individuals seeking to become involved in FOSS [26]. They also found that community membership and reputation is important to developers.

Joining FOSS projects is not without costs or hurdles [16]. Prospective contributors must familiarize themselves with the constantly changing software as well as any design decisions made or tools used. Von Krogh goes on to say that "the alleged hobbyist culture of open source may not apply at all" [17].

3   Methodology

In order to examine our two research questions, even in an exploratory fashion, we needed to carefully narrow our scope. The selection of projects was some concern to the design of the research. We found that many small and medium projects simply did not have enough contributors or sponsors to explore these issues. We therefore restricted our investigation to the Linux Kernel 2.6 and GCC.

We chose these projects because they use complete e-mail addresses in bugzilla and code repositories, data we needed to track contributors. These projects included a diverse enough population that we had a reasonable chance to find and study interesting behaviors. Finally these projects had open and widely available mailing list archives, for future exploration.

To gather data on participation in bug triaging (either as a reporter or as a debugger), we collected the complete bug report and revision history database for each project. We collected and analyzed more than 95% of the bug reports. The remaining bug reports were unavailable due to insufficient permissions, database errors or malformed content.

From these records we extracted the email addresses of anyone who contributed to bug reports. We took the domain from the email addresses and used the publicsuffix 1.0.2 python module (http://pypi.python.org/pypi/publicsuffix) to consolidate domains. The crowd-sourced public suffix effort by Mozilla helped us effectively collapse subdomains such as us.ibm.com and ca.ibm.com to ibm.com. For the purposes of this study we chose not to differentiate between different types of contributors to bug reports. While it is true that those reporting bugs have a different level of influence than those working to fix bugs, they all participate in the public debate about the improvement of the project.

Because we are interested in investigating the influence organizations have on projects, we chose to lump all contributors from an organization together. An organization with a very small number of very active contributors could have more influence than one having a large number of occasional contributors. In order to manage the long tail of occasional contributors, we capped our data such that each domain had to have at least five unique contributors to be included. While it is possible that this could lead to the exclusion of high-volume contributors, it is unlikely that this would affect our understanding of influence and sponsorship.

To make the analysis more meaningful, we grouped organizations together by type: email provider, corporate domain, FOSS project, FOSS umbrella organization, educational institution, government agency, technical association, and unknown. If an email account was provided through some paid relationship or free signup with no other membership requirement, the domain was categorized as an email provider. The same approach applied to domains that were clearly maintained by an individual. FOSS project domains received their own classification while domains that were specifically related to FOSS projects (or FOSS in general), but were not the project itself we categorized separately as a FOSS umbrella organization. Examples of this would be linux.com and gnu.org. Technical associations such as ieee.org and acm.org were categorized separately as well.

For code submissions we gathered the complete commit logs from the projects' code repository. From these we performed the same email parsing and categorization as we did for the bug repository. One central list of domains was used to reduce the risk of incorrect categorization between the two data sources.

Data from bug reports and code repository logs for the Linux Kernel 2.6 was collected from November 6th 2002, through July 29th, 2010. Data for GCC was collected from August 3rd, 1999 through July 30th, 2010.

4   Results and Discussion

If we look at the number of contributors by affiliation, those associated with email provider domains dominate bug reporting (Figure 1), with as many contributors in this category as there are in all the others combined. While the numbers are surprising, it is not an entirely unexpected result, as the barriers to submitting a bug report are generally low, and thus we expected broad participation. Second, a number of paid programmers are likely to not want to disclose their affiliation when reporting bugs in order to protect their employers, deflating the numbers for the other categories.

When we look at code contributions, we see a different trend. Contributors from email provider domains were eclipsed by those from corporate domains. This is also not surprising, since end-users are willing or able to contribute code. Furthermore, contributing code requires a greater time investment; therefore, we expect to see more dedicated, professional programmers. This matches the findings of the Linux Foundation's report that corporations are very active in the coding of the Linux Kernel [15].

When we compare bug reporting and code contribution for the Kernel, it is clear that there is a shift in participation, with corporations and other organizations being more involved in coding rather than identifying problems or addressing the complaints of users. Keep in mind that diagrams in Figure 1 are on a logarithmic scale, so seemingly small differences can be very significant.

Another interesting finding is that in the Kernel project there are more unique code contributors from each of the different domain categories than bug reporters. This is somewhat distorted by our filtering of data, but it is still amazing how big the difference there is. Furthermore, because we are only tracking successful code submissions, the number of people trying to contribute code could be even larger. We do not see the same pattern for the GCC project, except for corporate contributors.

Unique Bug Reporters

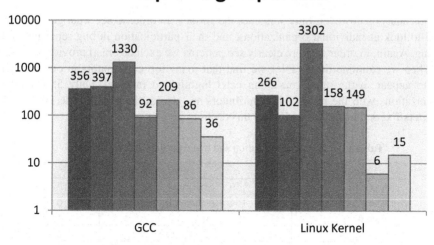

Unique Code Contributors

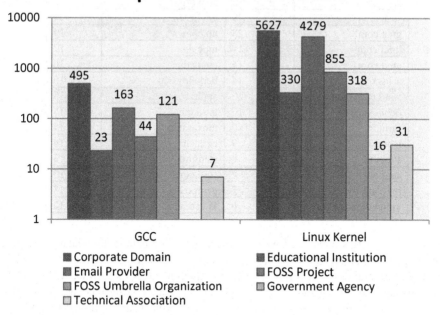

Fig. 1. Categories of participation for GCC and Linux Kernel. Logarithmic scale

So what is going on here? Assuming that bug reporters are not reporting massive numbers of bugs each while code contributors only ever submit one or a handful of code patches, it appears that the Kernel project is driven by a self-centered development philosophy rather than by community needs. By this we mean that people are contributing code because they think the features or improvements will be useful rather than because someone has requested such features or fixes. The discussion about the evolution of the project is not occurring in a public forum.

This analysis however, only scratches the surface. In order to see what goes on, we need to look at individual organizations, and their participation in bug reporting and coding. Again, in order to more clearly see patterns we exclude email providers.

When we examine these tables we find that many top contributors in one column fail to appear in the other (matching pairs highlighted in blue). Only 55% of the organizations with the most code contributors are also in the top 20 in terms of bug reporters/fixers. For the Linux Kernel this drops to 30%.

Table 1. GCC code contribution and bug reporting (top 20 domains)

Unique code contributors		Unique bug reporters	
redhat.com	150	gnu.org	174
gnu.org	104	redhat.com	61
ibm.com	70	ibm.com	55
adacore.com	55	debian.org	46
codesourcery.com	47	sourceforge.net	35
google.com	38	mit.edu	27
apple.com	30	acm.org	26
suse.com	29	intel.com	24
gnat.com	23	hp.com	19
intel.com	17	mpg.de	17
amd.com	14	cmu.edu	16
arm.com	14	berkeley.edu	16
sourceforge.net	12	apple.com	15
debian.org	10	nasa.gov	15
inria.fr	9	utexas.edu	14
ispras.ru	9	cern.ch	14
st.com	8	stanford.edu	13
acm.org	7	suse.com	13
hp.com	7	gentoo.org	13
kpitcummins.com	6	kth.se	12

So what does this mean, and why does it matter? We believe this data shows that some organizations are strategic in how they invest their efforts, choosing to either leverage their strengths (for instance hardware manufacturers like AMD, ARM and TI who have special insight into their own products) or addressing their needs without necessarily contributing to the overall needs of the project (as expressed in the bugs being reported), exemplified here by Google and Novell, among others.

Other organizations choose a different approach, working much closer with the community, regardless of whether they are a hardware provider or services companies. Exemplars here are IBM, Intel, and Redhat, among others, who despite having a vested interest in supporting their own needs balance coding with community engagement. The next step is to see whether participant numbers translate to actual activity, as some organizations can have few people contributing a lot, or a lot of people contributing very little. Table 3 shows us that for the GCC project at least, the number of organizations that have more people working on the code rather than contributing and addressing bugs is small, only 8 total. However, if we look at the average number of contributions, we see another source of distortion. Except for the organizations highlighted, the average number of bug contributions per bug reporter is much smaller than the average code contributions per coder. Most organizations may therefore be even more biased toward code contributions than initially thought.

Table 2. Linux Kernel code contribution and bug reporting (top 20 domains)

Unique code contributors		Unique bug reporters	
ibm.com	721	ibm.com	115
intel.com	571	osdl.org	112
fujitsu.com	478	intel.com	47
redhat.com	409	gentoo.org	36
kernel.org	367	redhat.com	32
google.com	228	sourceforge.net	30
ti.com	209	debian.org	26
sgi.com	203	suse.com	22
linutronix.de	187	hp.com	18
novell.com	145	kernel.org	13
suse.com	132	bigfoot.com	12
amd.com	130	linux.com	12
freescale.com	125	mit.edu	11
nokia.com	104	hut.fi	10
hp.com	96	ubuntu.com	9
atheros.com	89	amd.com	9
samsung.com	88	fujitsu.com	9
infradead.org	83	cornell.edu	8
mvista.com	81	ieee.org	8
oracle.com	78	tudelft.nl	7

When we turn our attention to the Linux Kernel project we see an even more biased situation. If we rank organizations by the ratio of code contributors to bug reporters/fixers, we find 33 organizations with a code bias, and then a very sharp drop-off. More importantly, the contributions of these code and bug contributors is even more lopsided than in the GCC case, with only the Kernel.org team having bug reporters who are more active than their code contributors.

Again, what does this mean? It is important to emphasize that there is nothing wrong with organizations contributing large amounts of code; these are very significant contributions. The concern however is that unless these organizations are otherwise engaged in the greater discussion about direction and governance, the contributions may not align with the needs of the project in question. Said another way, if organizations do not get involved in the community discussion (via bug reporting, in this case), they may be effectively ignoring the community.

One very likely situation is that these organizations are responding to bugs reported by their customers directly, or from internal users, circumventing the official bug reporting channels. While this might be understandable from a corporate perspective, this can make it harder to optimally allocate resources, prevent duplication of efforts and make debugging of complex problems difficult for the project overall.

Table 3. GCC contributions ordered by coder/bug reporter ratio

Domain	Unique Contributors			Contributions per contributor		
	Code	Bug	Ratio	Code	Bugs	Ratio
google.com	38	6	6.333	34.184	2.333	14.652
codesourcery.com	47	8	5.875	43.766	43.875	0.998
redhat.com	150	61	2.459	52.620	15.000	3.508
suse.com	29	13	2.231	221.103	9.077	24.359
apple.com	30	15	2.000	69.300	12.733	5.443
arm.com	14	7	2.000	14.000	1.571	8.912
ibm.com	70	55	1.273	21.314	4.945	4.310
columbia.edu	5	5	1.000	17.200	1.400	12.286
inria.fr	9	11	0.818	4.444	5.273	0.843
st.com	8	10	0.800	12.500	1.900	6.579
intel.com	17	24	0.708	138.765	1.958	70.871
kpitcummins.com	6	10	0.600	1.167	2.200	0.530
gnu.org	104	174	0.598	70.356	145.414	0.484
gentoo.org	5	13	0.385	2.800	3.538	0.791
hp.com	7	19	0.368	25.571	3.947	6.479
sourceforge.net	12	35	0.343	14.500	3.743	3.874
acm.org	7	26	0.269	16.286	2.423	6.721
debian.org	10	46	0.217	19.700	10.478	1.880

That said, we believe we see clear evidence of corporate strategies with regard to participation on FOSS emerging from our data. For instance, compare the participation of Google and IBM employees across both projects. While IBM does favor code contributions, they still actively participate in bug tracking. We could say that IBM seems to have a balanced approach to participation as the pattern is consistent across the two projects. Google on the other hand seems to consistently follow a very different policy, with very few people reporting bugs, and the bulk of employees focusing exclusively on code. While this could be a coincidence, the pattern seems clear, and it would be surprising to learn that there wasn't some corporate or incentive policy reinforcing this. Whether that is in the interest of the FOSS projects affected is an open question and one we don't attempt to answer, but it would likely be in the projects' interest to be aware of these patterns.

Table 4. Linux Kernel code commits to bug reporting ratio

Domain	Unique Contributors			Contributions per contributor		
	Code	Bug	Ratio	Code	Bugs	Ratio
fujitsu.com	478	9	53.111	18.866	1.333	14.153
google.com	228	5	45.6	18.741	1.400	13.386
sgi.com	203	7	29	42.291	12.857	3.289
kernel.org	367	13	28.231	41.507	70.692	0.587
amd.com	130	9	14.444	35.400	4.111	8.611
infradead.org	83	6	13.833	140.759	42.333	3.325
oracle.com	78	6	13	184.423	5.833	31.617
redhat.com	409	32	12.781	132.770	5.438	24.415
intel.com	571	47	12.149	79.783	29.319	2.721
vmware.com	43	6	7.167	23.442	2.333	10.048
ibm.com	721	115	6.270	43.431	7.530	5.768
suse.com	132	22	6	391.856	22.500	17.416
hp.com	96	18	5.333	54.448	3.778	14.412
mit.edu	45	11	4.091	44.800	4.455	10.056
linux.org.uk	20	5	4	723.850	87.600	8.263
cam.ac.uk	21	6	3.5	52.476	2.667	19.676
mandriva.com	21	7	3	57.857	1.286	44.990
ubuntu.com	25	9	2.778	16.160	2.222	7.273
acm.org	19	7	2.714	24.053	1.714	14.033
debian.org	67	26	2.577	9.299	3.192	2.913
gnu.org	17	7	2.429	36.588	1.571	23.290
helsinki.fi	13	7	1.857	159.154	1.857	85.705
sourceforge.net	54	30	1.8	21.857	1.000	21.857
cmu.edu	11	7	1.571	10.636	1.571	6.770
ieee.org	12	8	1.5	4.583	1.875	2.444
linux.com	17	12	1.417	90.588	6.750	13.420
gentoo.org	44	36	1.222	63.068	2.722	23.170
berkeley.edu	6	5	1.2	4.333	1.400	3.095
ethz.ch	6	5	1.2	3.833	3.800	1.009
cvut.cz	8	7	1.143	22.500	3.000	7.500
hut.fi	11	10	1.1	14.545	4.800	3.030
uio.no	6	6	1	39.000	28.500	1.368
altlinux.org	6	6	1	9.500	3.333	2.850
tudelft.nl	6	7	0.857	6.167	1.714	3.598
cern.ch	5	6	0.833	2.800	1.333	2.101
osdl.org	27	112	0.241	1193.074	43.795	27.242

It is entirely possible that some of these organizations have designated email addresses for reporting bugs, or employees dedicated to reporting such issues, thereby skewing our data. This is not entirely far-fetched. Submitting a bug report in the name of a development groups' email distribution list would ensure that the whole team is notified when someone comments or addresses the issue, as opposed to only the developer who reported the issue. Initial investigations suggest this is not the case, but this is an issue that should be explored in future studies.

5   Limitations

One of the problems we faced in this study was the categorization of contributors by organization type by looking at email domains. This may have led us to misclassify domains, something that would affect the data presented here. While this may have happened, we believe it to be an infrequent occurrence as our categories were relatively well defined.

One place where this may be an issue is in the case of ISPs, where it may be difficult to distinguish the emails of employees from customers. In most cases, additional investigation revealed business rules that dictated which addresses were available to customers and which were available only to employees. Second, participants may be contributing under a generic email address, even if their contribution is part of their work commitment. While we know this occurs, the scope should be limited as most organizations see being involved in FOSS projects as good publicity, or that their name adds extra credibility to their contributions.

A second potential limitation is our decision to exclude any domains with fewer than 5 contributors from the dataset. We did this because of the sheer number of domains we needed to categorize. By applying this filter we were left with some 500 domains from over 13,000 original domains. While we may have lost some high-impact contributors, our goal was to determine the impact of organizational, rather than individual, participation in FOSS projects. Given that these were very large projects, we feel that an entity dedicating so few resources out of the project total is unlikely to have that much influence. There will always be exceptions, but we believe the overall impact of this decision is negligible.

The projects included varying information in the CVS data. For example, the Linux Kernel has a very structured format for their code commits. Each code commit has an author as well as a list of additional individuals who sign-off, review, or are otherwise included in the commit log. GCC does not follow as rigorous of a process. This difference in practices could have had an effect on our results, with contributors being over or undercounted.

Finally, our analysis of contributions, both to the debate as well as to the code base was very simplistic; a simple count. We acknowledge the fact that not all code contributions or bug report interactions are created equal, some of these will be more important than others. A simple count gives a distorted view. However, without a rating or review system for contributions, we have no objective way of evaluating the impact of individual contributions.

6   Conclusions

We found that for these large projects, corporate developers dominate in terms of code contributions. This has important implications for project governance and our understanding of FOSS demographics. Large projects may not be accurately portrayed as grass-roots volunteer efforts.

The data suggests there exist two distinct communities within projects. While these communities may interact with each other through other means (e.g. mailing lists), there is a community of coders and a community of bug reporters. While this is not unexpected, it is unexpected to see that the most prolific code contributors seem not to interact with the bug reporters—we tracked any participation in bug reporting, not just the reporting of new bugs. This disconnect can in the long-term lead to alienation and declining participation of non-technical contributors.

We also found that many projects do not currently track this kind of data, or at least they do not make it publicly available. While there may be privacy concerns with posting email addresses or calling out individual developers or companies, this has to be balanced against users and other contributors' need to know. Without this information, FOSS users and possible contributors lack the necessary information to understand whether a project is well governed and healthy.

7   Future Work

In the future we plan to expand our scope both in terms of projects examined and metrics used. For instance, we hope to look at projects that range in size. Prior research has shown that projects studied are anomalies rather than the norm in the FOSS ecosystem. Examining how smaller projects are affected would give us a better picture and help their maintainers make better growth decisions.

Our research primarily used publicly available data. While this is important for evaluating the transparency and inclusiveness of decision-making, we know we are missing part of the picture, including any private deliberations between maintainers. We hope to get the direct cooperation of projects to determine if understanding participation in FOSS projects differs with an inside view.

The involvement of government agencies warrants further investigation, as we believe that these agencies have much to offer the FOSS community. We wish to explore how these organizations contribute, and how to get them more involved.

Recent events in the OpenOffice/LibreOffice project have brought the issue of forking and the role of corporations in FOSS to the forefront. We plan to investigate these projects as well as others that have forked over governance issues to determine if our metrics are meaningful. Retrospective analysis, before and after the split, could give key insights and early warning signs to enable corrective actions if desired.

Bug reports and code commits are not the only means by which individuals are involved in FOSS development. In the future we plan to look at mailing lists, project governance, project documentation, and conduct developer interviews. These will give us a broader picture of FOSS development work. This may help in answering more difficult questions relating to measuring project health and success. We hope to better understand healthy participation.

Acknowledgements. We would like to thank Andy Ko for his assistance with scripts to extract bug repository information from Bugzilla databases. We would also like to thank the Oregon State University HCI group for their input and feedback on the research.

References

1. Antoniol, G., Gall, H., Di Penta, M., Pinzger, M.(n.d.): Mozilla: Closing the Circle, `http://scholar.googleusercontent.com/scholar?q=cache:neQwzT9 UfPwJ:scholar.google.com/&hl=en&as_sdt=0,38` (retrieved)
2. Bergquist, M., Ljungberg, J.: The power of gifts: organizing social relationships in open source communities. Information Systems Journal 11(4), 305–320 (2001)
3. Bonaccorsi, A., Rossi, C.: Why Open Source software can succeed. Research Policy 32(7), 1243–1258 (2003), doi:10.1016/S0048-7333(03)00051-9
4. Crowston, K., Annabi, H., Howison, J., Masango, C.: Effective work practices for software engineering: free/libre open source software development. In: Proceedings of the 2004 ACM Workshop on Interdisciplinary Software Engineering Research, WISER 2004, pp. 18–26. ACM, New York (2004), doi:10.1145/1029997.1030003
5. Fischer, M., Pinzger, M., Gall, H.: Analyzing and Relating Bug Report Data for Feature Tracking. In: Working Conference on Reverse Engineering. p. 90. IEEE Computer Society, Los Alamitos (2003), `http://doi.ieeecomputersociety.org/10.1109/ WCRE.2003.1287240`
6. Gall, H., Jazayeri, M., Krajewski, J.: CVS release history data for detecting logical couplings. In: Proceedings of Sixth International Workshop on Principles of Software Evolution, pp. 13–23. IEEE (2003), doi:10.1109/IWPSE.2003.1231205
7. German, D.M.: An empirical study of fine-grained software modifications. Empirical Software Engineering 11, 369–393 (2006), doi:10.1007/s10664-006-9004-6
8. Ghosh, R.A., Prakash, V.V.: The Orbiten Free Software Survey. First Monday 5(7) (July 2000), `http://www.firstmonday.org/issues/issue5_7/ghosh`
9. Hars, A., Ou, S.: Working for Free? - Motivations of Participating in Open Source Projects. In: Hawaii International Conference on System Sciences, vol. 7, p. 7014. IEEE Computer Society, Los Alamitos (2001), `http://doi.ieeecomputersociety. org/10.1109/HICSS.2001.927045`
10. Jensen, C., King, S., Kuechler, V.: Joining Free/Open Source Software Communities: An Analysis of Newbies' First Interactions on Project Mailing Lists. In: 44th Hawaii International Conference on System Sciences (2011)
11. Jensen, C., Scacchi, W.: Role Migration and Advancement Processes in OSSD Projects: A Comparative Case Study. In: 29th International Conference on Software Engineering, ICSE 2007, pp. 364–374. IEEE (2007), doi:10.1109/ICSE.2007.74
12. Ko, A.J., Chilana, P.K.: How power users help and hinder open bug reporting. In: Proceedings of the 28th International Conference on Human Factors in Computing Systems, CHI 2010, pp. 1665–1674. ACM, New York (2010), doi:10.1145/1753326.1753576
13. Ko, A.J., Myers, B.A., Chau, D.H.: A Linguistic Analysis of How People Describe Software Problems. In: IEEE Symposium on Visual Languages and Human-Centric Computing, VL/HCC 2006, pp. 127–134. IEEE (2006), doi:10.1109/VLHCC.2006.3
14. Kogut, B., Metiu, A.: Open-Source Software Development and Distributed Innovation. Oxford Review of Economic Policy 17(2), 248–264 (2001), doi:10.1093/oxrep/17.2.248

15. Kroah-Hartman, G., Corbet, J., McPherson, A.: Linux kernel development: How fast it is going, who is doing it, what they are doing, and who is sponsoring it. The Linux Foundation Publication (2008), http://www.linuxfoundation.org/publications/ linuxkerneldevelopment.php
16. Krogh, G., von Spaeth, S., Lakhani, K.R.: Community, joining, and specialization in open source software innovation: a case study. Research Policy. Open Source Software Development 32(7), 1217–1241 (2003)
17. von Krogh, G., Spaeth, S., Haefliger, S.: Knowledge Reuse in Open Source Software: An Exploratory Study of 15 Open Source Projects. In: Hawaii International Conference on System Sciences, vol. 7, p. 198b. IEEE Computer Society, Los Alamitos (2005), http://doi.ieeecomputersociety.org/10.1109/HICSS.2005.378
18. Lakhani, K., Wolf, R.G.: Why Hackers Do What They Do: Understanding Motivation and Effort in Free/Open Source Software Projects. SSRN eLibrary (2003), http:// papers.ssrn.com/sol3/papers.cfm?abstract_id=443040 (retrieved)
19. Lessig, L.: CODE and other laws of cyberspace. Basic Books (1999)
20. Mockus, A., Fielding, R.T., Herbsleb, J.D.: Two case studies of open source software development: Apache and Mozilla. ACM Trans. Softw. Eng. Methodol. 11(3), 309–346 (2002), doi:10.1145/567793.567795
21. Nguyen Duc, A., Cruzes, D.S., Ayala, C., Conradi, R.: Impact of Stakeholder Type and Collaboration on Issue Resolution Time in OSS Projects. In: Hissam, S.A., Russo, B., de Mendonça Neto, M.G., Kon, F. (eds.) OSS 2011. IFIP AICT, vol. 365, pp. 1–16. Springer, Heidelberg (2011)
22. David, P., Watermann, A., Arora, S.: FLOSS-US: The Free/Libre/Open Source Software Survey for 2003. Technical Report. Standford Institute for Economic and Policy Research, Standford, USA (2003), http://www.stanford.edu/group/floss-us
23. Sandusky, R.J., Gasser, L.: Negotiation and the coordination of information and activity in distributed software problem management. In: Proceedings of the 2005 International ACM SIGGROUP Conference on Supporting Group Work, GROUP 2005, pp. 187–196. ACM, New York (2005), doi:10.1145/1099203.1099238
24. Scacchi, W.: Free and open source development practices in the game community. IEEE Software 21(1), 59–66 (2004), doi:10.1109/MS.2004.1259221
25. System Size - eLinux.org. (n.d.), http://elinux.org/System_Size (retrieved October 8, 2011)
26. Ye, Y., Kishida, K.: Toward an understanding of the motivation of open source software developers, pp. 419–429. IEEE (2003), doi:10.1109/ICSE.2003.1201220

Two Evolution Indicators for FOSS Projects

Etiel Petrinja and Giancarlo Succi

Free University of Bozen/Bolzano

Abstract. In this paper we introduce two project evolution indicators. One is showing an increase of downloads of the project and therefore a growing interest of users in the results of the project. The second indicator is predicting the future evolution of the project with the submission of new revisions to the concurrent versioning system. Both indicators can provide evidence of the sustainability of a software project. We used the General Linear Model method to statistically formulate the two linear equations that can be used to predict the two indicators. The predicting equations were build by using two stratified data samples one of 760 projects and the second of 880 projects extracted from the SourceForge repository. The six metrics included into the final version of the two models were extracted from a set of thirty project and product metrics as: the number of downloads, the number of developers, etc. We have validated the discriminant and the concurrent validity of the two models by using different statistical tests as the goodness-of-fit and we have used the two models to predict the indicators on two hold-out validation samples. The model predicting the increment of downloads was correct in 75 percent of the cases, the model predicting the submission of new revisions was correct in 93 percent of the cases.

1 Introduction

Software projects evolve according to different evolution processes. The Free Source Software [9] projects or the Open Source Software projects (FOSS) evolution differs in several aspects from closed source software (CSS) projects [11]. The success of closed source software projects is usually correlated with the number of copies of the software product soled [27]. FOSS projects are often considered successful if there is a large number of users of the FOSS product [18]. As proposed by DeLone and McLean in their Model of Information systems Success paper [28] the number of FOSS users can represent the 'Users satisfaction' factor that is included in their model. The number of users depends on the quality of the software product and on the quality of the development process that is followed inside the FOSS community [18], [6].

The number of FOSS projects has been growing rapidly in the last decade [29]. The aim of the presented research was to identify characteristics of successful FOSS projects focusing on the number of downloads of FOSS products and the vitality of the development process. Based on those characteristics we defined two indicators of the future evolution of the FOSS project. The success of a software product is a common dependent variable of the research of software

I. Hammouda et al. (Eds.): OSS 2012, IFIP AICT 378, pp. 216–232, 2012.

projects, and due to its dependency on several aspects, it should be modelled as a multidimensional factor. The number of downloads should be considered as a metric indicating the interest of users into a FOSS product, not necessarily its real usage. Not all downloaded projects are used and there is also a large number of users of FOSS products that have not downloaded them but obtained them as part of a software bundle; for example in one of the Linux distributions. Taking in consideration these two deviations, the number of downloads of FOSS projects is still a factor that is well correlated with the number of users of a FOSS product. The research presented in this paper was based on a empirical study of several thousands FOSS projects stored in the SourceForge repository. The characteristics of FOSS projects were identified by defining and validating two indicators of FOSS project evolution based on a set of thirty measurements. Two models were studied: one is focused on the interest of users in the FOSS product, the second is explaining the potential future survival of the FOSS project by inserting new revisions (working increments of the project) into the project's versioning system. Another important characteristic of FOSS projects is the sustainability. It depends on a large number of product and process aspects. The two indicators, presented in this paper, can provide evidence of the sustainability of the FOSS project. An growing number of users and a high probability of new revisions being published is correlated with the sustainability of the project. The data collected about the projects stored in SourceForge were used for building and validating the two models following a statistical approach.

Section two provides background information reviewed for the study. Section three contains information about the measures collected, the sources of information used, the building of the two evolution indicators, and their validation. In section four we discuss the results and consider the limitations of this study. Finally, in section five we conclude the paper.

2   Background

The quality of a FOSS product is an important factor considered when adopting it or planing to start contributing to the project. The open availability of project data has supported a large set of FOSS studies. Many of those studies were focused on software measurement and especially on the measurement of its quality. Scacchi [12], McConnell [26], Alshayeb and Li [10] published observations of the results of studies comparing Closed source software projects and FOSS projects showing the differences and similarities between the two development approaches.

The Lines of Code (LOC) and their variation through time was a metric often considered and analysed [22], [11]. Crowston and Scozzi [13] analysed the FOSS development process and proposed transitions between different phases of the FOSS development process. Several studies were conducted by statistically analysing a large sample of projects. Capiluppi et al. [15] conducted a horizontal study of 404 FOSS projects focusing on the change of the size of alive projects. They observed that only a small percentage of projects is in a growing phase.

Similar studies analysing large samples of FOSS projects were done by Koch [16] that identified a relationship between the size of the project, the number of participants, and the distribution of work in the development team. Robles-Martinez et al. [17] studied the MONO project by taking in consideration the lines of code, the commits, and the authorship of contributions.

Projects available on SourceForge were used for FOSS studies published by for example Grewal et al. [20], Koch [16], or Capiluppi et al. [15]. Raja and Tretter [25] have used the data of 290 projects available on SourceForge to build and validate a model of FOSS projects survivability. Their study allowed them to propose a stable model to define the survivability of a FOSS project. The model is based on three factors: the organization of the project, the resilience of the community, and its vigour. We have adopted a similar approach to build our models, however along the three factors we have included in the study several other FOSS software and process metrics.

Various publicly available data sources were used for studies of FOSS. The source code stored in versioning systems is one of them. Code level studies done by Godfrey and Tu [22] and Robles et al. [23] are often based on concurrent versioning system tools as CVS, Subversion, and recently GIT or Mercurial. Mishra et al. [24] proposed a quality model that analyses factors contributing to code quality, such as the number of developers, or the mix of talents involved in a FOSS community. Other studies include data from the issue management system as the number of issue contributors, the time necessary to solve an issue [25], etc. Mailing lists [23] and the information available on web pages are also an important source of information for studies on FOSS projects Koch [16].

Crowston et al. [18] proposed a framework for measuring the success of FOSS projects. The exact number and type of users of FOSS products is not well-known as it is in commercial projects, where customers are usually well profiled. Crowston et al.[19] proposed to insert an automatic feedback collection mechanism directly inside the software product. This functionality has been implemented in the last years in projects as Firefox, Ubuntu, Libre Office, and others. Grewal et al. [20] identified user and technical criteria for inferring the success of FOSS projects. In part similarly to our approach Polancic et al. [21] proposed a framework for evaluating OSS projects based on simple metrics.

The FOSS development process was studied by Taibi et al. [5] and Petrinja, et al. [6]. They proposed evaluation models as the MOSST and the OMM models based on FOSS product and process metrics. Deprez and Simons [8], and Petrinja et al. [7] have compared the models used to assess the FOSS development process and identified the critical aspects of the analysed models. Some of the issues identified were the subjectivity of the assessment process, and a difficult interpretation of some metrics. In the study presented in this paper we use a set of metrics to propose evaluation models that are based on a statistically significant sample of FOSS projects and are not biased by a subjective interpretation of factors.

3   Analysing Project Evolution

Based on a sample of project data extracted from concurrent versioning systems and web pages available on the SourceForge repository, we sudied which characteristics influence the number of downloads of a FOSS product, and which factors can be used to predict the evolution of the FOSS project. Based on identified characteristics we proposed two evolution indicators. We inferred the evolution of projects by counting the number of new revisions inserted into the versioning system. The number of downloads is indicating the user's interest in the project. New revisions indicate the further evolution of the FOSS project and therefore the interest in the project by the FOSS community. The two aspects shows the expansion or restriction of the development process. We considered the increase of the two aspects as an indication of improved quality of the FOSS project. We defined a dichotomous value for both characteristics and calculate them for each FOSS project included in the study. The Equation 1 shows the definition of the download increment factor and the Equation 2 shows the revisions indicator. In both cases k represents the time period. We decided to choose one year as the studied time period, in particular we used the data available for year 2011. For building the model and calculating the metrics we used all the data available for the considered projects from when they have started. Some projects included in the study exist already for more than ten years.

$$DownloadsIncrement(D_i) = \begin{cases} 1 & \text{if } \sum_k (Downloads_k - Downloads_{k-1}) > 0 \\ 0 & \text{otherwise} \end{cases} \tag{1}$$

$$Revisions(R_i) = \begin{cases} 1 & if\, Revisions_k > 0 \\ 0 & otherwise \end{cases} \tag{2}$$

The generalized linear model (GLM) is in statistics the generalization of the linear regression approach. It allows linking the variance of each factor included in the model (independent variables) to be linearly connected with the predicted value (the dependent variable). The dependent variable can be calculated using the Equation 3. The predicted value is the sum of the independent factors multiplied by a weighting factor β summed with an intercept constant.

$$PredictedValue = \sum_i \beta_i * IndependentFactor_i + Intercept \tag{3}$$

3.1   Data Sources

The SourceForge project repository contains currently nearly 360.000 projects and exists already for more than a decade. In spite of the high number of projects only a small percentage of those projects is still alive and evolving. The large majority of them is represented only by a name, and a brief description of an idea to be implemented inside the project. Half of the projects in SourceForge adopted the Subversion versioning system and the other half is using the CVS. The GIT, the Mercurial, and the Bazaar versioning systems are not yet largely used inside SourceForge. Out of the 150.820 projects using Subversion only 66.674 have at least one revision inserted into the versioning system. In several cases the projects that are inserted into SourceForge have also an external database and versioning system. The projects are not always promptly synchronised between the two repositories. A retrieval of external project data and comparison with the data available in SourceForge could provide an interesting indications of the life cycle of those FOSS projects. We limited our study just to the data stored in different data sources all composing the SourceForge system.

We have decided to considered just the projects stored in the Subversion system. We have collected different data as the number of revisions and the date when they were inserted, for each of the 66.674 projects with at least one revision. Another important source of information about the projects were the SourceForge web pages presentations available for each project. We have spidered the pages collecting metrics as: the name of the project, the staring date, the status of the project, the issues reported and solved, the developers involved in the process, the number of downloads, the time distribution of the downloads, and others. Joining all the data collected we have limited the number of projects useful for our study. The number of projects with all the characteristics necessary for our study stored in SourceForge was 5.905. We have performed several analyses on these data and we have additionally limited their number for some studies. For the two studies reported in this paper we have considered only projects that exist for a period longer than 1 year when calculating the download increase factor and for a period longer than 3 years for building the model related to the revisions and survival of the FOSS project. The factors included into the study are simple project metrics that do not need additional explanations. Three composed factors: vigour, resilience, and organization have been calculated following the equations proposed by Raja and Tretter [25].

3.2 Building the Two Models

We aimed to predict if the number of downloads in the considered period will be higher from the preceding period. We predicted this characteristic (dependent variable) from a set of factors characterising FOSS projects (independent variables). For building the model we adopted the General Linear Model (GLM). We used the R statistical evaluation tool to automate the GLM calculation. After restricting the projects to the one that exist for more than one or three years we have obtained a sample (with 760 projects) as inputs for building the downloading evolution model. Based on the number of downloads extracted from the SourceForge repository for the years 2010 and 2011 we calculated the downloading delta factor assigning a 1 if the number of downloads was higher in 2011 than in 2010 and 0 if the number was lower. For improving the correctness of the accuracy, and the precision of the proposed model it is important that the number of projects that have increased the number of downloads (having the download increase factor 1) and those that did not (having the download factor 0) should be equal. In our initial sample of projects the number of projects that did not increase the number of downloads was larger than the number of projects increasing the number of downloads. We had to limit the number of the first type of projects. We randomly selected projects from the first group to reach the number of projects in the second group. We have prepared both a modelling and a hold-out validation sample following the stratified sampling approach. We first selected all projects that exist for more than one year and divided them into two strata based on the increment of the number of downloads. We used two-thirds of the sample for building the model and one-third for validating the model.

We have considered 30 different factors for building the download increment model and 12 factors for building the model of the liveliness of the project by predicting the future revisions of FOSS projects. Due to space constraints we are unable to present in details all the metrics considered. However just few of the factors proved to be significant for building the two models. Four factors were dichotomous (with values 0 or 1) the other represented continuous metrics. In the continuation of this section we present basic statistics of the factors included in the final versions of the models developed.

The two dichotomous factors that were included into the download increment model were ActivityRev2011 and ActivityDowDelta2010. The first indicates either there were new revisions for the project in year 2010 and the second indicates if there was an increment of the number of downloads in the year 2010 in comparison with the number of downloads in the year 2009. The two continuous factors included into the model were: the number of new revisions inserted into the versioning system during the year 2010 (Rev2010) and the number of new opened issues in the year 2011 (OpenedIssues2011). The majority of characteristics of projects stored in SourceForge is strongly skewed to the right.

The 'step' function available in the R statistical tool was used to find the optimal combination of factors that should be included into the model. The 'step' function proceeds stepwise to identify the GLM model that has the lowest Akaike Information Criterion (AIC) number. The AIC factor indicates how well the data values predicted with the help of the parametric model fits the measured data. Better the model, better the predicted data, therefore smaller the difference between the predicted and the measured data. The optimal linear model for predicting downloads increment contained 9 different factors (activityRev2010, ActivityRev2011, activityRev2011delta, closedissues2010, averageclosuretime2010, openedissues2011, closedissues2011, averageclosuretime2011, and activityDow2010Delta). We limited the number of factors to four by loosing less than one percent of the prediction power of the model. We limited the number of metrics that have to be collected to improve the usability of the model. The statistical data characterising the factors included into the model are presented in Table 1. We see that the mean value of revisions in 2010 is 103 per project. There are some projects with zero revisions and one with 3431 revisions. The number of issues reported in the year 2011 for our sample of projects is not very large; the larger is 86 and the mean is just 2.6

issues. The percentage of projects that have more revisions in 2011 then in 2010 in our sample is 65 percent. The DownloadDelta Checker for 2011 is balanced for the correctness of the prediction as discussed previously.

We have designed the final GLM model by considering the prediction power of singular factors. We obtained a list of β factors for each of the 30 factors considered for predicting the downloading increment. The prediction power of factors were: projectLongevity (0.54), revisionsTotal (0.518), revisions2010 (0.575), revisions2011 (0.602), activityRev2010 (0.625), activityRev2011 (0.682), activityRev2011delta (0.595), vigorAverage2010 (0.589), vigorAverage2011 (0.607), openedissues (0.501), closedissues (0.501), openedissues2010 (0.587), closedissues2010 (0.595), averageclosuretime2010 (0.586), resilence2010 (0.570), openedissues2011 (0.616), closedissues2011 (0.595), averageclosuretime2011 (0.6), resilence2011 (0.597), organization (0.509), downloads (0.505), downloads2009 (0.501), downloads2010 (0.505), activityDow2010Delta (0.736), recomendedBy (0.506), createdbynumber (0.502), closedbynumber (0.504), averageclosuretime (0.516), averageclosuretimeabsolute (0.509), and numberOfContributors (0.509).

If for the download increment model we consider just one factor, we are able to predict correctly the percentage of projects shown in the brackets. We see that the increase of the number of downloads in year 2010 comparing it with the number of downloads in the year 2009 (activityDow2010Delta) factor is able to predict correctly the increase in the year 2011 in 73 percent of cases. With the combination of additional factors we tried to obtain a better prediction of the downloading model. We run the stepwise calculation of the optimal prediction model and obtained a model with four factors that are shown in Table 6. We see that the activityDow2010Delta has a strong influence in the prediction model. This is evident from the size of the β factor (1.83). The other factors have a smaller influence. Nevertheless the β factors of the Revisions 2010 factor and the OpenedIssues 2011 factor are small, they can still contribute considerably to the value of the prediction, if the number of revisions or the number of newly reported issues is large.

Table 1. Descriptive statistic data of the factors used for building the download incrementing indicator

	Revisions 2010	OpenedIssues 2011	Revisions Checker 2011	DownloadDelta Checker 2010
Mean	103.20	2.6	0.65	0.51
Median	18.00	0.00	1.00	1.00
Std Dev	252.99	8.17	0.48	0.50
Min	0.00	0.00	0.00	0.00
Max	3431.00	86.0	1.00	1.00
N	760	760	760	760

Table 2. Descriptive statistic data of the factors used for validating the download incrementing indicator

	Revisions 2010	OpenedIssues 2011	Revisions Checker 2011	DownloadDelta Checker 2010
Mean	127.10	3.77	0.67	0.51
Median	23.00	0.00	1.00	1.00
Std Dev	276.02	20.44	0.47	0.50
Min	0.00	0.00	0.00	0.00
Max	2444.00	352.00	1.00	1.00
N	379	379	379	379

Before building the revision prediction indicator we have first analysed the prediction power of 12 factors singularly: projectLongevity (0.57), revisionsTotal (0.59), revisions2010 (0.74), activityRev2010 (0.71), vigorAverage2010 (0.69), openedissues2010 (0.50), averageclosuretime2010 (0.50), downloads2009 (0.50), downloads2010 (0.50), createdbynumber (0.50), closedbynumber (0.52), and averageclosuretime (0.50). In brackets is shown the percentage of correctly predicted revision activity. We see that the number of revisions in the previous year and the checker of revision activity in the year 2010 have a high prediction power. Applying the step-by-step calculation of the optimal set of factors for best constructing the GLM revision model we identified four factors: the projectLongevity, the revisions2010, the activityRev2010, and the vigorAverage2010. The activityRev2010 is a dichotomous factor (values are 0 if there is no revision in a specific year or 1 if there is at least one revision), the other three factors are continuous metrics. We have subsequently trimmed the number of factors for simplifying the model. With the trimming the model has loosed less than one percent of its prediction power. Table 3 shows the descriptive statistics for the two factors used to build the model and Table 4 the descriptive statistics of the sample used for validating the revision model.

Table 3. Descriptive statistic data of the factors used for building the revisions indicator

	Revisions 2010	Vigor average 2010
Mean	101.50	107.90
Median	6.50	10.95
Std Dev	294.37	296.09
Min	0.00	0.00
Max	3431.00	3431.00
N	880	880

Table 4. Descriptive statistic data of the factors used for validating the revisions indicator

	Revisions 2010	Vigor 2010 average
Mean	109.2	120.10
Median	5.0	8.297
Std Dev	368.63	386.26
Min	0.0	0.0
Max	4337.0	4337.0
N	440	440

Table 5 shows the mutual correlations between the four factors used to define the download increment model. We calculated the Pearson correlation coefficient. We can consider the factors weakly correlated if the correlation is smaller than 0.4. As we can see in Table 5 all mutual correlations fulfil this requirement. All the tests were highly significant with the p value that was smaller than 0.00001 in all cases. We can consider the factors independent and therefore it is not superfluous including them all into the same prediction model.

Table 5. Correlation table of the factors used for constructing the download incrementing model

	Revisions 2010	OpenedIssues 2011	Revisions Checker 2011	DownloadDelta Checker 2010
Revisions 2010	-	0.364	0.276	0.157
OpenedIssues 2011	0.364	-	0.169	0.150
Revisions Checker 2011	0.276	0.169	-	0.305
DownloadDelta Checker 2010	0.157	0.150	0.305	-

Table 6 shows the β weights for the factors included into the download incrementing model. The biggest the β weight the largest is the influence of the related independent variable to the dependent predicted value. We see that the download delta checker from the previous year (2010) and the revisions checker from year 2010 have a strong influence on the predicted variable.

Using Equation 3 and the calculated weighting factors we can now write explicitly the linear equation of the model for predicting the increment of the downloads of a FOSS project as follows:

Table 6. General linear model coefficients for the download incrementing model

	Estimate	Std. Error	z value	$\Pr(>|z|)$
(Intercept)	-1.9040894	0.1774413	-10.731	<2e-16
Revisions 2010	-0.0009697	0.0003615	-2.683	0.00730
Revisions Checker 2011	1.4808722	0.1935980	7.649	2.02e-14
OpenedIssues 2011	0.0351792	0.0135808	2.590	0.00959
DownloadDelta Checker 2010	1.8329578	0.1749270	10.478	<2e-16

$$Increase of downloads = -1.904 -$$
$$0.001 * (Revisions 2010) +$$
$$1.481 * (Revisions Checker 2011) +$$
$$0.035 * (Opened Issues 2011) +$$
$$1.833 * (Download Delta Checker 2010)$$

Similarly as for the download model we have calculated the weighting factors for the revisions model. The Equation 2 can be used to predict the probability that the project will have new revisions in the following time period (in the year 2011 in our case).

$$Increase of Revisions = 1.201 +$$
$$451.49 * (Vigor Average 2010) -$$
$$452.252 * (Revisions 2010)$$

We can test the statistic significance of the weighting factors β by calculating the Wald statistics and checking the values obtained. In Table 7 we see the β values, their standard error, the Wald statistic, the p values, and the exponential factors of the β values which show how strongly each factor contributes to the change of the predicted value. We see that the p-values for all factors are marginal therefore the factors are statistically significant.

Table 7. Wald statistic for the download incrementing indicator

	β	St. Er.	Wald	df	Sig.	$Exp(\beta)$
(Intercept)	-1.9040894	0.1774413	115.2	1	0.0	0.1489582
Revisions 2010	-0.0009697	0.0003615	7.2	1	0.0073	0.9990307
Revisions Checker 2011	1.4808722	0.1935980	58.5	1	0.0	4.3967788
OpenedIssues 2011	0.0351792	0.0135808	6.7	1	0.0096	1.0358053
DownloadDelta Checker 2010	1.8329578	0.1749270	109.8	1	0.0	6.2523523

To be able to predict the increase of the downloads or the insertion of new revisions we have to define the threshold value of the prediction Equation 3 for which the model will predict the increase. We predicted the threshold value by drawing the receiver operating characteristics (ROC) curve for the prediction model and finding the point where the successful prediction of the model was reached. This value is optimal when the sum of the probability of a correct prediction of the model (the sensitivity of the model) and the correct prediction of the missing of the required conditions (the specificity of the model) is maximized. The ROC curve helps to graphically identify the maximum of both values (sensitivity and specificity). In the case of the model for download increment prediction this value is 0.43. After computing the Equation 3 for the values of a specific FOSS project, if the value is higher than 0.43, the model predicts that the number of downloads in a specific year will be higher than in the previous year.

3.3 Validating the Models

With the selection of only weakly correlated factors we guaranteed the discriminant validity of the two proposed models. The concurrent validity of the models can be tested by checking the goodness-of-fit of the two models and by comparing the measured and the predicted values. The goodness-of-fit of the model shows how well the prediction model identifies the correct values. Several tests exist that consider the difference between the observed and the predicted values. We have used three different tests.

The -2 Log Likelihood ratio is a statistical test for comparing the fit of the model to real data. For the model predicting the download increment the Log likelihood ratio is 224. The second test we have used was the Cox and Snell R^2 which gave for the download model the value 0.18. Which shows that the model has not a strong prediction power. The third test was the Nagelkerke R^2 test which gave for the download model the value 0.24. Based on the results of these tests we can not expect a high prediction power of the proposed download prediction model. We can see exactly how precisely the model can predict the values by using first the sample of FOSS projects used to build the model. Afterwards we will use the hold-out validation sample that was composed by one third of the initial sample.

Table 8 contains the measured and the predicted values about the increase of the number of downloads between the years 2010 and 2011 for 760 FOSS projects. We can see the percentages of correct and missed predictions. The overall prediction precision is 75 percent and it is far from mere guessing (which would be the case if the percentage rate would be 50 percent) but it is still not very precise.

The -2 Log Likelihood ratio for the revision download model is 177.56, the Cox and Snell R^2 value is 0.63, and the Nagelkerke R^2 value is 0.83. The three likelihood tests gave good results for the revision model showing that the model fits well to the measured data. Table 9 shows the results of the prediction and

Table 8. Classification table for the download incrementing indicator

		Predicted increase of downloads		
Measured increase of downloads	Yes	No		%
Yes	294	85		77
No	107	274		72
%	73	76		75

the measurement of the data used to create the Revision prediction model. The
number of FOSS projects included in this test was 880.

Table 9. Classification table for the Revision prediction indicator

		Predicted new revisions		
Observed new revisions	Yes	No		%
Yes	378	63		86
No	1	438		99
%	99	87		93

The predictions shown in the classification table 8 are biased while we have
used the same data to build the prediction model. By applying the download
prediction Equation 3 on the validation sample of 379 FOSS projects we have
obtained the results presented in Table 10. The percentages are comparable to
the data used for model creation, they are just slightly lower.

Table 10. Validation table for the download increasing indicator

		Predicted increase of downloads		
Measured increase of downloads	Yes	No		%
Yes	113	78		60
No	36	152		81
%	76	66		70

By applying the new revisions prediction Equation 2 on the validation sample
of 423 FOSS projects we have obtained the results presented in Table 11.

Table 11. Validation table for the new revisions prediction indicator

	Predicted new revisions		
Observed new revisions	Yes	No	%
Yes	166	35	83
No	6	216	97
%	97	86	90

4 Discussion

The further evolution of the FOSS project from the point of view of the user and from the point of view of the community provide two indications of the success of the project. It is important to take in consideration that FOSS users are sometimes also FOSS developers and that almost always the developers are also users of products they have contributed to develop.

The results of the validation show that the two prediction models can provide hints on the further evolution of the FOSS project. The equation for predicting an increased download number is less precise than the equation for predicting the availability of new revisions related to a FOSS project. One reason for this can be a higher uncertainty of the number of downloads in comparison with the number of new revisions. FOSS products are downloaded by individuals that are not always part of the FOSS community and it is therefore more difficult to predict precisely if their number will increase. On contrary the availability of new revisions depends on the past development and stability of the development process.

If the project is downloaded by a growing number of users it means that the community implements functionality that is needed and considered useful by a growing number of users. A larger number of users can afterwards provide new bug/issue reports, forum entries, or even code contributions. A growing number of downloads is a good indicator for the future development of a FOSS project. We were able to predict the future availability of new revisions more precisely than downloads. The proposed revisions prediction equation is precise and can identify projects that will stop evolving and the one that will have new revisions in the coming time period. Having an indication of the future availability of new revisions can be an important factor when deciding to download and start using a FOSS product. If the project is not going to be improved further with new revisions, the new bugs/issues reported might not be addressed and the new features proposed will never be implemented.

We can compare our results with the results reported by [25]. They achieved accuracy of 92.78 percent for predicting the survivability of projects they have included into their training and testing samples. We obtained a similar precision (93 percent) for the prediction of new revisions and a lower precision (75 percent) for the prediction of an increase of downloads. Our testing and training samples were between three to four times larger than the one used by [25]. A large sample allows us to be more confident when generalizing the results of our study.

The factors included into the two equations show also which aspects of the FOSS project influence the further evolution of the project. An increased downloading of the FOSS product depends on new revisions in the analysed time period. If there are no new revisions inserted into the versioning system most probably the number of downloads will decrease. If the project was downloaded in 2010 more often than in 2009 it will be probably downloaded more often in 2011 than in 2010. The majority of this type of projects are in a growing phase and they are attracting an increasing number of new users. The temporal existence of these type of projects was statistically shorter than the average existence of analysed FOSS projects. It means that they are new and they are growing. A large number of new issues reported by the user base is triggered by a larger number of users and downloads. The submission of new revisions depends on the number of revisions in the previous time period and the average vigour in the previous time period. The vigour is obtained from the number of revisions in a specific time interval and it shows how strongly the project is evolving.

4.1   Limitations

The construct validity is focused on the dependent and the independent factors and how accurately they are able to model the hypothesis. Most of the measures analysed are simple as the number of downloads, the number of revisions, or the number of issues reported. Problematic could be the assumption that an increased number of downloads or the submission of new revisions indicates a higher quality of the FOSS project. The number of users of a FOSS project is not equal to the number of downloads, however an increased download rate leads to an increased number of users. The same is true for the number of revisions. The total number of revisions is not an absolute indicator of the quality of the project, nevertheless it is indicating an evolution trend of the project. Another factor used was the number of issues which are usually bug reports or new feature requests. We did not distinguish between the two, however this was not an issue for our study, since both contributions indicate an interest of the users in the project. The factor organization and the factor resilience where not included into the final versions of the two models only the vigour factor is used for predicting new revisions. The validity of the three factors was demonstrated by Raja and Treter. Based on simply measured factors we have calculated four dichotomous measures about the change of downloads or revisions. These four measures do not present construct validity issues.

The internal validity is related to the link between the dependent and the independent variables. If the independent variables changes also the dependent variable should change. We have done rigorous testing of the factors included into the two models and the internal validity proved not to be an issue for this study.

The external validity is focused on the applicability of the results of the study to FOSS projects not included into the study. All projects used for the study have been extracted only from the SourceForge repository. This could prevent the applicability of the two equations on projects developed in other environments. However SourceForge is one of the largest and oldest FOSS projects repository and the quality of data available is good. The two models have been designed based on several hundreds of relevant projects and validated with two completely separate hold-out validation samples. Therefore we are confident that if the basic data necessary for the prediction is extracted diligently, the models should be valid also on FOSS projects contained in other FOSS repositories. An extended study replicated also on other FOSS repositories could anyway benefit the external validity of the proposed models.

5   Conclusions

In this paper we have presented an analyse of a large set of FOSS projects and identified two prediction equations. One for predicting the increase of product downloads and one for predicting the further development of the project with new revisions being submitted to the source code versioning system. The two indicators can provide a hint on the sustainability of the FOSS project. Based on simple project metrics users can understand if the project will evolve in the near future. The two predictions can be useful for the FOSS community that is developing the project and also for potential new users of the FOSS product. The community can benefit from the information about a potential risk of a diminishing number of downloads and can take preventive actions. A new user can decide to start using a product if there is a good chance of its further evolution proved by the probability of new revisions published in the future. The study presented in this paper is building on top of several other studies focused on predictors of FOSS projects sustainability and success. Some of the methods we have adopted for our study could be applied to similar research domains as for example the prediction of bug/issues in FOSS projects. A higher number of users and a growing number of revisions is intuitively correlated with the sustainability of the FOSS project. Further investigations are, however, necessary to quantitatively confirm this correlation. We have built the two models by collecting data from the web pages and the source code versioning system of the SourceForge repository. Thousands of projects have been analysed and subsets of the projects were used to design two samples for modelling the prediction equations and two samples for validating the predictions. The download increment prediction equation achieved a 75 percent correctness of predictions and the new revisions contribution equation achieved an average of 93 percent of correct predictions. Both models have been tested according to guidelines and best practices available in the literature for developing new software measurements.

References

1. Kajan, E.: Information technology encyclopedia and acronyms. Springer, Heidelberg (2002)

2. Broy, M.: Software engineering – From auxiliary to key technologies. In: Broy, M., Denert, E. (eds.) Software Pioneers. Springer, Heidelberg (2002)
3. Che, M., Grellmann, W., Seidler, S.: Appl. Polym. Sci. 64, 1079–1090 (1997)
4. Ross, D.W.: Lysosomes and storage diseases. MA Thesis, Columbia University, New York (1977)
5. Taibi, D., Lavazza, L., Morasca, S.: OpenBQR: A framework for the assessment of OSS. In: Open Source Software 2007, Limerick, Ireland (June 2007)
6. Petrinja, E., Nambakam, R., Sillitti, A.: Introducing the OpenSource Maturity Model. In: Workshop on Emerging Trends in Free/Libre/Open Source Software Research and Development collocated with 31st International Conference on Software Engineering, ICSE 2009, Vancouver, Canada, pp. 37–41 (2009)
7. Petrinja, E., Sillitti, A., Succi, G.: Comparing OpenBRR, QSOS, and OMM Assessment Models. In: Ågerfalk, P., Boldyreff, C., González-Barahona, J.M., Madey, G.R., Noll, J. (eds.) OSS 2010. IFIP AICT, vol. 319, pp. 224–238. Springer, Heidelberg (2010)
8. Deprez, J.-C., Simons, A.: Comparing Assessment Methodologies for Free/Open Source Software: OpenBRR and QSOS. LNCS, pp. 189–203. Springer, Berlin (2008)
9. Stallman, R.: GNU's Bulletin 1(1), 8 (1986), http://www.gnu.org/bulletins/bull1.txt
10. Alshayeb, M., Li, W.: An Empirical Validation of Object-Oriented Metrics in Two Iterative Processes. IEEE Trans. Software Eng. 29(11), 1043–1049 (2003)
11. Paulson, J.W., Succi, G., Eberlein, A.: An Empirical Study of Open-Source and Closed-Source Software Products. IEEE Trans. Software Eng. 30(4), 246–256 (2004)
12. Scacchi, W.: Understanding free/open source software evolution. In: Madhavji, N.H., Lehman, M.M., Ramil, J.F., Perry, D. (eds.) Software Evolution. Wiley, New York (2004)
13. Crowston, K., Scozzi, B.: Open source software projects as virtual organizations: Competency rallying for software development. IEE Proceedings Software Engineering 149(1), 3–17 (2002)
14. Stewart, K.J., Ammeter, A.P., Maruping, L.M.: Impacts of License Choice and Organizational Sponsorship on User Interest and Development Activity in Open Source Software Projects. J. Information Systems Research 17(2), 126–144 (2006)
15. Capiluppi, A., Lago, P., Morisio, M.: Evidences in the evolution of OS projects through Changelog analyses. In: Proceedings 3rd Workshop on Open Source Software Engineering, 25th International Conference on Software Engineering, pp. 19–24 (2003)
16. Koch, S.: Software Evolution in Open Source Projects A Large-Scale Investigation. J. Software Maintenance and Evolution: Research and Practice 19(6), 361–382 (2007)
17. Robles-Martinez, G., Gonzalez-Barahona, J.M., Centeno-Gonzalez, J., Matellan-Olivera, V., Rodero-Merino, L.: Studying the evolution of libre software projects using publicly available data. In: Proceedings 3rd Workshop on Open Source Software Engineering, 25th International Conference on Software Engineering, pp. 111–116 (2003)
18. Crowston, K., Annabi, H., Howison, J., Masango, C.: Towards a portfolio of FLOSS project success measures. In: Collaboration, Conflict and Control: The 4th Workshop on Open Source Software Engineering, ICSE 2004 (2004)
19. Crowston, K., Annabi, H., Howison, J.: Defining Open Source Project Success. In: Proc. Intl. Conf. Information Systems (2003)

20. Grewal, R., Lilien, G.L., Mallapragada, G.: Location, Location, Location: How Network Embeddedness Affects Project Success in Open Source Systems. J. Management Science 52, 1043–1046 (2006)
21. Polancic, G., Horvat, R., Rozman, T.: Comparative Assessment of Open Source Software Using Easy Accessible Data. In: Proc. 26th Intl. Conf. Information Technology Interfaces, vol. 1, pp. 673–678 (2004)
22. Godfrey, M.W., Tu, Q.: Evolution in open source software: A case study. In: Proceedings International Conference on Software Maintenance, pp. 131–142 (2000)
23. Robles, G., Gonzalez-Barahona, J.M., Merelo, J.J.: Beyond source code: The importance of other artifacts in software development (a case study). Journal of Systems and Software 79(9), 1233–1248 (2006)
24. Mishra, A., Mishra, D.: Software quality assurance models in small and medium organisations: a comparison. IJITM 5(1), 4–20 (2006)
25. Raja, U., Tretter, M.J.: Defining and Evaluating a Measure of Open Source Project Survivability. IEEE Trans. Software Eng. 38(1), 163–174 (2012)
26. McConnell, S.: Open-source methodology: Ready for prime time? IEEE Software 16(4), 6–8 (1999)
27. Yiftachel, P., Peled, D., Hadar, I., Goldwasser, D.: Resource allocation among development phases: an economic approach. In: Proceedings of the 2006 International Workshop on Economics Driven Software Engineering Research (EDSER 2006), pp. 43–48. ACM, New York (2006)
28. DeLone, W.H., McLean, E.R.: Information Systems Success: The Quest for the Dependent Variable. Information Systems Research 3(1), 60–95 (1992)
29. von Hippel, E., von Krogh, G.: Open Source Software and the 'Private-Collective' Innovation Model: Issues for Organization Science. Organization Science 14(2), 209 (2003)

Open Source Migration in Greek Public Sector: A Feasibility Study

Androklis Mavridis, Dimitrios Fotakidis, and Ioannis Stamelos

Software Engineering Group, Department of Informatics,
Aristotle University of Thessaloniki, Greece
Aristotle University Campus, PO Address 54124
amavridis@csd.auth.gr, dfotakidis@yahoo.gr, stamelos@csd.auth.gr

Abstract. Open Source software has been recently recognized by governments as a viable and cost effective solution. However, transition to open source is not a plug-and-play process but one that requires deep knowledge of open source dynamics and of organization's operations, budgetary constraints, capacities, ethics and political agenda. As with any IT transition, there are uncertainties and risks that need to be handled in order to maximize the gains for the organization and for the society through the provided services. In this paper we present a feasibility study conducted in 15 Greek public sector organizations with the aim to discover the value this transition brings to a typical public sector organization.

1 Introduction

The benefits of Open Source Software (OSS) within public sector (PS) have been highlighted by numerous studies [6],[12],[14],[15] focusing on the the fast growth of OSS projects and open standards which offer usable solutions able to support organizations in supplying high quality services to society. However the OSS migration is not a risk free plug and play process. According to [3], the uncertainty of the quality of the OSS applications [4], the dynamic nature of the majority of OSS projects [5] and the lack of technical support [9] are some of the obstacles faced by integrators. Furthermore, while there is an acknowledged demand for financial transparency that advocates the use of OSS, there is still lack of awareness of the feasibility and viability of OSS in the PS environment. In [13] authors argue that the majority of public sector shows little interest in financial performance.

To discover the value of OSS migration and to shed light to the uncertainties that affect its viability, we conducted a feasibility study in fifteen municipalities in Greece, where we calculated the value generated from three scenarios of OSS adoption namely *minimal, basic* and *massive* based on the number and type of the adopted software solutions. To do so, Real Options Analysis was employed as a decision making tool able to capture the uncertainties faced by integrators and calculate their impact on the anticipated revenues.

The paper is structured as follows. In section two we provide background information on the Real Options Theory and tools, followed by the proposed

I. Hammouda et al. (Eds.): OSS 2012, IFIP AICT 378, pp. 233–243, 2012.

approach. In section three we analytically present the results of the study and finally we share some ideas for further research in section four.

2   Background and Proposed Approach

We argue that the value of an OSS is generated and both affected by its project's dynamics [7]. As the OSS evolves over time, uncertainties related with its provided qualities such as usability, availability and maintainability, may be introduced or resolved. However, to what extend these uncertainties will affect the anticipated value is subject to organization's capacities, competencies, resources and constraints. Hence, selecting the right OSS solutions (the more profitable) depends on organization's resilience to these uncertainties. In this respect, finding the more profitable migration scenario is not simply a matter of accumulating the value generated from the number of OSS solutions to be adopted but of identifying which OSS solutions maximize and/or maintain their values over time.

Real options analysis is a valuable decision making tool capable of exploring the volatility of the anticipated OSS value in order to provide reasoning about the viability of the migration scenario. Real Options Analysis (ROA) is based on the analogy between investment opportunities and financial options. A real option is a right, but not an obligation, to make a decision for a certain cost within a specific time frame. A project is perceived as an option on the underlying cash flows (value) with multiple associated investment strategies to be exercised if conditions turned out to be favorable.

As option is an asset that provides its owner the right with out a symmetric obligation to make an investment decision such as growth, exit, wait, and learning etc. If conditions to investing arise, the owner can exercise the option by investing the strike price defined by the option. A call option gives the right to acquire an asset of uncertain future value for the strike price. There are two option mechanisms, namely the *call* and *put*.

A *call option gives* the buyer of the option the right to buy the underlying asset at a fixed price, called the exercise price, at any time prior to the expiration date of the option: the buyer pays a price for this right. If at expiration, the value of the asset is less than the strike price, the option is not exercised and expires worthless. If, on the other hand, the value of the asset is greater than the strike price, the option is exercised. The net profit on the investment is the difference between the gross profit and the price paid for the call initially.

In a similar manner, a put option gives the buyer of the option the right to sell the underlying asset at a fixed price, again called the strike or exercise price, at any time prior to the expiration date of the option. The buyer pays a price for this right. If the price of the underlying asset is greater than the strike price, the option will not be exercised and will expire worthless. If on the other hand, the price of the underlying asset is less than the strike price, the owner of the put option will exercise the option and sell the stock a the strike price, claiming the difference between the strike price and the market value of the asset as the gross profit.

Many authors appreciated the applicability of ROA in IT investments like in [1],[2] while others employed ROA in software engineering practices such as in

[8],[10],[11]. Following the same logic, we argue that an OSS migration scenario can be expressed as a *call option,* where the owner (the PS organization) has the right but not the obligation to make the selection within a given time frame.

Before proceeding to the analysis we translate the traditional ROA variables to fit to our context of use. Intuitively we have:

1. Current Value (Net Present Value) of migration scenario (So): The accumulation of the costs of the operational proprietary software are the cash flows generated from the adopted OSS.
2. Exercise Price (X): Total Cost of Ownership (TCO) of the adopted OSS.
3. Time to Expiration (T): The time frame decision makers have to select the optimum migration scenario.
4. Volatility of the Underlying Asset Value (σ): The percentage of the cash flows fluctuations due to uncertainties introduced from the dynamics of the adopted OSS.
5. Risk Rate (r): The Cost of capital

Our approach employs three consecutive steps. The first step commences with the discovery of the uncertainties. In the second we calculate the expected cash flows and their associated volatilities in the form of (%) standard deviation, and finally in the third step we calculate the call options for each OSS candidate and we compare the results. We present this steps in detail through our presentation of the case study.

3   Feasibility Study on the Migration to OSS in Greek Public Sector

3.1   Study Preparation

We examined 85 of the 325 (26.15%) municipalities in Greece where we recorded all proprietary applications currently in use and categorized these according to their provided functionalities and domain:

- Administrative Applications
- Office related Applications
- Resource Planning Applications
- Operating System

After conducting interviews with IT managers we produced a list of OSS applications capable of providing the intended functionalities and group these into three migration scenarios as shown in table 1:

- ➤ Scenario 1 - Massive Change
- ➤ Scenario 2 - Basic change
- ➤ Scenario 3 - Minimal change

Table 1. OSS applications capable of substituting the currently installed closed source applications

SOFTWARE	SCENARIO 1	SCENARIO 2	SCENARIO 3
Office Application	OpenOffice.org	OpenOffice.org	OpenOffice.org
Operating System	UBUNTU LINUX	-	-
Protocol	SCRIPTUM	SCRIPTUM	SCRIPTUM
Document Management			
Registries Managment			
Real Estate Tax			
Traffic code	OpenERP	OpenERP	-
Water/Sewer			
Irrigation			
Payroll			
Humman Resource Management (HRM)	OrangeHRM	OrangeHRM	

We then proceeded to a closer examination of fifteen municipalities (average in population size and in IT department staffing), to obtain the necessary financial data for our ROA application. For each scenario we calculated   the installation and maintenance costs as shown below (all calculations are in Euros):

Table 2. Installation and Maintenance costs for scenario 1

OSS Software	Installation Cost	Maintenance Cost	Total
Open Office	2,000	0	2,000
SCRIPTUM	12,000	5,000	17,000
Linux	11,000	5,000	16,000
ERP	15,000	5,000	20,000
OrangeHRM	15,000	5,000	20,000
Total	55,000	20,000	75,000

Table 3. Installation and Maintenance costs for scenario 2

OSS Software	Installation Cost	Maintenance Cost	Total
Open Office	2,000	0	2,000
SCRIPTUM	12,000	5,000	17,000
ERP	15,000	5,000	20,000
OrangeHRM	15,000	5,000	20,000
Total	44,000	15,000	59,000

Table 4. Installation and Maintenance costs for scenario 3

OSS Software	Installation Cost	Maintenance Cost	Total
Open Office	2,000	0	2,000
SCRIPTUM	12,000	5,000	17,000
Total	14,000	5,000	19,000

We proceeded with calculation of costs of the currently operational proprietary software for a twenty years period. As stated before, these costs will be attributed to the cash flows generated from the adopted OSS. Similarly for each scenario we have:

Table 5. Cash flows from migration scenario 1

Years	Proprietary Purchase Cost	Installation and maintenance cost	Total
2011	103,500.00	32,500.00	136,000.00
2012	0.00	34,125.00	34,125.00
2013	0.00	35,831.25	35,831.25
2014	36,225.00	37,622.81	73,847.81
2015	0.00	39,503.95	39,503.95
2016	0.00	41,479.15	41,479.15
2017	38,036.25	43,553.11	81,589.36
2018	0.00	45,730.76	45,730.76
2019	0.00	48,017.30	48,017.30
2020	39,938.06	50,418.17	90,356.23
2021	0.00	52,939.08	52,939.08
2022	0.00	55,586.03	55,586.03
2023	41,934.97	58,365.33	100,300.30
2024	0.00	61,283.60	61,283.60
2025	0.00	64,347.78	64,347.78
2026	44,031.71	67,565.17	111,596.88
2027	0.00	70,943.42	70,943.42
2028	0.00	74,490.60	74,490.60
2029	46,233.30	78,215.13	124,448.42
2030	0.00	82,125.88	82,125.88
Total	349,899.29	1,074,643.51	1,424,542.80

Table 6. Cash flows from migration scenario 2

Years	Proprietary Purchase Cost	Installation and maintenance cost	Total
2011	98,500.00	28,500.00	127,000.00
2012	0.00	29,925.00	29,925.00
2013	0.00	31,421.25	31,421.25
2014	34,475.00	32,992.31	67,467.31
2015	0.00	34,641.93	34,641.93
2016	0.00	36,374.02	36,374.02
2017	36,198.75	38,192.73	74,391.48
2018	0.00	40,102.36	40,102.36
2019	0.00	42,107.48	42,107.48
2020	38,008.69	44,212.85	82,221.54
2021	0.00	46,423.50	46,423.50
2022	0.00	48,744.67	48,744.67
2023	39,909.12	51,181.91	91,091.03
2024	0.00	53,741.00	53,741.00
2025	0.00	56,428.05	56,428.05
2026	41,904.58	59,249.45	101,154.03
2027	0.00	62,211.93	62,211.93
2028	0.00	65,322.52	65,322.52
2029	43,999.81	68,588.65	112,588.46
2030	0.00	72,018.08	72,018.08
Total	332,995.94	942,379.69	1,275,375.64

Table 7. Cash flows from migration scenario 3

Years	Proprietary Purchase Cost	Installation and maintenance cost	Total
2011	18,500.00	10,000.00	28,500.00
2012	0.00	10,500.00	10,500.00
2013	0.00	11,025.00	11,025.00
2014	6,475.00	11,576.25	18,051.25
2015	0.00	12,155.06	12,155.06
2016	0.00	12,762.82	12,762.82
2017	6,798.75	13,400.96	20,199.71
2018	0.00	14,071.00	14,071.00
2019	0.00	14,774.55	14,774.55
2020	7,138.69	15,513.28	22,651.97
2021	0.00	16,288.95	16,288.95
2022	0.00	17,103.39	17,103.39
2023	7,495.62	17,958.56	25,454.19
2024	0.00	18,856.49	18,856.49
2025	0.00	19,799.32	19,799.32
2026	7,870.40	20,789.28	28,659.68
2027	0.00	21,828.75	21,828.75
2028	0.00	22,920.18	22,920.18
2029	8,263.92	24,066.19	32,330.12
2030	0.00	25,269.50	25,269.50
Total	62,542.39	330,659.54	393,201.93

3.2   Applying Real Options Analysis

From the collected information we where able to calculate the total budget assuming a two year period within which all employees will operate the adopted OSS solutions:

Total Budget		
Scenario 1	Scenario 2	Scenario 3
99,850	80,550	24.700

Finally the Net Present Values with 10% cost of capital was found:

Net Present Value		
Scenario 1	Scenario 2	Scenario 3
134,001	169,445	42,199

To estimate the volatilities we took into account the following factors affecting the expected cash flows for each scenario:

⋏ Popularity of the OSS to be adopted
⋏ Awareness of the OSS from employees
⋏ Dependency of the substituted proprietary application with legacy applications

Based on the scores and weights provided by the IT managers we obtained a 30%, 20% and 10% volatility estimations for the three scenarios respectively.

With risk rate at 10% and Time to expiration 4 years (the time frame to select one of the three scenarios) we have:

Table 8. Data for ROA - scenario 1

Net Present Value	134,151.08
Exercise Price	99.850,00
Time to Option Expiration	4 Years
Risk rate	10,00%
Volatility	30,00%

Table 9. Data for ROA - scenario 2

Net Present Value	169,445.39 €
Exercise Price	80.550,00 €
Time to Option Expiration	4 Years
Risk rate	10,00%
Volatility	20,00%

Table 10. Data for ROA - scenario 3

Net Present Value	42,20 €
Exercise Price	24.700,00 €
Time to Option Expiration	4 Years
Risk rate	10,00%
Volatility	10,00%

To calculate the Option Values C_0 we employed the Black-Scholes model given as :

$$C_0 = S_0N(d_1)-Xe^{-rT}N(d_2) ,$$

where:

$$d_1 = [ln(S_0/X)+(r+\sigma^2/2)T]/\sigma\sqrt{T},$$

$$d_2 = d_1 - \sigma\sqrt{T} ,$$

and N(d) is the probability that a random draw from a standard normal distribution will be less than (d). Employing available Option Value calculators[1] we finally obtained:

Options Values		
Scenario 1	Scenario 2	Scenario 3
70,845.18	115,471.65	25,642.09

These option values represent the additional value that comes from the right not to implement immediately the migration scenario but only upon favorable conditions. Going a step further Option Value C_0 depends on two variables, the Intrinsic Value (IV) and the Time Value (TV), as such,

$$C_0 = IV + TV,$$

The intrinsic value (IV) of an option is the value of the option if exercising it now and is given as:

$$IV = S_0 - X,$$

Intrinsic value can be defined as the amount by which the exercise price of an option is "in-the-money". It is actually the portion of an option's price that is not lost due to the passage of time. While Time Value or "Option Premium" give as:

$$TV = OV - IV,$$

is the real cost of owning a stock options contract. It is the part of the price of an option which the seller of the option gets to keep as profit should the stock remain inactive until its expiration. In our context Time Value is the amount of money the PS organization will loose by waiting to see how the uncertainties associated with the migration scenario will evolve over the time to expiration. Calculating the option premiums for the three scenarios we have:

---

[1] http://www.soarcorp.com/black_scholes_calculator.jsp

	Option Premium
Scenario 1	36,694.10
Scenario 2	26,576.26
Scenario 3	8,143.09

What we can infer is that the third scenario is the one with the lowest cost of waiting. Nevertheless, the second scenario is the one that should be preferred as not only provides the highest Net Present Value but also a lower cost of waiting (option premium) in comparison to the first scenario.

4   Conclusions

We have presented an options based approach for the valuation of the OSS migration in a PS organization. The application of ROA addresses some fundamental issues, like the lack of accountability and risk averseness inherent in PS environments. The method provides an alternative view to the OSS migration process in the uncertain Open Source Software realm. By perceiving the OSS migration as a risky investment, a more accurate calculation of the anticipated value of OSS employment to PS environments can be achieved. It is our intention to extend this study to other public sector organizations and to examine the suitability and applicability of simulation techniques i.e. Monte-Carlo in volatility calculations.

References

[1] Amram, M., Kulatilaka, N.: Real Options: Managing Strategic Investment in an Uncertain World. Harvard Business School Press, Boston (1999)
[2] Erdogmus, H.: Valuation of Learning Options in Software Devel- opment under Private and Market Risk. The Engineering Economist 47(3), 308–353 (2002)
[3] Gosh, R.A., Glott, R., Schmitz, P.E., Boujraf, A.: OSOR Guide- lines, Public procurement and Open Source Software. Public draft version 1.0. Unisys Belgium, UNU-MERIT (2008)
[4] Immonen, A., Palviainen, M.: Trustworthiness Evaluation and Testing of Open Source Applications. In: Seventh International Conference on Quality Software (QSIC 2007), Portland, Oregon, USA (October 2007)
[5] Immonen, A., Palviainen, M.: Trustworthiness Evaluation and Testing of Open Source Applications. In: Seventh International Conference on Quality Software (QSIC 2007), Portland, Oregon, USA (October 2007)
[6] Kovacs, G.L., Drozdik, S., Zuliani, P., Succi, G.: Open source software for the public administration. In: Proceedings of the 6th International Workshop on Computer Science and Information Technologies, Budapest, Hungary (2004)
[7] Mavridis, A., Stamelos, I.: Real Options as tool enhancing Rational of OSS applications selection. In: IEEE-DEST 2009, Istanbul, Turkey, May 31-June 2 (2009)
[8] Ozkaya, I., Kazman, R., Klein, M.: Quality-Attribute Based Economic Valuation of Architectural Patterns, Technical Report CMU/SEI CMU/SEI-2007-TR-003 (2007)

[9] Singh, V., Twidale, B.M., Nichols, D.M.: Users of Open Source Software - How do they get help? In: Proceedings of the 42nd Hawaii International Conference on System Sciences, Hawaii, January 5-8 (2009)

[10] Shaw, M., Arora, A., Butler, S., Poladian, V., Scaffidi, C.: In search of a unified theory for early predictive design evaluation for software, Technical Reports CMU-ISRI-05- 114, Carnegie Mellon University (2005)

[11] Sullivan, K.J., Chalasani, P., Jha, S., Sazawal, V.: Software Design as an Investment Activity: A Real Options Perspective. In: Trigeorgis, L. (ed.) Real Options and Business Strategy: Applications to Decision Making. Risk Books (1999)

[12] Richter, D., Zo, H., Maruschke, M.: A Comparative Analysis of Open Source Software Usage in Germany, Brazil, and India. In: Fourth International Conference on Computer Sciences and Convergence Information Technology, Seoul, Korea, November 24-26 (2009)

[13] Van Der Wal, Z., Huberts, L., Van Den Heuvel, H., Kolthoff, E.W.: Central Values of Government and Business: Differences, Similarities and Conflicts. Public Administration Quarterly 30(3), 314 (2006)

[14] Waring, T., Maddocks, P.: Open source software implementation in the UK public sector: evidence from the field and implications for the future. International Journal of Information Management 25, 411–428 (2005)

[15] Wong, K.: Free/Open Source Software: Government Policy. In: Asia- Pacific Development Information Programme e-Primers on Free/Open Source Software, UNDP-APDIP (2004)

Free and Open Source Software Adoption in Emerging Markets: An Empirical Study in the Education Sector

G.R. Gangadharan[1] and Martin Butler[2]

[1] IDRBT, Hyderabad, India
grgangadharan@idrbt.ac.in
[2] University of Stellenbosch Business School, South Africa
martin.butler@usb.ac.za

Abstract. The adoption of Free and Open Source Software (FOSS) in the education sector in emerging markets holds much promise, but should be accompanied by a well-informed decision to ensure that the potential value is realized. The research conducted provides insight into the pragmatic factors driving the adoption of FOSS in the education environment, as well as those aspects inhibiting adoption. This study indicates an increasing readiness to accept FOSS in the education sector, where the more successful organizations show a readiness to adopt a comprehensive decision model to ensure the installation of appropriate ICT infrastructure, including FOSS, for the future.

1 Introduction

One of the business sectors that could benefit considerably from Free and Open Source Software (FOSS) is the education sector [3], in particular educational institutions within the developing world. This is mainly due to the fact that education systems around the world are experiencing a range of drivers for fundamental change, including (but not limited to) globalization, changing concepts around the role of knowledge, knowledge workers, knowledge citizens, innovation systems and learning organizations, the widespread need for quality life-long learning, and the relentless emergence of new information and communication technologies coupled with their growing penetration of, and impact on, all sectors of society, including the most disadvantaged [5].

The study by Satyarajan and Akre [6] analyzes the differences between the implementation of FOSS and proprietary software in educational institutions. According to them there are two distinct views on the academic acceptance of FOSS. One view favors the use of FOSS, while the other shows hesitancy about FOSS, suggesting that it could suppress the creativity of individuals.The study by Lakhan and Jhunjhunwala [4] focuses on open educational resources and open source learning management systems. They argue that, despite continuing technical challenges, FOSS offers an approach to addressing the technical problems by providing optimal delivery of online learning.

However, the factors influencing and inhibiting FOSS adoption in the education sector in the emerging markets has received significantly less academic attention. To

I. Hammouda et al. (Eds.): OSS 2012, IFIP AICT 378, pp. 244–249, 2012.
© IFIP International Federation for Information Processing 2012

the best knowledge of the authors of this paper, no published research exists in the context of FOSS adoption in the education sector of emerging markets. It therefore focuses primarily on the pragmatic reasons for adopting FOSS.

The paper is organized as follows: The research methodology adopted in this paper is described in Section 2. Section 3 elucidates the factors that influence the adoption of FOSS in the education sector of emerging markets. Section 4 presents the set of factors that inhibit the adoption of FOSS in the education sector of emerging markets, followed by concluding remarks in Section 5.

2   Research Methodology

A flexible research design was developed for this study with the purpose of exploring FOSS adoption in the education sector of emerging markets.

The research was completed in two phases. During the first phase, existing literature on FOSS adoption was reviewed and a set of structured questions was designed based on adoption factors identified during the literature review. The validity of the questions that emerged from the literature review was tested by conducting preliminary interviews with knowledgeable individuals in the areas of information and communication technology and FOSS. In the second phase, the questionnaire was emailed to the representatives of 40 universities and higher education institutions in emerging markets, including India, Brazil, Russia, South Africa, and China.

Queries from interviewees arising from the e-mail interviews were handled by the authors: respondents were contacted by telephone to discuss any points requiring clarification.

The small sample size of this study presents limitations in generalizing the results to all educational institutions in emerging countries. In addition, the authors recognize that different factors could prevail when considering the adoption of different types of FOSS and that these differences were not addressed in this study. Finally the impact of FOSS on the education process and the pedagogical considerations that should be brought into reckoning when doing an in-depth analysis of FOSS adoption did not form part of this research.

3   Factors Favoring the Adoption of FOSS

Several factors that favor the adoption of FOSS in education institutions of emerging countries were identified in the survey. Here follow summaries of responses favoring adoption, with accompanying discussions.

3.1   Software Code Access

Access to source code is an important adoption factor identified from the research. Users value the ability to change the source code. However, in general, educational institutions do not change the source code unless they want to become part of the

FOSS development community. It is interesting to note that the majority of respondents do not want to become part of the FOSS community. None the less, they state access to source code as an important motivating factor. There are limited instances where access to source code is seen as an opportunity to extend and develop software to suit an organization's particular needs. One example is the facility to customize software in local languages, although well-designed proprietary software provides the same facility.

3.2   Software Costs

The lower cost associated with adopting FOSS is the most common factor in favor of FOSS adoption, according to this research. The initial acquisition cost of FOSS is negligible and it is usually possible to download FOSS without any application cost, except the cost to download the data. Another cost benefit cited by respondents is that FOSS adheres to open standards and can be run on different platforms, thus reducing the reliance on a single vendor. This increases competition and further reduces adoption costs. The reduced cost of FOSS remains a contentious issue. There are immediate cost benefits in the adoption of FOSS. Educational institutions would be wise to obtain a fully inclusive view of the costs debate, since this complex issue remains at the forefront of the motivations.

3.3   Technological Factors

Technological factors relevant to FOSS adoption in the education sector identified from the research include software maturity, performance, stability, usability, security and availability. Respondents' opinions were divided on whether access to source code improves or degrades the security of FOSS. The usability of FOSS is generally considered by respondents to be either better or worse than proprietary software, again depending on the application.

3.4   Support Factors

The availability of support is an important factor in all technology adoption decisions. The responses indicated that educational institutions with a strong ICT capability were able to use FOSS without external support.Where they did not have the capabilities to support the FOSS themselves, institutions that adopted vendor-based FOSS obtained support similar to proprietary software solutions. Institutions with the appropriate skills and resources have taken the responsibilities of the software vendor upon themselves.

3.5   Human Factors (*Supporting*)

An important supporting factor is that a great deal of innovation traditionally originates from universities. In academic environments, where FOSS had its beginnings and where interested engagement with this technology is more likely, staff and students can tinker and experiment with, and participate in, its continued development. The return of FOSS to its original crucible for growth may eventually lead to further innovative solutions.

4   Factors Inhibiting the Adoption of FOSS

Several factors that inhibit the adoption of FOSS in education institutions of emerging countries were identified in the survey. The opinions of respondents, given in answer to the questionnaire, are summarized below.

4.1   Migration and Operation Cost

Although FOSS has a significant upfront cost advantage and in certain instances an operational cost advantage, the costs of migrating from proprietary software to FOSS could be substantial. It is especially the unknown, or hidden, costs within this transition that are cited as an inhibitor of FOSS adoption. Indeed, this study has revealed that institutions that have migrated to FOSS for the purpose of cost-efficacy have experienced the cost of migration and maintenance operation to often exceed expectations. The fact is, deep-rooted educational systems, sometimes rife with self-interested reasons to maintain the status quo, are difficult to replace.

4.2   Lack of Resources

It is widely believed that FOSS has vast market potential in emerging countries. However, very few FOSS programmers are present in these countries. According to this study, the lack of adequately skilled FOSS resources in emerging countries hinders the implementing of FOSS. A few major vendors dominate the higher education domain [1,7]. This creates the risk of monopoly in the future. Transitions are thus rendered even more difficult as the skills in these vendors dominate the market, and will continue to do so.

4.3   Satisfaction with Existing Software Products

Many of the educational institutions responding to the questionnaire stated that they were satisfied with existing non-open source or proprietary software products. Hence, they claimed to have no reason to migrate to FOSS. In addition, the challenges presently faced by these institutions are centered around servicing the growing and diverse needs of a technologically illiterate constituency. Institutions, with their limited resources and budgets, can ill afford to spend time and resources on new, unproven products to replace that which is currently meeting their requirements.

4.4   Human Factors (*Inhibiting*)

The foremost human barrier to any technology adoption is resistance to change, a concept very well researched in the ICT sphere. Different models of technology adoption are widely used by practitioners. Skeptical users remain a significant barrier to FOSS adoption, especially in large scale migrations [2]. This factor is confirmed by the respondents in this study and remains a stumbling block for FOSS adoption. Unfortunately, it seems from the responses obtained by this research that certain top managers within the academic environment refuse to acknowledge that the learning landscape has been fundamentally altered (by the advent of FOSS).

4.5   Other Factors (*Inhibiting*)

Some additional factors were listed by respondents as barriers to FOSS adoption, but not with the same frequency or level of importance as those highlighted above. These include the following:

- Poor integration with other software (software incompatibility)
- Incompatibility with different hardware platforms (hardware incompatibility)
- A lack of information on FOSS products
- A lack of case studies of successful FOSS adoption by similar organizations
- Bureaucracy in ICT decision-making

5   Concluding Remarks

Given the complexity of the arguments presented, it is highly unlikely that a wide adoption of FOSS to replace incumbent systems will sweep through educational institutions in emerging markets. What is more likely is that new ICT initiatives will give advocates of FOSS an equal voice at the table. Just as FOSS has matured over the past decade, so will those making decisions about new ICT adoptions – they will become more sensitive to the value contribution and challenges associated with FOSS, since this innovation has the potential to deliver considerable benefits for educational institutions in emerging markets.

References

[1] Courant, P., Griffiths, R.J.: Software and Collaboration in Higher Education: A Study of Open Source Software (2006), http://www.ithaka.org/about-ithaka/announcements/ooss-study-final-report
[2] Holck, J., Pederson, M., Larsen, M.: Open Source Software Acquisition: Beyond the Business Case. In: ECIS 2005 Proceedings (2005)
[3] Huett, J.B., Sharp, J.H., Huett, K.C.: What's all the FOSS?: How Freedom and Openness Are Changing the Face of Our Educational Landscape. International Journal of Open Source Software and Processes 2(1) (2010)

[4] Lakhan, S.E., Jhunjhunwala, K.: Open Source Software in Education. EDUCAUSE Quarterly 31(2) (2008)

[5] NACI. Free/Libre and Open Source Software and Open Standards in South Africa - A Critical Issue for Addressing the Digital Divide (2004), http://www.naci.org.za/pdfs/flossv269.pdf

[6] Satyarajan, D., Akre, V.: Open Source Software Adoption: An Academic Perspective. International Journal of Computer & Communication Technology 2(5), 38–42 (2011)

[7] Wheeler, B.: Open Source 2010: Reflections on 2007. EDUCAUSE Review 42(1) (2007)

Open-Source Technologies Realizing Social Networks: A Multiple Descriptive Case-Study

Jose Teixeira

University of Turku, Turku School of Economics, Rehtorinpellonkatu 3, 20500 Turku, Finland
Jose.Teixeira@utu.fi,
http://www.tse.fi

Abstract. This article aims at describing the role of the open-source software phenomenon within high-tech corporations providing social networks and applications. By taking a multiple case study approach, We address what are the open-source software technological components embedded by leading social networking players, and a rich description on how those players collaborate with the open-source community. Our findings, based on a population of three commercial providers of social networks a suggest that open-source plays an important role on the technological development of their social networking platforms. An open-source technological stack for realizing social networks is proposed and several managerial issues dealing with collaboration with open-source communities are explored.

Keywords: open-source, social networks, entrepreneurship, facebook, spotify, netlog.

1 Introduction

This article develops a deeper understanding on how providers of popular social networking Internet sites employ open-source technologies, that are freely available on the Internet and within the public domain, in their inner technological operations realizing social network services targeting a global community of Internet users.

Even thought studies on social networks have been conducted in fields like sociology and anthropology for decades (Oinas-kukkonen et al. 2010), only more recently it captured massive attention from computer scientists and information systems researchers.

In this paper, we cross the social networking phenomenon with the open-source phenomenon by assessing how social networking providers are employing open-source technological components in their in-house software development. The open-source phenomena also gather extensive research attention in the last decades such as Stallman(1993), Raymond (2001) and Lerner and Tirole (2005).

In this research, we engaged what is role that the open-source software phenomenon plays as a enabler of the social networks and its applications.

I. Hammouda et al. (Eds.): OSS 2012, IFIP AICT 378, pp. 250–255, 2012.

2   Literature Review

The existence of recent literature reviews on social networks and applications across different disciplines such as entrepreneurship (Hoang & Antoncic 2003); marketing (Cooke & Buckley 2008); computer science (Mislove et al. 2007); information systems (Parameswaran & Whinston 2007) and (Oinas-kukkonen 2010) facilitated the process of identifying relevant literature that guided this research.

A first stream of research address the topology of networks of open-source developers as investigated by Valverde and Solé (2007), Madey et al. (2002) and Xu et al. (2005). A second research stream addresses social aspects such as communication, socialization and motivation withing open-source social networks as explored by Ducheneaut (2005), Barcellini et al. (2008) and Crowston and Howison (2005).

Both streams of research, the researchers point their lenses to social networks of open-source software developers. In this paper however, we turn the lenses from a completely different perspective by looking at organizations developing digital technology that realize social networks and how they use and benefit from public domain software artifacts developed by the open-source community.

3   Methodology

The research question guiding the preliminary research efforts was: "what role the open-source software phenomenon plays as a enabler of the social networks and correspondent applications". In this paper we address first, what are the open-source software technological components embedded by social networking players; and second, how are those players collaborating with the open-source community.

This research efforts took the form of a multiple descriptive case-study in the molds of Eisenhardt (1989), Miles and Huberman (1994) and Yin (2002). In Table 1, we present the three unit of analysis from this multiple descriptive case study. By interviewing staff from those three social networking providers, we searched for consistent patterns of evidence across the three units taking a recognized role within the same phenomenon being studied.

Table 1. The multiple case-study organizational unit of analysis

Organization	Description	Country
Facebook	Biggest and most studied social network	USA
Spotify	The leading peer-assisted music streaming system	Sweden
NetLog	One of the most global social networks for the youth	Belgium

This research was guided by the case-study process proposed by Eisenhardt (1989), we simply and modestly aim at providing a rich description of the observed phenomenon. Also methodologically inspired by Dyer and Wilkins (1991), we seek to provide a good and rich phenomenological description, emphasizing on contemporary relevance over rigor. Therefore, this paper is detached of any generalization reasoning, but rather invites the readers to thereafter address it.

In the following sub-sections, we provide more detail on methodological issues embedded on the design and execution of this research.

3.1   Preparation and Fieldwork Strategies

This research was partially driven from an event organized by the Canada-Norway partnership program in higher education (CANOE) and hosted by the University of Oslo between 22 and 26 of August 2011 in Sundvolden, Norway. This event was a rare opportunity for researchers with interests on social networking topics to meet together with industry practitioners from major providers of social networks and services.

Both the case study protocol as described by Yin (2002) and phenomenological interviewing by Thompson et al. (1989) guided the author semi-structured interviews during the fieldwork phase of the study.

A total of five semi-structured interviews were conducted by the author in a very informal setting. Small pauses were requested by the interviewer to transcript important parts of the conversation. After each interview, the author rapidly produced several textual notes capturing information he considered relevant.

4   Findings

Directly addressing the first research question, the following Table 2 presents a stack of open-source technological components used by the studied organizations. Due to informal non-disclosing agreements with the interviews, we do not reveal what technologies are used specifically by each organization but by the overall set of three organizations.

Table 2. Technological stack realizing social networks

Technological function	Integrated open-source software packages
Client-side programing languages	C, C++, Java
Server-side programing languages	Python, Java, Scala, Ruby, PHP
Database/Persitence	Mysql, ext3 file-system
Server operating system	GNU Linux kernel
Web server	Apache, nginx, php-fpm, HipHop
Load balancer	haproxy
Object cache	jemalloc, memcached
Search and indexing	ubersearch, unicorn, sphinxsearch
Configuration management	Puppetlabs
Process orchestration	cron, gearman
Network monitoring	Zabbix
Backup systems	Bacula
Version control	CVS, SVN, GIT
Statistics/BI/DW	hadoop, hbase, HIVE, Sqlite
Testing	phpunit, seleniumhq, jenkins-ci

Addressing the second research question, even if the collected data was consensual with existing knowledge, we could observe some unexpected findings evidenced by patterns on the collected multi-organizational data. Following we report three descriptive findings with potential to rise debate among this paper readership.

First, the satisfaction of the studied organizations with open-source technologies seems quite high, specially among the R&D teams. It was observable that some of those organizations ownership and governance changes led to pressures on the R&D staff to roll-out from open-source software to proprietary technology.

"we been told several times to embrace cloud-computing technologies from a particular vendor, we tried and failed several times" ... "Many proprietary , expensive and complex solutions are designed as if one would fit all" ... "Vendors are focused in attracting user base over our specific needs"

Second, the collaboration with the open-source communities seems to be taken more at a personal level than at institutional level. As reported by one of the interviewees, the support provided by the open-source community is more ad-hoc and the solution for the problems is available earlier

"we have very good contacts with the open-source community, this enable us to fix complex problems just by chatting with key developers of the project" ... "In our experience in dealing with cloud computing vendors, bug reporting was tedious, passing over slow and complex processes, often resulting in nothing"

Finally, and for an entrepreneurship perspective. Open-source was present from the beginning of the organizations venture.

"We use a lot of open-source stuff. That's what made sense" ... "We never got together and discuss about open-source vs proprietary, it just came naturally" ... " startups need to get used to the idea of rapid-prototyping cycles ... open-source software development tools are friendly for rapid interactions".

Following we discuss the implications of the previous reported findings encompassing a set of open-source technological components and three descriptions regarding the collaboration of the social networking industry with the open-source community.

5   Discussion

5.1   Theoretical and Practical Implications

Our theory testing approach did not falsify any open-source theoretical proposition refereed in the literature review. As inspired by Dyer and Wilkins (1991) we focus more in providing a good description on the phenomena being studied, leaving out space for refined theoretical contributions.

From the practical point of view, industry players can benefit from the suggested technological stack realizing social networks and applications. Moreover, our limited but in-depth description raises managerial awareness for issues that might pop-up when collaborating with the open-source community.

5.2   Limitations of the Study and Future Research

Limitations of the sample in this regard do not allow us to make any substantial assertions but these initial findings certainly point to the value of examining this unexplored issue further. It matters to apply other theoretical lenses covering fields such as marketing, entrepreneurship and social science disciplines that already deal with social networks for decades.

6   Conclusions

In our sample, the satisfaction from social networking technological developers with the open-source phenomena is extremely high. The use of open-source technological components started from the beginning, as early as the company founders developed their first software pieces.

This research contributes with a technological stack for realizing social networks and applications as proposed by our sample organizations. In addition, and perhaps more prone to foment future research, we provide a simple and rich description on how three popular and innovative organizations integrate technological components from the open-source community into their social networking platforms.

References

Anon, Facebook's Uphill Battle for Big-Brand Advertisers - WSJ.com, http://online. wsj.com/article/SB10001424052970204294504576613232804554362.h tml (accessed March 14, 2012)

Barcellini, F., et al.: A socio-cognitive analysis of online design discussions in Open Source Software community. Interacting with Computers 20(1), 141–165 (2008)

Cooke, M., Buckley, N.: Web 2.0, social networks and the future of market research. International Journal of Market Research 50(2), 267–292 (2008)

Crowston, K., Howison, J.: The social structure of free and open source software development. First Monday 10(2) (2005)

Ducheneaut, N.: Socialization in an Open Source Software Community: A Socio-Technical Analysis. Comput. Supported Coop. Work 14(4), 323–368 (2005)

Dyer, W.G., Wilkins, A.L.: Better Stories, Not Better Constructs, to Generate Better Theory: A Rejoinder to Eisenhardt. The Academy of Management Review 16(3), 613–619 (1991)

Eisenhardt, K.M.: Building Theories from Case Study Research. The Academy of Management Review 14(4), 532–550 (1989)

Hoang, H., Antoncic, B.: Network-based research in entrepreneurship: A critical review. Journal of Business Venturing 18(2), 165–187 (2003)

Xu, J., et al.: A Topological Analysis of the Open Souce Software Development Community. In: Proceedings of the 38th Annual Hawaii International Conference on System Sciences, HICSS 2005, p. 198a (2005)

Lerner, J., Tirole, J.: The Economics of Technology Sharing: Open Source and Beyond. Journal of Economic Perspectives 19(2), 99–120 (2005)

Madey, G., Freeh, V., Tynan, R.: The open source software development phenomenon: An analysis based on social network theory. In: Americas Conference on Information Systems, AMCIS 2002, Citeseer, pp. 1806–1813 (2002), http://citeseerx.ist.psu.edu/viewdoc/download?doi=10.1.1.138.1547&rep=rep1&type=pdf

Miles, M.B., Huberman, A.M.: Qualitative data analysis: an expanded sourcebook. Sage Publications (1994)

Oinas-kukkonen, H.: Social Networks and Information Systems: Ongoing and Future Research Streams. Journal of the Association for Information Systems 11(2), 61–68 (2010)

Parameswaran, M., Whinston, A.B.: Research Issues in Social Computing. Journal of AIS 8, 336–350 (2007)

Raymond, E.S.: The Cathedral and the Bazaar: Musings on Linux and Open Source by an Accidental Revolutionary. O'Reilly & Associates, Inc. (2001)

Stallman, R.: The GNU Manifesto - GNU Project - Free Software Foundation, FSF (1993), http://www.gnu.org/gnu/manifesto.html (accessed March 14, 2012)

Thompson, C.J., Locander, W.B., Pollio, H.R.: Putting Consumer Experience Back into Consumer Research: The Philosophy and Method of Existential-Phenomenology. Journal of Consumer Research 16(2), 133–146 (1989)

Valverde, S., Solé, R.V.: Self-organization versus hierarchy in open-source social networks. Phys. Rev. E 76(4), 046118 (2007)

Yin, R.: Case Study Research: Design and Methods. Sage Publications (2002)

A Qualitative Method for Mining Open Source Software Repositories

John Noll, Dominik Seichter, and Sarah Beecham

Lero, The Irish Software Engineering Centre,
Department of Computer Science and Information Systems,
University of Limerick, Limerick, Ireland
{john.noll,sarah.beecham,dominik.seichter}@lero.ie

Abstract. The volume of data archived in open source software project repositories makes automated, quantitative techniques attractive for extracting and analyzing information from these archives. However, many kinds of archival data include blocks of natural language text that are difficult to analyze automatically.

This paper introduces a qualitative analysis method that is transparent and repeatable, leads to objective findings when dealing with qualitative data, and is efficient enough to be applied to large archives.

The method was applied in a case study of developer and user forum discussions of an open source electronic medical record project. The study demonstrates that the qualitative repository mining method can be employed to derive useful results quickly yet accurately. These results would not be possible using a strictly automated approach.

Keywords: Open Source Software, Electronic Medical Record, Qualitative Research.

1 Introduction

The sheer volume of data archived in open source software project repositories makes automated, quantitative techniques attractive for extracting and analyzing information from these archives.

However, some kinds of archival data - bug reports, commit log entries, email messages, and forum postings - include large blocks of natural language text that are difficult to analyze automatically. Software development is a human-intensive activity; these qualitative data convey important information about a project that cannot be explained by numbers alone. For example, analyzing project discussion forum postings can help to explain how users are supported, who is reporting and fixing bugs, who actually commits enhancements, and how requirements are elicited.

While qualitative techniques employing human interpretation are necessary to analyze such data, qualitative analysis is a labor-intensive activity; as such, the amount of data that can be analyzed is limited by the capabilities of human researchers.

This paper introduces a hybrid data-mining technique that combines automated data extraction with human qualitative analysis. The approach is transparent and repeatable, produces objective results from qualitative data, and is suitable for a reasonably large project archive.

I. Hammouda et al. (Eds.): OSS 2012, IFIP AICT 378, pp. 256–261, 2012.

At the core of the technique is a classification scheme for classifying natural language fragments such as mailing list messages An iterative process is employed to develop a set of categories to classify natural language text, such as discussion forum posts. Inter-rater agreement measures are used to refine the list until a high degree of agreement among researchers is achieved. The resulting categories are then used to classify a representative sample of text artifacts. The results can then be aggregated to provide a quantitative summary of qualitative data.

We describe the method in the next section, including use of inter-rater agreement analysis to refine the coding scheme. The last two sections present related work and conclusions.

2   Method

The method proposed by this study employs *content analysis* Krippendorff [10], a classification technique that is frequently applied to interview and focus group data. The objective of content analysis is to ask quantitative questions about qualitative data. The approach is similar to the grounded theory method, but differs from grounded theory in that the results are quantitative rather than qualitative: content analysis produces results such as, "49% of messages submitted to project mailing lists were sent by core developers."

Our method is adapted from Burnard [2] and comprises the following specific steps:

Develop Initial Code Set. The first step is to create an initial set of codes by analyzing a small, representative sample of text fragments. Typically these would be elements in the project repository, such as bug reports, discussion forum posts, commit log entries, etc.

This is an inductive step: the researcher reads a fragment and invents a code (word or phrase) that captures the meaning of the fragment. During this step, the list of codes grows and evolves as more fragments are read and the research becomes familiar with the content; the resulting list may be large and therefore require consolidation.

Coalesce Codes into Themes. A good coding scheme has a small set of codes, with clear definitions, so that the scheme is easy to apply and can be performed quickly. As such, the next step is iteratively coalesce codes with similar meaning into a single category, and assign a new code to the category. When the list has coalesced into a handful of categories with distinct meanings, the process ends and the category codes become the codes that are assigned to text fragments during the content analysis phase.

Create Checklist. A checklist describing how to categorize a given text fragment is developed from the set of disjoint codes from the previous step. This checklist guides the coding process, providing a step-by-step decision list for the researcher to use to code the data.

Refine Codes and Checklist. The set of codes and associated checklist are evaluated and refined using a series of trials involving two or more researchers. The goal is to achieve a high degree of agreement among researchers about which code should be assigned to a given text fragment. This is achieved by having two researchers apply the checklist to a small sample of text fragments independently. The results are then compared using

Table 1. Crosstabulation table comparing coding of two researchers

			Sarah			
John	fix	impl	issue	other	prop	Total
fix	3	0	0	3	0	6
impl	0	2	0	2	0	4
issue	1	1	15	0	0	17
other	1	1	2	21	2	27
prop	0	0	0	2	3	5
Total	5	4	17	28	5	59

crosstabulation to see how they agree; disagreements are discussed to determine how the checklist or set of codes could be refined to make the choice of correct code more clear, and the process is repeated until an acceptable level of agreement is achieved.

Table 1 is an example of a crosstabulation created from a trial coding exercise used to refine the coding scheme and checklist for the case study described in [14]. Both the rows and columns are labelled with codes from the coding scheme. The cells show the number of messages coded with the row label by the first researcher (John) that were coded with the column label by the second researcher (Sarah). The diagonal, therefore, represents agreement. The table shows that both John and Sarah assigned seventeen *issue* codes; of these, fifteen were assigned by both researchers to the same text fragments. This table makes clear where disagreements lie: *prop* has only 40% agreement ($frac25$), *impl* has 50% ($\frac{2}{4}$), and *fix* has 60% ($\frac{3}{5}$), while both *issue* ($\frac{15}{17}$) and *other* ($\frac{21}{27}$) have more than 75% agreement.

Assess Inter-rater Agreement. Cohen's kappa [1, 3] is a statistic that attempts to assess the degree of agreement between the codes assigned by two researchers working independently on the same sample. Cohen's kappa accounts for the reality that a certain level of agreement would be achieved even if codes were assigned at random; as such, it is more conservative than simply calculating the percentage of agreement between two researchers, which does not account for randomness.

Cohen's kappa produces values between 0 and 1, where 0 indicates poor agreement, and 1 perfect agreement. Landis and Koch [11] proposed an assessment scheme for determining strength of agreement from Cohen's kappa values: less than .2 represents "slight" agreement; a value between .4 and .6 represents "moderate" agreement; a kappa statistic above .8 is considered a sign of "almost perfect" agreement. Researchers have to balance agreement against the effort required to refine the checklist and coding scheme in order to achieve high agreement. If "good" agreement has been achieved (kappa value between .6 and .8), and successive refinement attempts produce incremental or no improvement, it may be best to move on to actual coding.

Code the Data. In this phase, several researchers apply the coding checklist to code a large sample extracted from the project archives.

Analyze Coded Data. For example, the case presented in [14], coded discussion forum posts were combined with author IDs extracted from the discussion forums and commit logs, to create a picture of what kinds of activities different groups of project participants were involved in.

2.1 Validation

The method was applied to a case study of an open source software project [14]. The case study results show that useful conclusions can be drawn from minimally structured natural language data that are not easily analyzed using an automated approach. Also, the method for iteratively developing a classification scheme using inter-rater agreement analysis proved to be an effective approach for developing a repeatable yet efficient coding scheme. Finally, we found that qualitative analysis techniques can be employed to derive results quickly and accurately through careful transparent and validated analysis, and dividing the work among several researchers.

3 Related Work

Testing inter-rater reliability is not a new concept, and has been used in software engineering qualitative research.

For example, Henningsson and Wohlin [9], used Cohen's kappa statistic to measure whether eight people could agree on how to classify faults independently. Other researchers used the same method to test the reliability of their fault classifications, with mixed results. However, in contrast to the approach described in this paper, both Henningsson and Wohlin [9], and Hall et al. [8], used the interrater measure to test agreement post hoc, and not as a tool to resolve problems with the coding scheme. However, El Emam and Wieczorek [4] were able to use poor kappa values to go back to look at specific fault types that were causing low repeatability of code defect classifications.

Researchers studying software process assessment have used Cohen kappa statistic to test the external reliability of interrater agreement [5–7, 12, 15]. As software process assessment can be subjective, researchers identify the need to check the reliability of the results. Kohen's kappa has also been applied in fuzzy systems [16], and in the subjective evolvability evaluation of object-oriented software [13]. Also, Vilbergsdóttir et al. [17] used kappa statistics over several iterations to revise their scheme defining usability attribute values.

To our knowledge this process has not been used in classifying data mined from software repositories, and therefore as we identify this to be an area that is potentially high in subjectivity, we think the community can benefit from assessing the quality of classifications prior to making any judgements about what the data are telling us.

4 Conclusions

This paper presented an approach to software repository data mining based on qualitative content analysis, a data analysis technique that is appropriate for situations where data cannot be easily quantified by automated data mining techniques. The approach was successfully applied in a case study of an open source software project.

260 J. Noll, D. Seichter, and S. Beecham

The results of the case study show that useful conclusions can be drawn from minimally structured natural language data that are not easily analyzed using an automated approach. Further, the application of inter-rater agreement analysis in the case study demonstrates how an effective coding scheme can be created that is transparent, repeatable, and consistent. This allows several researchers to work independently on content analysis, while still producing results that can be reliably aggregated. Finally, our experience shows the method is efficient as well as effective: researchers were able to code more than 60 messages per hour, meaning we were able to complete the coding and analysis in a week working part-time.

Acknowledgments. This work was supported, in part, by Science Foundation Ireland grant 03/CE2/I303_1 to Lero - the Irish Software Engineering Research Centre (www.lero.ie).

References

[1] Bakeman, R.: Behavioral observation and coding. In: Reis, H.T., Judge, C.M. (eds.) Handbook of Research Methods in Social and Personality Psychology, pp. 138–159. Cambridge University Press (2000)

[2] Burnard, P.: A method of analysing interview transcripts in qualitative research. Nurse Education Today 11, 461–466 (1991)

[3] Dewey, M.E.: Coefficients of agreement. British Journal of Psychiatry 143, 487–489 (1983)

[4] El Emam, K., Wieczorek, I.: The repeatability of code defect classifications. In: Proceedings, Ninth International Symposium on Software Reliability Engineering (November 1998)

[5] El Emam, K., Goldenson, D., Briand, L., Marshall, P.: Interrater agreement in SPICE-based assessments: some preliminary results. In: Proceedings, Fourth International Conference on the Software Process (December 1996)

[6] El Emam, K., Simon, J.-M., Rousseau, S., Jacquet, E.: Cost implications of interrater agreement for software process assessments. In: Proceedings, Fifth International Software Metrics Symposium (November 1998)

[7] Fusaro, P., El Emam, K., Smith, B.: Evaluating the interrater agreement of process capability ratings. In: Proceedings, Fourth International Software Metrics Symposium (November 1997)

[8] Hall, T., Bowes, D., Liebchen, G., Wernick, P.: Evaluating Three Approaches to Extracting Fault Data from Software Change Repositories. In: Ali Babar, M., Vierimaa, M., Oivo, M. (eds.) PROFES 2010. LNCS, vol. 6156, pp. 107–115. Springer, Heidelberg (2010)

[9] Henningsson, K., Wohlin, C.: Assuring fault classification agreement - an empirical evaluation. In: International Symposium on Empirical Software Engineering (ISESE 2004) (August 2004)

[10] Krippendorff, K.: Content Analysis: An Introduction to Its Methodology, 2nd edn. Sage Publications (2004)

[11] Landis, J.R., Koch, G.G.: An application of hierarchical kappa-type statistics in the assessment of majority agreement among multiple observers. Biometrics 33(2), 363–374 (1977)

[12] Lee, H.-Y., Jung, H.-W., Chung, C.-S., Lee, J.M., Lee, K.W., Jeong, H.J.: Analysis of interrater agreement in ISO/IEC 15504-based software process assessment. In: Proceedings Second Asia-Pacific Conference on Quality Software (2001)

[13] Mantyla, M.V.: An experiment on subjective evolvability evaluation of object-oriented software: explaining factors and interrater agreement. In: International Symposium on Empirical Software Engineering (November 2005)

[14] Noll, J., Beecham, S., Seichter, D.: A qualitative study of open source software development: the OpenEMR project. In: 5th International Symposium on Empirical Software Engineering and Measurement (ESEM 2011), Banff, Alberta, Canada (Septemebr 2011)

[15] Park, H.-M., Jung, H.-W.: Evaluating interrater agreement with intraclass correlation coefficient in SPICE-based software process assessment. In: Proceedings, Third International Conference on Quality Software (November 2003)

[16] Vieira, S., Kaymak, U., Sousa, J.: Cohen's kappa coefficient as a performance measure for feature selection. In: 2010 IEEE International Conference on Fuzzy Systems (FUZZ) (July 2010)

[17] Vilbergsdóttir, S.G., Hvannberg, E.T., Law, L.-C.: Classification of usability problems (CUP) scheme. In: Proceedings of the 4th Nordic Conference on Human-Computer Interaction, NordiCHI 2006 (2003)

The Impact of Formal QA Practices on FLOSS Communities – The Case of Mozilla

Adina Barham

Hitotsubashi University, Graduate School of Social Sciences, 2-1 Naka,
Kunitachi, Tokyo, 186-8601, Japan
adina.barham@yahoo.com

Abstract. The number of FLOSS projects that include a QA step in the development model is increasing which suggests that a new layer may be emerging in the classic "onion model". This change might affect the information flow within projects and implicitly their sustainability. Communities, the essential resource of FLOSS projects, have been extensively studied but questions concerning QA remain. This paper takes a step towards answering such questions by analyzing QA mailing lists and issue tracker data for the Mozilla group of projects. Because the Bugzilla data set contains over half a million bugs, data processing and analysis is a considerable challenge for this research. The provisional conclusions are that QA activity may not be increasing steadily over time but is dependent on other factors and that the QA team and other groups of contributors form a highly connected network that doesn't contain isolates.

Keywords: quality assurance, test, Mozilla, social network analysis, information flow.

1 Introduction

In recent years open source software has become a viable choice for a wider range of users, overcoming its initial status as a tool used only by experts and hackers. This phenomenon has led to higher expectations from end-users which translates into a greater need for responsible management, productivity over time, ease of maintenance, availability of support, increased quality and other features that now drive the success of FLOSS projects. This paper investigates whether and to what extent this change is affecting the way FLOSS communities develop software.

It is no longer a surprise when an open source project's community decides to adopt methodologies and policies that point more towards a hybrid development model than towards the bazaar model. This hybrid model combines development methodologies from traditional FLOSS development such as heavy community involvement, with those from proprietary development such as a QA phase comprising a series of elaborate steps taken to ensure a certain quality standard. Even though QA practices are becoming more and more present in FLOSS projects, their success or failure depends greatly on actual community development [7], in other

I. Hammouda et al. (Eds.): OSS 2012, IFIP AICT 378, pp. 262–267, 2012.

words on the project members. Furthermore, characteristics of the community such as its size [15] are important factors influencing the quality of a software product. We therefore need an up-to-date understanding of communities' structures and dynamics.

2   Background and Motivation

Open source software development has evolved substantially to keep up with the standards imposed by the continuously growing user base and the needs of the market. This implies refining the development process and pushing it towards a more sustainable model. But what does sustainability actually mean in this context? The Brundtland Commission's report defines sustainable development as development that "meets the needs of the present without compromising the ability of future generations to meet their own needs" [21]. In the context of open source software, this includes raising the quality standards of products by implementing more complex processes and rigorous methodologies. For example, it is safe to assume that as a project matures so does the testing process around it, which is a truism for both open source and proprietary software [11].

The importance of quality in open source is recognized as an important issue that needs to be further studied. This trend is illustrated by current research in the academic world [1-5], [13], [20] as well as research programs funded by various organizations and governments such as the Qualipso project [16] or Qualoss [10].

Another important trend in current research consists of analyzing the community that drives FLOSS using social network analysis. Although these studies focus on various aspects of the FLOSS community such as structure and dynamics [12], [14], communication patterns between core and periphery [17],[18] or migration within the hierarchy of FLOSS projects [9], none have sought to link QA with the rest of the community. This paper starts to fill that gap.

By analyzing the QA teams within one of the most famous FLOSS organizations (Mozilla) we can take a first step towards clarifying the position of QA within the open source community and further develop these findings into QA guidelines that can be applied to other FLOSS projects. Due to the particularities of each project there will not be a single recipe for success, but a study of this kind should provide important insights.

3   Research Questions

Q1: How does a QA contributor fit into the Mozilla community? Although recent research has defined more than three layers in the onion model [6, 9] it is generally accepted that a project's community can be split into: active users, co-developers and core developers. This research aims to investigate the extent to which QA is a step on the road from end-user to developer, or whether it has become established as a separate category of contributor.

Q2: What are the characteristics of QA activities within Mozilla? Members of the periphery also perform some QA tasks such as posting bugs on the issue tracker. It has been noted that for the case of Firefox the percentage is 20 to 25% [18] and it would be interesting to compare and see the percentage of periphery involvement for other Mozilla products. Another aspect that should be investigated is how participants' activities evolve over time considering that QA tasks can vary based on technical difficulty. For example users may provide automated test tools, which might suggest that QA may be divided into two subgroups based on activity type.

Q3: What are the characteristics of communication patterns between QA members as well as with other project participants? The goal of analyzing the characteristics of communication patterns between QA members is to find the central figures within the community and observe their evolution over time as social networks have a continuously changing structure [8]. As previous research has shown, information access by community members correlates with productivity [19], and for this reason, interaction of QA with other layers of the Mozilla organization should not be ignored.

4   Data and Research Method

Mozilla has a QA phase in its development in the sense that community members form a layer that is responsible for the QA process and it is easily identifiable [22] (meaning that information associated with the QA team such as web pages, wikis, mailing lists, forums and so on can be easily found). For conducting this study, QA mailing lists and the issue tracker were analyzed using quantitative techniques and social network analysis (SNA).

Mozilla QA has two dedicated mailing lists, Mozilla.dev-quality and Mozmill developer, which is addressed to more technically aware users. A total of 3689 messages were exchanged (February 2006 – July 2011) between 327 distinct authors. More specifically 2535 e-mails were exchanged by 293 authors on Mozilla.dev-quality and 1155 e-mails were exchanged by 61 authors on Mozmill developer. As expected, the traffic and number of users is higher on the Mozilla.dev-quality mailing list due to the fact that it is less technical.

The issue tracker (Bugzilla) data set covers all Mozilla products since 1998 containing 687,221 bugs with 5,834,507 associated comments which brings up processing challenges due to its size. Bug ids range from 0 to 724,339 making a total of 724,339 where collected bugs represent 94.87% of the id range. The remaining 5.13% were not collected because they were not publicly available or due to bad html that could not be parsed.

Approximately 4400 distinct project members were identified as assigned to fix bugs. Without getting the data associated with code commits it is not safe to assume that these members were also the members that posted the bug fix, but it is safe to assume that they are code commiters. These users are also active when it comes to posting bug comments as well as sending e-mails on the QA mailing lists. After cross-referencing members active on the mailing lists and code commiters, 883 bugs were found most of which belonging to Firefox.

An interesting detail that can be noticed after analyzing the data in Table 1 is that most activity levels show a steady increase, which may indicate a growth in the community as well as an improvement in the information flow between layers of the community. This improvement is also suggested by the fact that members active on the mailing lists have bugs assigned to them.

Table 1. Activity levels on a yearly basis

	2006	2007	2008	2009	2010	2011
Comments	328846	335323	467087	528199	658030	703857
Bugs	42015	41995	56785	60880	78089	78896
E-mails	343	361	556	1307	739	384
Dev bugs	119571	123234	174742	177776	227123	226555
Dev Comments	258458	271679	375729	449539	541707	561853
Dev e-mails	196	286	343	953	500	264

If we consider that 11 e-mails (average number of e-mails sent) is the lower limit for highly active users then Pareto's principle is somewhat applicable in the sense that only 16.8% of the users send more than 11 e-mails and 17.69% of users receive more than 11 replies. Following the same principle, only 4.39% of users show a higher than average activity posting more than 39 comments and 9.25% more than 6 bugs. From all the e-mails exchanged, 152 (4.12%) were sent by authors that had sent only one e-mail throughout the period taken into consideration for this research. On the other hand, 135466 bugs (19.70%) were posted by members that had posted only one bug throughout the period taken into consideration. Firefox was the Mozilla product with most of these "hit and run" bugs.

In this phase of the research, due to the fact that data collection and cleaning took longer than anticipated, social network analysis techniques could not be applied to the whole data set. Instead interaction was analyzed between active members on the mailing list (more than 10 e-mails sent – 55 users) and 10 members fairly active on the issue tracker. The resulting network does not depict relations between all QA members and its role is only to offer a sample of the interaction patterns within the community. After eliminating loops (replies to themselves) this sub-network had a number of 1433 participants with 2593 connections; 933 of these connections were formed by more than one interaction. The average degree is 3.16, which means that the average number of connections a member has is approximately 3.

5   Conclusions

Q1: How does a QA contributor fit into the Mozilla community? Considering the fact that the Mozilla QA team has dedicated communication channels, one can draw the conclusion that it represents a separate layer in the community model. Although, at this point of the research a clear definition of the tasks performed by QA members has not been made, evidence such as the existence of a QA mailing list oriented to more technically aware users might suggest that there is more than one type of QA task.

Q2: What are the characteristics of QA activities within Mozilla? As expected the activity of members of the community that "hit and run" (open one bug and never contribute again, send one e-mail and never contribute again) is higher on the Issue Tracker than on the QA mailing list. This may suggest that QA mailing list members have a more sustained activity in the Mozilla community. Another difference is that issue tracker activity has shown an increase over time while mailing list data showed a peak level. This might suggest that mailing list activity may not be related to time progression but to other variables that need to be found. On the other hand, the increase in activity on the issue tracker points out the community has grown over the years.

Q3: What are the characteristics of communication patterns between QA members as well as with other project participants? Data used for the social network analysis section of this study was performed only on a sample due to time related issues and thus a general conclusion regarding communication patterns can't be drawn at this point. However, the sample shows no small groups of people working together but a team spanning both mailing lists and issue tracker. In addition, judging by the activity of QA members and code commiters on the issue tracker it is safe to say that interaction with other community members has been increasing. This suggests that it is unlikely that there will be participants that control the flow of information, or bridges between the QA team and other layers of the community.

6   Limitations and Further Research

The purpose of this study is to create a precedent for further research in this direction in order to come up with general guidelines that can be applied on a wider scale. It is logical to conclude that by analyzing the structure and behavior of only Mozilla QA, one can't obtain a foolproof method to successfully implement QA practices due to the variety and uniqueness of every FLOSS project. In addition, community members might also use other communication channels that are not publicly available. This is one reason why findings should be confirmed with a qualitative follow-up. Another reason to go back to the community is to correlate data peaks and other anomalies with actual situations.

In the next phase, social network analysis will be applied to the whole data set using time frames and with consideration to time decay affecting connections between members of the community. Furthermore, in order to obtain an objective categorization of community members it is necessary to integrate previously acquired results with code comment data. It is essential to separate the QA members from developers and track their evolution within the community by monitoring their activity levels within different time frames and in different environments.

Whether the quality of Mozilla products have improved or not after the introduction of a formal QA step could represent a valuable assessment for other growing FLOSS communities. For this reason further phases should also include quality evaluation and measurement of Mozilla products as well as a classification and definition of QA procedures within Mozilla.

References

1. Halloran, T.J., Scherlis, W.L.: High quality and open source software practices. In: 2nd Workshop on Open Source Software Engineering (2002)
2. Hedberg, H., Iivari, N., Rajanen, M., Harjumaa, L.: Assuring Quality and Usability in Open Source Software Development. In: First International Workshop on Emerging Trends in FLOSS Research and Development, FLOSS 2007, p. 2 (2007)

3. Michlmayr, M., Hunt, F., Probert, D.: Quality practices and problems in free software projects. In: Proceedings of the First International Conference on Open Source Systems, pp. 24–28 (2005)
4. Schmidt, D.C., Porter, A.: Leveraging open-source communities to improve the quality & performance of open-source software. In: Proceedings of the 1st Workshop on Open Source Software Engineering (2001)
5. Chengalur-Smith, I., Sidorova, A., Daniel, S.: Sustainability of Free/Libre Open Source Projects: A Longitudinal Study. JAIS 11 (2001)
6. Wiggins, A., Howison, J., Crowston, K.: Social dynamics of FLOSS team communication across channels. In: Proceedings of the Fourth International Conference on Open Source Systems, vol. 275, pp. 131–142 (2008)
7. Kilamo, T., Hammouda, I., Kairamo, V., Räsänen, P., Saarinen, J.P.: Applying Open Source Practices and Principles in Open Innovation: The Case of the Demola Platform. In: Hissam, S.A., Russo, B., de Mendonça Neto, M.G., Kon, F. (eds.) OSS 2011. IFIP AICT, vol. 365, pp. 307–311. Springer, Heidelberg (2011)
8. Watts, D.J.A.: Twenty-first century science. Nature 445(7127), 489–489 (2007)
9. Jensen, C., Scachi, W.: Role Migration and Advancement Processes in OSSD Projects: A Comparative Case Study. In: Proceedings of the 29th International Conference on Software Engineering, pp. 364–374 (2007)
10. Quality in Open Source Software, http://www.qualoss.org/
11. DiBona, C., Cooper, D., Cooper, M.: Open Sources 2.0: The Continuing Evolution. O'Reilly, USA (2006)
12. Crowston, K., Howison, J.: The social structure of Free and Open Source software. First Monday 10(2) (2004)
13. Spinellis, D., Gousios, G., Karakoidas, V., Louridas, P., Adams, P.J., Samoladas, I., Stamelos, I.: Evaluating the Quality of Open Source Software. In: Proceedings of the International Workshop on Software Quality and Maintainability. Electronic Notes in Theoretical Computer Science, vol. 233 (2009)
14. Mockus, A., Fielding, R.T., Herbsleb, J.D.: Two Case Studies of Open Source Software Development: Apache And Mozilla. ACM Transactions on Software Engineering and Methodology 11(3), 309–346 (2002)
15. Sowe, S., Ghosh, R., Haaland, K.: A Multi-Repository Approach to Study the Topology of Open Source Bugs Communities: Implications for Software and Code Quality. In: 3rd IEEE International Conference on Information Management and Engineering, IEEE ICIME (2011)
16. Qualipso (Trust and Quality in Open Source Systems), http://www.qualipso.org
17. Oezbek, C., Prechelt, L., Thiel, F.: The Onion has Cancer: Some Social Network Analysis Visualizations of Open Source Project Communication. Psychology, Section 4, 4–9 (2010)
18. Masmoudi, H., den Besten, M.L., De Loupy, C., Dalle, J.M.: Peeling the Onion: The Words and Actions that Distinguish Core from Periphery in Bug Reports and How Core and Periphery Interact Together. In: Fifth International Conference on Open Source Systems (2009)
19. Aral, S., Brynjolfsson, E., Van Alstyne, M.: Productivity Effects of Information Diffusion in E-mail Networks. In: Proceedings of ICIS 2007 (2007)
20. Aberdour, M.: Achieving Quality in Open Source Software. IEEE Software, 58–64 (2007)
21. Burtland Comission: The Bruntland Report. United Nations (1987)
22. QMO, https://quality.mozilla.org

Do More Experienced Developers Introduce Fewer Bugs?

Daniel Izquierdo-Cortázar, Gregorio Robles, and Jesús M. González-Barahona

GSyC/LibreSoft, Universidad Rey Juan Carlos
{dizquierdo,grex,jgb}@libresoft.es

Abstract. Developer experience is a common matter of study in the software maintenance and evolution research literature. However it is still not well understood if less experienced developers are more prone to introduce errors in the source code than their more experienced colleagues. This paper aims to study the relationships between experience and the bug introduction ratio using the Mozilla community as case of study.

As results, statistical differences among developers with different levels of experience has not been observed, when the expected result would have been the opposite[1].

1 Introduction

Software development is a task that demands high intellectual effort. Fixing errors is in among those tasks that are especially difficult. Even more when those errors are located in parts of the source code with which the developer is not *familiar*. Being *familiar* with a piece of code can be considered as having some *expertise* on/with it or previous *experience* with it (or similar one).

The goal of this paper is to study this assumption from a quantitative point of view, studying differences among developers of different levels of experience using several modules from Mozilla. To this aim, three ways of measuring experience will be used: a) number of commits, b) number of fixing commits, and c) *territoriality* (measured as the number of files only *touched* by one developer). Six null hypothesis have been defined: correlation between the three ways of calculating experience and the *bug seeding ratio* (being the percentage of *buggy* commits out of the total number of commits), and another three with the relationship among the several experience metrics used.

2 Empirical Approach

Some Mozilla Foundation projects have been the selected case of study for this paper. The analysis is based on the Mercurial repository[2] which offers a list of

---

[1] This work been funded in part by the European Commission under project ALERT (FP7-IST-25809) and by the Spanish Gov. under project SobreSale (TIN2011-28110).

[2] http://hg.mozilla.org/

I. Hammouda et al. (Eds.): OSS 2012, IFIP AICT 378, pp. 268–273, 2012.

repositories that can be easily *cloned*. As a summary, 19 projects were analyzed, with more than 100,000 commits, more than 2,500 authors and around 4 years of history up to June 2011. In this scenario, we define following concepts:

- **Bug fixing commit**: commit that fixes an issue.
- **Bug seeding commit** (or *buggy* change): commit whose action has caused a later fixing action.
- **Bug seeding ratio**: the value represents the percentage of *buggy* changes done by a developer.
- **Territoriality**: number of files *touched* only by one committer.
- **Bug fixing activity:** this activity is detected analyzing the log message left by developers when performing a commit. In our case study, the developers of the Mozilla usually specify the fix of an error by means of the key word *Bug* followed by an integer. This integer matches with an *id* of an issue in the bug tracking system (BTS). We have validated our process and tested the heuristic we used, and have obtained 91,7% of precision and 89,65% of recall.
- **Bug seeding activity:** in general, the method is based on three steps: a) detection of fixing activity as previously detailed; b) identification of the lines involved; and, c) identification of previous commits where those lines were involved. The identification of commits inducing fixing actions is based on the *SZZ* algorithm [9], a method that has been also used in other research works [6]. The main assumption of this algorithm is that *modified* or *removed* lines in a fixing commit are the ones *suspicious* of having caused the fixing action (or being part of the error). Tracing back in the source code management system (SCM) to the time when they were *added* or *modified* results in the commit where the error was introduced. That commit is the one that is considered as the bug seeding commit.

3 Related Research

Expertise in developing teams is a recurrent piece of study. As claimed by some authors: "Finding relevant expertise is a critical need in collaborative software engineering, particularly in geographically distributed developments" [8].

From a quantitative point of view, experience has been found to be measured in several ways: a) *Number of commits* [8,7,2]; b) *Fixing activity* [1]; and, c) *Ownership* of the source code [3,4].

Regarding our methodology, the approach used follows the assumption made by the SZZ algorithm where the lines that are part of a fixing activity are suspicious of being causing the fixing action (or being at least part of the problem) [9].

4 Results

Testing hypothesis $H_{0,a}$, $H_{0,b}$ and $H_{0,c}$: these hypotheses say that there is not correlation between bug seeding ratio and a) number of commits, b) number of fixing commits, and c) territoriality.

Table 1. Testing hypothesis $H_{0,a}$: Number commits *vs.* bug seeding ratio and $H_{0,c}$: Correlation of bug fixing activity and bug seeding ratio

textbfProject	R^2	p-value	R^2	p-value
ActionMonkey	0.006	0.432	0.019	0.166
ActionMonkey Tamarin	0.193	0.276	0.409	0.088
Camino	0.004	0.825	0.083	0.319
Chatzilla	0.001	0.953	0.005	0.876
Comm Central	0.007	0.557	0.037	0.157
Dom Inspector	0.000	0.941	0.238	0.077
Graphs	0.038	0.712	0.480	0.127
Mobile Browser	0.000	0.978	0.004	0.794
Mozilla Central	0.010	0.068	0.041	0.000
Tamarin Central	0.329	0.065	0.402	0.036
Tamarin Redux	0.009	0.651	0.001	0.897
Tamarin Tracing	0.419	0.043	0.005	0.849

Table 1 shows the results we have obtained, offering the values of R^2 and the p-value for the projects under study. This table provides information about the comparison between bug seeding ratio and two types of experience: number of commits and number of fixing commits. Regarding to the territoriality study ($H_{0,b}$), all of the projects dataset is aggregated given that there are few values of study per project. In this case the R^2 is 0.037 and the p-value is 0.06. In all of the cases the inspection of the values provides low correlation.

When visually analyzing the graphs for the projects, we have observed a behavior that is worth mentioning. We expected that developers with a high number of commits would have lower bug seeding ratios, graphically appearing on the left upper corner of the charts. However, some of the projects present a surprising pattern: the area the dots covers is similar to a triangle. This can be observed especially well in the case of *Mozilla Central* (see Figure 1), where those developers contributing with more than 800 commits have values of bug

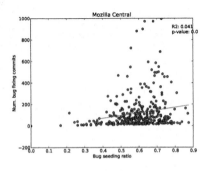

Fig. 1. Correlation study between number of commits and the bug seeding ratio. Each dot represents a developer of the Mozilla Central repository (Firefox project).

Table 2. Testing hypothesis $H_{0,a-c}$: Study of the correlation between typical activity and fixing activity

Project	R^2	p-value
ActionMonkey	0.885	0.000
ActionMonkey Tamarin	0.076	0.510
Camino	0.880	0.000
Chatzilla	0.987	0.000
Comm Central	0.963	0.000
Graphs	0.676	0.045
Mobile Browser	0.995	0.000
Mozilla Central	0.967	0.000
Tamarin Central	0.033	0.592
Tamarin Redux	0.980	0.000
Tamarin Tracing	0.630	0.006

seeding ratio between 0.5 and 0.75, while we can find developers with less than 200 commits mostly in the range that goes from 0.25 to 0.85.

Although the pattern is not that clear as with the *Mozilla Central*, due probably to having a lower number of developers, the rest of the projects show a similar behaviour.

Testing Hypothesis $H_{0,a-b}$, $H_{0,a-c}$ **and** $H_{0,b-c}$: these hypotheses say that there is not correlation among the three ways of measuring experience. Table 2 shows the results for the comparison between the number of commits and number of fixing commits. In addition, the comparison between number of commits and territoriality has provided a R^2 of 0.085 and a p-value of 0.004. Besides the study of the correlation between the number of bug fixing commits and the territoriality has raised a R^2 of 0.006 and a p-value of 0.444.

Table 2 has shown that a high linear correlation between these two variables exist, with high values of R^2. As the p-values are below the specified threshold, the results are statistically significant. On the contrary, no significant values were found when correlating territoriality with number of commits and number of fixing commits.

5 Discussion

Results are detailed in Table 3. It is surprising to find that there is no correlation between any of the ways we measure experience and the bug seeding ratio. Our intuition and related research (see Eyolfson *et al.* [2]) had made us expect that developers would increase the quality of their code the more they contribute to a project. However, both results could be compatible. Eyolfson *et al.* study developers on an individual basis and consider their evolution, finding that the quality of the contributions improve over time. Our study is done in a specific snapshot and does not consider changes over time.

Our results raise some very interesting research questions. One first question is to look for the reason for which experienced and less-experienced developers

Table 3. Null Hypotheses and results. BSR: bug seeding ratio. FR: fail to reject.

ID	Null hypothesis	Result
$H_{0,a}$	No correlation between BSR and # commits	FR except in Tam. Tracing
$H_{0,b}$	No correlation between BSR and territoriality	Rejected, although no linear correlation is found
$H_{0,c}$	No correlation, BSR - fixing activity	FR except in Mozilla and Tamarin Central
$H_{0,a-b}$	No correlation, # commits - territoriality	Rejected, although no linear correlation is found
$H_{0,a-c}$	No correlation, # commits - fixing activity	Rejected and strong linear correlation is found
$H_{0,b-c}$	No correlation, territoriality - fixing activity	FR

introduce bugs to the same extent. This may lie in the peer review policy that some of the Mozilla Foundation projects follow[3].

A second question is related with the tendency observed in several graphs where more experienced developers tend to a constant bug seeding ratio. This could mean that there exists an inherent difficulty for any software project that will make developers introduce a given number of bugs, and that this cannot be circumvented with more experienced developers.

Our results show that among the various ways of defining experience, territoriality may be the better choice. But further research should study if other aspects, such as an optimized peer review process, would not provide better output.

According to the reproducibility classification criteria proposed in [5], detailed information can be obtained at http://gsyc.urjc.es/~grex/oss2012.

6   Conclusions

In this paper we have analyzed the relation between various ways of measuring developer experience and the ratio at which bugs are introduced into the code. We have found no linear correlation between experience and bug seeding ratio; more experience does not imply that less buggy code is included in the project.

We have seen that for the various ways of measuring experience (number of commits, territoriality, bug fixing activity), territoriality seems to be the best choice to have low number of bugs introduced, although this fact is not strongly supported by our results. Number of commits and bug fixing activity are highly correlated, so for studies that handle developer experience one of them can be left out.

Our study opens the door to new research, among which we propose to study the importance of peer reviewing, the existence of a project-specific characteristics that make more experienced developers tend towards a value of bug seeding

---

[3] http://www.mozilla.org/hacking/committer/

ratio, a better understanding of developer territoriality and implications of our findings in recommender systems.

References

1. Ahsan, S.N., Afzal, M.T., Zaman, S., Gütel, C., Wotawa, F.: Mining effort data from the oss repository of developer's bug fix activity. Journal of Information Technology in Asia 3, 67–80 (2010)
2. Eyolfson, J., Tan, L., Lam, P.: Do time of day and developer experience affect commit bugginess. In: Proceeding of the 8th Working Conference on Mining Software Repositories, MSR 2011, pp. 153–162. ACM, New York (2011)
3. Fritz, T., Murphy, G.C., Hill, E.: Does a programmer's activity indicate knowledge of code? In: Proceedings of the the 6th ESEC-FSE, pp. 341–350. ACM, New York (2007)
4. German, D.M.: Using software trails to reconstruct the evolution of software: Research articles. J. Softw. Maint. Evol. 16, 367–384 (2004)
5. González-Barahona, J.M., Robles, G.: On the reproducibility of empirical software engineering studies based on data retrieved from development repositories. Empirical Software Engineering 17(1-2), 75–89 (2012)
6. Kim, S., Whitehead Jr., E.J., Zhang, Y.: Classifying software changes: Clean or buggy? IEEE TSE 34(2), 181–196 (2008)
7. Minto, S., Murphy, G.C.: Recommending emergent teams. In: Proceedings of the 4th International Workshop on MSR, p. 5 (2007)
8. Mockus, A., Herbsleb, J.D.: Expertise browser: a quantitative approach to identifying expertise. In: Proc of the 24rd ICSE, pp. 503–512 (May 2002)
9. Śliwerski, J., Zimmermann, T., Zeller, A.: When do changes induce fixes? In: Intl. Workshop Mining Software Repositories, pp. 1–5 (2005)

Perspectives on Code Forking and Sustainability in Open Source Software

Linus Nyman[1], Tommi Mikkonen[2], Juho Lindman[1], and Martin Fougère[1]

[1] Hanken School of Economics, Helsinki, Finland
firstname.lastname@hanken.fi
[2] Tampere University of Technology, Tampere, Finland
tommi.mikkonen@tut.fi

Abstract. The ability to create high-quality software artifacts that are usable over time is one of the essential requirements of the software business. In such a setting, open source software offers excellent opportunities for sustainability. In particular, safeguarding mechanisms against planned obsolescence by any single actor are built into the definition of open source. The most powerful of these mechanisms is the ability to fork the project. In this paper we argue that the possibility to fork serves as the invisible hand of sustainability that ensures that code remains open and that the code that best serves the community lives on. Furthermore, the mere option to fork provides a mechanism for safeguarding against despotic decisions by the project lead, who is thus guided in their actions to consider the best interest of the community.

1   Introduction

Sustainability is a concept which is often automatically associated with open source software. Access to the source code allows developers to build solutions that are better protected from potentially harmful actions of any single developer, company, or organization. The openness of the source code also means that decisions concerning the software artefact become transparent to the developer community.

In this paper we address the role of code forking – a situation in which several versions of a piece of software originating from a single, shared code base are developed separately – in ensuring the long-term sustainability of a software system. Furthermore, we advocate the freedom that enables developers to create novel features that may go well beyond what the original developers anticipated. This freedom, a key factor in the promise of open innovation that builds on open source software, can nurture open source projects through difficult times and extreme events that could otherwise prove lethal. An example is a hostile acquisition, which may cause radical changes in the project.

2   Sustainability and Planned Obsolescence

The link between software and sustainability is not evident if considering sustainability as something related to raw materials or energy in design, use or

I. Hammouda et al. (Eds.): OSS 2012, IFIP AICT 378, pp. 274–279, 2012.

maintenance [1]. Indeed, sustainability is an "essentially contested" concept [2, 3, 4], and thus sustainability of a product can be interpreted in many ways. We take the view of the consumer and focus on two central elements: quality and staying power – how to create a high-quality product that is usable as long as possible.

This approach to product sustainability conflicts with what is known as "planned obsolescence", a term popularized in the 1950s by American industrial designer Brooks Stevens [5]. Stevens defined planned obsolescence as the act of instilling in the buyer "the desire to own something a little newer, a little better, a little sooner than is necessary" [6]. From the fashion industry, where last year's models are designed to look out-of-date by the time this year's models come around, to the software industry, where the norm is for software to be compatible with older models but not with newer ones, planned obsolescence – considered by some "an engine of technological progress" [7] – has become an inescapable part of the consumer's everyday life, which is increasingly problematized in business ethics literature [8].

Digital artifacts, of course, differ substantially from the end products of 1950s industrial design, or even those of today. The main differences are related to their characteristics as editable, interactive, reprogrammable, distributed, and open [9]. These characteristics dictate that software as an artefact is prone to being changed, repaired and updated rather than remain fixed from early stages of the design process (see also [10]). The software marketplace has transferred planned obsolescence to the digital realm by creating ways to benefit from these artefact characteristics. The revenue models of companies that operate in the software marketplace thus welcome versioning, lock-ins, competition, and network effects [11].

Open source software offers an alternative to some of the pitfalls of planned obsolescence. Rather than needing to buy something "a little newer, a little better", the open source community can simply make the existing product a little – or a lot – newer and better. In open source, anything, once invented, once written, need never be rewritten. On the other hand, the software product is never ready but can become stable and mature enough for the developer community. With community interest, the software can always be improved.

The right to improve a program, the right to make it portable to newer as well as older programs and versions, and the right to combine many programs into an even better entity are all fundamental privileges built into the very definition of open source, and these rights are often exercised by the involved parties [12]. Therefore, in open source systems any program that has the support of the open source community will enjoy assured relevance rather than planned obsolescence. In fact, planned obsolescence in open source is impossible without community consent, due to a practice which is at once both the sustainer and potential destroyer of open source programs: the code fork.

3   Code Forking

A popular metaphor in economics is Adam Smith's "invisible hand", a self-regulating force that guides the marketplace [13]. We claim that open source software has its own invisible hand: the fork. In fact, even the *possibility* of a fork usually suffices. A broad definition of a code fork is when the code from an existing program serves as the basis for a new version of the program; more specifically, a version which seeks to continue to exist apart from the original[1]. Forking can (though need not) be the result of a split in the developer community regarding the software artefact, its development practice, or the direction of the development, and is in such cases usually followed by a split in the user community. With open source, one can always fork a project: an inclusion of the right to fork is a prerequisite of all open source licenses. Furthermore, the licensing terms impose no conditions which would in any way require developers to adhere to the original development line.

Forking is paradoxical in nature; it is simultaneously both one of the greatest threats that an individual project faces, and the ultimate sustainer: a guarantee that as long as users find a program useful, the program will continue to exist. The threat to the program comes mainly in the form of the (potential) dilution of both users and developers. As Fogel [15] has noted, it is not the existence of a fork that hurts a project, but rather the loss of developers and users. The benefits of a fork come in ensuring that the program can continue to exist regardless of external circumstances. If, for instance, the developers of a program under a permissive license decide to relicense it under either a proprietary license or a license otherwise perceived to be less favorable, the community can fork a new version and continue development. Forks can also serve as an escape hatch for projects and developers who find themselves cornered or unable to continue on a planned course. In the case of a program remaining under an open source license, but where the people or company shepherding the code make decisions which run counter to the interests of the larger community and developers, forking ensures the continued development, as the community and developers can fork a new version on which to continue working[2].

While there are no guarantees that a fork will become accepted or used by the community – forks of popular software in particular are likely to face considerable obstacles to their sustainability in the form of trademarks and the brand value of the main branch – the mere possibility of forking a program has a huge impact on how open source programs projects are governed [15]. A better-managed project increases chances of sustainability – even a project viewed as important and necessary can become unsustainable if people no longer want to be a part of the group working on the program. In successful projects, however, a dynamic seems to exist where developers are happy enough to follow the project leader as long as the project leader listens to developers' views enough to keep them on board: while the individual members of the development team all *could* fork the program, they choose not to. This balance creates continuity for long-term cooperation.

---

[1] A branch is problematic to categorize at the time of its 'creation': it can be considered a fork if it is not, at some later point, merged back into the main branch. The intricacies of comparing and defining forking versus fragmentation, light forking, 'pseudo-forking' [14], branches, and versions is the topic for a paper under development, but beyond the scope of this one.

[2] In recent years, examples of using a fork for the sustainability of a community include high-profile cases such as the forking of OpenOffice into LibreOffice and the creation of various projects from the code base of MySQL. projects from the code base of MySQL.

4   Code Forking and Sustainability

The first of Lehman's laws of program evolution is that of change or decay – a program must continue to evolve in order to remain useful [16]. Brooks notes not only that all successful software gets changed, but also that successful software "survives beyond the normal life of the machine vehicle for which it was first written" [10, p. 185]. Forking can offer solutions to the aforementioned concerns. The possibility of forking provides the community with the tools it needs to handle situations in which a program could become obsolete (for the community as a whole or a particular segment of the community) either through stagnation, a change in licensing, or any other reason by enabling the creation of a new version of the system, a porting to a new hardware environment, a change in program focus, and many other possible solutions to avoid decay and obsolescence (see [17] for examples).

If several developers leave a project and start their own fork, benefits to sustainability can still be found. Among the more obvious is that the developers are still working on the program, be it on a different version. Had forking not been possible, they might have stopped their work on the program entirely. Also, as long as the licenses are compatible, any breakthroughs or developments in a fork can be incorporated into the original version. While there may be duplicated efforts involved, all versions can still benefit from the work done on others.

Given that the reuse of existing code is a common practice in open source [18], one could contrast the evolution of code with the evolution of species since open source software, like living species, can be seen to "reproduce" and pass on certain traits through forking and reuse. In discussing natural selection, one of the central tenets resulting from Charles Darwin's research, Darwin notes that each variation of a species, if useful, is preserved, while "any variation in the least degree injurious would be rigidly destroyed" [19, pp. 130-131]. The same can be said of code forks – if a new variation is considered useful by developers and community it will endure, while forks considered "injurious", or at least less favourable than an available alternative, will not endure[3]. Open source, however, is not as unforgiving as Darwin's nature in the sense that even if a program falls into disuse, it may still continue to exist (for instance in the form of source code on a forge). An abundance of similar yet unique forks of the same program may prove useful for its sustainability through an increased likelihood of survival if some forks, by chance or design, are better protected than others against adversity, be it in the form of a virus, unfavourable corporate or community actions, or any other form.

A greater amount of similar yet distinct forks may also help bring about new functionalities, even innovations. Disruptive innovations – innovations which improve a product or service in a way that the market does not expect, eventually displacing the earlier technology – are commonly not so much advances in technology as they are new combinations of existing technology [20]. Code forking as a practice could both create programs better suited to benefit from disruptive

---

[3] Variations which are "neither useful nor injurious [...] would not be affected by natural selection, and would be left a fluctuating element", Darwin [19, p. 131] notes. In the case of code forking, these "fluctuating elements" could conceivably become either useful or injurious in the event of new developments in the environment.

innovations by other actors, as well as create enough building blocks – variations of programs – to make new functionalities as well as innovations more likely to occur. Indeed, is there any other area or field in which the combining in new ways of existing technologies, in this case computer programs, is as catered to and as ingrained in community practice as in open source development? The plethora of forges online offer hundreds of thousands of programs, available for forking and reuse in any new, creative way the user can imagine.

Perhaps the greatest potential threat to the practice of forking and combining different open source programs is the question of license compatibility. The so-called copyleft, or viral, licenses, chief among them the GPL family of licenses, set restrictions regarding which types of licenses they can be combined with, while permissive (or non-viral licenses) like the BSD and the MIT licenses impose no such restrictions (see, for instance, [21, 22, 23]). For practical use, there are well-established ways to overcome some of the restrictions [24].

For an open source project to remain sustainable it must evolve with its user base. The same goes for the developers, whose actions must also evolve along with the evolution of the project as well as the users. The possibility to fork is one of the key factors that ensure that open source will continue to evolve and thus remain sustainable. Open source programs can also cease to develop; some programs and pieces of code live on while others die out. Forking, as well as the effect of the possibility of forking, ensures that the selection lies in the hands of the community. At its best, open source software, guided by the invisible hand of forking, may well render planned obsolescence itself obsolete.

5   Conclusions

Forking has the capability of serving as an invisible hand of sustainability that helps open source projects to survive extreme events such as commercial acquisitions, as well as ensures that users and developers have the necessary tools to enable change rather than decay. Code forking may also have other, less foreseeable benefits, as some variations of a program may be better suited either to surviving adverse events or to aiding in achieving new functionalities and innovations, for instance through the novel combining of programs. The possibility of forking is a powerful incentive for ensuring continuity and the long-term viability of an open source development, and thus the sustainability of the resulting software artefacts.

References

[1] Murugesan: Harnessing Green IT: Principles and Practices. IT Professional 10(1), 24–33 (2008)
[2] Connelly: Mapping Sustainable Development as a Contested Concept. Local Environment: The International Journal of Justice and Sustainability 12(3), 259–278 (2007)
[3] Davison: Technology and the contested meanings of sustainability. State University of New York Press, Albany (2001)
[4] McManus: Contested terrains: Politics, stories and discourses of sustainability. Environmental Politics 5(1), 48–73 (1996)

[5]   Planned obsolescence, The Economist (March 23, 2009), http://www.economist.
      com/node/13354332 (accessed September 14, 2011)
[6]   Brooks   Stevens   biography,   http://www.brooksstevenshistory.com/
      brooks_bio.pdf (accessed September 14, 2011)
[7]   Fishman, Gandal, Shy: Planned Obsolescence as an Engine of Technological Progress.
      Journal of Industrial Economics 41(4), 361–370 (1993)
[8]   Guiltinan: Creative Destruction and Destructive Creations: Environmental Ethics and
      Planned Obsolescence. Journal of Business Ethics 89, 19–28 (2009)
[9]   Kallinikos, Aaltonen, Attila: A theory of digital objects. First Monday 15(6-7) (June
      2010)
[10] Brooks: The mythical man-month. Addison-Wesley, Boston (1995)
[11] Shapiro, Varian: Information Rules: A Strategic Guide to the Network Economy.
      Harvard Business School Press, Boston (1998)
[12] Fitzgerald: The Transformation of Open Source Software. MIS Quarterly 30(3), 587–598
      (2006)
[13] Smith: The Wealth of Nations (Bantam Classic Edition March/2003). Bantam Dell, New
      York (1776)
[14] Raymond: The Cathedral & the Bazaar: Musings on Linux and Open Source by an
      Accidental Revolutionary. O'Reilly, Sebastopol (2001)
[15] Fogel: Producing Open Source Software. O'Reilly, Sebastopol (2006)
[16] Lehman: Programs, Life Cycles, and Laws of Software Evolution. Proc. IEEE
      68(9), 1060–1076 (1980), http://www.cs.uwaterloo.ca/~a78khan/cs446/
      additional-material/scribe/27-refactoring/Lehman-
      LawsofSoftwareEvolution.pdf
[17] Nyman, L., Mikkonen, T.: To Fork or Not to Fork: Fork Motivations in SourceForge
      Projects. In: Hissam, S.A., Russo, B., de Mendonça Neto, M.G., Kon, F. (eds.) OSS
      2011. IFIP AICT, vol. 365, pp. 259–268. Springer, Heidelberg (2011)
[18] Haefliger, von Krogh, Spaeth: Code Reuse in Open Source Software. Management Sci-
      ence 54(1), 180–193 (2008)
[19] Darwin: The Origin of Species (1985 Penguin Classics edition). Penguin Books, London
      (1859)
[20] Christensen: The Innovator's Dilemma. Collins, New York (1997)
[21] Meeker: The Open Source Alternative: Understanding Risks and Leveraging Opportuni-
      ties. Wiley, Hoboken (2008)
[22] Sinclair: License Profile: BSD. International Free and Open Source Software Law Re-
      view 2(1) (2010), doi:10.5033/ifosslr.v2i1.28
[23] Lindman, Rossi, Puustelli: Matching Open Source Software Licenses with Correspond-
      ing Business Models. IEEE Software 28(4), 31–35 (2011)
[24] Hammouda, Mikkonen, Oksanen, Jaaksi: Open Source Legality Patterns: Architectural
      Design Decisions Motivated by Legal Concerns. In: Proceedings of the 14th Internation-
      al Academic MindTrek Conference: Envisioning Future Media Environments. ACM,
      New York (2010)

Open Source Prediction Methods:
A Systematic Literature Review

M.M. Mahbubul Syeed, Terhi Kilamo, Imed Hammouda, and Tarja Systä

Tampere University of Technology, Finland
{mm.syeed,terhi.kilamo,imed.hammouda,tarja.systa}@tut.fi

Abstract. For the adoption of Open Source Software (OSS) components, knowledge of the project development and associated risks with their use is needed. That, in turn, calls for reliable prediction models to support preventive maintenance and building quality software. In this paper, we perform a systematic literature review on the state-of-the-art on predicting OSS projects considering both code and community dimension. We also distill future direction for research in this field.

Keywords: Open Source, Systematic Literature Review, Prediction.

1 Introduction

The use of Open Source Software (OSS) is increasingly becoming a part of the development strategy and business portfolio of IT organizations.To adopt an OSS component effectively, an organization needs knowledge of the project development, composition and possible risks associated with its use, due to its unconventional and complex development process and evolution history [1]. This in turn, calls for building reliable prediction models and methods supporting error prediction, measuring maintenance effort and cost of OSS projects.

In this paper, we present a literature Review on prediction studies to analyze OSS projects both from the point of view of the product and the community. The contribution of this work are as follows, (a) a study on the state-of-the-art in OSS prediction methods and approaches; (b) future directions of research work in this field; (c) developed a reusable literature review protocol following the guideline of [2] that can be used as a model for review studies in software engineering. Only key contributions of the work is presented in this paper. Detail discussion on the review process, associated thread to validity and elaborated results with more research questions can be found in *http://literature-review.weebly.com/*.

2 Review Methodology

For this review, we developed a review protocol by keeping perfect alignment with the guidelines suggested by Kitchenham [2]. We briefly discussed the review protocol here. A detail discussion on this along with the list of 36 articles reviewed, can be found at *http://literature-review.weebly.com/*.

I. Hammouda et al. (Eds.): OSS 2012, IFIP AICT 378, pp. 280–285, 2012.

2.1 Research Questions

For this review, we defined a set of research questions as presented in Table 1.

Table 1. Research Questions

	Research Questions	Main Motivation
Q1.	What are the main focuses/purposes of the study?	To identify the focus area of the prediction work (e.g., fault prediction, effort prediction).
Q2.	What are the datasets of OSS projects exploited in prediction?	To identify the data sources of an OSS project that are used for the prediction models.
Q3.	What kinds of methods are used in predicting OSS projects?	Explore the trends and methods used for prediction in the context of OSS.
Q4.	What kinds of metrics are used in predicting OSS projects?	To identify the trend and usage of different types metric suits for prediction in the context of OSS.

2.2 Article Selection

Inclusion Criteria. For assessing the suitability of the articles are as follows:

- Articles must explicitly state the study type (e.g., fault, quality, effort prediction) and provide evidence of metrics, methods, data sets exploited.
- Articles must exhibit a profound relation to OSS projects and take into account the aspects that can be attributed to the OSS community and projects.

Automated Keyword Search. At first a broad automated keyword search based on the title, keywords and abstract was performed to get the initial set of articles. Six digital libraries are searched within the time period of January, 1980 and 31st June, 2011. Search terms can be found in *http://literature-review.weebly.com/*.

Manual Selection. To filter out the irrelevant ones from this set of articles, we performed a manual selection by reviewing the title, keywords, abstract and conclusion.

Reference Checking. To ensure the inclusion of other relevant but missing articles, we performed a non-recursive search through the references of the 32 articles. Finally, we selected 36 articles (12 journal and 24 conference articles) for this review.

2.3 Attribute Framework

Attribute Identification. The attribute set was derived based on: (a) The domain of the review and (b) The research questions. For this, a pilot study consisting of following activities was run: first, an exploratory study on the structure of 5 randomly selected articles was performed to identify initial set of attributes. Then, this list of attributes was refined further into a number of specific sub-attributes employing a through study of the same set of articles. The sub-attributes were then generalized further to increase their applicability. The final attribute set can be found at *http://literature-review.weebly.com/*.

2.4   Article Assessment and Characterization

Appropriate set of attributes are assigned to the articles to effectively capture the essence in terms of the research questions and allow for a clear distinction between (and comparison of) the articles. The data colleciton table can be found at *http://literature-review.weebly.com/*.

3   Review Result

3.1   Answering the Research Questions

Q1. What are the main focuses/purposes of the study?
Research interest toward predicting OSS projects predominantly dedicated to traditional defect/fault prediction studies (66%) , with minimal exploraion of the impact of OSS community in these prediction studies.

Q2. What are the datasets of OSS projects exploited in prediction? What else to be explored?
OSS development process produces repositories consisting of source code, bug reports, mailing lists, change logs, forums, wikis and so on. Due to such wide variety of data sources, we group them into different categories, such as, Contribution refers to bug reports, patches, feature requests.

According to our results, the highest utilized data sources are, source code version control systems (49%) and contribution (36%), with CVS repositories and the Bugzilla tool having the maximum exploration count. These sources are mainly used for fault or defect prediction. But the two sources, communication channels and knowledge sources (e.g., mail, chat, wikis), are yet to get attention confirming the fact that OSS community dynamics was not explored in prediciton studies.

Q3. What kinds of methods are used in OSS and prediction?
As can be seen from Figure 1(a), around 50% of the articles exploited statistical methods for prediction, whereas only 24% of the articles used machine learning algorithms. This result contradicts with the survey on fault prediction studies

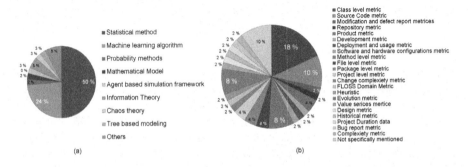

Fig. 1. (a) Methods employed for prediction (b) Metric suites studied

[3], where it was noted that machine learning algorithms are gaining more interest (increased from 18% to 66%) over statistical methods (decreases from 59% to 14%). This difference may be for two reasons, (a) the survey in [3] focused on fault prediction, whereas our survey covers the entire domain of prediction studies on OSS projects, and (b) OSS is relatively new area to explore for prediction studies. However, it will be promising to see the exploration of machine learning methods in OSS prediction studies which is also suggested in [3].

Q4. What kinds of metrics are used in predicting OSS projects?
The distribution of metrics which have been used in research for predicting OSS projects are shown in Figure 1(b). As shown in this figure, the class level metric and the source code metric suites got the highest priority for prediction (18% and 10% respectively). Among other metric suites, file level and package level, and project level metrics were also exploited. All these metric suits are prevalently used for fault prediction studies, hence confirms the findings presented in Q1.

3.2   Open Questions and Research Agenda

Q1. Are the generalizability of the prediction models hold across the domain of OSS projects? Or are they subjected to specific project(s)?
This research question evolved due to the fact that most of the reviewed articles (67%) admitted the necessity of external validity of the prediction models studied. To be specific, in [4] generalization of the findings was not done because the study is subjective and is dependent on how the errors are classified in the project. Again in [9], it is acknowledged that further replication across many OSS projects is required to establish the cross project validity of the prediction model. It is also noted that the prediction models are not general and are not applicable to different software systems [10]. Specially for defect prediction models there exists very little evidence on their cross project applicability [5]. Thus a comprehensive study on the generalizability issue of the prediction models across the domain of OSS projects is an area of future research.

Q2. Is the prediction accuracy of metrics remains consistent among the studies, or is there any contradictory results exist?
Each metric used for prediction, either being positively or negatively associated with prediction results. For example, in case of fault prediction, a metric signifies a module as either being faulty or not faulty. In either case, the metric's prediction recital is judged as a best, significant or bad predictor. In this regard, our review results show inconsistency on some metric's performance. For instance, the metric LOC (Line of Code) was evaluated as a best or good predictor in [1][9], whereas in [11] it was noted as a bad predictor. Moreover, DIT (Depth of Inheritance Tree) was noted as a significant predictor in [6], but classified as a bad predictor in [1][4]. Possible causes behind these differences in results might be the variations in OSS systems [9], differences in implementations of the metrics [9], or different prediction models used. However, an indeepth investigation and resolution of such conflicting issues would be a future research agenda.

Q3. What metrics persist across the domains of the OSS projects?
Researchers studied the effectiveness and accuracy of several metric suites using

data from one or more OSS projects. Despite of their esteemed contribution in predicting OSS projects, they suffer from lack of generalizability due to diverse nature of OSS projects and the project specific nature of the metric suites. Also it is quite difficult to ensure the availability and quality of metric data, which makes the results incomparable [10]. Thus, a future research agenda would be to perform an indeepth analysis on (a) cross project validity of the studied metric suits, and (b) to propose methods to ensure the quality of metric data.

Q4. Contradiction or complementary?: (a) metric suit rely on a snapshot or (b) metric suit derived from the evolution of a project.
Traditionally defect prediction models rely on metrics that represent the state of the software system at a specific moment in time [11].These metrics are used to capture a particular snapshot or release of a project to predict the next one. But metrics capturing changes over time in projects also play a significant role in prediction. For example, metrics presenting the software evolution were used to predict the need of refactoring [12] and quality of OSS projects with significant accuracy. Thus a future research direction would be to explore a comparative study for identifying either (a) which form of metrics are more suitable for prediction models in terms of accuracy, reproducibility, and generalizability, or (b) are these metrics complementary to each other and should be used in combination to get better prediction results.

Q5. What does the community structure predict for the OSS projects?
What sets open source development apart from the traditional proprietary software is the developer community behind it. Although the social structure and communication of OSS communities have gained significant research interest, the research efforts to the community in relation to prediction appear quite the opposite. Evolution of communities is of interest starting from the paper introducing the community structure [13] but our search did not find much focus on community evolution tied to prediction. In [14] the authors investigate the impact of social structures between developers and end-users on software quality and their results give support to thinking that social structures in the community do hold prediction power in addition to the source code centric approaches. It is also suggested that combining metrics focusing on code and social aspects work as a better prediction model than either alone. This gives support that the question has research value and is worth looking into further: what does the community and the community structure predict for the software?

4   Discussion

SLR concerning software fault prediction was first conducted by [3] and was extended with new results in [7]. However these works were limited to fault prediction of closed source projects and fall short of exploring OSS domain.

This SLR will help researchers to investigate prediction studies from the perspective of metrics, methods, datasets, tool sets in an effective manner. Future research should focus on establishing external validity and consistent accuracy of prediction models, incorporation of social aspects of OSS projects, and building tool support to automate the prediction process.

References

1. Gyimothy, T., Ferenc, R., Siket, I.: Empirical Validation of Object-Oriented Metrics on Open Source Software for Fault Prediction. TSE 30(10), 897–910 (2005)
2. Kitchenham, B.A., Pretorius, R., Budgen, D., Brereton, O.P., Turner, M., Niazi, M., Linkman, S.: Systematic literature reviews in software engineering- A tertiary study. Information and Software Technology 52(8), 792–805 (2010)
3. Catal, C., Diri, B.: A systematic review of software fault prediction studies. Expert Systems with Applications 36(4), 7346–7354 (2009)
4. Shatnawi, R., Li, W.: The effectiveness of software metrics in identifying error-prone classes in post-release software evolution. TSE 81(11), 1868–1882 (2008)
5. Turhan, B., Menzies, T., Bener, A.B., Stefano, J.D.: On the relative value of cross-company and within-company data for defect prediction. ESEM 14(5), 540–578 (2009)
6. Subramanyan, R., Krishnan, M.S.: Empirical Analysis of CK Metrics for Object-Oriented Design Complexity: Implications for Software Defects. TSE 29(4), 297–310 (2003)
7. Catal, C.: Software fault prediction: A literature review and current trends. Expert Systems with Applications 38(4), 4626–4636 (2011)
8. Capiluppi, A., Adams, P.J.: Reassessing Brooks Law for the Free Software Community. IFIP AICT, pp. 274–283 (2009)
9. English, M., Exton, C., Rigon, I., Cleary, B.: Fault detection and prediction in an open-source project. In: PROMISE (2009)
10. Askari, M., Holt, R.: Information theoretic evaluation of change prediction models for large-scale software. In: MSR, pp. 126–132 (2006)
11. Knab, P., Pinzger, M., Bernstein, A.: Predicting Defect Densities in Source Code Files with Decision Tree Learners. In: MSR, pp. 119–125 (2006)
12. Ratzinger, J., Sigmund, T., Vorburger, P., Gall, H.: Mining Software Evolution to Predict Refactoring. In: ESEM, pp. 354–363 (2007)
13. Nakakoji, K., Yamamoto, Y., Nishinaka, Y., Kishida, K., Ye, Y.: Evolution Patterns of Open-Source Software Systems and Communities. In: IWPSE, pp. 76–85 (2002)
14. Bettenburg, N., Hassan, A.E.: Studying the Impact of Social Structures on Software Quality. In: ICPC, pp. 124–133 (2010)

From Open Source Software to Open Source Hardware

Robert Viseur

UMONS, Faculté Polytechnique,
Service d'Economie et de Management de l'Innovation
robert.viseur@umons.ac.be
CETIC
robert.viseur@cetic.be

Abstract. The open source software principles progressively give rise to new initiatives for culture (free culture), data (open data) or hardware (open hardware). The open hardware is experiencing a significant growth but the business models and legal aspects are not well known. This paper is dedicated to the economics of open hardware. We define the open hardware concept and determine intellectual property tools we can apply to open hardware, with a strong focus on open source licenses and practices. We next conduct some case studies in order to determine which licenses and business models are used by open hardware companies. We show some strong similarities with open source software and propose new opportunities for future works.

1   Introduction

The open hardware concept covers new practices for hardware creation inspired by open source licenses and development models. The concept is not totally new. Bruce Perens (co-author of the Open Source Definition) already discussed the concept in the book "Open sources: voices from the open source revolution" published in 1999, and describes open hardware from open source model. Open source later gives rise to new initiatives such as open access (in the scientific field), open data (for data owned by companies, produced by research or published by public sector) or free culture [3, 4].

Open, or open source, hardware is known by popular projects such as LEON3 (free processor compatible with SPARC v8 specifications) or Arduino (free electronic board for prototyping and do-it-yourself works). There also were some recent articles in popular newspapers or conferences for professionals. In 2010, the sector was estimated at $50 millions, for 13 main companies and 200 active projects [10]. The potential growth was estimated at one billions dollars in 2015. However, business models and legal aspects of open hardware have not been studied in detail.

The paper is organized as follow. We define the open hardware concept and determine intellectual property tools that we can apply to hardware. We then conduct eleven case studies in order to determine business models and licenses that companies use for their projects. Finally we discuss our results and propose future works about open source hardware.

I. Hammouda et al. (Eds.): OSS 2012, IFIP AICT 378, pp. 286–291, 2012.

2   Definitions

The concepts of "free software" and "open source" were defined by two well-known organisms: the Free Software Foundation (fsf.org) and the Open Source Initiative (opensource.org). Such organisms do not exist in the open hardware field, so several definitions can be found. Fortunately a more complete definition was recently created by the participants of the Open Hardware Summit (openhardwaresummit.org). The definition is named "open source hardware definition" and can be considered as reference. It defines 12 criteria and clearly draws on the Open Source Definition.

Note that two kinds of open hardware projects can be found: the "open source IP" and the "open source designs". The projects of "open source IP" are electronic components such as cores (DSP, cryptography, etc.), controllers (Ethernet, I2C, VGA, etc.) or processors (LEON3, OpenRISC, etc.). The projects of "open source designs" are more or less complex designs such as specialized boards (OGP1), prototyping boards (Arduino, Beagleboard, etc.), electronic devices (Ben Nanonote, OpenMoko, etc.) or machines (Makerbot, Reprap).

3   Intellectual Property and Business Models

The open source hardware consists of some items to protect: (1) the source code for electronics (e.g.: VHDL or Verilog source codes), (2) the source code for associated softwares (e.g.: development tools, SDK, etc.), (3) the schematics, the design files and the technical drawings (what we named "hardware design"), (4) the aesthetic value, (5) the documentations, and (6) the brands.

Several intellectual property tools can be applied (see inpi.fr and [6]). The source codes are protected by copyrights and sometimes by patents. The technical innovations on machines can also be protected by patents. The aesthetic value of a machine can be protected by industrial design rights. The documentation are covered by copyrights. The name can be protected as a trademark. Note that it exist a legal protection for the topographies of semiconductor products (europa.eu). Some similarities with open source softwares can be found, for example for the protection of source codes (electronics and associated softwares).

The open source software licenses are based on copyright. They allow the authors to fix the softwares user's rights and obligations. Patents can sometimes cover the software [6]. The free and open source licenses can include clauses about patents (such as documentation or automatic license) and trademarks.

Two families of open source licenses exist: the academic licenses and the copyleft licenses. The fist one (e.g.: BSD, MIT, etc.) allows the user to change the license of the software (a proprietary license can be applied). The second one (e.g.: LGPL, GPL, etc.) requires the conservation of the license. There are a lot of open source licenses, and some of these licenses are incompatible between them [7, 9]. That is a problem in the software developments based on reusable components and, by extension, with open source hardwares (e.g.: IP cores sharing).

The licenses strongly influence the business models. The license determines the possibilities for creating value and capturing revenues by modulating the appropriability conditions [8]. Free software companies generally create revenues with the distribution of softwares, the services and the software edition [2, 13]. The software editor sells add-ons for its open source software or applies dual licensing model [8, 12, 13]. The dual licensing model implies the software is published under both copyleft and proprietary licenses. The proprietary version benefits from its license, simplifying the reuse in other proprietary developments, or technical differentiation (more features) [13].

Some licenses are specific to open hardware field, for example the TAPR Open Hardware License and the CERN Open Hardware License (www.ohwr.org; www.ohwr.org). TAPR OSH also exists in a Non Commercial version.

4   Methodology

We aim to identify emergent practices and determine which business models and licenses are used by companies. We conducted eleven case studies by analyzing organizations with commercial activities in the open hardware field. We presented a draft with partial results in an international conference about free softwares in order to give feedback from more specialized audience.

We mainly used information from the projects Web site or information from projet's owners (presentations, interviews, etc.). We then searched documents published or relayed by newspapers, specialized in computer science or not. We also collected public documents highlighting particular aspects of projects such as relations between companies, relations between companies and communities or important events
(conflict, license change, etc.).

We refer to Troxler about the business models of fab labs, Malinen, Mikkonen, Tienvieri et Vadén about open source hardware developers' motivations, and Baldwin, Hienerth and von Hippel about the way from innovations by users to commercial products [1, 5, 11].

5   Results

Most of the business models in open source hardware have an equivalent in open source software, except for the distribution of manufactured third party products, and the manufacture and the sell of products, which are inapplicable for softwares.

We find, as we would expect, some open source software licenses: BSD, GPL and LGPL. They are used for source codes (electronics and softwares). They sometimes cover hardware design (it is not the intended use for that kind of license).

Hardware design is also covered by Creative Commons licenses (creativecommons.org). The chosen license is often CC-BY-SA. That one allows to copy, to distribute and to modify the work, with a commercial goal or not. It requires to name the original author (BY, for Attribution) and to keep the same license (SA, for Share Alike). That version of Creative Commons applies the copyleft principle (as GPL does with open source software).

Table 1. Examples of business models for open source softwares and hardwares

Business model	Example (OSH)	Example (OSS)
Distribution of designs	Opencores (OpenTech)	Red Hat, Novell (SuSe)
Dual licensing edition	Gaisler (Leon3)	Trolltech (QT), MySQL
Services (support, porting,...)	Gaisler	IBM, Novell, Linagora
Online services (Cloud, SaaS,...)	Bug Labs	Nexedi (ERP5 Free SaaS), OpenERP (OpenERP Online)
Distribution of manufactured third party products	Farnell	-
Manufacture and sell of products	Smart Projects (Arduino)	-

One project use a license written for open source hardware (TAPR OSH, for OGP1). The use of licenses forbidding commercial use is uncommon. No one reference to protection of the topology of semiconductor products was found.

Note that the license is not always clearly indicated. When the source code is available, it is often hosted on shared platforms such as Github (github.com), Google Code (code.google.com) or Sourceforge (sourceforge.net).

6   Discussion

The use of Creative Commons licenses for protecting hardware design raises the question of the protection which is really provided. Indeed, it is not the intended use for that kind of license: Creative Commons licenses were written to cover cultural contents (musics, books, movies, etc.). Moreover a CC-BY-SA license brings freedom to users but that freedom can be canceled by a patent covering the product. The free software and open hardware licenses often prevent or limit this by including clauses about patent, and requiring documentation or automatic patent license.

The use of GPL probably causes less difficulties for open source hardware companies. The companies revenues also come from the manufacture and the sell of products developed in a collaborative way and published under free licenses. The manufacture implies the quality control of the industrial process and the ability to manage the distribution of products. Those capacities can be reached with difficulty by a community. However the customers critical mass and the attraction power of popular brands allow to benefit from economies of scale, to offer lower prices and to invest in new products developments. Moreover quality control allows to face poor quality copies (e.g.: Arduino Asian knockoffs).

The forks are well known in the software field [14]. They are a consequence of the four freedoms given by free and open source licenses which allow to create a new project by forking source code and community. Malinen and al. note that forking is harder with open source hardware because of the need of physical copies [15]. However forking is still possible with smaller open source hardware projects. Two studied open hardware projects had been forked: OpenSPARC and Arduino. The OpenSPARC fork is a "friendly" fork. That one was made to simplify product. Several forks was made with Arduino. They were motivated by trademarks issues and by the desire to offer lower price version of products.

7   Future Works

The relation between companies and users (sometimes gathered in communities) is not well known. Some companies, such as Arduino, created business ecosystems, playing the role of leader and receiving positive externalities. Other projects seems more closed. Their owners seem less wanting to exploit the returns from collaborative development than benefit from open source hardware label and capitalize on the commercial attractiveness of documented materials which simplify the developers' work. The interactions between open hardware companies and developers should be further studied. That research could be based on questionnaires sent to the projects leaders or on activity in the collaborative tools.

References

[1] Baldwin, C.Y., Hienerth, C., von Hippel, E.: How user innovations become commercial products: a theoretical investigation and case study. Research Policy 35(9), 1291–1313 (2006)

[2] Elie, F.: Économie du logiciel libre. Eyrolles (2006)

[3] Lessig, L.: Free Culture - The Nature and Future of Creativity. Penguin (2005)

[4] Lindman, J., Tammisto, Y.: Open Source and Open Data: Business Perspectives from the Frontline. In: Hissam, S.A., Russo, B., de Mendonça Neto, M.G., Kon, F. (eds.) OSS 2011. IFIP AICT, vol. 365, pp. 330–333. Springer, Heidelberg (2011)

[5] Malinen, T., Mikkonen, T., Tienvieri, V., Vadén, T.: Community created open source hardware: A case study of "eCars — Now!". First Monday 16(5) (2011)

[6] Messerschmitt, D.G., Szyperski, C.: Industrial and Economic Properties of Software: Technology, Processes, and Value (2000)

[7] Montero, E., Cool, Y., de Patoul, F., De Roy, D., Haouideg, H., Laurent, P.: Les logiciels libres face au droit. Cahier du CRID (25) (2005)

[8] Muselli, L.: Le rôle des licences dans les modèles économiques des éditeurs de logiciels open source. Revue Française de Gestion 34(181), 199–214 (2008)

[9] St.Laurent, A.M.: Understanding Open Source and Free Software Licensing. O'Reilly Media (2004)

[10] Torrone, P., Fried, L.: Million dollar baby - Businesses designing and selling open source hardware, making millions, O'Reilly's foo camp east 2010, Microsoft's NERD center, MIT campus (2010), http://www.adafruit.com (read: March 6, 2012)

[11] Troxler, P.: Commons-Based Peer-Production of Physical Goods: Is There Room for a Hybrid Innovation Ecology? In: 3rd Free Culture Research Conference, Berlin, October 8-9 (2010)

[12] Välimäki, M.: Dual licensing in open source software industry. Systèmes d'Information et Management 8(1), 63–75 (2003)

[13] Viseur, R.: La valorisation des logiciels libres en entreprise, Jeudis du Libre. Université de Mons (September 15, 2011)

[14] Viseur, R.: Forks impacts and motivations in free and open source projects. International Journal of Advanced Computer Science and Applications (IJACSA) 3(2) (February 2012)

[15] von Hippel, E.: User toolkits for innovation. Journal of Product Innovation Management 18(4), 247–257 (2001)

Does OSS Affect E-Government Growth?
An Econometric Analysis on the Impacting Factors

Spyridoula Lakka, Teta Stamati, and Draculis Martakos

National and Kapodistrian University of Athens,
Department of Informatics and Telecommunication,
Panepistimioupolis, Ilisia 15784, Athens, Greece
{lakka,teta,martakos}@di.uoa.gr
http://www.di.uoa.gr/

Abstract. Inspired by the OSS values, an increasing number of different forms of open initiatives have come to the fore. In the context of eGovernment the notion of open government has met wide acceptance among nations and became closely related to one of its goals. Open government shares with OSS the notions of collaboration, participation and transparency and many actions towards OSS into eGovernment reform policies, have been recorded worldwide. The study investigates the relationship between OSS growth and eGovernment. A theoretical framework of the theories of institutionalism, growth and human capital is proposed as the guiding theoretical lens to identify possible influencing factors that together with OSS are evaluated for their magnitude of impact on eGovernment growth across different economic environments.

Keywords: Open source software, eGovernment adoption, institutionalism, growth theory, human capital theory.

1 Introduction

Being "computer-based innovation"[1], open source software (OSS) is marked by ideologies and values of collaboration and sharing, adopting a different value creation model, in which value is an outcome of collective intellect achieved through the OSS community. The OSS model is able to deal with costs and short product life cycles, attracting organizations and governments to use these value added services, without compromising the required levels of quality. Inspired by the OSS values, a number of other forms of open initiatives have been gaining momentum. Open source systems now extend beyond software to include open access, open documents, open innovation, open government and more. Open government is defined as the governmental response to citizens' demands for information and services from government organizations [2].

In the context of eGovernment (eGov) the notion of openness has met wide acceptance among nations and became closely related to one of its goals. eGov refers to the transformation of traditional public sector services and processes into an

I. Hammouda et al. (Eds.): OSS 2012, IFIP AICT 378, pp. 292–297, 2012.
© IFIP International Federation for Information Processing 2012

electronic format with greater accessibility and interactivity to citizens [3]. eGov aims at more efficient, transparent and accessible public services to citizens and businesses. Implementation of eGov initiatives requires substantial reform in public organizations because the typical form of a bureaucratic organization with conservative cultures, make it resistant to change. The choice and design of new technologies constitute important carriers of eGov reform aims and a number of actions show that OSS is one of these innovative technologies. Also, OSS diffusion as infrastructure software of the web (e.g Apache and Linux), shows that OSS establishes an advanced technological framework upon which eGov services can be build.

As a result, many actions and policies that promote OSS in the public sector have been recorded worldwide [4]. Recently, the US government has introduced the open government initiative declaration, which focuses on the institutionalization of the principles of transparency, participation, and collaboration into the culture and work of eGov [5]. Also, in Europe, the EU Ministerial Declaration [6] of eGov goals define a more open, flexible, and collaborative eGov, paying particular attention to the benefits of the use of open source model and specifications. Both declarations, contain principles (like accessibility, transparency and openness) and methodologies (like collaboration and sharing), that are obvious references to OSS. The commonalities of OSS and open government have even lead to a new political philosophy, which advocates the application of the principles of the OSS and open content movements to the democratic principles, that enable any citizen to add to the creation of policy.

Taking into account the above evidence, the relation of eGov growth and OSS technology is considered of great interest. Even though prior studies [7] have already identified technological factors that determine eGov diffusion, none has attempted to assess the impact of OSS technology. The study proposes a theoretical framework of the theories of institutionalism, growth and human capital as the guiding theoretical lens to identify possible influencing factors that together with OSS are evaluated for their magnitude of impact onto eGov growth.

2   Theoretical Framework

A country is conceptualized as a socio-economic system within which eGov growth occurs. The model is based on the idea that the forces of growth to an economic system comprise of institutional, human capital and growth theory factors and is specified as:

$$eGov_{it} = F(X^{inst}, X^{hc}, X^{gr}) \qquad (1)$$

Where $eGov$ is the eGovernment growth determined by a vector of all factors relevant to institutional X^{inst}, human capital X^{hc} and growth X^{gr} theories, for each country i, at time t. The corresponding conceptual model is illustrated in Fig. 1.

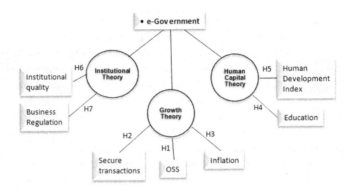

Fig. 1. Conceptual model for eGovernment growth

Growth Theory indicates that economic growth is generated from within a system as a result of internal processes [8]. This study examines the impact of technological and economic factors within a country. Firstly, as discussed in section 1, OSS is expected to have an impact on eGov growth (H1). Secondly, security in transactions is also important [9], as possible security pitfalls of eGov services could retain users from the use of electronic services (H2). Finally, economic conditions like the cost of living or a country's inflation rates could influence eGov. For instance, higher costs of internet access would hinder its use (H3).

Human Capital Theory stresses that education, health, and skills are forms of capital, the human capital, that can explain the differences in growth among individuals and nations [10]. The study examines the impact of both the education level (H4) and the quality of human capital in terms of social development (H5).

Institutionalism considers the processes by which structures, rules, norms, and routines, become established as authoritative guidelines for social behavior [11]. Prior studies [12] found that from an institutional view, public services are likely to adopt eGov due to the pressures from regulation and competition environment. Thus, the impact of institutional quality (IQ) and business regulations are evaluated. IQ is considered as an indication of government effectiveness to enact regulations and laws (H6). Also, regulations and actions that enable business creation and improve competition are assumed to improve acceptance of eGov services (H7).

3   Data Description, Statistical analysis and Results

The factors are evaluated by means of a panel data analysis of 25 countries selected so as to represent different regions and economic status[1], over the period 2003-2008. The data, measures and sources for each of the factors are provided in Table 1.

---

[1] Belgium, Finland, France, Germany, Greece, Italy, Netherlands, Spain, Sweden, United Kingdom (UK), Romania, Russia, Turkey, Argentina, Brazil, Canada, Mexico, United States (US), Australia, China, India, Japan, Korea, South Africa, Tunisia.

Table 1. Data Labels, variables' Definitions, Measures, and Sources

	Variable	Measure	Sources
eGov	e Gov Development Index encompasses the capacity and the willingness of the public sector to deploy ICT for improving knowledge in the service of the citizen.	Measured in the range of 0 and 1.	United Nations eGov data center[2].
OSS	Number of subscribed per country users in the SourceForge portal.	Natural log	University of Notre Dame[3]
sserv	Servers using encryption technology in Internet transactions	Natural log	World Bank Indicators[4]
HDI	Human Development Index (HDI) reflects social and economic development.	Ranging between 0 and 1	United Nations [5]..
educ	Operating expenditures in education	Percentage of GNI.	World Bank Indicators
inf	Inflation, measured by the consumer price index, is the annual percentage change in the cost to the average consumer.	Percentage rate.	World Bank Indicators
IQ	Institutional quality measured by the mean value of the six dimensions of governance. Higher values indicate higher quality.	Ranging from -2.5 to +2.5 units.	Worldwide Governance Indicators[6]..
B_R	Business regulation expresses policies to improve market entry conditions and competition. Higher values indicate less restrictions and higher competition.	Values ranging from 1 to 10.	Economic Freedom Network[7].

$$eGov_{it} = a + b_1OSS_{it} + b_2sserv_{it} + b_3HDI_{it} + b_4educ_{it} + \qquad (2)$$

$$b_5inf_{it} + b_6IQ_{it} + b_7B\_R_{it} + u_i + \varepsilon_{it}$$

Initially, data were successfully tested for correlations among the variables. The econometric model is given by equation (2), where u_i is the country specific effect and ε_{it} is the idiosyncratic error. Next, specification tests were performed. The Hausman test [13] indicates that the fixed effects model should be preferred ($\chi^2(7)=15.89$, p <0.05). The Breusch and Pagan test [14] indicated the significance of the individual specific effects($\chi^2(1)=135.6$, p=0, H_0: Var(u)=0). The Durbin-Wu-Hausman test [13,15] showed no evidence of endogeneity of the regressors. Panel models often violate standard Ordinary Least Squares assumptions. The Wooldridge test [16] showed evidence of serial correlation in the idiosyncratic errors: F(1, 24)=100.4, p=0.

[2] http://www2.unpan.org/egovkb/datacenter/CountryView.aspx
[3] http://zerlot.cse.nd.edu
[4] http://data.worldbank.org
[5] http://hdr.undp.org/en/
[6] http://www.govindicators.org
[7] http://www.freetheworld.com/datasets_efw.html

Also, the modified Wald test [17] indicated heteroscedastic disturbances ($\chi^2(25)=720.8$, p=0). The tests indicate that the optimal method choice is the feasible generalized least squares (FGLS), which is consistent for autocorrelation errors and panel heteroscedasticity, provided exogeneity of the independent variables [16].

Table 2. FGLS regression results

Dependent variable: eGov ***	No of Observations:150		Wald $\chi^2(7) = 272.26$
Variables	Coef.	Std. Err.	Z
OSS	0.014	0.004	3.75***
sserv	0.012	0.004	3.21***
educ	0.012	0.006	1.95*
HDI	0.662	0.094	7.02***
inf	0.001	0.001	1.18
IQ	0.055	0.018	3.00**
B_R	-0.002	0.002	-0.7
_cons	0.045	0.072	0.63

Notes. Significance levels are denoted by: *=p<0.1, **=p<0.05, ***= p<0.01.

Regression results are provided in Table 2. It can be deduced that there is a significant and positive impact of OSS on eGov (z=3.75 at p<0.01). Implementation of eGov initiatives requires substantial reform in public organizations, such as the bureaucratic organization with conservative cultures, and innovative technologies. OSS combines technological innovation and quality characteristics and cost efficiency. It also carries the values and ideas of collaboration, participation and code sharing, which aligns with the notions of open eGov. This philosophy is expected to increase transparency, trust and citizen's participation in electronic services. The commonalities between the two entities, show that their growth follow parallel trajectories and that countries with higher OSS penetration are more probable to exhibit higher eGov adoption. It can be elicited that OSS is an emerging technology into the eGov context, that challenges the potential of eGov reforms. This, n turn, creates new direction fields and opportunities for OSS growth and long term sustainability.

Other factors that show a positive and statistically significant impact are the use of secure servers (H2), social development (H4), education (H5) and IQ (H6). *HDI* has the highest coefficient in the regression (0.66), reflecting the importance of social development for the achievement of cultural and political leaps in the UN's five stage model. Finally, inflation and B_R variables don't show any statistical significance, rejecting hypotheses H3 and H7. It can be deduced, that well organized societies, exhibiting effectiveness in governess and in policies related to social development are more prone to lead eGov initiatives that earn citizen's trust and willingness to adopt.

4   Conclusions

The study evaluates factors for eGov adoption. Grounded on the findings, OSS showed a significant impact on eGov, indicating that OSS is an emerging technological approach into the eGov context. This, in turn, would create more opportunities for OSS growth and long term sustainability. In addition, the use of secure servers, IQ, social development and education proved to be drivers that lead eGov growth.

Results provide with useful input for research and practice. For research it brings in a new theoretical framework for the study of eGov growth and new directions on the technological approaches for eGov reforms. For practice, it emphasizes on positive effects of the use of OSS for the implementation of eGov projects. The study constitutes an initial evaluation of country specific factors affecting eGov, limited by the small number of countries and possible missing factors. However, findings are still important, as they give an insight of the factors that positively affect the diffusion mechanism. Future research, could explore more inhibitory or favouring factors, by extending the current theoretical framework.

References

1. Von Hippel, E.: Innovation by user communities: learning from open source software. MIT Sloan Management Review 42, 82–86 (2001)
2. La Porte, T.M., Demchak, C.C., De Jong, M.: Democracy and bureaucracy in the age of theWeb - Empirical findings and theoretical speculations. Administration & Society 34, 411–446 (2002)
3. Huang, Z., Bwoma, P.O.: An overview of critical issues of e-government. Issues of Information Systems IV, 164–170 (2003)
4. Lewis, J.A.: Government Open Source Policies, http://csis.org/publication/government-open-source-policies
5. McDermott, P.: Building open government. Government Information Quarterly 27, 401–413 (2010)
6. EU-Ministerial-Declaration: EU Ministerial Declaration on eGovernment. In: 5th Ministerial eGovernment Conference, Malmoe, Sweden (2009)
7. Siau, K., Long, Y.: Factors Impacting E-Government Development. In: International Conference on Information Systems (ICIS), Washington, DC (2004)
8. Romer, P.M.: Increasing returns and long run growth. Journal of Political Economy 94, 1002–1037 (1986)
9. Smith, S., Jamieson, R.: Determining Key Factors in E-Government Information System Security. Information Systems Management 23, 23–32 (2006)
10. Schultz, T.W.: Human Wealth and Economic Growth. The Humanist 19, 71–81 (1959)
11. Scott, W.R.: Institutional theory. In: Ritzer, G. (ed.) Encyclopedia of Social Theory. Sage, Thousand Oaks (2004)
12. Gil-Garcia, R.J., Martinez-Moyano, I.J.: Understanding the evolution of e-government: The influence of systems of rules on public sector dynamics. Government Information Quarterly 24, 266–290 (2007)
13. Hausman, J.A.: Specification tests in econometrics. Econometrica 46, 1251–1271 (1978)
14. Breusch, T.S., Pagan, A.R.: The Lagrange multiplier test and its applications to model specification in econometrics. Review of Economic Studies 47, 239–253 (1980)
15. Durbin, J.: Errors in variables. Review of the International Statistical Institute 22, 23–32 (1954)
16. Wooldridge, J.M.: Econometric Analysis of Cross Section and Panel Data. MIT Press, Cambridge, MA (2002)
17. Greene, W.: Econometric Analysis. Prentice-Hall, New York (2000)

Open Source, Open Innovation and Intellectual Property Rights – A Lightning Talk

Terhi Kilamo[1], Imed Hammouda[1], Ville Kairamo[2],
Petri Räsänen[2], and Jukka P. Saarinen[3]

[1] Tampere University of Technology
firstname.lastname@tut.fi
[2] Uusi Tehdas/New Factory
firstname.lastname@hermia.fi
[3] Nokia Research Center
jukka.p.saarinen@nokia.com

Abstract. Open innovation projects are fast paced aiming at producing a quick proof of concept of an innovative software product. This need for speedy results makes the use of open source components as a basis for the work appealing. Open source brings with it an inherent risk of license conflicts that may become an issue when aiming to develope an innovative demo into an actual product. In this study, the first results of investigating the knowledge the participants of innovation projects have on intellectual property are presented. The effect this may have on the project results is also discussed.

1 Introduction

Ongoing and fast-paced innovation is becoming a vitality to companies in the software business. Innovation can lie in any commodity; it commonly is a novelty that can be put into actual, practical use. Many companies rely on innovation projects to create better products and to improve their internal processes [2]. Open innovation environments allow businesses to reach beyond the company scope in the search for new concepts, ideas and business opportunities.

Innovation, and open innovation especially, comes with a number of challenges such as motivation, integration and exploitation of the results [13]. It needs a governance framework [4] that enables organizational alignment of the different partners, proper handling of intellectual property rights (IPR) issues, and the emergence of new kinds of business opportunities. These challenges have to be taken into account when building any open innovation platform with the goal of driving future development and solutions. One major issue affecting exploitation and emergence of business opportunities is the handling of intellectual property.

A natural requirement for a open innovation environment is a mutually beneficial and agreeable IPR model. In addition, the IPR issues need to be further taken into account in development of innovation projects and when commercializing their results. The focus in this paper is to investigate to what extend do the university student participants of open innovation projects consider IPR issues

I. Hammouda et al. (Eds.): OSS 2012, IFIP AICT 378, pp. 298–303, 2012.

such as licensing in their development. The paper motivates the problem and gives some preliminary results.

The rest of the paper is structured as follows. Section 2 provides background for and motivates the study. Section 3 explains the research setting and some preliminary results are presented in Section 4. Finally Section 5 discusses the findings and concludes the paper.

2   Research Motivation

This section discusses the background for the study including related work. The motivation for the study is given with the research goal and research questions the study aims to answer.

2.1   Background

Demola [11,9] is an open innovation platform intended for academic students. It aims to develop innovative products and demos within multidisciplinary and agile project teams. The project ideas are initiated by local businesses and public organisations and thus have practical business importance. Demola also gives support for emerging business ideas and encourages start-ups based on these projects. A model for managing immaterial rights that supports all this and respects the authors is offered. Demola is now in its third year of operation with several successful projects completed.

The Demola IPR Model. One significant factor in building an innovation environment that is attractive to all of its participants is the management of intellectual property within. The Demola IPR agreement maintains the authors rights to their work giving the project partner company full utilization rights, if they so want, at the same time. Only the project results are under this kind of agreement, prior knowledge is excluded. The agreement entered also states that the project results must not contain third party trade secrets, third party owned parts or otherwise copyrighted material and should be usable without any IPR protected material. Software licenses from the open source perspective are not addressed in the IPR agreement. All immaterial rights are handled the same.

Related Work. With the rise of free/libre/open source software (FLOSS) and FLOSS components utilized in software projects the importance of legality concerns has risen. The focus in research has mainly been to license analysis on the software level to either identify the licenses [8] or to check the code against license compatibilities [5,12]. These methods do not support license awareness at the time of development but focus at final source code instead. Research effort has also been directed to finding ways of documenting the legal rules [7,10]. Our aim here is on the individual developers and how they regard IPR and licensing in a short and hectic innovative software project. These topics are scarcely taught in standard software engineering degree program curricula which increases the interest to study the current level of knowledge. With works such as [3,6,1] it is evident that further legality research is needed.

2.2 Research Goals

The goal of this paper is to investigate to what extent students from different academic levels take intellectual property rights into account when working in quick paced open innovation projects. These projects are run in Demola and the results should be usable by the companies in their further commercial products.

The Demola contract model allows the project partner to purchase rights to the project results. The project perspective is however more on getting the project completed and to show a functional end result or at least a demo level proof of concept. This may direct the project groups to not take IPR issues such as licensing and license compatibility into account while working on the project. Furthermore, as the projects are relatively short framed the likelihood of utilizing open source licensed components is notable. Not having to implement everything from scratch leaves the projects more freedom to focus on the actual innovation in the project.

The research questions are:

Q1 How much prior knowledge the participating students of the Demola innovation projects have in IPR issues?

Q2 Do they utilize open source components in the projects?

Q3 Are the IPR issues characteristic to software and open source taken into consideration?

Q4 Based on the three first questions: does IPR cause inherent risks to the project partners in acquiring rights to the end product?

3 Research Design

In order to map out the project groups' attitudes towards IPR issues while working on the project, we conducted a survey targeted towards local technology students, who had completed a Demola project. A survey available online[1] was used.

The survey consisted of 14 questions that queried the project participants' background (Q1), usage of open source components in the project (Q2), prior knowledge in IPR issues in software (Q3) and how significant the risk for different software IPR violations is estimated as (Q4).

The survey was sent to students who have completed a Demola project in the past. The initial phase of the research reported in this paper targeted only a small sample group of students who have recently completed or are just completing a Demola project. A wider study of all Demola project participants is planned in the near future based on the experiences collected here.

4 IPR Knowledge in Projects

At this trial round of the survey, in total nine people answered the survey. There were in addition nine incomplete answers that are left out of the results presented

---

[1] Survey available at: `ossli.cs.tut.fi/survey/index.php?sid=44979`

here and one with most of the fields left empty. Each of the respondents came from a different project so in total nine projects are represented. Four of them had had their project licensed by the company behind it and one was still in progress.

Four of the respondents had utilized open source components in their work and described a pattern we had predicted where open source software was used in order to avoid writing large amounts of code. Also open source development tools were mentioned. There were three respondents who answered this with "uncertain" and one left the field unanswered.

Table 1. Knowledge of legality issues

	knowledgeable	quite a lot	a little	none	no answer
Patents and licences	2	3	2	1	1
License compatibility	1	1	3	3	1
Specifics of FLOSS	2	1	5	0	1
Copyleft in FLOSS	1	3	3	1	1

Prior knowledge in legality aspect varied but the specifics of open source were less familiar than licences and patents as general concepts. Only one respondent answered to be knowledgeable in the FLOSS licenses' copyleft requirement. Five had only a little knowledge in FLOSS specifics. License compatibility was a little known issue to 67% of the respondents, The knowledge reported by the respondents is listed in Table 1

The risks were all in all considered significant. The risks evaluated and the answers are listed in Table 2. License terms infringement and third party risks were considered as the highest risks while quite a high risk was also seen in patent infringements in general. Open source related questions saw a rise in unanswered questions. License incompatibility was considered as a risk by two respondents still, while four saw the courtroom as a risk.

Table 2. Risks considered in replies

Risk	Seriousness			
	Extreme	Moderate	Not relevant	No answer
Product infringes on a software patent	2	2	3	2
Product contains code that unbeknownst to you belongs to third party	2	4	2	1
Product contains code that unbeknownst to you is covered by third parties trade secret	3	2	3	1
Product contains code that unbeknownst to you is violating its license terms	3	2	2	2
Open source licenses are incompatible with each other	1	1	3	4
Open source licenses do not stand up in court	2	2	2	3
Patent law suits	2	1	0	1

5 Discussion and Conclusion

The replies into the initial study were scarce and thus it is difficult to draw any major conclusions based on the results. We can give initial answers to the research questions but no real weight is there yet. However, the results do indicate only a little care is given to IPR issues when working on the project which supports our hypothesis that there is an inherent risk there. Furthermore, we are going to add more data into the final version of the paper.

The result seems to indicate a problem also in regard to the risks themselves. The participants find the most significant risks where there should not be none given the IPR agreement, such as third party code, trade secrets and patents. Open source – while utilized – is not deemed as such a high risk which itself gives a reason to suspect there is one. Furthermore in FLOSS related issues the number of no answers increases which leads to suppose a knowledge gap is there.

Part of the reason why the complete answer percentage was so low may be in the feedback we got from the students that they had not understood some of the questions. While the survey itself can be improved in some respects, this indicates that there may very well be a large gap in the participants' IPR knowledge. Overall the results themselves suggest that the participants don't have a sufficient knowledge in IPR matters and what knowledge there is dwindles significantly in FLOSS related issues.

What the study already shows is that there is a need for a wider survey of open innovation project participants. There seems to be a need for a set of recommendations to the participants to take into account when working on the projects regarding the intellectual property rights issues. Currently, the project participants at least are vary of the product not being sound in IPR. Mapping out what the participants know would help in giving recommendations and supporting the projects also in respect to IPR. This could further enforce the IPR and software legality matters to be mode widely included more into the software engineering curricula.

References

1. Alspaugh, T.A., Asuncion, H.U., Scacchi, W.: Analyzing software licenses in open architecture software systems. In: Proceedings of the 2009 ICSE Workshop on Emerging Trends in Free/Libre/Open Source Software Research and Development, FLOSS 2009, pp. 54–57. IEEE Computer Society Press (2009)
2. Chesbrough, H.: Open Innovation: Researching a New Paradigm, chapter Open Innovation: A New Paradigm for Understanding Industrial Innovation. Oxford University Press (2006)
3. Di Penta, M., German, D.M., Guéhéneuc, Y., Antoniol, G.: An exploratory study of the evolution of software licensing. In: Proceedings of the 32nd ACM/IEEE International Conference on Software Engineering, ICSE 2010, vol. 1, pp. 145–154. ACM (2010)
4. Feller, J., Finnegan, P., Hayes, J., O'Reilly, P.: Institutionalising information asymmetry: governance structures for open innovation. Information Technology & People 22(4), 297–316 (2009)

5. Fossology, http://fossology.org (last visited March 2012)
6. Germán, M., Di Penta, D., Davies: Understanding and auditing the licensing of open source software distributions. In: Proceedings of the 18th International Conference on Program Comprehension, pp. 84–93. IEEE (2010)
7. Hoekstra, R., Breuker, J., Di Bello, M., Boer, A.: The LKIF Core Ontology of Basic Legal Concepts. In: Proceedings of LOAIT, pp. 43–63 (2007)
8. A license code indetification tool for source code, http://ninka.turingmachine.org/ (last visited March 2012)
9. Facilitating Innovation at Demola. Open Threads: Open Innovation Newsletter (April 2009)
10. The Qualipso Project, http://www.qualipso.org/licenses-champion (last visited March 2012)
11. Demola Innovation Platform, http://www.demola.fi (last visited March 2012)
12. Tuunanen, T., Koskinen, J., Kärkkäinen, T.: Automated Software License Analysis. Automated Software Engineering 16(3-4), 455–490 (2009)
13. West, J., Gallagher, S.: Challenges of Open Innovation: The Paradox of Firm Investment in Open-Source Software. R&D Management 36(3), 319–331 (2006)

OSS Adoption in South Africa:
Applying the TOE Model to a Case Study

Jean-Paul Van Belle and Mark Reed

Department of Information Systems, University of Cape Town
Private Bag, 7701 Rondebosch, South Africa
Jean-Paul.VanBelle@uct.ac.za

Abstract. This paper presents a case study on the factors that influence the initial adoption of Open Source Software (OSS) in a large South African organization when implementing an OSS PBX platform. The theoretical foundation for this research draws on a number of academic frameworks and models, thus not only providing a practical illustration but also validating their usefulness in guiding OSS adoption.

1 Introduction

This paper explores the adoption of OSS in South Africa with a view to finding out how a South African (SA) company went about adopting OSS, uncovering what factors influenced the adoption and contributed to its sustainability in the post-adoption period, and investigating how supportive theoretical OSS models are of successful adoption. The OSS adoption was ascertained within the Technology, Organisation and Environment (TOE) framework, with factors drawn from a number of other OSS models as discussed in below.

The research hopefully offers practical insights to organisations who are considering adopting OSS. Researchers may find that it sheds light on the usefulness of some theoretical frameworks and models.

2 Theoretical Framework

The theoretical framework was beased on the Technology, Organisational and Environmental (TOE) framework, which identifies three contexts in which an organisation functions and therefore may influence its ability to adopt technology and affect the process by which it accepts [12] and implements a new technology [17]. These contextual factors also influence the organisation's intent to adopt an innovation, and affect its assimilation process as well as the impact of the innovation on organisational performance [17].

The **technological** context refers to the internal and external technologies available to the organisation which have a bearing on its productivity [12] and encompasses existing technologies, both those in use within the organisation and the relevant

I. Hammouda et al. (Eds.): OSS 2012, IFIP AICT 378, pp. 304–309, 2012.

technologies the organisation can draw on externally [18]. They include elements of open source maturity and technology readiness. Dedrick & West [4] consider five technological factors, namely compatibility, complexity, relative advantage, trialability and observability. They identify the three most common variables linked to technology adoption as compatibility with existing technologies, relative advantage over current technologies and with complexity negatively influencing adoption. Relative advantage is the measure of how much of an improvement the new technology is relative to the existing one and is primarily measured in terms of cost and reliability [18]. The software cost and risk model determines the cost and the risks of using open source [9]. Failure to optimally manage the potential risks and rewards of open source will put IT organisations at an increasingly serious risk in the coming years [5].

The **organisational** context is characterised by a few descriptive measures, i.e. scope, size of the organisation and the slack resources available internally. Organisations have different competitive positions and roles for IT, and a high level of IT intensity has been shown to be proportional to open source adoption [11]. The innovation orientation of an organisation is related to the timing of adoption and the triggers prompts pertinent to adoption decision [3]. The centrality of IT to the business strategy is core to the willingness of the organisation to adopt open source [4]. Choice set and selection occur as a response to software adoption policy, but more importantly arise within the application context. This context exhibits the strategic significance of the specified system and consequently the equivalent weighted value for features, risk, cost and available products where the predilection of the buyer is restricted by a limited number of available choices [11].

The **environmental** context refers to the arena in which the organisation operates and conducts its business [17]. The organisation is influenced by its competitors and by the industry itself [12]. Environmental factors encompass factors such as rivalry and relations with buyers and suppliers [18]. A regionally available appropriate skill set reduces the time investment and the cost of using open source [9], although few certification programs exist for computer and network support professionals wanting to specialise in open source software [1]. A useful conceptual framework for exploring the OSS skills is the Open Source Skills and Risk Tolerance model. This ascertains the capacity of the organisation to handle the risks intrinsic in open source adoption and produces a risk tolerance plan and profile [9]. However, developer skills may be improved by the intellectual challenge of contributing to software development when they are granted access to source code [2]. Other barriers to the successful adoption of open source are the lack of resources and/or the availability of external technological resources as well as the lack of compatibility with current technologies and skill [10].

3   Research Methodology

In this research, a deductive, explanatory and qualitative research approach was taken. A qualitative case study approach was chosen because of the interdependence between variables and the non-measurability/intrinsic complexity of some of the variables. The aim is to provide richer and more subtle explanations than statistics can provide. The case study was a recent implementation of an open source PBX system, Asterisk, in one of the leading and largest medical health administrators in South Africa. The supporting data for the case study comes from semi-structured interviews with nine key decision makers within the organization: the Managing Director (Scheme Administration), MD (IT), Head of IT Infrastructure, Head of Telephony Solutions, the enterprise architect, the principal specialist, the senior manager, the software architect and the solutions architect in charge of the project.

4   Applying the TOE Model to the Adoption of an OSS PBX Platform in a South African Financial Services Company

The case takes place in one of the largest medical aid administrators in South Africa, with more than 2500 employees. They administer close to one million members and are one of the leaders in their field. They were faced with the important and high-risk decision to replace their PBX system in their 800-seat call centre. Negotiations with a number of proprietary vendors ensued, including their preferred communications provider, but no proprietary vendor could promise them the tight delivery times or required customizations. At that stage, they investigated Asterisk, an open source PBX system. The system was piloted, extensively customized and successfully put in production by the end of 2008. The case study was analyzed using the TOE framework and demonstrates the empirical validity and relevance of the factors outlined above.

4.1   Technology Factors

Access to source code – The ability to access the source code was a key positive factor mentioned by most respondents in the case study: *"The product itself is very basic, we're building around that to create exactly what we want"; "the ability to customize";* and *"to be able to be creative"* (Developer). They develop, maintain and support the OSS internally and they additionally post fixes for Asterisk PBX source code back into the community.

Complexity – Although the skill set to develop customized solutions around OSS products may require additional resources *"the skills that you deploy to customize the solutions need to be a lot more experienced"*, the software architect did not perceive OSS products to be intrinsically more complex: *"they are not more complex, it depends what level you look at it. At a source code level, I don't think they are more complicated."* On the other hand, the head of Telephony opined that OSS may often lack a user-friendly GUI to administer it: *"the only complexity that OSS PBXs introduce is that they don't have the easy or simplified configuration interfaces like proprietary PBXs"*.

Cost – The cost factor was never the initial key consideration. The major drives for the adoption were the quick deployment capability and the flexibility the solution provided: *"the cost factor over time is not a huge factor, for me it was about getting a solution that can deal with the growth of the business"* (MD of Schemes). In fact, management was nuanced about distinguishing between the zero licensing costs and the Total Cost of Ownership *"Nothing in life is free. You got to have somebody who is supporting it ... a Linux person, an Asterisk person... It's got a different cost of ownership model but, on the whole, in the end, as the maturity of the product grows, it does tend towards to being cheaper over time"* (MD of IT). However, the cost savings were significant: *"expensive carrier grade switches don't differ substantially in functionality to what Asterisk can do."* An internal cost benefit analysis revealed a saving of OSS over proprietary in the region of R30 million (about US$ 4 million) over the 36 month budgeting period.

Compatibility – Because of the existence of standards bodies, compatibility was assured: *"in the environment, they work with the de facto standards anyway"* (MD of IT). Critical to building an open source telephony platform was the fact that telephony equipment is produced to open telephony standards and the ability to source non-proprietary telephony components: *"If that [standard peripheral devices] didn't exist, open source for this specific application would never have been an option."* (Head of Telephony Solutions)

Trialability – This was important as indicated by the IT Infrastructure Manager: *"We started playing with it (OSS PBX), and we realized that it was one hell of a product... that actually, this could work for us as an organization..."*

Reliability – Although initially there were stability problems, in the end they achieved a stable solution: *"you just have to keep working at it to achieve the same amount of reliability"* (Developer).

Maturity –Digium's commercialization of Asterisk PBX support was an important influencing factor. The fact that a third party organization had built a business around packaging and supporting the OSS solution signalled the broader market acceptance and continuity: *"There is a 'keep alive' of the product [since] Digium has built a business around Asterisk. [...] This tells me Asterisk will not drift sideways."* (MD IT) This was in spite of the fact that they did not use nor intend to use Digium's services.

In this particular case study, some of the other technology factors (e.g. potential project forking, security issues and observability) did not seem to play a role.

4.2   Organisational Factors

Firm context – Being in the highly competitive financial services industry, the organization is very IT intensive. One of the key differentiating factors in the industry is customer service and the ability to deliver new products and services quickly. The two MDs put it as follows: *"Technology plays a big role in [our] positioning [for competitive advantage]"* and *"Technology is very dominant in our strategic thinking"*. However, the Senior Manager confirmed that the specific decision to go for Asterisk was not driven by competitive pressure explicitly.

Centrality of IT – IT and the ICT infrastructure is critical to the day-to-day functioning of the business. The communications infrastructure in particular is a critical business infrastructure component, so the replacement decision had a high risk profile. *"... when the PBX is down, you are dead ... it is the most business critical along the lines of our applications ..."* (Head of IT Infrastructure).

Open Source attitudes – The organization uses a combination of OSS and commercial applications so there were no critical attitudes to content with: *"I don't think they had an attitude about Open Source Software. I don't think they were pro or against it"* (Head of IT Infrastructure).

Standards attitudes – This is an important consideration in favour of open source: *"I am very comfortable with [open source], they don't just change standards. I mean if you are busy using an API, they are not all of a sudden going to make it incompatible, that is something that happens with Microsoft"* (Solutions Architect).

Boundary spanners – These are very important. A number of staff had already gained positive prior experience with OSS implementations. The OSS PBX was introduced to the company by an external telephony consultant, who also supported the solution in the initial deployment phase.

4.3   Environmental Factors

Vendor Support – Although the existence of an independent support service provider is an important consideration in establishing product maturity, it is not a factor in procuring actual support: *"[Digium provides] that enterprise level of support. But we still do it ourselves"* (developer).

OSS Support – The need to collaborate with the OSS community was emphasized: *"If we hit a major bug we would try and find some helpers ... but I don't think we will get it here in [South Africa]. We will have to go on to forums and communities"* (Developer).

Firm size – The organization is a large organization with over 2500 employees. The PBX platform serves 800 call centre seats. *"Because we are so large, we can throw a lot of resources at it, so it takes a lot of risk out of the equation."* (MD of IT)

Technology skills – The lack of skills in the market place made the decision a challenging one: *"We just go look for VoIP engineers ... they are so difficult to find and that's the risk."* (Head of Telephony Solutions) As a result, they mostly developed their own skills by providing hands-on experience and training: *"There was a training course that people went on ... again, very much a self-learning exercise"* (Head of Telephony Solutions). However, the key (Linux and VoIP) skills were available in the market: *"OSS would never have been an option if we weren't able to source skills externally and bring them in-house."*

Environmental factors that did not play a role in this particular case study were political splintering, legitimacy and availability. Perhaps these factors are more important to adopting organizations of a smaller size.

5   Conclusion

The TOE framework takes cognisance of the internal and external context in which the company operates and comprehensively covers the adoption process. It served as a useful framework when looking at the full scope of OSS adoption. Although this research involved only a single system adoption in one large organization, almost all of the factors identified in the TOE framework were found to be of significance. Hopefully this research will give other organisations a comprehensive overview of factors to consider when contemplating OSS adoption.

References

[1] Bruggink, M.: Open source in Africa: towards informed decision-making. IICD: The International Institute for Communication and Development 7, 1–4 (2003)

[4] Dedrick, J., West, J.: Adoption of open source platforms: an exploratory study. In: HBS - MIT Sloan Free/Open Source Software Conference: New Models of Software Development, pp. 1–27 (2003)

[5] Driver, M.: Key issues for open-source software in 2007. Gartner, Stamford, CT (2007)

[7] Glass, R.: A look at the economics of open source. Communications of the ACM 47(2), 25–27 (2004)

[9] Guliani, G., Woods, D.: Open source for the enterprise. United States of America. O'Reilly Media, Inc., Sebastopol (2005)

[10] Holck, J., Larsen, M.H., Pedersen, M.K.: Identifying business barriers and enablers for the adoption of open source software. Frederiksberg, Copenhagen Business School, Department of Informatics (2004)

[11] Kwan, S.K., West, J.: A conceptual model for enterprise adoption of open source software. In: Enterprise Adoption: The Standards Edge: Open Season (2004)

[12] Lipert, S.K., Govindarajulu, C.: Technological, organizational and environmental antecedents to web services adoption. Communications of the IIMA 6(1), 146–157 (2006)

[17] Zhu, K., Kraemer, K., Xu, S.: Electronic business adoption by European firms: A cross-country assessment of the facilitators and inhibitors. European Journal of Information Systems 12(4), 251–268 (2003)

[18] Zhu, K., Kraemer, K.L., Gurbaxani, V., Xu, S.X.: Migration to open-standard inter organizational systems: Network effects, switching costs, and path dependency. MIS Quarterly 30 (Special Issue), 515–539 (2006)

Forking the Commons: Developmental Tensions and Evolutionary Patterns in Open Source Software

Mehmet Gençer and Bülent Özel

İstanbul Bilgi University, Turkey
{mgencer,bulent}@cs.bilgi.edu.tr

Abstract. Open source software (OSS) presents opportunities and challenges for developers to exploit its commons based licensing regime by creating specializations of a software technology to address plurality of goals and priorities. By 'forking' a new branch of development separate from the main project, development diverges into a path in order to relieve tensions related to specialization, which later encounters new tensions. In this study, we first classify forces and patterns within this divergence process. Such tensions may stem from a variety of sources including internal power conflicts, emergence of new environmental niches such as demand for specialized uses of same software, or differences along stability vs. development speed trade-off. We then present an evolutionary model which combines divergence options available to resolve tensions, and how further tensions emerge. In developing this model we attempt to define open software evolution at the level of systems of software, rather than at individual software project level.

Keywords: Forking, Divergence, Specialization, Software Evolution.

1 Introduction

Beginning with its popularity as a commercially viable form of software innovation, open source development model has been often praised for its suitability for evolution and adaptation to fast moving demands on software products. On the other hand, understanding of software evolution in OSS research and practice remains to be confined to its closed source counterpart. This traditional conceptualization, in turn, uses the term software evolution as a synonym for software maintenance [8]. It acknowledges the environmental pressures on a single piece of software, and primarily concerns unpredicted changes in software through its life cycle.

This conceptualization is inadequate for systems of open source software. Unlike closed source software, open source software packages are forked or combined in a variety of ways. As such, environmental pressures and evolutionary processes work through systems of software, rather than a single software. In the face of openness, one needs a higher level unit of analysis to understand software evolution.

I. Hammouda et al. (Eds.): OSS 2012, IFIP AICT 378, pp. 310–315, 2012.

In this paper, we develop a theoretical model for evolution of systems of open software. We limit ourselves to cases of forking, re-forking, and occasionally, merging of forked variants. In our model we identify environmental or internal tensions on an OSS project, and patterns of consequent forking. Such forking may create separate species which no longer may exchange -genetic- code with one another (e.g. when fork uses a different, incompatible license, or is a result of power conflict), or may be a variant which can share code with its parent or sibling species (e.g. when fork is caused by stability/feature-richness trade-off).

Within this scope, we attempt to map essential elements of evolutionary framework to software. We suggest that through such models a better understanding of software evolution within the contextual dynamics of broader software ecosystem is possible, and can contribute to improve management and resource allocation in a variety of cases where OSS model is employed.

In this paper, we present our mapping of evolutionary elements to software, in the backdrop of existing literature. Summarizing empirical findings about forking patterns in OSS, we propose a model of evolutionary processes and dynamics around forking.

2 Software Evolution vs. Evolution in Software Ecosystems

Darwinian framework for biological evolution have been employed in explaining a variety of non-biological phenomena, primarily in economics. In doing so one needs to map the principal processes of variation, selection and inheritance. There is no random mutation in such social and economic systems but instead there are rational actions of human (or organization) actors. Thus the overall evolutionary analogy may be contested on the ground that variations are purposeful unlike those in biology. However, rationality in such complex systems is limited to information available to actors' to predict outcomes of their actions [6]. Complexity of outcomes in such systems make Darwinism particularly relevant to understand them [7]. Such an evolutionary framework has been used to explain economic and organizational systems [1].

In the field of software, the evolution concept has been used primarily through variations of Lehman's original conception [8], and almost interchangeably with the term 'software maintenance' [5]. Such usage of evolutionary framework, although weak, may be appropriate for proprietery software. On the other hand, in the case of OSS, life cycles of software projects exhibit complex patterns in which software packages are forked, merged, split, or combined in a variety of ways, thanks to their permissive copyleft or copycenter licenses. Apart from case studies on genealogy of certain OSS projects [5], however, attempts to analyze evolution above the unit of single software projects are rare.

On the other hand open source software seems to be particularly suitable for employing evolutionary framework. For any piece of software, creation and employment of its copies can be considered as corresponding to replication in biological evolution. What is different in OSS is the fact that many users modify it to fit their particular needs, thus mutating software. Depending on how common such a need is, some modifications find their way into the main development branch of the software project. Such changes are replicated thereafter, hence becoming part of the species' gene pool. Certain others may correspond to unique needs, and may never leave the single site they are created. More interestingly there may be a variant which is demanded by a considerable user base, but it may not be possible to converge the mutated software with the main development stream for a variety of reasons (such as licensing, stability, target platform, feature incompatibilities, or power conflicts with leadership). Such are cases which correspond to creation of new species.

The brief articulation above lays out the parts of Darwinian analogy corresponding to variation and inheritance processes. With the selection process, the situation is even more similar to biological evolution. In OSS projects, even when corporate actors are involved [3], a species' access to resources in the environment corresponds to user and developer interest attracted to an OSS project. An OSS software project develops and becomes more appealing to a larger user base as developers prefer to contribute to it (rather than another software), unlike a proprietary software whose development may depend on corporate investment. Such developer support may depend on a variety of factors including appeal of design choices by initiators. However, the major factor is how the functionality provided by a new software corresponds to a niche need in the ecosystem, and how it compares to alternatives. Given the complexity of such an ecosystem, it seems plausible to assume that such correspondence (i.e. fitness in biological evolution) is largely unpredictable.

3   The Open Source and Forking Patterns

Since open source software is based on a commons based property regime, anyone can forgo to modify such a software technology for a special need. One way to to do this is to extend software capabilities in desired direction. In this process, which is called 'forking' in the open source community, a developer/group/firm starts (forks) a branch of development work separate from the rest of collaborators (the main branch). Such a fork faces an inherent paradox: (1) one may disregard what is going on in the main branch entirely, thus reducing constraints in terms of developing a capability, or (2) try to modify as few modules as possible to achieve the desired capability, using the rest of the modules from the main branch. The latter method keeps immediate constraints but allows one to continue using –hopefully useful!– collaborative development of the main branch. In many situations, one cannot evaluate and choose a subset of constraints beforehand (at least not easily), hence facing a choice between staying interdependent with others or going independent, with little or no shades of gray in between.

Current state of OSS licenses adds further complication to the matter. In contrast to a commercial license which was used to keep software innovation within a proprietary sphere of a firm, open source licenses were designed to keep them in public space. Thus first commercial firms who were interested in adaptability and innovation advantages of OSS were faced with a dilemma between the power of collaborative innovation on the one hand and keeping competitive advantage on the other. Industry's answer to the problem was creating a variety of hybrid licenses (ie. copycenter licenses). While solving a range of competitive positioning problems, however, this introduced a new problem due to incompatibility of licenses preventing code sharing among projects in many cases [2]. Thus license incompatibilities enters OSS forking process as a potential complication.

In summary, independence and legitimacy 'to fork' under open source licensing regimes accommodates innovation and agility because it allows diversification to address tensions due to conflicting demands on development. It provides an assurance for each collaborator that they can go their way when there is a conflict of development goals.

In a previous study [4], we have observed various strategies based on forking, in response to a variety of tensions. We have found two broad categories. First one, *interdependent forks*, are the cases where the forked branch stays compatible with the parent branch. Such forks were triggered by needs of further specialization, differences in terms of stability/agility choices, etc. Further forks of the forks was possible, each with varying degrees of compatibility and mutual empowerment with other siblings. There were even cases of merging after a certain period of separation. The second category, *independent forks*, included cases where the fork became independent of the main branch. These were triggered by power conflicts, license issues, etc. In most cases in the latter category, only one of the branches survived.

New cases of forking has appeared since that study, some of which are more public than others. Among those are, for example, the Android system for mobile phones. Android forks the Linux kernel due to demanding requirements of mobile platforms, such as power consumption and user interface. In its current standing, the project have difficulties maintaining common code with the main branch, which introduces the danger of many vendors maintaining multiple versions of their hardware drivers for two different systems. Another example was the windowing system for Unix variants. Once dominant windowing system of XFree86 have changed its licensing scheme. The new license were incompatible with the copyleft licenses of many other software components in the Unix software ecosystem, of which it was a part. As a result the OSS community has created a fork named X Org, which soon became the dominant variant as the community abandoned the former one.

These observed cases of software divergence through forking can be classified as follows:

Variation - The fork creates two software variants which remain more or less compatible with one another. In effect, they become variations within the same species which retain advantage of code reuse or sharing. There are two major groups in this category: (1) Forks due to *specialization tensions*: An example is NetBSD fork of BSD Unix operating system. The fork was created to serve as a specialized variant which provides features for networking and security. The forked variants shared a large code base and kept empowering one another. (2) Forks due to *stability/agility tensions*: An example is Debian/Ubuntu Linux fork.

Ubuntu Linux was created to satisfy demands for using a feature rich Linux on the desktop systems, where Debian's focus was on stability and reliability. The two projects shared a large set of utility programs as well as benefiting from each others software package repositories.

Speciation -The fork creates two software species which are incompatible with one another, or effectively unable to share code. There are two major groups in this category: (1) Forks due to *licensing tensions*: An example is XFree86/XOrg fork. The fork was created when XFree86 project has adopted a licensing scheme which created a compatibility tension in the Unix ecosystem. The XOrg fork was created due to this tension, which eventually replaced the former. (2) Forks due to *power conflicts* within the leadership: An example is Emacs/Lucid Emacs fork. Lucid, a private company, has forked Emacs editor, triggering a series of power conflicts and trust issues with the original project's team. The two projects were not successful in aligning their efforts, hence went on their own way.

4   A Model of Divergence

Each fork, whether interdependent or independent, results from a tension. In time it ignites a new round of tensions. Several patterns are suggested by our previous study [3]. For example, in the case of GCC/EGCS fork, the fork was created due to differences in terms of stability and flexibility. While the fork served its purpose, the user community demanded the two projects to merge, hence creating a new tension. In contrast, the case of Debian/Ubuntu fork faced a different tension from its user base which valued usability promises of the Ubuntu fork over backwards compatibility with its parent.

In each of the cases (except the forks due to personal power conflicts), a fork, the consequent co-existence of two branches, and possible future mergers, seem to encounter tensions related to conflicting demands of specialization (flexibility, innovation speed, etc.) on the one hand and demands of compatibility (stability, collaborative efficiency, etc.) on the other. Our model, visualized in Figure 1, frames these observed patterns in a unified process.

The model visualization roughly corresponds to a timeline of events. An existing software community evaluates tensions regarding specialization, and a decision emerges about whether to fork, and if so whether in an interdependent or independent manner. In either case, but particularly interesting for us in the case of a fork, the -forked- project will continue for a while, with tensions are now relatively relaxed.

Survival of a forked branch faces several challenges such as being able to generate or sustain quality, keeping up attention of commercial or non-commercial users. If the targeted specialization corresponds to a growing niche and delivers the expected quality, it is likely that the project will survive and grow (in terms of users, and in turn in terms of developer resources contributing to it). Such a growth is likely to create new tensions of specialization. Depending on how the parent project is growing, it may also face demands to merge with its parent as well, since such a move will create certain advantages. However, if the fork was

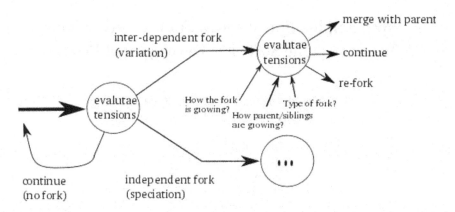

Fig. 1. A model of open software divergence in the face of tensions between plural interests/goals

an independent one (due to power conflicts, licensing differences, etc.) a merge is less likely even if it is desirable.

In summary, each phase of evaluating tensions of specialization and its result is effected by three factors: (1) how the fork is growing?, (2) how the parent or siblings are growing, and (3) the type of fork. The growth of fork itself possibly creates internal tensions for further specialization. The state of parent or sibling projects on the other hand causes developers to weigh advantages of staying separate versus advantages of merging with parent/siblings. Finally, the type of fork (interdependent/independent) further constrains the options to resolve tensions.

References

1. Aldrich, H.: Organizations Evolving. Sage (1999)
2. de Laat, P.B.: Copyright or copyleft?: An analysis of property regimes for software development. Research Policy 34(10), 1511–1532 (2005)
3. Gencer, M., Oba, B.: Organising the digital commons: a case study on engagement strategies in open source. Technology Analysis & Strategic Management 23(9), 969–982 (2011)
4. Gencer, M., Ozel, B., Tunalioglu, V.S., Oba, B.: Forking: The gpl coherent technology for flexible organizing in foss development. In: European Group of Organizational Studies Colloqium in Bergen, Norway (2006)
5. Godfrey, M., Tu, Q.: Evolution in open source software: a case study. In: Int. Conf. on Software Maintenance, pp. 131–142 (2000)
6. Hayek, F.A.: The use of knowledge in society. The American Economic Review 35(4), 519–530 (1945)
7. Hodgson, G.M., Knudsen, T.: Why we need a generalized darwinism, and why generalized darwinism is not enough. Journal of Economic Behavior & Organization 61(1), 1–19 (2006)
8. Lehman, M.M.: Programs, life cycles, and laws of software evolution. Proceedings of the IEEE 68(9), 1060–1076 (1980)

A Novel Application of Open Source Technologies to Measure Agile Software Development Process

Luis Corral, Andrea Janes, Tadas Remencius,
Juri Strumpflohner, and Jelena Vlasenko

Free University of Bozen-Bolzano
Piazza Domenicani 3
39100 Bolzano-Bozen, Italy
luis.corral@stud-inf.unibz.it,
{andrea.janes,tadas.remencius,juri.strumpflohner,
jelena.vlasenko}@unibz.it

Abstract. In the last 10 years Open Source products have been widely used in industry. New methodologies and best practices to develop Open Source software appeared. In this work, we present an application that runs on Android-based mobile phones and collects proximity data with other devices via Bluetooth. The application gives new insights into measuring proximity inside a team of software developers. Data collection process is automatic so that the team members are not distracted from their daily activities. The collected data represent time frames when developers work alone at their machines and when they do Pair Programming with their colleagues.

1   Introduction

In the last 10 years Open Source based products have been widely used in industry [7], including platforms for mobile devices. For example, from the several operating systems for mobile phones (iOS, RIM OS, Windows Mobile, Android, etc), Open Source Android OS stands out as one of the leading platforms. Android is based on Linux, and ships with tools that provide significant support support for mobile-oriented software development. Moreover, Android OS supports many technologies, e.g. 3G, WiFi, Bluetooth, and many others, making it a powerful platform. Taking advantage of such technologies and its Open Source nature, it opens a new space for mobile software development. In this work, our focus is to take advantage of these characteristics and exploring how Open Source platforms and tools can be leveraged for measuring software development process.

Starting in the early '90s there have been several proposals for metrics for software processes and products [1, 3, 4, 12]. Since then, the way in which people develop software has changed dramatically. To determine how software is developed, there have been several studies that have been dedicated to automatic and non-invasive observation of behavior of software developers [3], in terms of code quality [9], time to market, effort distribution [1], knowledge transfer, etc.

I. Hammouda et al. (Eds.): OSS 2012, IFIP AICT 378, pp. 316–321, 2012.

The purpose of our research is to take advantage of such experience and to propose a new set of tools and methodologies to collect and interpret software metrics coming from emerging software production environments [8], making use of technologies and possibilities that mobile resources offer. In this paper, we present DroidSense, a mobile application for Android based smartphones, that utilizes Bluetooth technology to measure proximity between team members. Using these data we can detect when developers work alone and when they do Pair Programming, working collaboratively on one task using a single machine.

2   Related Work

There have been several works aiming to compare existing mobile operating systems in terms of different quality characteristics. In [2], authors evaluate architectural openness of iPhone, Windows Mobile, Android, and others. The results evidence that Android and Symbian are more open for modifications than other platforms, making them attractive to carry out research and experimentation.

In [13], authors explore Bluetooth potentials for designing interacting systems. Several benefits and weaknesses of this technology have been identified, for example, Bluetooth chips can be carried by a person or placed in a specific location. Device names can be easily changed to uniquely identify persons or groups. With this, from the obtained data it is always possible to detect what kind of device has been encountered. However, Bluetooth is limited by short-range radio technology, so that only nearby located devices can be detected. Several scans might be needed to identify all the participating devices. For product assessment, in [11] authors developed BlueMonarch, an application to evaluate Bluetooth-based applications.

In this study, we take advantage of such technologies and to apply them for software metrics collection. There is also a significant number of devices supporting Bluetooth communications: phones, headsets, hand-helds, laptops, etc. Some of such devices, like phones and headsets, very often are carried by people wherever they go, thus, the presence of such devices can provide a detailed map of the physical activities that developers do during their work, meetings, etc. Tools using Bluetooth to determine proximity exist, like ReduxComputing-Proximity [5], Where's Blue [6], and Proximity Data Gathering For Android Through Bluetooth [10]. However, they are primitive and not yet adopted to extract detailed software metrics.

3   DroidSense

DroidSense is a system for the automated collection of proximity information between developers for software process analysis. DroidSense consists of a mobile Android application and a central server component responsible for receiving, storing, and analyzing the data. The collected data can then be viewed and analyzed through an according web interface providing different kinds of visualizations. The structure of the system is shown in Figure 1:

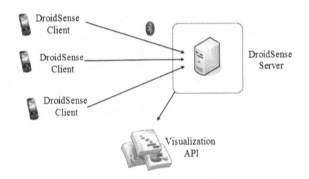

Fig. 1. High Level System Architecture

DroidSense Android client is the core component of the system, being responsible for the data collection. It has been designed to be easily extensible to allow the development of future Android activities that are able to attach to its functionality. The end-user mainly interacts with the Android client that collects and uploads the data to the server. The main user interface presented to the user when he starts the application is the list showing all of the discovered Bluetooth devices.

By selecting an entry of the device list, the according device detail view opens. In addition to the device's detail information, it presents the collected proximity raw data in descending order, showing the most recent value on top of the list. Each entry shows the calculated value on top, followed by the raw value that has been returned from the Bluetooth adapter as well as the time stamp of the discovery.

DroidSense server, on the other hand, is responsible of storing and analyzing the collected values by all of the DroidSense Android clients. It has been implemented by using a conjunction of Open Source-only application frameworks, on top of J2EE and Spring. Spring supports Hibernate, which has been used to perform the object-relational mapping to the underlying MySQL database. Open source technologies JDOM and Castor prepare the XML received from DroidSense services into Java objects that can be understood by JDBC to communicate with the database instance. For the web front-end, the Spring Web MVC framework has been used with JSP and jQuery.

4   DroidSense in Action

4.1   Case Study

To gain experience on the collection of data using our tool, as well as to prove their practical usability for the purpose of software process measurement, it was conducted an experiment of the use of DroidSense by a professional team. An initial implementation of the prototype took place on a team of 10 programmers, members of a software development team in a University Research Center which uses Agile practices such as Extreme Programming, Pair Programing, and Test-Driven Development. All participants joined the experiment in a voluntary basis.

The experiment covered a period of 3 months. Through the whole phase, more than 240,000 proximity values have been transmitted by the 10 participants. The samples were analyzed with the purpose of reconstructing the whole -or at least significant parts- of the software development process, based on human interaction. For privacy reasons, all personal names have been obfuscated.

4.2   Interpretation of Data Samples

An example on how data are interpreted is depicted in Figure 2, which shows a visualization of the raw data collected on a regular working day, from the viewpoint of developer U_E at the University, our experimental setup. The y-axis shows the RSSI indicator, where lower values indicate shorter distances. The x-axis shows the time of the day in hours.

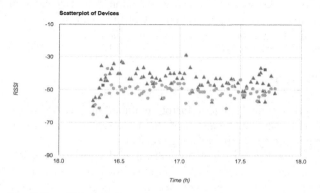

Fig. 2. Raw Values Collected at the University Research Center

The visualization contains data of the devices:

- P_E: U_E's personal laptop, used at work (triangles)
- M_M: DroidSense-equipped Android phone of a member of U_E's team (points)
- M_S: Android phone with DroidSense, member of U_E's team (squares)

Figure 3 shows an interpretation of the data acquired by DroidSense, saying that M_M was near to P_E during the whole period of the scan, while M_S dropped in for a small amount of time at the beginning and the end of the scan (as seen in Figure 2). A pair programming session between user U_E and M_M can be inferred:

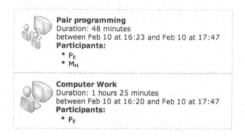

Fig. 3. Calculated Sessions at the University Research Center

On the other hand, another pair programming session took place in front of the workstation of U_E itself, while the pair programming session shown previously was in front of the teammate's computer. The output is not presented as a list of detailed session detections, but rather the aggregated information of all of them. This helps on giving an overview of the activities performed through the day. It can be seen that the raw data is correctly interpreted, showing the user M_S only appear for a small amount of 5 minutes during the scan period, while there is a longer pair programming session with M_M.

Project's team managers at the Research Center reported a clearer identification of the execution of pair programming sessions, recognizing how devices group in front of a particular workstation for a given amount of time. DroidSense was useful to understand the interaction among developers: the distance between users and devices can be appraised, allowing to observe how such distance shifts when one user approaches a colleague, leaving his own workstation. This visualization was reported by the team managers as suitable to conduct further analysis on the importance of people's physical distribution in the way a team collaborates.

5   Conclusions

Measurement has become a major factor of importance in software development. Project deadlines, limited budget and high customer expectations require the continuous search for optimizing existing processes.

In this work we presented a new approach in collecting data about Agile software development process by leveraging proximity measurements gathered using the Bluetooth technology through DroidSense, a system for Android OS which implements a software solution to characterize developer's interaction using data gathered from their own mobile devices. Thanks to an experiment with several developers conducting an Agile software development project, we present the practical use of DroidSense and the resulting process analysis. Using DroidSense shows that the collected data provides a valuable insight in the stakeholder's interactions within the process by automatically detecting a developer's involvement in computer work or pair programming sessions.

Using a widely spread technology such as Bluetooth, an Open Source operating platform like Android, and a wide range of Open Source frameworks and tools allows a team to slim down the development investment without losing the functionality required by architecture, design and implementation demands. Moreover, there is no costly setup required but installing a mobile app, and engineers do not have to undergo a major training phase or adapt their working habits.

References

1. Abrahamsson, P., Moser, R., Pedrycz, W., Sillitti, A., Succi, G.: Effort prediction in iterative software development processes–incremental versus global prediction models. In: Empirical Software Engineering and Measurement (2007)

2. Anvaari, M., Jansen, S.: Evaluating architectural openness in mobile software platforms. In: ECSA 2010, Copenhagen, Denmark (2010)
3. Coman, I.D., Sillitti, A., Succi, G.: A case-study on using an automated in-process software engineering measurement and analysis system in an industrial environment. In: ICSE 2009, Vancouver, Canada (2009)
4. Fenton, N.: New directions for software metrics. In: PROMISE Workshop, Invited Keynote, ICSE 2007, Minneapolis, USA (2007)
5. Google, http://code.google.com/p/reduxcomputing-proximity (retrieved March 10, 2012)
6. Engelsma, J.R., Ferrans, J.C., Hans, M.C.: EncounterEngine: Integrating Bluetooth user proximity data into social applications. In: IEEE International Conference on Wireless and Mobile Computing, WIMOB 2008, pp. 502–507 (2008)
7. Gurbani, V.K., Garvert, A., Herbsleb, J.D.: A case study of open source tools and practices in a commercial setting. In: Proceedings of the 5th Workshop on Open Source Software Engineering (2005)
8. Janes, A., Scotto, A., Pedrycz, W., Russo, B., Stefanovic, M., Succi, G.: Identification of defect-prone classes in telecommunication software systems using design metrics. Information Sciences 176(24) (2006)
9. Moser, R., Sillitti, A., Abrahamsson, P., Succi, G.: Does refactoring improve reusability? Reuse of Off-the-Shelf Components, 287–297 (2006)
10. Pullabhatla, A., Gomes, H.: Proximity data Gathering for Android through Bluetooth. Department of Computer Science Engineering. University of California, San Diego (2010)
11. Smith, T.J., Saroiu, S., Wolman, A.: BlueMonarch: A System for evaluating Bluetooth applications in the wild. In: MobiSys 2009, Kraków, Poland (2009)
12. Succi, G., Pedrycz, W., Liu, E., Yip, J.: Package-oriented software engineering: a generic architecture. IT Professional 3(2), 29–36 (2001)
13. Sundstrom, P., Taylor, A.S., O'Hara, K.: Sketching in Software and Hardware Bluetooth as a Design Material. In: Mobile HCI 2011, Stockholm, Sweden (2011)

A Linguistic Analysis on How Contributors Solve Software Problems in a Distributed Context

Héla Masmoudi[1] and Imed Boughzala[2]

[1] Paris Dauphine at Paris,
Place du Maréchal de Lattre de Tassigny 75116, Paris, France
hela.masmoudi.09@campus.dauphine.fr
[2] Telecom EM Research Center, Institut Mines-Télécom,
9 rue Charles Fourrier, 91011 Evry, France
Imed.boughzala@it-sudparis.eu

Abstract. There is a little understanding of distributed solving activities in Open Source communities. This study aimed to provide some insights in this way. It was applied to the context of Bugzilla, the bug tracking system of Mozilla community. This study investigated the organizational aspects of this meditated, complex and highly distributed context through a linguistic analysis method. The main finding of this research shows that the organization of distributed problem-solving activities in Bugzilla isn't based only on the hierarchical distribution of the work between core and periphery participants but on their implication in the interactions. This implication varies according to the status of each one participant in the community. That is why we distinguish their roles, as well as, the established modes to manage such activity.

1 Introduction

Distributed problem-solving in Open Source context is a complex phenomenon and a fundamental issue at the organizational level. Research in this field was conducted from different theoretical and methodological perspectives. Realized on several projects Open Source such as Apache, Mozilla, Linux, researchers stated that organization of the work in this project is not totally democratic and observed that the coding is reserved to core developers (a limited number of developers which have code source access), when repairing defects and reported problems are periphery tasks (a large number of users/developers members). This distinction between Open Source community members tasks by previous results are interesting but need more empirical investigation and validation concerning the characterization how distributed problem-solving is organized in Open Source context by core and periphery contribution categorization and using linguistic techniques.

We have considered the case of Free/Libre Open Source Software (FLOSS) development as an open and distributed process. Mostly, we were interested in software problems found in Bugzilla' bug reports. This study investigates particularly the interaction between contributors in the case of the community associated with

I. Hammouda et al. (Eds.): OSS 2012, IFIP AICT 378, pp. 322–330, 2012.

Mozilla's Firefox Internet browser. It analyzes the activities related to the participants in Bugzilla, the Mozilla's bug tracking system.

The rest of this paper is structured as follows: Section 2 presents the related research works. Section 3 describes our research method that has been used for conducting the linguistic analysis. Results are discussed and summarized in section 4. It describes linguistic specificities used in bug reports to identify the division of labor and contributors' roles in the organization of problem-solving. Section 5 includes concluding remarks and sketches the limits of this work as well as its future perspectives.

2   Related Research

A lot of research has been done on coordination in Open Source Software community. If Raymond [21, p.4] describes the software debugging task in Open Source development style as "*self-correcting systems of agents*", an open model that he qualifies as a "*bazaar*" and argues, from a Linux experience, that "*Given enough eyeballs, all bugs are shallow*". In contrast, some research suggests that the openness in Open Source development does not imply necessarily democratic processes.

In a study on Linux Kernel, Cox [2] reveals that the access to exchanges is not granted to all the participants but reserved only for a category of developers (core developers). The resultant structure of exchange is quite hierarchical. Mockus and colleagues [15] have examined two Open Source projects and studied a division of labor in Mozilla and Apache. They have observed that the coding is reserved to a limited number of developers. Only 15 developers have contributed for the greater part to the design, the coding (80 %), and the validation of the solutions. They suggest that "*a group larger by an order of magnitude than the core will repair defects, and a yet larger group (by another order of magnitude) will report problems*" [18, p.9]. Crowston and Howison [4] have focused on social organization of Open Source projects and proposed a general description of this organization by providing the "Onion Model" of software development. According to this model, a small group of core developers is surrounded by several layers of peripheral helpers ranging from occasional problem solvers (close to the core) to mainstream users whose contribution is limited to the occasional submission of crash reports.

In a study on the governance of the Open Source Software (OSS) projects, Markus [16] proposes a definition according to which the mechanisms of coordination are perceived as answers to the problems of control and more generally as solutions to manage the development work: "*In the operational coordination literature, OSS governance is understood as a solution to [... the problem of] loss of operational control and the solution is techniques for managing the process of OSS development work*" [16, p.156]. Grinter and colleagues [8] said that "*the coordination of a distributed activity, bases on the communication and the interaction between developers*" [8, p.308]. Malone and Crowston [15] underline that coordination is an activity that is not directly observable. It is often studied through the communication in particular contexts where artifacts, e-mails, forums or lines of code, shape the structure of interaction and favor the teamwork. In a study of the Mozilla project,

Gasser and collegues [7] shows that interactions participate to realize the coordination process and made through negotiation between contributors.

Until now according to our knowledge, little focused research has been done to understand how problems are being solved and described in OSS communities by using linguistic analysis. Indeed, apart from the interesting studies of Ripoche and Sansonnet [22], Ko and colleagues [10] and recently Maalej and colleagues [11,17], linguistic techniques have not really been used to describe the organization of distributed problem-solving related to Open Source software by interaction categorization.

3   Method

In this study, the bug report is the primary unit of analysis. We suppose that the organization of the community is reflected through the used tools that enable coordination of its activities. The traces of the structure should be visible in the community's bug tracking system. Therefore, a sample of 4109 bug reports was extracted from Bugzilla bug report repository. These bugs are selected in 2008 and specified the problems mentioned in Mozilla's CVS code archive before 2007 with a high complexity level (i.e. number of patches upper to 4) which were declared as solved. The analysis of our sample allows identifying the roles of participants in this activity according to their hierarchical statutes in the community. We specifically studied linguistic aspects of Bugzilla' traces since each bug report generates a discussion and all the exchanged messages between participants in the bug solving were recorded. Inspired by register linguistics analysis [1], our method is based on language categorization. A register is a variety associated with a particular situation of use and described for her linguistic features (lexical and grammatical characteristics). Registers can be identified and described based on analysis of texts or a collection of text. Especially, we look statistically at words that people use in Bugzilla to discern differences in the discourse and representation between participants (core and periphery).

4   Results through the Linguistic Analysis: Characterizing Core and Periphery Contribution

The emerging empirical literature on OSS communities indicates that a majority of code writing and communication activity is concentrated on a few individuals, the "core". Yet, these communities allow and encourage wide scale participation by anybody in their community, the periphery. Actually a large number of organizations and projects contribute to Bugzilla. The aim of this section is to explain by defining the roles of contributors, the division of labor amongst the core and periphery in a distributed problem-solving community and in essence to determine the value of the periphery to the core.

4.1 Contribution Frequency

Table 1 shows that 8072 individuals participated in our selection of 4019 bugs whose numbers are identified in comments to revisions to code belonging to the Firefox branch, or Firebird or Phoenix branch (as Firefox was formally known) in a version of Mozilla's CVS code archive dating from 2007. One hundred and twelve of these participants had CVS commit access, that is, the decision right to make changes to the community's software repository, were considered core community members.

Participation was defined by contributing code to the OSS community or more exactly by technical contribution such as patches submission [3, 16]. In our sample, a majority (91%) of patches are provided by core contributors (approximately 28471 patches). Similarly Table 1 shows, according to the bug status, that core dominate discussion. Considering all emails posted by contributors in our selection of bug reports, approximately 89% (182369 messages) of all messages provides from core.

We notice on the basis of this first result, that the contribution of the core members is globally more significant than the periphery. We observe that the technical work (submission of patches) is made by the core participants and the contribution of the periphery is not significant at this level. Consequently, if problem-solving activity is mostly technical and do not impose normally frequent exchanges, the core developers multiply nevertheless the exchanges with others contributors because only 16% of posted messages from the core contain patches. These observations approve the need of the core participants to communicate with the periphery, and to strengthen the hypothesis according to which the contribution of the periphery is also important as that of the core, in the problem-solving activity [11]. To characterize better these contributions, we tried to study in the second part of this section, the exchanges through an analysis of e-mail discussions.

Table 1. Core and periphery contribution

Community status	Number of participants	Number of messages	Number of patches
Core	112	182369(89%)	28481(91%)
Periphery	7960	22538(11%)	2796 (9%)
Total	8072	204908(100%)	31277(100%)

4.2 Contribution Categorization

In this section, we characterize core and periphery with language categorization. In order to do so, we first define a subset of organizational proprieties identified in linguistic analysis and encode these proprieties as description, directives, activity and interaction. We then code bug reports into proprieties strings made up of this categorization. As expressed, we consider four proprieties:

1) Diagnosis and evaluation by description (**DESCR**): supply a maximum of information to the community to orient the problem-solving. The participants contribute to the activity by proposing information which allows:

- To describe the problem context: states provoked by the problem and the environment in which it is located (e.g. *"frequently the ad server that is used* by one of the forums I read is down, and when the request for the ad fails; Firebird shows a modal dialog telling me the connection was refused or something like that").

- To display and reproduce the problem (e.g. "go to www.mlb.com and click on a 'gameday' icon").

- To validate the state of normal functioning of the module further to integrate solution (e.g. "I downloaded the latest release today (V 1.0.7) installed it and it works exactly the way it did previously with regard to this bug!").

2) Coordination by the directives which (**DIREC**):

- To conduct the execution of some tasks (e.g. "make it listen to command rather than click, add Alt+Down / Up and F4 as equivalents to the dropdown button").

- To attribute some tasks to a particular contributor by explicit requests (e.g. "Tim could you review this and land it on branch and trunk").

- To verify that the instructions are correctly led ("The patch can bereviewed I tested it today and didn't run into any problems").

3) Activity explicitness (**ACTIV**): to perform an action directly or report on the performance of an action by:

- The creation of a patch, i.e. a suggested change in the code base (e.g. "Created an attachment (id=135235) [details]").

- The update of a designed solution: to indicate the link which allows to download the update of the solution (e.g. "From update of attachment 135235 [details]").

- The verification of the conceived solutions: when one or several solutions are proposed, several stages of reviewing and tests are implemented (e.g. "review=me,superreview=brendan@mozilla.org for trunk checkin).

- The fixing of bugs: after checking, the solution is validated to fix the bug (e.g. "verified, fixed").

4) Activity articulation by direct interaction (**INTER**): Communication between participants, is transformed into dialogue between two or three contributors by the use of expressive linguistic forms such as:

- Agreement or disagreement (e.g. "Actually, I'm not sure I agree with Gerv here. I understand that RMS agrees Mitchell").

- Interrogative forms (e.g. "Benjamin, could you explain why?").

- Forms which express the emotion or gratitude (e.g. "Thanks for writing this, Daniel! I'd say it's a pretty good starting point; Nice one :-) That's what I couldn't work out. Go to it. I'm away for the next nine days; thank you so much for clearing up after me :-) Gerv").

Having thus transformed the sample, we focus the frequency of the occurrence of organizational proprieties according contributors status. Figure 1 reveals that when considering organizational categorization, as a percentage, the used language by core members is essentially descriptive (42,45%). If we consider the language from the point of view of action, we notice that the core contributors often use the linguistic units, to clarify an action or to anticipate the actions to be realized (26,30%) with equivalent proportions of directives (28,19%). Finally, we note a small proportion

(3%) of linguistic units indicating the presence of direct interactions between core members, and other contributors. Figure 1 also reveals that proportions of actions, descriptions, and directives are even more important after the conception of the first patch. These observations confirm our first observations , indicating that the core members intervenes not only in the critical phases of software design, but also in the phases of reviewing, validation and integration of solutions, realized in the last phases of the problem-solving. These reports can be understandable by the fact that the Mozilla project is strongly structured, and that the integration of contributors is not completely free and requires the downstream of administrators of the project.

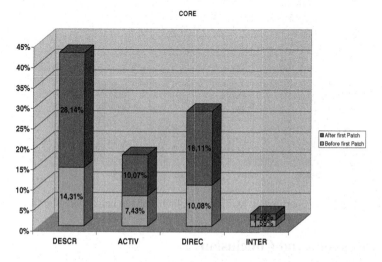

Fig. 1. Core contribution to manage problem-solving before and after the first patch

Figure 2 shows that peripheral members use an important rate of descriptive words (49,39%) in comparison with the other categories. Besides, we observe less important rates of interactive words (18,47%) and linguistic forms reporting action performed (15,68%). We note finally of small proportions (8,91%) of directives in comparison with the core contribution.

These results support works supporting that the contribution of the periphery in Open Source communities consists mainly in declaring problems, asking for instructions, or for instructions concerning it, without intervening in a significant way in its solving (patch submission) [22,4]. This thus explains the high frequencies of messages of the category description, followed by the category interactivity, and particularly before beginning to conceive a solution to the problems. The contribution of the periphery is thus more significant and important in the first phases of the problem-solving, which are characterized by a very strong rate of description.

Our results suggest that most common forms employed by the core are used for assigning explicitly tasks to developers and asking questions about problems. In general, the core members use more professional languages to ask questions about program output and purpose technical solutions. However, it is important to have a detailed understanding of problems by identifying problem context. Our results suggest the peripheral role to perform this categorization by use descriptive words as an indicator. For example, to reproduce contextual elements by using words such as "when", "during", and "after", in order to indicate the situation in which a problem is occurred.

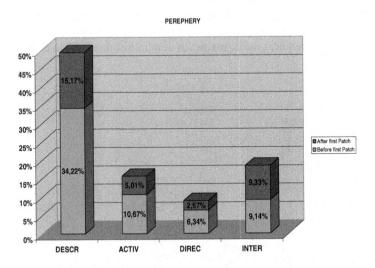

Fig. 2. Periphery contribution to manage problem solving before and after first patch

5   Discussion and Conclusion

This study serves as a starting point of a larger effort to better understanding of how the core and the periphery of an online community contribute to manage software problem-solving by focusing on Bugzilla community, and using several methodologies derived from computational linguistics. We have observed in this study same differences in the structure and content of language used by contributors in our dataset. This difference has a variety of implications to describe the organization of Bugzilla activities in the case of Firefox and distinguish between the core and periphery roles. Many research works found that most of the technical activities with respect to bug solving are carried out by a small minority of core members while periphery contributions are less significant.

We have initially suggested that collaboration and interaction between the core and periphery of the community is an important aspect of problem-solving in the Bugzilla, and then identified the peripheral role in managing this activity. The main difficulty in managing reports is how to determine the most qualified developer for each report. There have been attempts to automatically match developers with specific action or task, based on the correspondence between the task and the contributor's skills.

This study provides an empirical validation of previous results concerning the role of core and periphery OSS community members using a different analysis technique: linguistic categorization. It shows that if the writing of the code and more globally the technical work are the principal role of the core members. Peripheral members play also an important role in the problem-solving activity. Indeed, we examined that the role of the periphery is not only in helping to formulate the exact context by describing problems, but also in proposing potential information on solutions. The results presented here are interesting, but still very preliminary. Further investigations are so needed, for example, to analyze higher level issues in problem-solving processes such as roles' evolution according problem-solving phases.

References

1. Biber, D., Conrad, S.: Registre, genre and style, p. 344. Cambridge University Press, Cambridge (2009)
2. Bird, C., Gourley, A., Devanbu, P., Swaminathan, A., Hsu, G.: Open borders? immigration in open source projects. In: MSR 2007: Proceedings of the Fourth International Workshop on Mining Software Repositories. IEEE Computer Society, Washington, DC (2007)
3. Cox, A.: Cathedrals, bazaars and the town council (1998), http://www.linux.org.uk/Papers_CathPaper.cs
4. Crowston, K., Howison, J.: Hierarchy and centralization in free and open source software team communications. Knowledge, Technology & Policy 18(4), 65–85 (2006)
5. Ghosh, R.: Managing rights, in free/libre/open source software (2006), http://www.infonomics.nl/FLOSS/papers/20060423/GHOSH-licensing.pdf
6. Gasser, L., Gabriel, R.: Distributed Collective Practices and Free/Open-Source Software Problem, Management: Perspectives and Methods. In: Conference on Cooperation, Innovation & Technologie (CITE 2003), p. 17 (2003)
7. Grinter, R.E., Herbsleb, J.D., Perry, D.W.: The geography of coordination: Deling with distance in R&D work. In: Proceedings of SIGGROUP Conference on Supporting Group Work, pp. 306–315. ACM Press, New York (1999)
8. Herbsleb, J.D., Cataldo, M.: Factors leading to integration failures in global feature-oriented development: an empirical analysis. In: Proceedings, International Conference on Software Engineering, Honolulu, HI, pp. 161–170 (2011)
9. Ko, A.J., Myers, B.A., Chau, D.H.: A Linguistic Analysis of How People Describe Software Problems in Bug Reports. In: Visual Languages and Human-Centric Computing, Brighton, United Kingdom, September 4-8, pp. 127–134 (2006)
10. Lakhani, K.R.: The core and the periphery in distributed and self-organizing innovation systems. Thesis (Ph. D.) from Sloan School of Management, p. 331. Massachusetts Institute of Technology, Cambridge, MA (2006)
11. Lanzara, G.F., Morner, M.: Artifacts rule! how organizing happens in open source software projects. In: Czarniawska, B., Hernes, T. (eds.) Actor-Network Theory and Organizing, pp. 67–90. Copenhagen Business School Press (2005)
12. Maalej, W., Happel, H.-J.: Can Development Work Describe Itself? In: Proceedings of the 7th IEEE Conference on Mining Software Repositories (MSR 2012), pp. 191–200. IEEE CS (2012)
13. Malone, T.W.: Toward an interdisciplinary theory of coordination, Tech. Rept. CCS 120, MIT Sloan School of Management, Cambridge, MA (1991)
14. Markus, M.L.: The governance of free/open source software projects: monolithic, multidimensional, or configurational? Journal of Management and Governance 11(2), 151–163 (2007)

15. Masmoudi, H.: La résolution distribuée dans les communautés Open Source: propriétés organisationnelles et modes de coordination. Thesis (Ph. D.) from Paris Dauphine University, Paris, France, p. 265 (2011)

16. Mockus, A., Fielding, R.T., Herbsleb, J.D.: Two case studies of open source software development: Apache and mozilla. ACM Transactions on Software Engineering and Methodology 11(3), 309–346 (2002)

17. O'Mahony, S., Ferraro, F.: The emergence of governance in an open source community. Academy of Management Journal 50(5), 1079–1106 (2007)

18. Pagano, D., Maalej, G.: How do developers blog?: an exploratory study. In: Proceedings of the 8th Working Conference on Mining Software Repositories (MSR 2011), pp. 123–132. ACM, New York (2011)

19. Raymond, E.S.: The cathedral and the bazaar. First Monday (3) (1998)

20. Ripoche, G., Sansonnet, J.-P.: Experiences in automating the analysis of linguistic interactions for the study of distributed collectives. Computer Supported Cooperative Work 15, 149–183 (2006)

Examining Turnover in Open Source Software Projects Using Logistic Hierarchical Linear Modeling Approach

Pratyush Nidhi Sharma[1], John Hulland[2], and Sherae Daniel[1]

[1] University of Pittsburgh, Joseph M Katz Graduate School of Business,
229 Mervis Hall, Pittsburgh, 15232, USA
{pns9,sld54}@pitt.edu
[2] University of Georgia, Terry College of Business,
104 Brooks Hall, 310 Herty Drive, Athens, 30602, USA
jhulland@uga.edu

Abstract. Developer turnover in open source software projects is a critical and insufficiently researched problem. Previous research has focused on understanding the developer motivations to contribute using either the individual developer perspective or the project perspective. In this exploratory study we argue that because the developers are embedded in projects it is imperative to include both perspectives. We analyze turnover in open source software projects by including both individual developer level factors, as well as project specific factors. Using the Logistic Hierarchical Linear Modeling approach allows us to empirically examine the factors influencing developer turnover and also how these factors differ among developers and projects.

Keywords: Open Source Software, Turnover, Logistic Hierarchical Linear Modeling.

1 Introduction

Developer turnover in open source software (OSS) projects is a nontrivial issue because of the frequency with which it occurs and the difficulties new developers face in contributing to a project. Robles and Gonzales-Barahona [8] analyzed the evolution of some popular OSS projects (such as GIMP, Mozilla etc.) over a period of 7 years and found that these projects suffered from yearly turnover in core development teams and had to rely heavily on regeneration. Turnover is a critical problem in software development projects because it can lead to schedule overruns [1] and regenerating teams is a complicated issue [7]. A majority of the OSS research concerns itself with a developer's motivation to contribute to OSS development [2; 3].

Prior studies have tended to focus on the explanation of developer activity levels using either the individual perspective [2; 3] or the project perspective [10]. However, since OSS participants are embedded in projects it is important to relate characteristics of individuals and the characteristics of projects in which they function. Disaggregating all project level variables in an individual level analysis may lead to the violation of the assumption of independence of observations, since all developers will have the same value on each of the project variables. On the other hand, aggregating

I. Hammouda et al. (Eds.): OSS 2012, IFIP AICT 378, pp. 331–337, 2012.
© IFIP International Federation for Information Processing 2012

developer level variables to a project level analysis may lead to unused within group information [6]. None of the research studies have attempted to model turnover behavior in OSS in a comprehensive fashion taking into account both the developer level and project level factors. In order to address these limitations and expand the existing research, this exploratory study develops a model of turnover behavior in OSS by focusing on two levels: the developer level, which examines factors that may affect developers' decisions to become inactive, and the project level, which examines the factors that may influence the rates of turnover among projects.

2   Methodology

To explore and explain the nature and impact of a developer and project variables on turnover, we used archival data. The sample of projects and participants was drawn from SourceForge (www.SourceForge.net). The sample contained data for 40 currently active projects on SourceForge and 201 developers.

2.1   Developer Level Variables

The following five developer level (level 1) variables, including the outcome variable, turnover, were collected –

- Turnover –Turnover was operationalized as a binary outcome variable. A developer was deemed active, coded as 0, if at least one CVS/SVN commit was made by him/her in a 2 month period; otherwise coded as 1. Joyce and Kraut [10] also followed a similar approach in their study of turnover from online newsgroups, however they chose an observation period of six months to determine turnover.

- Role of the Developer –A project may employ developers for various roles that range in the level and kind of expertise required[1]. We created two dummy variables *Developer* and Admin with the base group *Other* (which included all other roles)[2].

- Number of Projects –The number of OSS projects undergoing active development that the developer was involved in.

- Past Activity Level –Past activity was operationalized as a binary variable[3]. A developer was deemed active in the past, coded as 0, if at least one CVS/SVN commit was made by him/her in the previous 10 month period; otherwise, we coded it as 1.

- Tenure – We approximate the tenure of a developer in months by using the date of joining SourceForge.net.

---

[1] Some examples of roles developers may perform in the project are as administrators, developers, document writers, project managers, packagers, web designers, etc.
[2] Roughly 25% roles belonged to the *Other* category. Since *Developer* and *Admin* dummies are correlated we also analyzed the data by merging *Other* and *Admin* categories to create a single *Developer* dummy variable. In doing so we found that the HLM results did not change appreciably.
[3] Using a binary dummy variable for measuring turnover and past activity results in loss of variance information and right censoring of data in developer activity levels. Please see the limitations section for how we intend to remedy this problem in the future.

2.2   Project Level Variables

The following project level variables (level 2) were collected –

- Project Age – The date the project was registered is available on SourceForge. We calculate the age in number of months since its registration on SourceForge.

- Size of Project – The number of developers with commit access to the project's CVS/SVN code repository.

2.3   Statistical Models and Results

The Hierarchical Linear Modeling (HLM) technique allows researchers to model developer level outcomes within projects and model any between project differences that arise. The study was carried out in two parts and follows the approach recommended by Rumberger [9]. In the first part a developer model of turnover was developed and tested with logistic regression using only developer level variables. This allows an analysis focused only on developer level variables. However, this not only ignores project level variables but also assumes that the effects of developer level variables on turnover do not vary from project to project. This assumption was tested in the second part of the study using logistic HLM analysis. The developer level model used in this part of the study was based on the results of the first part. It allowed us to focus the analysis on explaining between project differences in the predicted mean turnover rates (turnover characteristics adjusted for differences in developer characteristics between projects) and between project differences in the effects of developer level variables on turnover rates.

2.4   Logistic Models

A series of linear logistic models were developed and tested to measure the effect of developer level variables on turnover behavior. Turnover is a binary dependent variable that can be expressed as a probability p_i, which takes on the value of unity if the developer i becomes inactive in the project, zero otherwise. The probability p is transformed into log of odds (or logit) which is expressed as:

$$Log\ [p_i/(1-p_i)] = \beta_0 + \beta_1\ Past\_Activity + \beta_2\ Tenure + \beta_3\ Developer + \beta_4\ Admin + \beta_5\ Number\_of\_Projects$$

Table 1 presents the exponentiated logistic coefficients, which represent the ratio of predicted odds of turnover with a one unit increase in the independent variable to the predicted odds without one unit increase. Thus, a value of one signifies no change in the odds of turnover. A value greater than (less than) one indicates that the odds of turnover increase (decrease) due to a unit change in independent variable.

Table 1. Predicted odds of turnover

Variable	Univariate estimates	Multivariate estimates
Past_Activity	371.429**	431.724**
Admin	.443*	.989
Developer	1.104	.548
Tenure	1.008	1.007
Number_of_Projects	.981	1.038
-2LL (initial = 266.583)		109.008
Cox and Snell R^2		.543
Nagelkerke R^2 $\Delta\chi^2 = 157.57\ (p < .001)$		.740

$*p < 0.05, **p < .001.$

The univariate and multivariate estimates of *Past_Activity* are both significant. The univariate estimate suggests that inactive developers have 371.42% higher odds of turnover than developers that were active. Unsurprisingly, inactive developers did not become active at a later stage. The univariate estimate of *Admin* is also significant and suggests that administrators have 44.3% lower odds of turnover than the *Other* category. This means that administrators are more than twice as likely to remain active than developers with *Other* roles. Since *Past_Activity* and *Admin* were significant in the univariate estimates they were retained for further HLM analysis.

2.5   HLM Models

HLM analysis requires two types of models: a level 1 model to estimate the effects of developer level variables on turnover and a level 2 model to estimate the effect of project level variables on the coefficients of the level 1 analysis. We begin the analysis by modeling the unconditional model (base model) with no predictors at either level.

2.6   Unconditional Model

$$Log\ [p_{ij}\,/\,(1\text{-}p_{ij})] = \beta_{0j}$$
$$\beta_{0j} = \gamma_{00} + u_{0j}$$

This model allows us to ascertain the variability in the outcome variable at each of the two levels i.e. within project and between project variability. The results are shown in Table 2.

Table 2. Unconditional Model

Fixed effect		Coefficient	se	p value
Average project mean γ_{00}		.484	.183	0.012
Random effect	**Variance component**	**df**	**$\chi 2$**	**p value**
Project mean, u_{oj}	.314	39	57.48	.028
Deviance (-2LL) Estimated parameters	631.288 2			

The Null hypothesis H_0: $\tau_{00} = 0$ is rejected (p = .028). This suggests that significant variation exists among projects in their turnover rates. The intraclass correlation coefficient (ICC) measures the proportion of variance in the outcome that is between projects [11]. ICC values for our analysis suggest that 8.71% variation in turnover that can be explained by level 2 predictors resides between projects. Further, for a project with a typical turnover rate (with $u_{0j} = 0$), the expected log odds of turnover is .484. This corresponds to a probability of $1/ (1 + e (.484)) = .38$. This means that for a typical developer in a typical project there is a 38% chance of turnover in a 2 month period.

2.7 Conditional Model

This model allows part of the variation in the intercept β_0 (mean turnover rates) to be explained by project level variables (project age and size),

$$Log\ [p_{ij}/(1-p_{ij})] = \beta_{0j} + \beta_{1j}\ Past\_Activity + \beta_{2j}\ Admin$$
$$\beta_{0j} = \gamma_{00} + \gamma_{01}\ Proj\_Age + \gamma_{02}\ Proj\_Size + u_{0j}$$
$$\beta_{1j} = \gamma_{10}$$
$$\beta_{2j} = \gamma_{20}$$

All the variables were grand mean centered to reduce multicollinearity concerns in group level estimation [5]. Table 3 presents the results of the conditional model.

Table 3. Conditional Model

Fixed effect	Coefficient	se		p value
Average project mean γ_{00}	1.86	.49		0.001
Proj_Age Slope γ_{01}	.005	.006		0.461
Proj_Size Slope γ_{02}	-0.012	0.008		0.154
Past_Activity Slope γ_{10}	5.951	1.161		0.000
Admin Slope γ_{20}	0.041	0.527		0.938
Random effect	**Variance component**	**df**	**$\chi 2$**	**p value**
Project mean, u_{oj}	0.057	37	29.48	>.500
Deviance (-2LL) Estimated parameters	477.808 6			

The Null hypothesis H_0: $\tau_{00} = 0$ fails to be rejected ($p > .500$). This means that after controlling for project size and age no significant variation remains to be explained. The proportion of reduction in variance or variance explained at level 2 is .8184, implying that project size and age account for 81.84% of the explained variance at level 2. The Deviance (-2 Log Likelihood) is also significantly improved from the base model ($\Delta D = 153.48$, $\chi2_{df} = 4$, $p < .001$), suggesting a good model fit and a fully identified model[4].

3   Limitations and Future Directions

Like all empirical work this study is limited in many ways. First, the sample is biased toward more active projects. Such projects may have well developed infrastructures allowing retention of active members and/or a constant inflow of newer active members. Including less active projects in the future should allow for more robust and generalizable results. Second, the use of binary variables for turnover and past activity leads to loss of variance information and right censoring of the data. To address this critical issue in the future, we will rely on techniques such as survival modeling that allows inference from right censored data. Finally, we will seek a conceptual integration of developer and project level factors in modeling turnover rather than just an empirical integration.

4   Conclusion

In this preliminary study, we argued that taking both the developer and the project level factors into account will lead to a richer understanding of the issue of turnover in open source projects. Our analysis suggests that past activity, developer role, project size and project age are important predictors of turnover. We find that there exists a significant variation in mean turnover rates among projects on SourceForge and that project age and project size account for a sizable proportion of this variation.

References

1. Collofello, J., Rus, I., Chauhan, A., Smith-Daniels, D., Houston, D., Sycamore, D.M.: A System Dynamics Software Process Simulator for Staffing Policies Decision Support. In: Proceedings of the Thirty-First Hawaii International Conference on System Sciences, Hawaii (1998)
2. Hars, A., Ou, S.: Working for Free? Motivations for Participating in Open Source Projects. International Journal of Electronic Commerce 6(3), 25–39 (2002)
3. Hertel, G., Niedner, S., Herrmann, S.: Motivation of Software Developers in Open Source Projects: an Internet-Based Survey of Contributors to the Linux Kernel. Research Policy (32), 1159–1177 (2003)

---

[4] A conditional model that included all developer level variables did not further improve deviance and was rejected in favor of the more parsimonious model presented here.

4. Joyce, E., Kraut, R.E.: Predicting Continued Participation in Newsgroups. Journal of Computer Mediated Communication (11), 723–747 (2006)
5. Raudenbush, S.W.: Centering Predictors in Multilevel Analysis: Choices and consequences. Multilevel Modeling Newsletter (1), 10–12 (1989)
6. Raudenbush, S.W., Bryk, A.S.: Hierarchical Linear Models, 2nd edn. Sage Publications, Thousand Oaks (2002)
7. Reel, J.S.: Critical Success Factors In Software Projects. IEEE Software 16(3), 18–23 (1999)
8. Robles, G., Gonzalez-Barahona, J.M.: Contributor Turnover in Libre Software Projects. In: Open Source Systems 2006. IFIP, vol. 203, pp. 273–286. Springer, Boston (2006)
9. Rumberger, R.W.: Dropping Out of Middle School: A Multi-Level Analysis of Students and Schools. American Educational Research Journal 32(3), 583–625 (1995)
10. Stewart, K.J., Ammeter, T.A., Maruping, L.: Impacts of License Choice and Organizational Sponsorship on User Interest and Development Activity in Open Source Software Projects. Information Systems Research 17(2), 126–144 (2006)
11. Snijders, T., Bosker, R.: Multi Level Analysis: An Introduction to Basic and Advanced Multilevel Modeling. Sage Publications (1999)

A Study on OSS Marketing
and Communication Strategies

Vieri del Bianco, Luigi Lavazza, Valentina Lenarduzzi,
Sandro Morasca, and Davide Taibi, and Davide Tosi

Universita' degli Studi dell'Insubria,
Dipartimento di Scienze Teoriche e Applicate (DISTA)
via Mazzini, 5 Varese, Italy
{vieri.delbianco,luigi.lavazza,valentina.lenarduzzi,
sandro.morasca,davide.taibi,davide.tosi}@uninsubria.it

Abstract. The goal of every open source project is to gain as many satisfied users as possible. To this end, open source software producers should focus on both product development and communication. Currently, most open source projects are mainly concerned with developing code using the most appealing technologies and introducing fancy features. On the contrary, open source software producers seem to lack good communication strategies. In this paper we describe the communication strategies adopted by three successful companies that are active in open source software development. The goal of the paper is to provide some hints that could help other open source software producers identify communication strategies that are effective in promoting their products on the market.

1 Introduction

The usage of Open Source Software (OSS) has been continuously increasing in the last few years, mostly because of the success of a number of well-known projects. However, the diffusion of OSS products is still limited if compared to Closed Source Software (CSS) products. Most consumers are still hesitant in the adoption of OSS. Final users are often skeptical in trusting and adopting software products that are typically developed for free by communities of volunteer developers, who are not supported by large business companies. Moreover, OSS developers often do not pay attention to communication, marketing, commercial, and advertising aspects, since these activities require a huge amount of effort without being gratifying. For most developers, creating attractive websites and leaflets, or spending time on social advertisement is not as much fun as coding might be.

In this work, we analyze marketing and communication strategies of three OSS producers, namely a large software company, a SME and an Open Source Community. Our goal is to provide OSS producers and maintainers with a set of case studies concerning effective and low-effort marketing strategies on how to promote and advertise their OSS products.

I. Hammouda et al. (Eds.): OSS 2012, IFIP AICT 378, pp. 338–343, 2012.

The remainder of this paper is structured as follows. In Section 2, we report a concise literature review. Section 3 reports on the case studies analyzed. Finally in Section 4 we draw conclusions and outline future work.

2   Literature Review

Although there is a good deal of research on marketing in general, when it comes to software, traditional marketing and communication strategies still mainly focus on CSS [1]. Since implementing a complete marketing strategy is quite a complex process, large industries have undeniable advantages over smaller ones.

SMEs, often managed by technical people, usually adopt simplified marketing strategies because of lack of resources, skills [2], and marketing expertise [4]. Thus, marketing strategies are in some cases based on managers' decisions or personal preference, instead of a strategic and objective assessment of the environment [5].

Moreover, software products evolve quickly, often with decreasing intervals between releases, and become obsolete in a short time [3]: this fast and competitive market pushes companies to focus on product development rather than marketing aspects.

Usually, people who would like to adopt an OSS product are influenced both by opinions and the website of the product itself [6]. The website acts like a shopping window: so, if it is not effective in adequately and completely displaying information on the OSS product, it has very low probability of attracting customers [6]. In fact, the quality of a website is very important for the success of an OSS product, as websites are the main information centers for OSS products.

Moreover, as in CSS, OSS often relies on viral marketing. In viral marketing users are personally involved in the process of acquiring new customers as they are influenced by a sort of "love" for the product and act as direct promoters of the product itself. In this case, users directly encourage friends, relatives and acquaintances to acquire or adopt a product and refer them to the project website from which the OSS product can be downloaded [7]. This strategy is largely adopted by several OSS projects such as Debian, Postgres and Drupal: users act as promoters of the product, for instance by spontaneously adding a footer message to emails advertising the product they are in love with [7].

3   Case Studies

In this section, we analyze the marketing strategies adopted by two companies and an OSS community when they launch a new product on the market. We carried out several semi-structured interviews with people, ranging from CEOs to marketing manager about marketing strategies applied to both OSS and CSS. During the interviews we asked the following questions:

Q1: Number of company employees
Q2: How do you come up with ideas for new products or services?

Q3: On what grounds do you decide to develop a product or not? Do you decide by studying the results of a market analysis or do you make the decision yourself?

Q4: How do you decide if a new project should be released with an OSS license?

Q5: Which marketing strategies do you take into account during the lifecycle of a product or a service?

Q6: Which communication channels do you adopt?

All interviewees also expressed their own opinion on OSS in general and on which strategy should be applied in order to succeed on the market with OSS.

The software company we analyzed is Engineering S.p.A. (ENG). ENG is quoted at the Milan Stock Exchange and generated a revenue above 750M€ in 2010. Engineering is a global player and Italy's largest systems integration group and a leader in the provision of complete integrated services throughout the software value chain. We first interviewed the director of Communication and Marketing to get general information on the adoption of strategies concerning CSS products and services for the whole company. Then, we interviewed the Architectures & Consulting Director of the Research & Innovation Division of the ENG group in Padua (Italy) and founder of SpagoWorld (www.spagoworld.org), the free/open source initiative by ENG. SpagoWorld includes six OSS projects: SpagoBI, Spagic, Spago4Q and Spago, available in the OW2 Consortium forge, and eBAM, eBPM available in the Eclipse Foundation forge. The initiative adopts a 100% open source version (LPGL).

The SME case study was carried out by interviewing professionals of QWERTY S.r.L., an Italian SME located in Pavia. QWERTY has grown its revenue over the last years with an average annual rate of 6.6% up to 1.2M€ in 2010. QWERTY has a team of professional a remarkable experience in different platforms, both CSS (Microsoft, IBM, Oracle and others) and OSS (Linux). Some of QWERTY employees have worked for many years in the development of software applications, including integrated ERP systems such as Adempiere, which is also funding partner of the Italian Community (Adempiere Italia). QWERTY does not have employees who are competent in commercial communication, so it outsources   marketing and communication to an external communication agency.

We also took analyzed marketing and communication strategies of Ubuntu -one of the biggest OSS communities- by interviewing a member of the Italian Ubuntu marketing and promotion group. Ubuntu is led by Canonical Ltd, which estimates that the product has over 12 million users worldwide and is used to run more than ten thousand applications. Moreover, Canonical supports the user community with websites providing tutorials, a paid support option, and much more. Canonical delivers two Ubuntu releases per year, co-ordinates security and trouble-shooting, and provides an online platform for community interaction. In this work, we took into account the entire work carried out both by Canonical and the community.

Table 1 schematically shows the results of the interviews.

Table 1. Case Study comparison

	Industry		SME	Community
	CSS	OSS		
Choice of new features to be developed (Q2)				
On request (job order)	✔	✔	✔	
Based on user's needs		✔		
Based on team's ideas			✔	✔
Team decision; Tested components developed by community are included				✔
Marketing techniques adopted to support development decisions (Q3)				
Marketing outsourced to an external agency			✔	
Customer's feedback collection	✔		✔	✔
Market share analysis			✔	
Competitors analysis			✔	
Community ideas				✔
Communication strategies (Q4)				
Announcement before product launch		✔		
Announcement for product launch		✔		
Announcement for new releases		✔		
Events for product launch	✔	✔	✔	
Events for new releases		✔		✔
Decision to release as OS (Q5)				
BU decide	✔			
Software always released as OS		✔		✔
If service is based on OSS product			✔	
Communication Channels (Q6)				
Website	✔	✔	✔	✔
Specialized magazines	✔	✔		
Press release	✔	✔		✔
Newsletter			✔	
Social Media		✔		✔

The result showed different approaches to communication. Looking at how different organizations come up with ideas for new products or services, industry and SME introduce new features only in case of job orders, while Ubuntu follows decisions by Canonical, and integrates community developed components only if they are already tested.

Ubuntu community and ENG OSS BU develop only OSS, while for QWERTY the decision to release software as OSS depends on the service requested.

The role of marketing before product release is marginal for the ENG CSS BU, while the OSS BU does not apply marketing strategies at all. Marketing is fundamental for QWERTY, which employs a communication agency for analyzing the market and making surveys on potential competitors. For Ubuntu, marketing is performed by Canonical, and ideas from the community are rarely taken into account.

During the lifecycle of a product or service, ENG CSS BU makes a survey only on already published services and products. On the contrary ENG OSS BU, QWERTY and Ubuntu issue an announcement two months before the product launch and plan some events.

Websites and specific events are adopted by all the interviewed organizations for communication and are considered very useful. Ubuntu is oriented also to using online channels, like twitter and forums, while QWERTY takes advantage of newsletters as well. Both the OSS and CSS business units of ENG exploit the traditional communication channel when the client is a Public Administration and the online channels otherwise.

4   Conclusion

This is a unique study comparing OSS communication models which illustrate communication strategies employed by different OSS producers.

The results shown different approaches used in the case studies with some similarities in SME and big industry on communication channel and several differences from the open community.

Of course, this work leaves room for further research. In fact additional case studies, including failure cases, could be explored in the future to further confirm or complement our findings.

Finally, correlations between communication, project diffusion and project maturity could be investigated further.

Acknowledgements. The research presented in this paper has been partially funded by the FIRB project "ARTDECO," sponsored by the Italian Ministry of Education and University and by the project "Metodi e tecniche per l'analisi, l'implementazione e la valutazione di sistemi software" funded by the Università degli Studi dell'Insubria. We are especially grateful to Costanza Amodeo and Gabriele Ruffatti of Engineering group, Adelio Trabella of QWERTY, Monia Spinelli and Paolo Sammicheli of the Ubuntu Foundation.

References

[1] Helander, N., Ulkuniemi, P.: Marketing challenges in the software component business. International Journal of Technology Marketing 1(4), 375–392 (2006)

[2] Dwyer, M., Gilmore, A., Carson, D.: Innovative marketing in SMEs. European Journal of Marketing 43(1/2), 46–61 (2009)

[3] Kulmala, H.I., Uusi-Rauva, E.: Network as a business environment: experiences from the software industry. Supply Chain Management: An International Journal 10(3), 169–178 (2005)

[4] Simpson, M., Padmore, J., Taylor, N., Frecknall-Hughes, J.: Marketing in small and medium sized enterprises. International Journal of Behaviour & Research 12(6), 361–387 (2006)

[5] Chaston, I.: Small firm performance: assessing the interaction between entrepreneurial style and organizational structure. European Journal of Marketing 31(11/12), 814–831 (1997)

[6] Lavazza, L., Morasca, S., Taibi, D., Tosi, D.: OP2A: How to Improve the Quality of the Web Portal of Open Source Software Products. In: Filipe, J., Cordeiro, J. (eds.) WEBIST 2011. LNBIP, vol. 101, pp. 149–162. Springer, Heidelberg (2012)

[7] Guo, S., Wang, M., Leskovec, J.: The role of social networks in online shopping: information passing, price of trust, and consumer choice. In: ACM Conference on Electronic Commerce 2011, pp. 157–166 (2011)

The Effect of Open Source Licensing on the Evolution of Business Strategy

Tetsuo Noda[1], Terutaka Tansho[1], and Shane Coughlan[2]

[1]Shimane University
nodat@soc.shimane-u.ac.jp, tansho@riko.shimane-u.ac.jp
[2] Founder at Opendawn,
Visiting Researcher at Shimane University and Executive Director /
Vice-President Far East at OpenForum Europe
shane@opendawn.com

Abstract. This paper explores how the approach underlying Open Source development has encouraged a greater sharing of knowledge in related business and legal affairs, and subsequently leads to the emergence of Open Source-driven collaboration by enterprises to address challenges. We use an Economic approach to propose a theoretical framework for Open Source business analysis and provide a defined sample of real-world developments to support its initial findings. We conclude that the need to develop effective Open Source governance solutions has led to widespread collaboration regarding business and legal challenges by stakeholders in the field, and that this collaboration will increase to improve efficiency as the market matures.

1   Introduction

In spite of the increased adoption of Open Source technology in businesses, most enterprises do not yet have formal processes in place regarding its management. According to research by Gartner (2011), over 50% of organizations are using Open Source as part of their IT strategy, while only 33% have a policy to address it. OpenLogic (2010) reported 65% of organizations who think they do not use Open Source actually include technology licensed under its terms.

It is possible that one of the reasons Open Source has such extensive market penetration is that initial adoption is not associated with a licensing fee. Nevertheless, while users are free to use, study, share and improve the technology, these freedoms are conditional on various terms associated with individual Open Source licenses.

The most common license - and therefore the most illustrative - is the GNU GPL. This latter requirement originated in Open Source and is termed "Copyleft", a play on words that refers to its formal provision of lasting freedom to subsequent users, as opposed to traditional restrictions applied by copyright law. Copyleft as a principle facilitates on-going collaboration on projects like Linux, though as pointed out by Hatta (2007), understanding its scope or definition is not sufficient to explain how and why Open Source itself works. This paper explores this question via the application of

I. Hammouda et al. (Eds.): OSS 2012, IFIP AICT 378, pp. 344–349, 2012.

historical and logical analysis, asking what conditions are necessary to sustain Open Source dynamics and to encourage the applications of multiple business models - and therefore participants - in the global Open Source community.

2   Open Source Licensing and the Facilitation of Business Models

2.1   Copyleft and Its Evolution

Richard Stallman, the originator of the formal definition of the Copyleft licensing provision, wanted to ensure that the GNU Operating System would be available to everyone with a lasting set of freedoms. This is not to suggest that the concept of Copyleft itself is uncontroversial. Some would suggest that Open Source licenses without this provision are best because the cooperative model does not require formal statements of subsequent sharing. Some maintain that they want an explicit Copyleft requirement applied to their code.

Of course licenses using provisions like Copyleft have been modified occasionally - with a good example being the GNU GPL, now on its third revision - but the core grants and the principle of maintaining those grants has been consistently maintained, allowing relatively certainty in the development and use of software under its terms. The same principles and the same expectations also apply to derived licenses such as LGPLv2 and AGPLv3. Where the former takes steps to loosen the conditions applied to linking software packages and the latter increases the Copyleft conditions into the sphere of network-based software (including cloud computing), they are consistent with the core values of Open Source and offer the same pre-conditions that facilitate collaborative development.

2.2   Copyleft and the Cooperation of Labor

The Internet has allowed people to communicate and to work together across great distances at a lower cost and at a higher speed than ever before. It has been a powerful driver in reducing barriers to working with partners and customers to accomplish goals, what is sometimes referred to as co-innovation. In the software field it is difficult for a single vendor to meet all the requirements of multiple customers, and it is more effective for several parties to cooperate on developing and enhancing a shared platform. This is what increasingly happens, and it has led to the commercial sustainability of Open Source projects such as the Linux kernel. This is because Open Source, a software paradigm build on the inherent assumption of cooperation and sharing, is a natural beneficiary of trends towards cooperation.

The dynamics of the software industry have altered in the last two decades. Twenty years ago the dominant proprietary paradigm resulted in a small number of providers controlling innovation and serving a large number of users in a fairly static relationship. However, the emerging Open Source paradigm encouraged new development models and new software development processes that moved the decision-making emphasis to users. Since the Open Source paradigm gained mainstream traction this has had a profound effect on the market as a whole.

2.3   The Cooperation of Labor in Software Development

The proprietary software and Open Source paradigms facilitate the establishment and improvement of various software development models and processes. These development models may be hierarchical, loosely managed or unstructured depending on the given software paradigm and the requirements of the individuals or organizations working on a project. It would be incorrect to attempt to associate Open Source exclusively with one development or business model, though such an approach has in the past been unfortunately common.

There are many business models applicable to Open Source. This is for the same reason that Open Source facilitates multiple development models; as a paradigm Open Source draws a wide set of parameters that participant operate inside. The cooperation of labor in software development indeed evolves a variety of business model in Open Source. And business models corresponding to the market needs, open source businesses as revenue generating model can be formed into practice.

Ultimately the numbers of possible business models applicable to Open Source make it impossible to pick out any one as a clear favorite. As with any field of business, the correct model depends on market segment analysis, an understanding of skills, and a prudent balance between maximization of profit and sustainability. As have been discussed, open source licenses in the meta-level, strongly expressed in the Copyleft concept, have led to the natural consequences of cooperation of labor and collaboration.

3   Open Source Business Models and Licensing Strategy

3.1   Intellectual Property Rights and Business Strategies around Licensing

Business enterprises have always exercised their Intellectual Property Rights (IPR), especially around patent properties, in compliance with their business strategies. Takahashi (2007) indicates that the monetary value of patent properties primarily depends not on the scientific value per se but rather on the business assessment regarding its worth and the processes that frame such understanding. This means that aggression is possible with patents of low worth, but also that the opposite holds true. For example, even if a patent with value in terms of monopolizing a technology implementation is possessed by a business enterprise, the exertion of it is determined based on a strategic understanding of the requirements of the enterprise.

There are occasions when Open Source software packages or projects primarily governed by copyright licenses come into potential conflict with patent issues. Some Open Source licenses address this matter by the inclusion of patent provisions providing non-aggression pledges between collaborators on the licensed software, but the larger issue of whether a business makes a strategic decision to leverage patents aggressively essentially remains open. This is especially true of parties not collaborating on the same Open Source packages, or of third parties who may have minimal investment - and therefore understanding or sympathy - for Open Source approaches as a whole.

Such challenges have led to an evolution in the governance applied to Open Source. Early legal concerns around Open Source focused on copyright issues.

3.2   Open Source and Transition of Governance

(1) Early Cases of Open Source Governance
The governance of Open Source in the late 1990's to early 2000 was naturally focused on the licenses that govern Open Source transactions. The emphasis was on compliance as this was regarded as the critical issue for minimizing potential risk in adoption and deployment.

(2) Growing Up Stage in Open Source Governance – Supply Chain Consideration
As Open Source stakeholders became more understanding of how Open Source derived value - namely through collaboration between an ever-changing pool of third parties - they also became more nuanced in their understanding of the governance necessary to provide maximum benefit. This encouraged an alteration in their approach to governance, and there was a shift in perspective towards using governance as a tool to assist in maximizing value throughout the supply chain while honoring obligations in procurement and deployment.

(3) Market Solutions
There are many services, products and collaborative platforms that contribute to governance in the Open Source marketplace. None is a panacea but many are useful for new entrants and relatively experienced participants alike, providing avenues for discovering and comparing approaches to minimizing risk, improving understand and dealing with suppliers or customers.

3.3   Open Source and Remaining Governance Challenges

The trend in Open Source legal affairs is aware from copyright licensing matters - which are essentially solved though not yet fully refined - and towards broader questions of governance and business management. One key challenge from this perspective remains the aforementioned tension between Open Source concepts and IPR, especially in the context of third parties who do participate in Open Innovation or direct invests in Open Source. Leveraging IPR against Open Source-derived technologies - whether as a business strategy to obtain new revenue streams or to hinder competition - is a significant potential challenge to the future growth and lasting viability of Open Source solutions.

The majority of these actions is rather passive and may introduce further complexity, perhaps by diminishing the perceived value of collaboration around Open

Source or by creating complex tangles of Open Source licensing obligations and proprietary licensing conditions. An alternative strategy is to seek other ways to engage with tension between Open Source and IPR, in particular by seeking to find collaborative solutions to this challenge.

3.4   Collaboration to Sustain Open Source Business Models

It is observable that in issues related to Open Source license compliance various checks and measures have been created to provide adherence to the rules and to discourage imbalances in the market. Examples include the lawsuits initiated by GPL-violations.org in Europe and later followed by Software Freedom Law Center in the USA, or the knowledge-sharing communities fostered by Linux Foundation and Free Software Foundation Europe.

One similar collaborative approach that has arisen in Open Source to be engaged with IPR tensions is Open Invention Network (OIN), established in 2005 by Red Hat, IBM, NEC, Sony, Novell and Philips. Initially conceptualized as a shared pool of defensive patents and a common agreement not to litigate over a defined set of Linux System technologies, OIN has since grown to lead a community of over 400 companies and projects that formally pledge non-aggression to each other over the Linux System, and to hold hundreds of patents important to all sectors of technology.

While it makes sense for companies investing in the development of new technology to formally register such innovation in the form of patents what these companies subsequently seek to do with these patents is another matter. The aggressive enforcement of rights may provide initial advantage, but it reduces the ability of parties to collaborate in the mid to long-term, thus undermining the central precept behind obtaining lasting returns in Open Source. Taking this into account, the defensive holding of patents - and the strengthening of shared defensive pools and risk mitigation methods - is only logical. It is likely that OIN and perhaps similar entities will remain significant contributors to Open Source legal matters, and that the extent of its shared patent pool may increase as well. The reduction of potential risk from other collaborators on the Linux System in combination with the deterrent against aggression from third parties alone makes this reasonable.

From a broader perspective, it is possible to contextualize the modern governance activity around Open Source as being characterized by stakeholders seeking to efficiently maintain the rules inherent to deriving value between stakeholders, and to mitigate the risk of disruption from third parties wherever possible. This ensures the sustainability of value through collaboration, a state that facilitates a business environment with a wide range of applicable models and investors. As with the intersection between IPR portfolio decisions and Open Source business imperatives, the tension between commercial and collaborative life-cycle knowledge provision may be an interesting vein of potential further study, as may be the multi-layered relations between Open Source and proprietary software companies moving forward.

4   Conclusion

We analyzed the evolution of business engagement with Open Source as a paradigm for the creation, distribution and shared evolution of software platforms. The inherent value provided by Open Source appears to be that it provides rules for collaboration between multiple parties with multiple motives. While the propositions behind Open Source challenge preconceptions from the perspective of proprietary software development, and while some parties would question the necessity of Open Source-derived measures like Copyleft, there is no doubt Open Source as a concept and licenses like the GNU GPL have in practice delivered tremendous value.

With Open Source now maturing and collaboration moving into avenues of legal and business intelligence, the dynamics of the field are changing. A reoccurring theme is that Open Source and proprietary approaches to software and IPR management increasingly brush against each other, and inevitably will seek some form of coexistence. This will not necessarily be without further tension, though from a rational perspective it is hardly feasible that destructive conflict would be the preferred outcome from either side. It is therefore our conclusion that the need to effectively engage with improvements in Open Source governance will see increased collaboration on all forms of legal issue by the stakeholders in the field, and those stakeholders from both Open Source and proprietary business perspectives will ultimately reach a form of accommodation and equilibrium.

References

Andrew, M.: Understanding Open Source & Free Software Licensing. O'Reilly Publishing (2004)

Guadamuz, A.: Viral Contracts or Unenforceable Documents? Contractual Validity of Copyleft Licenses. E.I.P.R 26(8), 331–339 (2004)

Hatta, M.: Software License and the Development Style. Manufacturing Management Research Center of Tokyo University (2007)

Takahashi, N.: General Theory of the Strategy of Licensing Business, Software License and Development Style. Manufacturing Management Research Center of Tokyo University (2007)

Binoculars: Comprehending Open Source Projects through Graphs

M.M. Mahbubul Syeed

Tampere University of Technology, Finland
mm.syeed@tut.fi

Abstract. Comprehending Open Source Software (OSS) projects requires dealing with huge historical information stored in heterogeneous repositories, such as source code versioning systems, bug tracking system, mailing lists, and revision history logs. In this paper, we present Binoculars, a prototype tool which aims to provide a platform for graph based visualization and exploration of OSS projects. We describe the issues need to be addressed for the design and implementation of a graph based tool and distill lessons learned for future guideline.

1 Introduction

Open Source Software (OSS) has gained interest in both commercial and academic world over the past decade due to its high quality. Successful OSS projects produce a rich set of software repositories, coming with a large number of versions reflecting their development and evolution history. These repositories consist of the source code, change logs, bug reports and mailing lists.

To know the facts related to such OSS project development, composition, and the possible risks associated with its use, one has to explore the huge information stored in the repositories. But often such repository contains heterogeneous information with different data representation, which also varies significantly from project to project. Thus a tool support for uniform data representation and customizable visualization mechanism is required to ease the comprehension of OSS projects.

In this paper, we present the tool Binoculars as the first step towards a graph based platform to comprehend and visualize OSS projects. Video demonstration of the tool Binoculars can be seen from [11].

2 Tool Support for Comprehending OSS Projects: A Review

This section presents a review on tool supports that offer different visualization approaches for comprehending OSS projects.

The tool, CodeSaw [10] provides a time series representation of social interaction data in juxtaposed displays. This tool explores links between one's contributions to that of social interactions. In this context, the tool Tesseract [10]

I. Hammouda et al. (Eds.): OSS 2012, IFIP AICT 378, pp. 350–355, 2012.

explores the multi-perspective relationships in a project for a user-selected time period (i.e., the evoluiton), and represents them via four juxtaposed displays.

In [10], FASTDash was proposed as an interactive conflict management tool which provides a spatial representation of the shared code base by highlighting team members current activity. The tool CollabVS [10] addresses this issue at editing time, and provides a visual representation of conflicting code and a communication mechanism. The tool Palantir [10] performs similar task by graphically displaying the shared workspace to the developers with the information of what others are doing, and calculating the severity of such activities. Also the tool Augur [10] provides a line oriented view of the source code with colors for each pixel line indicating the location of the modification work and how recently it was conducted. This visualization allows to see how much activity has taken place recently and where that activity has been located.

In [10], the tool Ariadne utilizes call-graph approach to visualize social dependency of the developers due to code sharing. Similarly, the tool Expertise Browser [10] determines developers expertise from historical contributions.

Though the tools discussed above provide useful insight of OSS projects through different visualization approaches, yet none effectively explores graph based visualization of OSS projects. We thus add another dimension towards the comprehension of OSS projects by providing a graph based data representation and visualization. The principal argument here is that graph structures are most suitable for analyzing data that exhibits inherent relationships. In this context, the repository data produced by OSS projects exhibit strong relationships among them due to common work space sharing and exchange of information. For example, community members often share many technical competencies, values, and beliefs over online discussion forums. Similarly, code artifacts have interrelationships due to architectural dependency as well as due to contributions from multiple community members. Thus, OSS projects can be effectively comprehended through graph based representation and visualization.

3 Graph Based Visualization

In this section we concentrate on the available methods and techniques exploited in literature for graph based data representation and visualization. We also put a discussion on pros and cons of such techniques.

Graph based data representation and visualization can be effectively utilized when there exists inherent relations among data elements [3]. In such visualization, one can generate any number of links (i.e., edges) between two data points (i.e., nodes), and can easily traverse a given path through the data. This visual experience can be enhanced further by using layout algorithms, navigation and interaction methods, and incremental exploration mechanisms [3].

A significant amount of libraries, frameworks and toolkits are developed to support such visualization. To mention a few, GraphEd [4],the Tom Sawyer Software Graph Editor Toolkit [5], Graphlet [6], JUNG [1] provide APIs with different layout algorithms, customization, generic graphics and interprocess communication to create task-specific tools. Libraries and frameworks like GTL,

LINK, GFC, GDT, and GVF provide support for both general and specific purpose graph visualization [3]. Within open source domain, Graphviz [10] and Zest [10] provides comprehensive set of APIs to support such visualization. Although there is no widely used standard for graph description formats, GML [7] and GraphXML [8] are available.

Despite of such benefits and supports for graph visualization, there are inherent shortcomings to such techniques. This includes, (a) difficulties in visualizing and comprehending large graphs. For example, a graph with thousands of nodes would cause performance bottleneck of the platform used and decrease the viewability (or usability) of such visualization significantly. In general, comprehension and detail analysis of data in graph structures is easiest when the size of the displayed graph is small [3]; (b) efficiency of a graph layout algorithm may be scale upto several hundred nodes, not beyond that; (c) time complexity for visualization, interaction and update of a graph is relatively high and increases with increase in graph size.

So far no single toolkit or framework mentioned above has proved to be sufficient to cope with these problems. Thus design decision for implementing an efficient graph visualization tool should ruminate the followings, (a) provide appropriate level of data abstraction. This keeps the graph structure small enough for effective comprehension and increase the efficiency of layout algorithms. To explore the graph, incremental exploration mechanism should be implemented, (b) time complexity of an algorithm should be measured accurately.

4   Binoculars: A Graph Based Platform

This section describes the requirements to design and implement a graph based visualization tool and presents Binoculars as a representative example. These requirements are derived considering the characteristics of OSS projects and the shortcomings of graph visualization techniques. The usability features of Binoculars are also presented. Fig. 1 shows the main interface of Binoculars.

First requirement is to provide an architectural model supporting well defined extension points for extending functionalities. As OSS analysis tools of this kind operate on project data, thus a good starting point is to model a generalized and standard data representation. This forms the system kernel and provides interfaces to build functionalities over it. The conceptual architecture of Binoculars is shown in Fig.2. In Binoculars, we defined a data repository structure to store both project and graph data (Fig.2), and use XML data format for representation (Fig.3(a)). XML is chosen over others due to (a) its inherent power of extensibility with new tags, (b) standard formating, and (c) graph generation and manipulation seems flexible with XML.

Having modeled such a repository, the next step is to decide what data to represent and how. For current implementation of Binoculars, we explored CVS or SVN checkouts, bug reporting system and mailing list. To represent data we adopt the following approach- first identified each entity within an OSS project which plays a role (either active or passive). For example, a community member

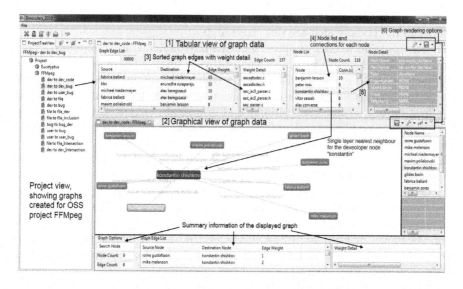

Fig. 1. User interface of Binoculars

(e.g., developer, user as active entities), and a code file, a single thread of mail and bug report (as passive entities). Then we identified unique set of attributes to describe each entity and provide values with the data mined from the sources presented above. In XML each such attribute is presented as a tag. Fig.3(a) shows an example of a code file representation.

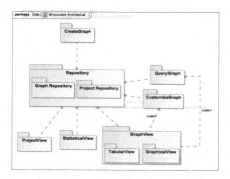

Fig. 2. Conceptual architecture of Binoculars

Third, a set of methods should be derived to transform repository data into graphs. These methods and the graph data should be reusable in a sense that one or more graph data can be reused by a method to generate new graphs. In Binoculars, graph data are stored using XML representation (example, Fig. 3(b)). As the methods operates on XML tags, thus one interface works for all repository data. As shown in Fig 2, CreateGraph module implements these graph generation methods, which are discussed in [9].

Fourth, provide a GUI support to visualize, render and manipulate graph data. This GUI design for graph visualization is often constrained by the limiting factors of the available visualization techniques discussed in section 3. To cope with these issues we took the following measures. We provided a two-way visualization of a graph, e.g., tabular and graphical (Fig.1 items 1,2). Tabular view provides complete graph information consisting of (a) Graph with nodes and (weighted) edges; (b) Node list with degree count for each node; (c) description of each node; (d) Summary data on graph; and (e) Options to render a graph (Fig.1, item 3,4,5,6, respectively). Thus user can get complete graph data with detail information in real time for large graphs with thousands of nodes. Then, depending on the option selected for rendering a graph, a modified (or abstracted) version of the graph (in tabular view) can be viewed in graphical form. As shown in Fig.1 item 2, a single level nearest neighbor graph showing the developers to whom developer "Konstantin" has direct communication in FFMpeg project [10]. Hence the graphical view (Fig.1 item 2) always shows a tailored version of the complete graph provided in tabular view (Fig.1 item 1), thus minimizing the performance bottleneck of layout algorithms.

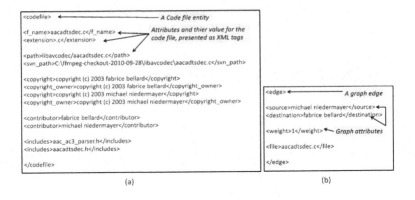

Fig. 3. (a) XML representation of a code file repository in FFMpeg project. (b) XML presentation of a developers relationship graph generated from (a).

Other options for rendering a graph includes (Fig.1, item 6), customization based on (a) given range of edge weights, (b) selected set of nodes or edges from the original graph, (c) a given attribute value (e.g., gio-location= "america").

None-the-less, searching, sorting, zooming, and saving graph data in XML format can also be performed. As in Fig. 2, rendering mechanisms are implemented in QueryGraph and CustomizeGraph module, and the visualization are handled by ProjectView, GraphView and StatisticalView modules.

Fifth, selection of platform and packages for implementation should be steered by it's easy extension and distribution. Our choice in this issue is to release

Binoculars as an OSS. Thus we utilized well established and maintained OSS platforms and packages, e.g., Eclipse, Eclipse RCP, ZEST, DOM, and JFreeChart. Reference to these platforms can be found here [10].

5   Discussion and Future Work

In this paper we put a discussion on the requirements to model and implement a graph based platform for comprehending OSS projects, and present the tool Binoculars as a first step towards establishing such a platform. Our starting point is the design of a repository to capture the essence of OSS projects and then built tool functionalities over it to operate on repository data. We also discuss the inadequacy of graph visualization techniques and distill possible solution.

Future extension of this tool includes, (a) visualization on the evolution of socio-technical aspects of OSS projects, (b) Incremental exploration mechanism on the displayed graph, and (c) a formal language query support.

References

1. Souza, C.R.B., Quirk, S., Trainer, E., Redmiles, D.F.: Supporting collaborative software development through the visualization of socio-technical dependencies. In: ACM SIGGROUP Conference on Supporting Group Work, pp. 147–156 (2007)
2. Mockus, A., Herbsleb, J.: Expertise browser: A quantitative approach to identifying expertise. In: ICSE, pp. 503–512 (2002)
3. Herman, I., Melancon, G., Marshall, M.S.: Graph visualization and navigation in information visualization: A survey. In: TVCG, IEEE, vol. 6(1), pp. 24–43 (2000)
4. Di Battista, G., Eades, P., Tamassia, R., Tollis, I.G.: Graph Drawing: Algorithms for the Visualization of Graphs. Prentice Hall (1999)
5. Becker, R.A., Eick, S.G., Wilks, A.R.: Visualizing Network Data. In: TVCG, IEEE, vol. 1(1), pp. 16–28 (1995)
6. Argawal, P.K., Aronov, B., Pach, J., Pollack, R., Sharir, M.: Quasi–Planar Graphs Have a Linear Number of Edges, pp. 1–7. Springer, GD (1995)
7. Himsolt, M.: GML — Graph Modelling Language. University of Passau (1997)
8. Herman, I., Marshall, M.S.: GraphXML. Reports of the Centre for Mathematics and Computer Sciences (1999)
9. Syeed, M.M., Aaltonen, T., Hammouda, I., Systä, T.: Tool Assisted Analysis of Open Source Projects: A Multi-Faceted Challenge. IJOSSP 3(2), 43–78 (2011)
10. References (2012), http://rajit-cit.wix.com/syeed#!refrences
11. Binoculars Demo (2012), http://www.youtube.com/watch?v=cMoYq6J0pQE

OSSLI: Architecture Level Management of Open Source Software Legality Concerns

Alexander Lokhman, Antti Luoto,
Salum Abdul-Rahman, and Imed Hammouda

Tampere University of Technology
{firstname.lastname}@tut.fi

Abstract. This paper presents a tool that addresses the legality concerns of open source at the level of software architecture, early in the development activity. The tool demonstrates the significance of licensing concerns at the architectural level by extending existing modeling tools with support for open source licensing issues.

1 Introduction

The overall research problem we investigate in this work is twofold. First, we study the significance of licensing concerns at the architectural design phase. Second, we investigate what kind of tool concepts are needed for addressing open source licensing issues in architectural models.

Our goal is to develop a new kind of open source legality support tool, named OSSLI (Open Source Software Licensing)[1], focusing especially on validating architectural models against open source legality and proposing remedial architectural solutions. The OSSLI tool provides mechanisms to express licensing constraints, detect violations while application model is being constructed, and provide possible remedies and alternative solutions to resolve possible license violations. The tool is implemented as a plug-in to existing CASE tools.

2 Background

The Open Source Initiative lists about 70 licenses[2]. Popular licenses include the GNU General Public License (GPL), the Lesser GNU General Public License (LGPL), the Apache license, the Massachusetts Institute of Technology license (MIT), and the Berkeley Software Distribution license (BSD). The terms of different licenses vary considerably. Typically licenses are categorized as permissive (e.g. MIT), weak copyleft (e.g. LGPL), and strong copyleft (e.g. GPL).

There are a number of ontologies and standards proposed for documenting the legal rules and constraints of software systems, with respect to open source

---

[1] http://ossli.cs.tut.fi/

[2] http://opensource.org/licenses

I. Hammouda et al. (Eds.): OSS 2012, IFIP AICT 378, pp. 356–361, 2012.

software. Examples include Legal Knowledge Interchange Format (LKIF [4]), Software Package Data Exchange (SPDX)[3], and QualiPSo Intellectual Property Rights Tracking (IPRT)[4]. These works could contribute to the foundation of our work, but nevertheless should be enhanced for better ties with the work processes and methods of software architects.

Licenses can be conflicting [3]. As an example, a software component under the terms of GPL cannot be directly linked with another under the terms of the Apache license. The reason is that GPL'ed software cannot be mixed with software that is licensed under the terms of a license that imposes stronger or additional terms, in this case the Apache license.

When integrating third party open source components, possibly together with own work, the restrictions and obligations which the used licenses impose may depend on whether the work is considered as derived (derivative) or combined (collective) [1]. Also the interpretation may depend on how the component is used: as a redistributable product, as a hosted service, as a development tool, or for internal use [8]. Furthermore, Open Source legality interpretations are subject to the way software is implemented, packaged, and deployed [3,5].

The legality challenge of FLOSS has been partly addressed using so-called license analysis techniques and tools. These tools provide functionality to identify the licenses (e.g. Ninka[5]) used and to verify license compliance in source code packages (e.g. FOSSology[6], OSLC[7], and ASLA [7]). These techniques however are mostly useful in analyzing ready packaged software systems but give little guidance, with respect to licensing issues, for software developers during the development activity itself.

3   OSSLI Tool Architecture

Our goal is to develop a new kind of open source legality support tool, OSSLI, focusing especially on validating architectural models against open source legality constraints and proposing remedial architectural solutions. Figure 1 depicts the overall architecture of the tool. Here we assume that the tool is capable of managing the legality concerns at the architectural level (i.e., application design is expressed as an UML component diagram for example).

Table 1, in turn, explains each of the architectural components. A part from Core, each component is associated with an extension point. The architecture is made extensible so that the tool is able to work with different licenses. The License Profile component allows for attaching different licensing concepts to the architectural model. Different implementations of License Model give different interpretations of clauses based on local law. Different open source components

---

[3] http://spdx.org/

[4] http://qualipso.org/licenses-champion

[5] http://ninka.turingmachine.org/

[6] http://fossology.org/

[7] http://sourceforge.net/projects/oslc

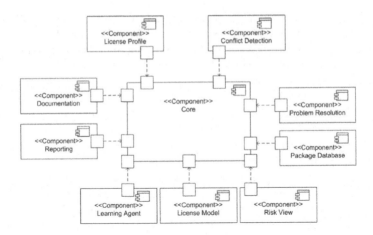

Fig. 1. An Open Architecture for Open Source Compliance

can be registered to the tool via the Package Database component. The Risk View extension point allows the plug-in of different risk analysis methods. The tool also integrates different techniques for detecting conflicts among licensed components (Conflict Detection) and proposes remedial actions (Problem Resolution). These actions can be recorded for future exploitation (Learning Agent). Finally, the tool is capable to report the analysis results in different pluggable formats (Reporting) and links to relevant documentation resources (Documentation).

The OSSLI tool is built on top of Eclipse and is integrated to Papyrus[8], which is an open source tool for graphical UML2 modeling. The plug-in architecture of the tool allows users and developers to extend its functionality beyond the support that comes as part of the base version. Any new feature that corresponds to any of the extension point shown in Figure 1 can be developed as an Eclipse plug-in and deployed to an own version of Eclipse. A video recording of a number of usage scenarios of the tool is available in the OSSLI project website.

4   Example Usage Scenarios

In the following we present a number of usage scenarios of the OSSLI tool.

4.1   Annotating Design Models with Licensing Information

Using the OSSLI tool, UML models can be extended with license and IPR related information by applying a UML profile. The profile introduces concepts related to the properties of open source licenses in the form of stereotypes and meta-attributes. This allows the user to create a UML model that takes into account

---

[8] http://papyrusuml.org/

Table 1. Architectural Components

Component	Description
Core	Handles interactions between the application model, licensing information and the user.
License Profile	A UML extension to include license information.
License Model	Describes in computable format the clauses, restrictions, rights and their interdependencies of a license.
Package Database	A repository of containing information on which license and copyright information is associated with which package.
Risk View	Assess legal risks related to use of component for variable purposes re-licensing, sale, internal use etc.
Conflict Detection	Analysis whether license terms of different licenses conflict when linked into the same software.
Problem Resolution	Suggests operations that can be performed to remove license conflicts from model.
Learning Agent	Records user actions so that they can be later used to improve program performance.
Reporting	The analysis results from the different components can be output in different formats.
Documentation	Linking to internal and external documentation on open source licensing concerns.

what licenses each component is associated with. For example, a software package could be annotated with information such as copyright holder, license type, and the risks associated with its use in different usage scenarios. Figure 2 shows an example annotation of example components.

4.2 Visualizing the Risk Levels of Open Source Components

Once the components in the UML diagram have been annotated with the information defined in the profile, the user can activate a risk view plug-in. The user selects the concrete risk evaluator s/he wants to use. The user can also choose to analyze part of the model. The user is prompted for the intended application domain, e.g. "internal use", "redistribution" or "as a hosted service". The tool analyzes the information in the UML diagram using the fields defined in the profile to evaluate the level of legal risk of using each component for the selected application domain. The legal risk level is displayed by changing the background color of the components analyzed. In Figure 2, for example, three packages show no risk (green color) and one package is of a clear risk.

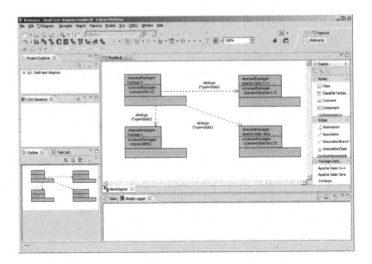

Fig. 2. Risk view analysis

4.3 Identifying License Conflicts

Using the OSSLI tool, it is possible to identify conflicts related to how software components are integrated. This is based on the licensing information attached to the components themselves and the inter component links. The tool can either analyze the whole diagram or just a selected set of components. The detected conflicts are presented to the user and are highlighted in the UML diagram in red color.

The identified conflicts can be analyzed and possible remedial actions can be suggested. For example the way two conflicting components communicate could be changed from static linking to dynamic linking. Another example remedial action could be to add an intermediate layer with a neutral license between two conflicting components.

4.4 Logging Decisions for Future Recommendation

The OSSLI tool is capable to record the detected conflicts and the corresponding remedial actions for future recommendation. An example logged session is given in Figure 3. In the background picture shows a conflict detected between two software packages. In order to address the conflict, the user has changed the type of dependency (named DEP 9) from static to dynamic.

In the foreground dialog, a new conflict has been detected between two other software packages licensed under the terms of Apache 2.0 and LGPL v2.1 licenses respectively. The OSSLI Tool suggests two solutions of which the first one corresponds to the recorded remedial action taken in the background picture, i.e. hanging the link type from static to dynamic. The second recommendation is to relicense Barcode 4J under the terms of LGPL v2.1. This is of course subject to ownership of the copyrights.

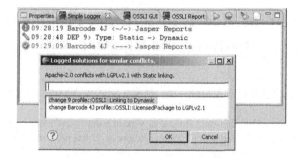

Fig. 3. Logging solutions and recommendation

5   Discussion

In this paper we have presented a tool that is capable of expressing, analyzing, and managing open source licensing constraints in architectural design models. As future work, we are planning to enhance the OSSLI tool with new features. For example we plan to investigate how the proposed concepts could be the basis for building novel techniques to devise optimal architectural solutions taking into consideration the legality constraints. This could be achieved, for instance, through the use of genetic algorithms [6]. We are also enhancing the tool recommendation capabilities with more advanced techniques, for example by applying search-based heuristics such as Tabu search [2]. Also we plan to apply the tool to a number of industrial case studies.

References

1. German, D., Hassan, A.: License integration patterns: Addressing license mismatches in component-based development. In: Proc. ICSE 2009, pp. 188–198 (2009)
2. Glover, F., Laguna, M.: Tabu Search, Reading. Kluwer Academic Publishers, Boston (1997)
3. Hammouda, I., Mikkonen, T., Oksanen, V., Jaaksi, A.: Open source legality patterns: Architectural design decisions motivated by legal concerns. In: Proc. AMT 2010, pp. 207–214 (2010)
4. Hoekstra, R., Breuker, J., Di Bello, M., Boer, A.: The LKIF core ontology of basic legal concepts. In: Proc. LOAIT 2007, pp. 43–63 (2007)
5. Malcolm, B.: Software interactions and the GNU General Public License. IFOSS L. Rev. 2(2), 165–180 (2010)
6. Hadaytullah, O.R., Koskimies, K., Makinen, E.: Synthesizing architecture from requirements: A genetic approach. In: Avgeriou, P., et al. (eds.) Relating Software Requirements and Architecture, ch. 18, pp. 307–331 (2011)
7. Tuunanen, T., Koskinen, J., Karkkainen, T.: Automated software license analysis. Automated Software Engineering 16(3-4), 455–490 (2009)
8. von Willebrand, M., Partanen, M.: Package review as a part of free and open source software compliance. IFOSS L. Rev. 2(2), 39–60 (2010)

Hybrid Business Models in Software Product Industry: Patterns and Challenges

Swanand J. Deodhar[1], Kulbhushan C. Saxena[1], and Mikko Ruohonen[2]

[1] Fortune Institute of International Business, Vasant Vihar, New Delhi, 110057, India
[2] CIRCMI, Department of Computer Sciences, University of Tampere,
Kalevantie 4, 33014, Tampere, Finland

Abstract. Operating in software product industry is becoming an increasingly risky proposition. Compressed timeline for product development combined with need to reduce cost has compelled organizations to look at new ways of doing business. One such avenue is combining the erstwhile conflicting practices of open source and closed source software. This industry paper highlights common patterns and challenges encountered in operationalizing such business models. The findings are based on a larger multiple case study research involving six such software products.

1   Introduction

Software product industry represents organizations that develop software products and build business models around these products. These business models are influenced by two dominant and contrasting licensing regimes, namely proprietary and open source licensing. These two approaches have spawned diverse mechanisms for software development and distribution.

Although the two approaches are highly contrasting, they have an ironic capability of complimenting each other's weaknesses. In proprietary approach, vendors are in control of development and distribution and therefore vendors have to bear the cost for the same. In return vendors are assured of larger chunk of economic rents as only they can sell software licenses. On the other hand, open source approach allows for faster development and distribution channel as large pool of voluntary developers would contribute the software code and place the same in public domain thus removing any practical chance of selling licenses. Clearly, if a proprietary software vendor can benefit from development and distribution practices of FOSS and vice versa.

Such attempts are increasingly becoming necessary with organizations' survival in software industry becoming increasingly uncertain. Established software product vendors are threatened by reduced barriers to entry. With software product innovations happening rapidly [1] and leadership positions in software product industry becoming fragile [2], software product industry is increasingly becoming a risky proposition with firms ending up in bankruptcy in a short span of time. For

I. Hammouda et al. (Eds.): OSS 2012, IFIP AICT 378, pp. 362–367, 2012.

example, from 1995 to 2007, exit rate in software product industry was three times that of pharmaceutical industry and two times that of hardware industry [1].

Hybrid business models provide one form of innovation adopted by organizations to survive in such troubled environment [3]. Such merging represents number of challenges. How can organizations combine two approaches that were designed to be incommensurable? And are there any common patterns in such hybridization? These questions were the starting point of the study

1.1   Hybrid Business Models

Before we explain challenges in operationalizing hybrid business models, it is important to elaborate on notion of hybrid business models. Hybrid business models form a special class of business models. Software product business models are often divided into four categories: product development, product distribution, revenue model, and maintenance [4]. A business model hence can be treated hybrid if one or more its dimensions combines practices from both open source and proprietary software ecosystems.

Commonly reported example is dual licensing model where software is released under multiple editions with each edition governed by different licensing norms [5]. However we observed that most organizations adopted a single licensing approach. The generic form of such business model can be described as follows.

The software was available under multiple editions, each edition governed by the same licensing norms but different in functionality and support. The low-cost edition (often termed as community edition) was available for free and provided what one respondent called *commodity functionality*. The professional edition on the other hand extended such commodity functionality through extensions and contractual agreements for service provision. Most organizations studied had developed partner networks for providing services. Partners also participated in developing specific extensions which were also packaged with professional editions or could be purchased separately. The professional edition could be bundled with such partner-developed and at time proprietary editions owing to the terms of the customized permissive licensing. Users could avail professional edition on the basis of subscription. In the next two sections, we describe common patterns and challenges in operationalizing such business models.

1.2   Research Methodology

Owing to the contextual adherence of the phenomenon, we chose case study as the research methodology. Case study was adopted as research methodology. In disciplines such as medicine and law, case study research has been the most favored mode of investigation while organizational and social sciences, case study research is gaining acceptance [6-8]. The increasing importance of case study research as methodology is rooted in its potential to expose phenomenon and researcher to each other in myriad of empirical avenues that otherwise are not possible through positivistic paradigm.

Case study research is suitable under certain conditions only. According to [8], case study research is appropriate to investigate a phenomenon within its real-life context, when the investigator has little control over the events. As the goal of the study was to expose trends and challenges experienced by organizations in operationalizing hybrid business model, it was hence imperative to examine hybrid business model in its context. Therefore, a case study method was chosen as the most appropriate approach for this research.

Before any case study endeavor is undertaken, important considerations have to be handled. In the subsequent sections, treatment of these considerations in the context of the study is explained. First issue is about the number of cases. As outlined by [8], multiple case study approach is suitable for a theory development exercise where each case is a separate experiment in itself. Each case compares the theoretical understanding and the new empirical evidences. On the other hand, single case study is suitable when phenomenon requires studying a unique, critical or revelatory case. Because we were interested in pattern identification, multiple case study approach was considered as the ideal choice. The cases were chosen as per replication logic (all cases having a hybrid business model), to improve on external validity of the findings.

Second consideration in case-based research pertains to the case selection criteria. Explicit mention of case selection criteria is key indicator of rigor in case research [8]. Overarching selection criteria for this study were presence of a hybrid business model associated with a software product. The idea was to ensure the fit of the case with the research questions at hand.

Thirdly, case study protocol was used to guide data collection. We wanted to capture data on operationalization of hybrid business model. Hence the protocol was developed accordingly with most questions began with 'how' and 'why'. We used interviews as the primary data collection vehicle. It is considered particularly suitable for the interpretive case studies [9]. Due to geographical limitations, interviews were conducted and recorded through video conferencing. Later these interviews were transcribed. We also used data from the published news articles and social media platforms.

We began the analysis process with open coding. The interview transcripts were coded for either operational practice of hybrid business model or an indicator of challenge in doing so. Once the open coding was done, we tried to examine the linkage across codes to identify axial linkages across coded excerpts. The exercise ended up with a set of operational practices and challenges related to hybrid business models.

1.3   Summary of the Cases

A total of six cases were studied. The cases belonged to four different product categories. One of the cases was an enterprise resource planning software. Three belonged to the content management system product category. One belonged to the business process management system while the last one was a customer relationship management system. The organizations were geographically diverse as well. Two cases were from mainland Europe, one was located in Scandinavian Europe, one was from South American continent, and two were headquartered in USA.

In all the cases, one of the top members of top management (preferably CEO) was interviewed. The idea was to get an overall description of the business model. To understand the operationalization, personnel from business development, and product engineering were also interviewed. As external resources such as community members play a key role in open source approach, personnel from community management were also interviewed. Lastly, to understand the distribution management, personnel responsible for managing partner network was interviewed.

In some cases, single person represented more than one functions. So he/she was contacted for collection data on all relevant dimensions. A total of 23 full-length interviews were conducted across 6 cases. The primary data was substantiated with secondary collected through secondary sources such as forum interactions between different stakeholders, product roadmap document, and release policy document.

1.4   Hybrid Business Models: Patterns

OSS is largely governed by two forms of licensing: permission and restrictive [10] (Lerner & Tirole, 2005). In all the cases, we observed *adoption of customized permissive licensing*. Such licensing allowed community members freedom to choose licensing of their respective contributions. As one of the respondents stated it acts as an incentive for commercial organizations participating in the community. The licenses however were customized to provide legal protection to the brand name of the product. Common permissive licenses that were used as basis included Mozilla Public License and Lesser GNU Public License.

Secondly, we observed *community to be made up of multiple segments*. Unlike the traditional notion of community as a uniform social collection of developers, hybrid business model fostered communities made up of business partners, customers of professional edition, customers of free edition, and partners of free edition. Each segment participated in development of product with distinct motivations.

Technological proximity to open source was another pattern observed. Most organizations studied did not start out with hybrid business model. It emerged later as suitable way of doing business. However, organizations already were technologically closer to open source than proprietary with software product being created using open source technologies. As stated by most of the interview respondents, migration to hybrid model was therefore a natural choice.

Phased release was another common feature. Organizations would often release their community edition before corresponding release of professional edition. This allowed the organizations to capture the user-feedback (for example, bug reports and feature requests) which was often incorporated for the professional edition, along with few more extensions.

Finally, most organizations were attempting to *create ecosystem around their products*. Towards this, they had developed a customized development and distribution platform. These platforms provided infrastructure for developing and hosting extensions for sales. Customers could search specific extensions through enhanced search functionality. In other words, entire ecosystem of the product could be developed around such platforms.

1.5   Hybrid Business Models: Challenges

Operationalization of such business models however involved certain challenges. Owing to the dichotomy of mixing open source with proprietary, most of these challenges were dichotomous.

Software products were released in multiple editions. Some of these editions were freely available while others came at a cost. Intended purpose of each edition was defined. The community edition was meant to achieve a faster rate of diffusion and to gather customer's feedback before releasing the professional editions. Usually community editions were not meant to be used in mission critical applications. Accordingly, organizations had to devise functional coverage of each edition. This functional differentiation across editions had to be wide enough for community edition users to perceive professional edition as valuable and upgrade. On the other hand, it also had to be narrow enough for community edition to qualify as a usable piece of software. Naturally, a community edition that did not have critical pieces of functionality would not allow for intended faster rate of diffusion. We observed that attempts to resolve this challenge led to differences of opinions between community members and the organization. We term this challenge as an extends the concept of *selective revealing* [11].

We have already posited segmented structure of community as a outcome of hybrid business models. In such segmented communities, different segments participated for different motivations. The challenge was to coordinate product development and distribution across these segments. For example, partners with interests in community edition only could package the edition and under certain licensing terms could also release the same as their own product. As one of the respondents stated, this led to a fractured user-base where multiple versions of the same editions were floating around in the market. One may be tempted to install strong appropriation regimes and take control of the product development and distribution. However, this would significantly take away benefits of hybrid business model. We term this challenge as *segmented meshing* where different community segments need to be meshed into a single entity. We observed adoption of a customized permissive license as a common approach to tackle this situation. Such a license provided intellectual property protection for the brand of the software product but still allowed community members to add proprietary functionality.

1.6   Conclusion

The paper focuses on emergence of hybrid business model in software product industry. It also provides some patterns and challenges in operationalizing such business models. The findings are based on data collected for a larger empirical study carried out as first author's doctoral work. Authors hope that reported findings would act as quick-start guidelines for software product organizations to looking to adopt hybrid business models.

References

1. Li, S., Shang, J., Slaughter, S.A.: Why Do Software Firms Fail? Capabilities, Competitive Actions, and Firm Survival in the Software Industry from 1995 to 2007. Information Systems Research 21(3) (2010)
2. Schmalensee, R.: Antitrust Issues in Schumpeterian Industries. American Economic Review 90(2), 192–196 (2000)
3. Campbell-Kelly, M., Garcia-Swartz, D.D.: The Move to the Middle: Convergence of the Open-Source and Proprietary Software Industries. International Journal of the Economics of Business 17(2), 223–252 (2010)
4. Rajala, R., Rossi, M., Tuunainen, V.: A Framework for Analyzing Software Business Models. In: Proceedings of the ECIS 2003, European Conference on Information Systems - New Paradigms in Organizations, June 18-22, Markets and Society, Naples (2003)
5. Välimäki, M.: Dual Licensing in Open Source Software Industry Systemes d'Information et Management 8(1), 63–75 (2002)
6. Lee, A.: A Scientific Methodology for MIS Case Studies. MIS Quarterly 13(1), 33–50 (1989)
7. Eisenhardt, K.M.: Building Theories from Case Study Research. Academy of Management Review 32(4) (1989)
8. Yin, R.: Case Study Research: Design and Methods, 4th edn. SAGE Publication (2009)
9. Walsham, G.: Interpretive case studies in IS research: nature and method. European Journal of Information Systems 4(2), 74–81 (1995)
10. Lerner, J., Tirole, J.: The Scope of Open Source Licensing. Journal of Law, Economics, and Organization 21(1), 20–56 (2005)
11. Henkel, J.: Selective Revealing in Open Innovation Processes: The Case of Embedded Linux. Research Policy 35(7), 953–969 (2006)

Two Modes of Product Development: Head-Oriented vs. Release-Oriented

Masayuki Hatta

Surugadai University,
Faculty of Economics,
698, Azu, Hannou, Saitama, Japan
hatta.masayuki@surugadai.ac.jp
http://about.me/mhatta

Abstract. In this paper, the concept of two different modes for product development process is proposed. One is "release-oriented" product development, which is a fairly common way to develop various products up to now. The other is "head-oriented" product development, which is recently observed especially in the field of software/content development. The distinguishing difference and possible merits and demerits of two modes are scrutinized.

1   Introduction

In the manufacturing industry, the product development is typically performed in aiming at the market release of a product. That is, trial experimentations are repeated inside the company, and a prototype is created when the concept and key features are stabilized to some extent (or scheduled deadline is imminent). After the so-called Quality Assurance work and some fine tuning are done, a final product is released to the market. This is mostly the same in the software industry until recently (Brooks 1975, Krishnan 1994).

However, recently, a different mode of product development has emerged, especially in the area of Open Source software/contents development and the development of on-line services such as SaaS (Software as a Service). In this mode, the target of development (typically the source code or running service) is always open to the public, and the insider developers and mere users share the same "forefront of development", or often called as "HEAD" in the developers' circle (Fogel & Bar 2003).

2   Release vs. Head

In this paper, the former, more conventional type of the product development process will be called "Release-oriented". The release-oriented product development process has an independent Quality Assurance (QA) process and a discrete release (Fig.1).

I. Hammouda et al. (Eds.): OSS 2012, IFIP AICT 378, pp. 368–370, 2012.

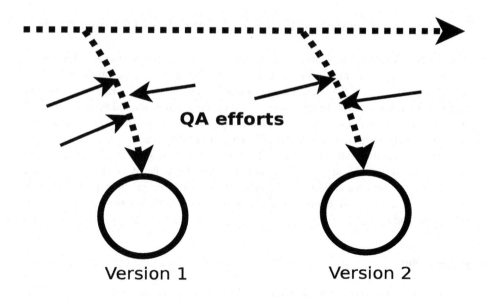

Fig. 1. The Release-oriented mode of product development. The dotted arrow indicates non-disclosed development. The solid circle means an officially released version of product.

By contrast, the latter one will be called "Head-oriented". The head-oriented way has no QA, no official releases, but the HEAD is open to the public (Fig.2).

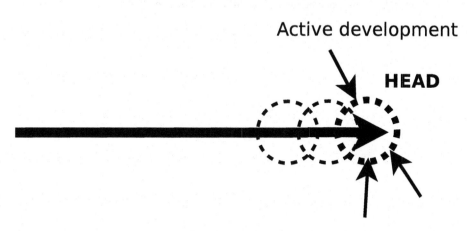

Fig. 2. The Head-oriented mode of product development. The head never released officially (except "snapshots"), thus indicated in the dotted circle.

The current development (writing/editing) process of Wikipedia is an excellent example of Head-oriented mode of product development. There are no "official releases". Instead, what you can see is always the latest edition.

3   The Key Elements Which Enabled the Head-Oriented Mode

The head-oriented mode enables the project to grow fast and mostly developer-friendly, however it is highly probable that imperfect and unstable products will be delivered to the users if the head-oriented mode has taken place. In order to realize the head-oriented product development, some external conditions should be ready. In this research, the author emphasizes the importance of technical progress in the realm of development infrastructure, and especially, the attribution of users.

Finally, the author will investigate the recent confusion at the scene of the KDE Desktop 4.0 release. Some Open Source projects have faced strong and sudden criticism from users when they put the new release out. This can be explained by the difference of orientation toward product development and releases, between core developers and users.

References

1. Brooks, F.P.: The Mythical Man-Month: Essays on Software Engineering. Addison-Wesley, New York (1975)
2. Krishnan, M.S.: Software release management: a business perspective. In: CASCON 1994: Proceedings of the 1994 Conference of the Centre for Advanced Studies on Collaborative Research, vol. 36 (1994)
3. Fogel, K., Bar, M.: Open Source Development with CVS, 3rd edn. Paraglyph Press, New York (2003)
4. Von Hippel, E.: Democratizing Innovation. MIT Press, Boston (2005)

OSS in 2012: A Long-Term Sustainable Alternative for Corporate IT

Didier Durand, Jean-Luc Vuattoux, and Pierre-Jean Ditscheid

Eranea SA, Chemin de Mornex 2, 1001 Lausanne, Switzerland
{didier.durand,jl.vuattoux,pjditscheid}@eranea.com
http://www.eranea.com

Abstract. The current internet leaders (Google, Facebook, etc.) all have OSS in their DNA. Traditional corporations still rely mostly on proprietary software for their mission-critical IT systems. But, situation is changing: as tip of the iceberg, major stock exchanges of the world have announced successful migrations to OSS. Many traditional corporations can now follow the OSS path because this market has clearly matured in many relevant aspects for them. In addition, solutions are here to achieve quick, efficient and secure mutations to OSS which must be undoubtedly considered by CIOs as the technological state of the art for 2012.

1 Historical Situation

Current high-tech leaders like Google and Facebook were born with Open Source Software. They massively leveraged it to develop their huge infrastructure with an incredibly high price-performance ratio:

- Google is known for having an infrastructure in the million-range of servers[1]. They are equipped with a customized version of Linux[2].
- Facebook is relying on Linux and the Cassandra NoSql database, that it initially created[3], to accumulate and manage the incredible amount of content uploaded daily on its hundreds of thousands of servers.

It was obvious for their founders that OSS software was the way to go when those giants of 2012 were very nimble startups: the cost of OSS, mostly free (like in "free beer"), is clearly one of its major advantages for a nascent company.

For more traditional and well-established corporations, origins of OSS and its inception mode made it clearly suspicious in its early days. How can you rely for the mission-critical part of your business on an OS like Linux, initially conceived by Linus Torwald, a student, as a personal project to make better use of its new 80386 PC[4]? More generally, major components of Linux were built by Internet-connected communities of individuals who very often never met each other and who tend to make the software, that they develop, evolve in the direction that best suits their own needs first. Their project dies or succeeds if its functions match the needs of a vast community, if its quality is high and if its improvements / versions appear quickly.

I. Hammouda et al. (Eds.): OSS 2012, IFIP AICT 378, pp. 371–376, 2012.

This very Darwinian evolution clearly doesn't meet the usual and traditional corporate requirements where suppliers have to be reliable, foreseeable and dependable. This is the reason why OSS was mostly limited to students, researchers and hobbyists until recent years.

But, things have started to change: London Stock Exchange announced in 2011 the successful end of its migration to Linux. It is part of a pack of similar achievements in the financial community[5]: NYSE, Deutsche Börse, Qatar Exchange, Shanghai Stock Exchange, etc. also migrated. Many of those systems claim to run at rate over 1 million transactions/second !

A very professional and corporation-oriented approach of OSS in the recent years is clearly the catalyst of these changes.

2   OSS: Now Run by Professionals

OSS, exemplified by Linux, has clearly left its hobbyist status. A study by Linux Foundation of December 2010[6] demonstrates that the vast majority of developments and patches around the 13.5 millions of source code of the Linux kernel is achieved by regular IT suppliers: Redhat, IBM, Oracle, Intel, HP, etc.

Because the adoption of Linux is growing rapidly, traditional leading IT suppliers didn't have any other choice: they must get seriously involved in this common resource.

They can't take the risk that their hardware equipment or software solution would work less efficiently or less reliably than those of competitors on this platform aimed at very strong growth: about 5 times faster than the global server market for years to come[7].

Additionally, not taking advantage of a common resource, valued at more than 11 billions dollars[8] for a leading Linux distribution like Fedora, would clearly demonstrate poor business abilities in R&D optimization...

The plethora of distributions can really be perceived as a mess: Distrowatch counts 321 distributions[9] at time of writing. This abundance could repel many corporations frightened by the fear of doing the wrong choice.

So, as his founder Robert Young explains, companies like Redhat have taken early on the role of becoming the "Heinz" of Linux in comparison with tomato ketchup[10]:*"All leading companies selling commodity products, including bottled water (Perrier or Evian), the soap business (Tide), or the tomato paste business (Heinz), base their marketing strategies on building strong brands. These brands must stand for quality, consistency, and reliability. We saw something in the brand management of these commodity products that we thought we could emulate."* The role of Redhat was not initially to develop Linux per se but to create a solid, credible and reliable brand around it in order to foster its adoption in the corporate world. The figures of IDC already mentioned and achievements of Redhat as flagship Linux company just reaching the billion dollars in yearly revenues[11] , demonstrate clearly that this approach has succeeded.

Beyond the important factors of image, credibility and dependability, Linux has also demonstrated leadership by the usual technical measurements:

- in the scientific world, the K system, leader of the Top500 supercomputers for October 2011[12] , is running Linux on its 705'000 Sparc cores to reach peak computations at 10.51 petaflops. Its 9 followers in this list are also running Linux.
- In the corporate world, Linux reaches around 50% of the top 10 spots for benchmarks like those of Transaction Processing Performance Council[13]. It is mostly due to the fact that suppliers tend to demonstrate for obvious commercial reasons that their proprietary systems perform as well as Linux for their equipment by publishing close results for both situations.
- Reliability surveys demonstrate clearly that Linux is at least as reliable as its proprietary counterparts if not more.[14]

Those exhaustive criteria have validated over time that OSS in general and Linux in particular have become a fully viable and even premium solution for large, critical and sophisticated corporate IT system.

3   OSS for Traditional Corporations: The Way Forward

Behind the leaders, the crowd of traditional corporations is by far not on OSS / Linux for their mission-critical activities yet[15]. All companies nowadays have Linux somewhere in house but it is most of time limited to serving the corporate web site or running the email gateway and DNS server.

Our analysis of this situation through meetings and business cases with many prospects and customers demonstrates that the question is not willingness but ability to migrate.

Most CIOs are today under a pressure of an intensity never felt before to produce massive savings in their IT budget[16]. All of them want to reduce their cost of operations, often amounting up to and even beyond 80% of their total budget. They want to compress this dominant section of their costs in order to return savings to their management and users but also to free up new resources for innovation projects desperately needed in a world where competition never stops increasing.

For most CIOs in this situation, the major virtue of OSS is its costs: they clearly care much more for its quasi-gratuitousness (compared to the proprietary world where their current system currently exist) and its licensing simplicity than for its other virtues (access freedom, changeability, etc.).

But, most of those CIOs are trapped already because the savings are required today with no allowance for transient budget increase in order to produce them. So, an evolutionary path where a system built over decades (of economic stability) would be progressively replaced over decades (of economic tension) by its OSS equivalent is clearly excluded.

In parallel, those CIOs, especially those in the information processing business (finance, media, etc.), have to protect the massive investments represented by their current IT system, where all the expertise and distinctive features of their business lie. Their value is embedded in sophisticated algorithms and processes "engraved" in millions of lines of source code over decades. Their teams also assembled over long periods of time represent the associated knowledge and competences. No way that a mutation to Open Source could jeopardize any of those 2 assets!

Finally, when solutions are demonstrated to protect the current assets, the final issue to be solved for CIOs is the path forward to this new world. It must be quick, secure and safe.

Truly, safety is a must. No CIO will embark such a massive mutation when it puts the business of his company, and consequently his own job, at risk.

Our analysis over many years has proven that this safety for quick mutations to Open Source Software can only come from 2 factors combined jointly in those projects:

- Automation: the new OSS system is generated by a translating automaton that will analyze the old proprietary system to generate its OSS equivalent via some kind of translation / cross-generation.
- Iso-functionality: the new OSS system must be fully equivalent to its proprietary predecessor. It processes and stores data in the exact same way, the user interactions are strictly identical and the processing algorithms remain unchanged.

We have applied this methodology for migration to OSS in various projects, perfecting the translating technology that we rely on over time. Our last project is the migration of a sophisticated banking system composed of over 10 millions lines of source code.

Each time, in those projects, we obtain very similar feedback from CIOs:

- Quick mutation to OSS for a mission-critical system must be a repeatable industrial process (via full automation) and clearly not a "1-shot best-effort trial" in order to succeed. The repeatability guarantees that the quality level and also allows safe parallel construction of the new OSS system by repetition of translation on a nightly basis (to include last maintenance of legacy system).
- Iso-functionality is key to the safety of the process : the new OSS system can share the same database as the old system because the source of modified data is indistinguishable. So both, old and new system can harmoniously cooperate to jointly host the user crew while it is smoothly migrating from the old to the new system.

Combining those 2 characteristics foster success:

- massive savings are achieved, up to 90% of the costs of the original system, so millions of dollars / euros per year on a recurring basis,
- competitive software assets are moved to state-of-the-art technology for a "second life" with big potential for further evolution,

⋏ people (both end users and IT staff) also migrate with very moderate effort
  and resistance because their adaptation needs are minimized,
⋏ risks to achieve the objectives have been reduced to a strict minimum.

4 Conclusion

This paper demonstrated that traditional corporations can and should nowadays catch
up technologically with current high-tech stars of the Internet. The pioneering path for
OSS has been paved by Google, Facebook when they had no assets to protect and
when they had to leverage all available opportunities to succeed. It is no longer the
sole ability of this technological elite: OSS road is now open to all corporations!

The OSS world is now also open to more traditional companies that were initially
more reluctant because of their already existing assets: OSS is now dependable upon
because reliable brands have emerged around it and because its technical qualities and
abilities have been clearly demonstrated for large-scale traditional applications.

With market solutions automating the migration to OSS, the last barrier is
removed: CIOs can migrate quickly and securely to the technology that they must
recognize as state-of-the-art for their systems in 2012.

References

[1] "Where the cloud meets the ground", The Economist (October 2008), http://www.
   economist.com/node/12411920?story_id=12411920
[2] "Google Platform", Wikipedia,
   http://en.wikipedia.org/wiki/Google_platform
[3] "Apache Cassandra", Wikipedia,
   http://en.wikipedia.org/wiki/Apache_Cassandra
[4] "History of Linux", Wikipedia,
   http://en.wikipedia.org/wiki/History_of_Linux
[5] "The London Stock Exchange moves to Novell Linux", ZDNet (February 2011),
   http://www.zdnet.com/blog/open-source/the-london-stock-
   exchange-moves-to-novell-linux/8285
[6] "Linux Kernel Development, How Fast it is Going, Who is Doing It, What They are Doing, and Who is Sponsoring It", Linux Fondation (December 2010), https://www.
   linuxfoundation.org/sites/main/files/lf_linux_kernel_develo
   pment_2010.pdf
[7] "Linux in New Economy", IDC sponsored by Linux Fondation,
   http://www.linuxfoundation.org/sites/main/files/publication
   s/Linux_in_New_Economy.pdf
[8] "Estimating the total development cost of a Linux distribution", Linux Fondation
   (October 2008), http://www.linuxfoundation.org/sites/main/files/
   publications/estimatinglinux.html
[9] "Distrowatch Page Hit Ranking",
   http://distrowatch.com/dwres.php?resource=popularity

[10] "How Red Hat Software Stumbled Across a New Economic Model and Helped Improve an Industry", Voices from the Open Source Revolution. O'Reilly (1999) ISBN 978-1565925823, also online at http://oreilly.com/openbook/opensources/book/young.html

[11] "Red Hat Becomes Open Source's First $1 Billion Baby", http://www.wired.com/wiredenterprise/2012/03/red-hat/

[12] Top 500 Supercomputer sites (November 2011), http://www.top500.org/

[13] Transaction Performance Processing Council benchmark results, http://www.tpc.org/information/results.asp

[14] 2008 Server OS Reliability Survey, Yankee Group study on server reliability, http://www.iaps.com/2008-server-reliability-survey.html

[15] "More on Today's COBOL", Microfocus, http://www.microfocus.com/aboutmicrofocus/pressroom/releases/pr20100120709820.asp

[16] "State CIO Priorities for, ", National Association of State Chief Information Officers, NASCIO (2012), http://www.nascio.org/publications

Discussion on the Problems to be Solved toward the Migration to OSS Productivity Software in the Business Enterprises

Jun Iio[1] and Tomotaka Ogawa[2]

[1] Mitsubishi Research Institute, Inc., Advanced Business Promotion Unit
2-10-3 Nagatacho, Chiyoda-ku, Tokyo, 100-8141 Japan
iiojun@mri.co.jp
[2] K.K. Ashisuto, 4-2-1 Kudankita, Chiyoda-ku, Tokyo, 102-8109 Japan
togawa@ashisuto.co.jp

Abstract. In recent years, there is a tendency to migrate from proprietary productivity software to open-source productivity software, especially in government offices and municipal offices. ODPG (OpenOffice.org & OpenDocument Format Promotion Group, Japan) is an organization founded in order to promote the migration to the OSS productivity software in private enterprises as well. In the case evaluation work group of ODPG, business solutions about use of OpenOffice.org have been discussed many times, for the purpose of supporting the migration to OpenOffice.org, by collecting and feeding back the information of case studies useful for the member companies. This paper reports several subjects and solutions, such as promotion strategy for OpenOffice.org to be widely used, the problem in file exchange with the other stakeholders, preparation of use environment, and security issues, which were discussed in the work group.

1   Introduction

Open-Source Software (OSS) has become popular as a part of server solutions, operating systems, and middle-ware. In addition, it is widely used for embedded systems, such as home information appliances and cell phones. However, OSS desktop applications are not popular except for famous web browsers and mail agents; OSS productivity software[1] on which we focus in this paper is still not widely used as expected.

In recent years, there is a tendency to migrate from proprietary productivity software to OSS productivity software, especially in government offices and municipal offices in the world. In Japan, several local government offices have decided to adopt the OSS productivity software instead of the proprietary one. Cost saving is considered as the principal engine of this movement. Due to the protracted recession, not only public sectors but also private sectors begin considering the benefit of the migration to OSS productivity software.

---

[1] It is also called "office software" or "office suites."

I. Hammouda et al. (Eds.): OSS 2012, IFIP AICT 378, pp. 377–382, 2012.

ODPG (OpenOffice.org & OpenDocument Format Promotion Group, Japan)[1] is an industry organization founded in 2010, in order to promote OpenOffice.org and the OpenDocument Format (ODF) that is adopted by the OpenOffice.org as its file format. As of Mar. 2012, it consists of 23 business enterprises and associations. The members of ODPG exchange information on the usage of OpenOffice.org in their organization and discuss the problems that they have faced in their activities.

At the beginnings of fiscal 2011, the case study working group (CS-WG) was organized in the ODPG. The aim of CS-WG is to support adopting OpenOffice.org as standard software in the member organizations by collecting valuable information for the members and by giving feed back to the other members.

In this paper, we report summarized information and the results of discussions by CS-WG. Although we represent "OpenOffice.org" as the transitional object in this paper, it is not restricted to OpenOffice.org. That is, LibreOffice and similar OSS productivity software can be also considered as the target of the migration.

2   Problems and Solutions in the Migration

In this section, we report the problems and its solutions to realize smooth migration from the organizational usage of Microsoft Office (MS-Office), which is widely used as proprietary productivity software, to the organizational usage of OpenOffice.org, which is also typical OSS productivity software. In the practical discussion by CS-WG members, many problems and solutions about promotion strategy, file exchange with other organizations, preparation of the environment for the usage, security, and so on were confirmed.

2.1   Promotion Strategy

Firstly, we mention about choice of OpenOffice.org and its derivations, gradual or partial migration, document preparation useful for the migration.

Although some members considered that the migration from a product to another product was easy, the other members considered it was not easy. It depends on the size of organization and on the type of businesses. In regard to the style of the migration, gradual migration and partial migration, or the combination of both, were supported by most of members. Documents, which are training materials, guidelines, and the other articles, tend to be prepared in advance of the migration. The other method of the preparation of documents reported from some members is to compile inquiries from employees.

2.2   File Exchange with Other Organizations

Secondly, we point out the problems and solutions on the file exchange with other organizations.

In earlier discussions on this issue, one-to-one or one-to-few file exchange was supposed in many cases. Under these conditions, the problems are considered solved if such files are converted by person in charge or if restricted use of MS-Office is allowed as necessary. However, it costs too much man-hour to solve this problem by the method previously mentioned, if the solution for one-to-many file exchange is required. Also, if casual use of MS-Office is permitted under the migration to OpenOffice.org, the significance of the migration would be spoiled. In the discussion for the OpenOffice.org migration at the large business enterprises, one-to-many file exchange should be considered.

We have proposed two solutions. The first one is to make guidelines for keeping interoperability among ODF, OOXML, and traditional MS-Office files. The guideline claims that over-elaborate documents inhibit conversion from OOXML to ODF, from traditional MS-Office file format to ODF, and vice versa. This approach can be expected as the solution of the interoperability problem between different versions, so that it has a possibility to enable long-term use of office documents.

The other solution is decomposing and restructuring OOXML file. The data structure of OOXML is open to the public as is the case with ODF. Therefore, it is possible to construct a system to take required part of data content from OOXML file and to recompose a file in ODF to deliver the file within the organization.

2.3   Preparation of the Environment for the Usage

What the environment for the usage should we prepare to use OpenOffice.org, instead of other proprietary productivity software? Here we discuss printing and version upgrade.

Regarding the printing, when OpenOffice.org outputs printed image directly to the printer, there still remains some defects, such as misalignment. However, these defects are slight and ignorable. If a complete image is required, the file should be created as a PDF file and printed by a PDF viewer.

The problem in upgrading versions is that we have to distribute a large size file for version upgrade installation because current method to upgrade OpenOffice.org is overwriting installation so that whole image file is required. This would be problematic in the organization where the intranet connection is relatively poor. The bandwidth of the network is exhausted for transferring install files and it results in a negative consequence for network operations.

In addition, we have to prepare some particular systems to consolidate version numbers in an organization or to make all software upgraded, since OpenOffice.org's policy for the upgrade is that users themselves run an install program on an autonomous basis. It is important that a framework to make smooth upgrade, including distributed deployment of install image files to avoid congestion of the intranet, is considered beforehand with the migration.

However, other software upgrades such as Windows Update, the upgrade of Java Runtime package, the upgrade of Adobe Reader, require the large image files as well. If the network environment is rich enough and there are no problems in such software upgrades, the network bandwidth problem in upgrading OpenOffice.org is also ignorable.

2.4   Security

Security issues are not ignorable if the software is used in the business enterprises. How do we deal with the situation if a vulnerability is found in OpenOffice.org, especially with the targeted attack like APT (Advanced Persistent Threat) attack, which is frequently occurs in recent years.

First of all, once an APT attack targeted at zero-day vulnerability is reached at the internal of an organization, the attack to PCs in the network will be successful. It is better to consider that any attack to PCs will result in a higher rate of success even if the attack is not zero-day vulnerability, because many of anti-virus systems, anti-SPAM systems, and gateway systems of the intranet can not prevent from the APT attacks. Then, it is an effective approach to construct a framework to shield outgoing data, in order to protect the intranet from APT attacks.

In regard to dealing with vulnerability issues, the only way to solve the issue on vulnerability of OpenOffice.org is "upgrading OpenOffice.org," at the moment. In addition, the next version of OpenOffice.org has not been released for a while. However, the vulnerability of OpenOffice.org pointed out at Mar. 2012, is just the problem that the particular MS-Office file makes OpenOffice.org crashed. The patch program that can fix this vulnerability has already been developed and will be adopted in the next release of OpenOffice.org. The current version of LibreOffice, which was forked from OpenOffice.org, has already been fixed this problem.

2.5   Productivity

It is a considerable issue whether the productivity of business transactions is not decline after the migration to OpenOffice.org from existing productivity software with a familiar user interface. However, even the companies which have already succeeded in the migration to OpenOffice.org do not have clear values measuring the productivity of their business.

In addition, the productivity of office work is different from that of production lines in the factory. It depends on several factors, so that the values measured in other companies is not necessarily correspond to another company.

Anyway, the discussion to determine the productivity factors to be considered for the successful migration results in the following issues:

- depression of productivity due to human factors;
- conflict against existing business systems;
- appropriate target for comparison.

Depression of Productivity Due to Human Factors. It is concerned that decline in the productivity of document preparation occurs after the migration from MS-Office to OpenOffice.org, due to inexperience in the operation. According to the person who had succeeded in the migration, although depression of productivity comes out in any organization, operators have become accustomed to the new interface just for about three months.

Furthermore, in order to keep performance of office work after the migration, it is effective to make business process simple and not to require complicated documents. Moreover, the decline in productivity tends to occur in the parallel operation of MS-Office and OpenOffice.org because there are frequent opportunities to convert data format to each other. It should be careful if the parallel operation will be required.

Conflict against Existing Business Systems. There exist some business systems which suppose that the data is conveyed in MS-Office format. That may become a factor to decline the productivity of business transactions after the migration to OpenOffice.org. However, the risk can be eliminated by business process analysis (BPA) before the migration. Furthermore, it is possible to calculate how much man-hour should be required to migrate by the migration support services (MSS).

Utilizing BPA and MSS previously conducted, we can understand how much the productivity will be declined, what are the workaround plans, how many functions should be fixed to accept ODF files. These understandings reduce the risk of the problems involved in the migration.

Appropriate Target for Comparison. When we consider the migration from MS-Office 2003 to OpenOffice.org, they are often easily compared and it comes to a conclusion from the comparison of them. However, some CS-WG members pointed out that MS-Office 2007/2010 should be compared with OpenOffice.org (and/or its derived products) to make practical decisions especially in planning the migration to OpenOffice.org.

3   Related Work

Many academic studies about the migration to OpenOffice.org[2-8] have been conducted in recent decades. However, in almost of all studies, the case studies are the migrations in the public administration offices. Ven *et al.*[2] studied the case study at the ministerial cabinets of the Brussels Capital Region. Karjalainen[7] reported the Finnish case. Perry and Margoni [8] reported the case of the Canadian government.

Some of these studies were executed under the Consortium for Open Source Software in the Public Administration (COSPA)[9] project, which is supported by the European Union's Sixth Framework Program.

On the other hand, the case examples discussed in the activities of ODPG significantly differ from these case studies. ODPG mainly focus on the ODF-based migration in private sectors, and it is a private organization with no recourse to public funds.

4   Conclusions

ODPG promotes information exchange by organizations that plan the large scale migration to OpenOffice.org each other. In this paper, we report the results of the discussion on the problems and solutions faced in the migration, as a part of ODPG's activities.

Issues on promotion strategy, file exchange with other organizations, preparations of the environment for the usage, security, keeping productivity are pointed out by the discussion of the working group of ODPG. In these issues, some problems have not been solved. However, most of problems are solvable and it is confirmed that they are not large obstacles to realize the trouble-free migration.

References

[1] Iio, J., Shimizu, H., Kobayashi, K., Ogawa, T.: ODPG: A Grass Roots Approach for the Introduction of Open-Source Productivity Suites. Journal of Economics, Memoirs of the Faculty of Law and Literature (39), 51–58 (2011)

[2] Ven, K., Nuffel, D.V., Verelst, J.: The Introduction of OpenOffice.org in the Brussels Public Administration. In: Open Source Systems. IFIP International Federation for Information Processing, vol. 203, pp. 123–134 (2006)

[3] Huysmans, P., Ven, K., Verelst, J.: Reasons foProceedings of the First International Conference on Open Source Systems,r the Non-adoption of OpenOffice.org in a Data-intensive Public Administration. First Monday 13(10) (2008)

[4] Rossi, B., Scotto, M., Sillitti, A., Succi, G.: An Empirical Study on the Migration to OpenOffice.org in a Public Administration. International Journal of Information Technology and Web Engineering 1(3) (2006)

[5] Zuliani, P., Succi, G.: An Experience of Transition to Open Source Software in Local Authorities. In: Proceedings of e-Challenges on Software Engineering, Vienna, Austria (October 2004)

[6] Rossi, B., Russo, B., Succi, G.: Open Source Software Migration in Integrated Information Systems in Public Sector. In: Research and Practical Issues of Enterprise Information Systems. IFIP International Federation for Information Processing, vol. 205, pp. 683–689 (2006)

[7] Karjalainen, M.: Large-scale Migration to an Open Source Office Suite: An Innovation Adoption Study in Finland. Academic dissertation. University of Tampere, Finland (2010)

[8] Perry, M., Margoni, T.: Free-Libre Open Source Software as a Public Policy Choice. International Journal on Advances in Internet Technology 3(3&4), 212–222 (2010)

[9] Morgan, L.: Analysis of COSPA — A Consortium for Open Source in the Public Administration. In: Scotto, M., Succi, G. (eds.) Proceedings of the First International Conference on Open Source Systems, pp. 125–129 (2005)

How Can Open Standards Be Effectively Implemented in Open Source?

Challenges and the ORIOS Project

Björn Lundell[1], Admir Abdurahmanovic[2], Stefan Andersson[4],
Erik Bergström[1], Jonas Feist[4], Jonas Gamalielsson[1], Tomas Gustavsson[2],
Roger Kahlbom[3], and Konstantin Papaxanthis[2]

[1] University of Skövde, Skövde, Sweden
{bjorn.lundell,erik.bergstrom,jonas.gamalielsson}@his.se
[2] PrimeKey Solutions AB, Solna, Sweden
{admir,tomas,konstantin}@primekey.se
[3] Pro4u Open Source AB, Stockholm, Sweden
roger.kahlbom@pro4u.com
[4] RedBridge AB, Kista, Sweden
{stefan.andersson,jonas.feist}@redbridge.se

Abstract. Many organisations are currently restricted in their choice of software because of restrictions imposed by existing systems. Challenges include a lack of interoperability and a risk of technological lock-in, which many small companies seek to address by utilising Open Standards and Open Source implementations of such standards when developing and deploying systems. This paper presents an overview of how the industrial research project ORIOS (Open Source software Reference Implementations of Open Standards) seeks to address identified challenges. An overarching goal of the project is to improve understanding within organisations of Open Standards, Open Source Reference Implementations, and the ecosystems around them. This will be done by developing a reference model of necessary and desirable features of an Open Standard, and how Open Standards and their implementations can be utilised by small companies in different usage contexts. An action case study approach will be used as a core strategy for evolving a reference model together with Swedish companies.

1   Introduction

Amongst many small companies it is widely recognised that Open Standards inherently open up markets by counteracting monopolies based on proprietary technologies. They also offer increased opportunities through promoting interoperability (Ghosh, 2005). Such approaches are being reinforced by a number of international initiatives, including the European Interoperability Framework (EIF version 1.0) which promotes Open Standards as part of a strategy for interoperability (EU, 2004). Previous research has shown the importance of using Open Standards for maintenance of digital assets in long-term usage scenarios (Lundell et al., 2011).

I. Hammouda et al. (Eds.): OSS 2012, IFIP AICT 378, pp. 383–388, 2012.

The paper presents an overview of the ongoing ORIOS (Open Source software Reference Implementations of Open Standards) project, an industrial collaborative research project, which addresses a number of challenges experienced by small companies that relate to Open Standards and the potential for their implementation in Open Source software, including different types of lock-in and a lack of interoperability.

The central concepts and the scope for a reference model on Open Standards and their implementations in Open Source software which is to be developed during the project is presented in Figure 1. It clarifies that Open Standards can be implemented in Open Source Reference Implementations, and outlines that implementations of such standards can be used in different applications that are provided under different (proprietary and Open Source) software licenses.

The anticipated reference model characterises desirable properties for Open Standards and Open Source Reference Implementations for different usage scenarios and thereby provides guidance to different stakeholders groups and organisations in this domain. Somewhat simplified, an Open Standard is a standard which possesses certain 'openness' properties, and an Open Source Reference Implementation is a reference implementation of the specification of a standard that is licensed under an Open Source license. A Reference Implementation is an implementation of a specification which can be used as a definitive interpretation of the standard's specification.

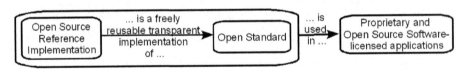

Fig. 1. Central concepts and the scope for a reference model to be developed

2   Why Open Standards?

According to the European Commissioner for Competition Policy: "Interoperability is a critical issue for the Commission, and usage of well-established open standards is a key factor to achieve and endorse it." (Kroes, 2008) A number of European countries are currently adopting national policies on Open Standards and some even require Open Standards in public procurement. For example, both the current and previous Swedish governments have expressed their support for Open Standards. With the directive ("Delegation för e-förvaltning", Dir. 2009:19) and SOU (2009:86) it is likely that Open Standards will play a much more significant role in the Swedish IT sector. The Swedish minister responsible for the e-Government Delegation has expressed strong support for Open Standards as defined in SOU (2009:86) and EIF version 1.0 (Odell, 2009).

Today, many companies and public sector organisations provide services to citizens and organisations that are dependent upon a well-functioning underlying

IT-infrastructure. Much of this infrastructure is based on Open Standards, with the Internet and the web at its core. Many organisations, especially small companies, would simply not have existed without infrastructure and systems based on Open Standards. In essence, Open Standards drive innovation (Berners-Lee, 2010).

However, there is evidence of considerable confusion amongst software providers, software procurers and politicians about the meaning and impact of openness in standards (Lundell, 2011, 2012). This lack of clarity can have many negative impacts, from clouding the public debate over appropriate legislation to confusing potential customers about the importance of software compliance (Lundell, 2012). Therefore, whatever position is taken about Open Standards it seems clear that there is a pressing need for informed legislation on the one hand and informed decision making by purchasers and providers of software on the other. Anything less has the potential to reduce competitiveness in the hugely important global market in ICT.

3   Challenges and Effects of Open Standards

During the last decade, a number of European governments have adopted Open Standards in their policies in order to address a number of fundamental challenges in the ICT marketplace, such as lock-in, interoperability and procurement. There are a number of stakeholder roles in the marketplace that affect and are affected by the provision and adoption of Open Standards. The project addresses such challenges.

It is widely recognised that Open Standards, and especially when implemented in Open Source software, have the potential to address a number of fundamental challenges which are especially troublesome for small companies. First, a *primary motivation* for Open Standards is that they promote a *healthy competitive market* (Ghosh, 2005; Krechmer, 2005; Simcoe, 2006; Lundell and Lings, 2010). For example, the existence of an Open Standard reduces the risk and cost of market entry, and so encourages multiple suppliers. According to Simcoe (2006), this in turn leads to lower prices and improved product quality. A *second motivation* is that insistence on Open Standards *reduces the risk* to an organisation of being technologically locked-in. Open Standards increase control by supporting migration, thereby reducing an organisation's reliance on a single product or supplier (Ghosh, 2005; Krechmer, 2005; Berkman, 2005; Bhattacharya et al., 2007; Simon, 2005; West and Dedrik, 2001; Lundell, 2011). A *third motivation* is that Open Standards are a basis for *interoperability*. A significant current problem in many organisations is that they are restricted in their choice of software because of restrictions imposed by existing or legacy systems. Interoperability supports systems heterogeneity, thereby increasing options for organisations (Bird, 1998; Ghosh, 2005; Krechmer, 2005; Fomin et al., 2008). A *fourth motivation* is that Open Standards offer a basis for *long-term access* and *reuse of digital assets*, and in particular when supported by Open Source Reference Implementations (Behlendorf, 2009; Lundell et al., 2011). Having a precise definition of a digital format clearly offers some protection for the long-term interpretation of digitally stored materials; in extremis a converter could be written against the specification in the Open Standard. This is becoming an increasingly well recognised issue for many organisations, especially in the public sector (Gamalielsson and Lundell, 2010; Lundell, 2011; Lundell and Lings, 2010; National Archives Australia, 2006).

From these arguments, it is evident that different authors have expressed (and experienced) a variety of different desirable effects from the use of Open Standards, either in general or related to specific Open Standards. However, different views on and experiences related to these desirable effects have been expressed by different stakeholders in different roles related to an Open Standard. This is perhaps unsurprising given potentially different motives, goals and usage contexts for a specific Open Standard.

So, the question arises: *what are the necessary and desirable features of an Open Standard, and how can Open Standards and their implementations be utilised by small companies in different usage contexts?*

4   The ORIOS Project

The ORIOS project has two primary scientific objectives. The first is to explicate the concept of Open Standard and its implementation as Open Source Reference Implementations, thereby making it easier for stakeholders to communicate unambiguously about the costs, benefits and effects of different adoption options. This includes investigation of specific examples of Open Standards and Open Source Reference Implementations, and their effects on the market: in terms of penetration, support and overall impact. One important dimension of the study constitutes an investigation of impact within the Open Source area; particularly with respect to tools, implementations and platforms utilising the standards. The second is to develop a reference model, based on the investigations of specific examples of Open Standards and Open Source Reference Implementations, for guiding organisations on how to utilise Open Standards and Open Source Reference Implementations. The reference model provides detailed guidance, with concrete strategies, for how organisations can utilise Open Source Reference Implementations and Open Standards in different usage scenarios. The project focuses on Open Standards and Open Source Reference Implementations that are of particular interest to all partner companies.

The project undertakes an analysis of organisations and networks that are involved in realising the potential offered by adoption of Open Standards and Open Source Reference Implementations, as users and providers of software systems. In doing so, the study aims to galvanise existing knowledge of Open Standards, particularly in the context of Open Source Reference Implementations, and identify a critical path for Swedish organisations wishing to exploit these in a variety of business models. At root, the major issues around Open Standards and Open Source Reference Implementations exploitation are socio-technical and business oriented rather than purely technical.

To meet the objectives we will utilize an action case research approach (Braa and Vidgen, 1999). For the first objective this will be supplemented by a study of the appropriate literature reinforced with feed-in from interactive workshops, seminars, and a review of relevant projects (Open Standards, Open Source software, and Open Reference Implementation projects) in order to identify their different characteristics.

5   Discussion and Implications

The project will provide a comprehensive understanding of the business models emerging from open strategies within specific usage contexts, and have immediate practical implications for business decision makers. Specifically, the project will establish an increased awareness in society and partner companies about opportunities and threats related to Open Standards and Open Source Reference Implementations. Such knowledge is especially important as it directly affects business conditions for small companies. For partner companies, the project will specifically raise awareness of interdependencies between Open Standards and the Open Source software ecosystems, and how this might impact on efforts to build a competitive software market.

It is expected that the project's overall approach will promote significant stakeholder and organisational learning, and improve Sweden's position for taking full advantage of the major international developments in Open Standards and Open Source Reference Implementations, their effect on Open Source software applications and the associated business opportunities which are likely to emerge with growing awareness and policy regulation.

Through our development of a reference model, we will establish key enablers and inhibitors for companies working in the Swedish context. The project will result in considerably increased exposure of Swedish organisations to the true potential of Open Standards and Open Source, which fundamentally affect all Swedish and international organisations.

References

Behlendorf, B.: How Open Source Can Still Save the World, Keynote Presentation, In 5th IFIP WG 2.13 International Conference on Open Source Systems, OSS 2009, Skövde, Sweden, 5 June (2009)

Berkman: Roadmap for Open ICT Ecosystems, Berkman Centre for Internet & Society at Harvard Law School (2005)

Berners-Lee, T.: Long Live the Web: A Call for Continued Open Standards and Neutrality, Scientific American, 22 November, http://www.scientificamerican.com/ article.cfm?id= long-live-the-web&print=true (2010)

Bhattacharya, J., Ilavarasan, P. V., Gupta, S.: Open standards and accessibility to information: a critical analysis of OOXML in India, In Proceedings of the 1st international Conference on theory and Practice of Electronic Governance, ICEGOV'07, vol. 232. ACM, New York, pp. 151-154 (2007)

Bird, G. B.: The Business Benefit of Standards, StandardsView 6(2), 76-80 (1998)

Braa, K., Vidgen, R.: Interpretation, intervention and reduction in the organizational laboratory: a framework for in-context information system research, Accounting, Management & Information Technology 9, 25-47 (1999)

EU: European Interoperability Framework, European Commission, Version 1.0 (2004)

Fomin, V. V., Kühn Pedersen, M., de Vries, H. J.: Open Standards and Government Policy: Results of a Delphi Survey, Communication of the AIS 22(25), 459-484 (2008)

Gamalielsson, J., Lundell, B.: Open Source Software for Data Curation of Digital Assets: a case study. In Proceedings of the 14th International Digital Media & Business Conference: MindTrek 2010 (Lugmayr, A. et al., Eds.), ACM, New York, pp. 53-56 (2010)

Ghosh, R. A.: An Economic Basis for Open Standards, FLOSSPOLS, December, http://www.flosspols.org/deliverables/FLOSSPOLS-D04-openstandards-v6.pdf (2005)

Krechmer, K.: The Meaning of Open Standards, In Proceedings of the 38th Hawaii International Conference on System Sciences – 2005, IEEE Computer Society, Los Alamitos, 10p (2005)

Kroes, N.: Being Open About Standards, Brussels, SPEECH/08/317, 10 June, European Commissioner for Competition Policy (2008)

Lundell, B.: e-Governance in public sector ICT-procurement: what is shaping practice in Sweden?, European Journal of ePractice 12(6), http://www.epractice.eu/en/document/5290101 (2011)

Lundell, B.: Why do we need open standards?, In Proceedings of the 17th EURAS Annual Standardization Conference, European Academy of Standardisation, The EURAS Board, (to appear) (2012)

Lundell, B., Lings, B.: How open are local government documents in Sweden? A case for open standards. In Agerfalk, P. et al. (Eds.) Open Source Software: New Horizons, Springer, Berlin, pp. 177-187 (2010)

Lundell, B., Gamalielsson, J., Mattsson, A.: Exploring Tool Support for Long-term Maintenance of Digital Assets: a Case Study, In Fomin, V. & Jakobs, K. (Eds.) Proceedings: 16th EURAS Annual Standardization Conference, European Academy of Standardisation, The EURAS Board, pp. 207-217 (2011)

National Archives Australia: Digital Preservation: illuminating the past, guiding the future, National Archives of Australia, Australian Government, June, http://www.naa.gov.au/images/XENA_brochure%5B1%5D_tcm16-47233.pdf (2006)

Odell, M.: Innovations for Europe: Increasing Public Value, Speech by Minister responsible for central government administration and local government issues, 5 Nov., Maastricht, http://www.regeringen.se/sb/d/11678/a/134858 (2009)

Simcoe, T. S.: Open Standards and intellectual property rights. In Chesbrough, H., Vanhaverbeke, W. and West, J. (Eds.) Open Innovation researching a new paradigm, Oxford University Press, Oxford (2006)

Simon, K.D.: The value of open standards and open-source software in government environments, IBM Systems Journal 44(2), 227-238 (2005)

West, J., Dedrick, J.: Proprietary vs. Open Standards in the Network Era: An Examination of the Linux Phenomenon, In Proceedings of the 34th Hawaii International Conference on System Sciences - 2001, IEEE Computer Society, Los Alamitos, 10p (2001)

Future Smart Metering Runs on Open Source – Challenges and the GuruxAMI Project

Mikko Kurunsaari

Gurux Ltd, Hermiankatu 6-8 H 33720
Tampere, Finland
http://www.gurux.org/

Abstract. More and more devices are coming to Internet and organizations are using more devices to measure things. Challenges include a huge amount of different protocols and a risk of technological lock-in. Because of new innovations and demands new protocols are coming out all the time. Increasing amount of protocols makes it harder to collect data from different data sources and save it to one place. If we want to make tailored reports it is important that we can save all collected data to the one place. This paper presents an overview of how the industrial research project GuruxAMI (Gurux Advanced Metering Infrastructure) tries to solve this problem. An overarching goal of the project is to make an open platform that can be used to collect data from different data sources using different protocols and save collected data to the one place. This will be done by developing Open Source platform that can handle different protocols.

1   Introduction

Protocols are like languages. There are lots of different protocols and if you speak one protocol other devices that speak other protocols do not understand you. It would be easy to say that we will build one universal protocol and everyone should use it but it is not possible. Demands that are expected from the protocol are changing a lot depending where protocol is used. A sensor has different needs than a paper mill for example. Sensor can measure only one variable and only purpose of it is measure it. From sensors point of view protocol must be very light and simple whereas paper mill can consist of lots of different variables and its protocol can be much bigger and more comprehensive.

The paper presents an overview of the ongoing GuruxAMI (Gurux Advanced Metering Infrastructure) project [1] and summarizes our open source experiences related to the project.

2   GuruxAMI Project Details

The goal of GuruxAMI is to offer an open platform that can be used to collect data from various data sources. The basic idea is that multiple protocols can be used simultaneously and more can be added on the fly. Thanks to this idea data can be collect from various data sources and save to one place and make tailored reports etc.

I. Hammouda et al. (Eds.): OSS 2012, IFIP AICT 378, pp. 389–394, 2012.

GuruxAMI

The Purpose of GuruxAMI is collect data from different data sources and made tailored reports so peoples can save energy. Basic idea is that if you want to save energy you must know where it is used or otherwise you are saving in wrong place.

Basic idea of GuruxAMI is that we can collect data from the meters using different kind of protocols. GuruxAMI can be used to collect data from other data sources than electricity meters but for the sake of clarity we are talking only them. So there is no need to have multiple concentrators for different meters/manufacturers: DLMS/COSEM, MBus, Modbus, etc. This saves time and money.

Basic difference between "Automatic Meter Reading" and "Advanced Metering Infra-structure" Systems is that AMR reads meters AMI can control them as well. In this moment biggest problems for meter reading are: different protocols and static IP addresses. GuruxAMI can handle both problems. Figure 1 shows the main parts of GuruxAMI.

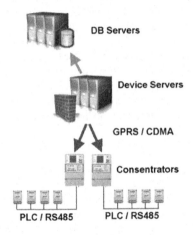

Fig. 1. GuruxAMI platform components

Database Server(s)

There is a uniform database where collected data is saved. From collected data is generated all kind or reports. Sometimes collected data is inserted directly to the SAP system.

Device Server(s)

Device servers collect data from meters. Device servers are also known as data collectors. In this moment they are polling data from the meters. Polling is problem when using GPRS/CDMA connection because concentrators' needs static IP address and this is expensive because mobile phone operators are charging quite a lot from static IP address. Additional some mobile operators do not give static IP addresses for smaller companies.

Concentrator(s)

The purpose of concentrator is connecting local meters to the data collecting system. Concentrators can be "dummy" when they only transport data between device server and meters. Problem is if there are lots of different meters. This is usually not a problem in energy utilizations but factories want to use different kind of meters from different manufacturers.

Because there are lots of concentrators without intelligence, data collecting systems must poll meters. This is a big problem is you have lots of meters. First if meters be-hind concentrators are using ex. Power Line Communication (PLC) it is really slow and causes that you must have lots of data collector devices. Second they must use Static IP addresses and this is very expensive.

Our idea is that we replace Concentrators with embedded Linux device where is GuruxAMI inside. In this way there is no need for static IP addresses (or concentrators) because device servers do the collecting work and after data is send they will send data to the database servers.

We are collecting data "on the field" and then we send collected data to the database server. It is faster and cheaper because we can use dynamic IP addresses. Data collector does not make connection to the concentrator and device server. Device server connects to the Database Servers and this makes possible to use dynamic IP addresses. Additionally we can build intelligence to the collector so concentrator does not need send data so often. Basic idea is not to invent concentrator again but to expand it. There are just some cases where plain concentrator is not enough. This is illustrated in Figure 2.

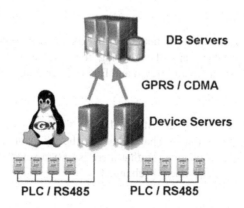

Fig. 2. Data collection using GuruxAMI

3   GuruxAMI Project Working

GuruxAMI lies on the Gurux Communication structure. We have developed it more than ten years now. Basic idea is that there is a thin layer where changes are made when protocol changes. All other parts are remaining same. Because of this developing and testing is faster because there is much less work to be done. The structure of GuruxAMI layers is depicted in Figure 3.

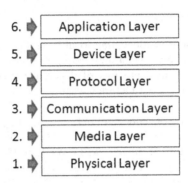

Fig. 3. Structure of GuruxAMI layers

Physical Layer

The physical Layer represents physical device.

Media Layer

Media layer presents different communication channels, ex. TCP/IP, serial port, USB, etc. basic idea is that media layer must implement IGXMedia interface. When media implements this interface Media can be changed to the other and there is no need to make any changes. Basic idea of media layer is offer transforming channel that is used to send and receive byte stream.

Communication Layer

Purpose of communication layer is take care that data is sent and received correctly. Communication layer takes care of resending if packet is lost and it also parses packets from the data stream using Begin and End of Packet markers and checksum.

Protocol Layer

Purpose of protocol layer is to transform data to the byte stream and vice versa. Protocol layer is the layer that is changed when the protocol is changed. Idea of Protocol Layer is to isolate changes so that there is only a small part of the code that needs to be tested when the protocol is changed.

Device Layer

Purpose of Device layer is represent all properties that device supports. All properties of device are saved to the xml file, so it can be easily modified for users needs. Because device's properties are saved to the xml-file it can be used to easily create user depend devices. Example: a developer needs to read much more data from the meter than an ordinary user. Thanks device Layer we can have two different xml-files. One for the developer and one for other users. There is no need to make changes for the actual source code only changing the xml-file will do the trick.

Application Layer

Application layer is usually User Interface. Basic idea is that if UI is changed rest of the application remains the same. Because of this developing is much faster and it is much faster to implement custom UIs. Gurux's products: GXDeviceEditor, GXDirector and GuruxAMI are relaying this idea. User uses GXDeviceEditor to tell what data is collected from the device. After that user uses GXDirector or GuruxAMI to collect data and visualize it.

We are collecting more and more data from various data sources. Companies are putting lots of money to collect data, but is it worth the cost? Is data used enough? Very easily costs are much higher than the benefits.

(a)

(b)

Fig. 4. Data collection and associated costs

The current situation is that costs and efforts on data collecting are high without Value of the data (Figure 4-a). The optimal situation would be that there are no more data collecting investments, but rather the focus should be on data utilization and value (Figure 4-b).

4   Why Open Source?

We are receiving lots of questions why we are Open Source Company. Reason for this is quite simple. We believe that we have made something great and if we succeeded GuruxAMI system can be a success story. Our problem was advertising. How a small company from Finland can be known around the world? Problem for software companies in Finland is that we have only 5 Million people and it is very hard or almost impossible to make software only for local markets. So if Finnish software companies want to live they must find bigger markets.

We considered this problem for over a year. What to do? How we could let people to know what we have done? After considering various options, we decided that the source code is not our most valuable asset.

We have learned a lot from Open Source during these years. One important thing what we have learned is that in Open Source world there usually is only one king at the time. We want to be that king of AMI systems.

5   Discussion

We have been Open Source Company over three years now and we are still learning. I believe that most important thing is publicity. It is very important for Open Source projects. I believe that biggest problem in Open Source projects is how people can find you. In internet there are lots of projects and big challenge is how you get visibility for your project. In picture below is visualized growth of users in our community. It took very long time from us to start grows, over a year. After we grow over critical point we started grow faster. I believe that reason for this is people talk and when they talk it increased people's awareness from us.

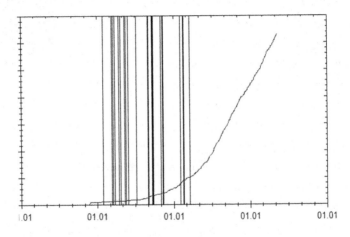

Fig. 4. GuruxAMI community growth

Reference

1. GuruxAMI, http://www.gurux.fi/index.php?q=AMIIntroduction (last accessed May 2012)

Open Source Software in Research and Development
(Guidelines for Postgraduate Students)

Michael Adeyeye[1] and Oluyomi Kabiawu[2]

[1] Cape Peninsula University of Technology, South Africa
[2] University of Cape Town, South Africa
adeyeyem@cput.ac.za, oluyomi.kabiawu@uct.ac.za

Two case studies were used in our study; they were two postgraduate projects that exploited FoSS but lacked proofs of concept. In addition, a survey was also conducted to investigate the level of usage of OSS in research. The sample population was quite small; hence, there should be some level of caution in generalizing the knowledge level of students as represented by the survey. 39 respondents out of the total 65 respondents said their works require prototype development; 26 respondents needed to develop their works ground-up, while 39 respondents needed to modify existing projects/codebases; 52 respondents leverage OSSD in their works, while 13 respondents do not; 40 respondents have access to sample/similar projects on the Internet, while 25 respondents do not; 35 respondents consider themselves proficient with the tools they use, while others are not. Lastly, the numbers of respondents that chose conceptualization, identification of tools, implementation and evaluation of a research work as the most challenging aspect of the research were 8,16,15,26, respectively.

In the two case studies, the researchers were required to present a proof of concept and access to the source code of their works. However, the researchers could not meet up with the requirements. In addition, they could hardly pitch their contributions to the existing body of knowledge and evaluate their works using comparisons. An exemplary OSS project that followed the core principles required in using OSS in a research is TransferHTTP+CAS. The work claimed that content sharing, session handoff and their control services in the Web-browsing context can encourage collaboration and interaction among the Internet users. The work contributed to the state-of-the-art in its domain by comparing the implemented prototypes[1] with emerging industry works, such as WebRTC, Google Wave, and Open APIs.

The OS project components that a researcher should be aware of include: the project community, its developers, source code and license(s). The first author considered all the components during his work to produce the artefacts and show a proof of concept. As a result, this paper proposes the following guidelines for using open source in research: visiting related project and wiki websites for information, joining their communities of developers; providing access to one's source code so that different individuals can contribute in different ways to the cohesive whole; and taking cognisance of the license used by the software that is being extended.

---

[1] http://www.ngportal.com/micadeyeye/index.php/2009/09/13/projects-videos/

I. Hammouda et al. (Eds.): OSS 2012, IFIP AICT 378, p. 395, 2012.

Development Style of Open Source
and Econmies of Connection

Keisuke Tanihana and Tetsuo Noda

Faculty of Law and Literature, Shimane University, Matsue, Japan
{keisuke_tanihana,nodat}@soc.shimane-u.ac.jp

Recently, Open Source Software (OSS) becomes indispensable resource in the information service industry. Moreover, OSS development also consists of the contribution and participation by information service enterprises. While the development of OSS style has spread, participation of information service enterprises toward OSS has also increased. In our research, we will consider the relation between OSS use and its effect in terms of economic theory.

As is noted in Coase (1937), when enterprises trade through a market, it is necessary to collect the information about goods, search a partner, etc. In other word, uncertainty which arises from trade through a market will cost enterprises. This is known as "Transaction Cost". We think that computerization decreases their transaction cost. As a result, computerization will cause enterprise's business strategy from closed style toward open one. The change of business strategy, economies of scale is the strategy of pursuing economy of scale. This strategy will have closed and independent management style. On the other hand, as is noted in Miyazawa (1988), "Economies of Connection" is the viewpoint that many companies cooperate and consider the synergistic effect of technology or know-how as important. The computerization, such as the Internet, serves as this background. In "Bazaar Model", a develop participant is not limited but a development process is exhibited generally. The developer can be connected by the Internet worldwide. Computerization such as the Internet enables source code to spread worldwide. Therefore these "Bazaar Model" will suggest "the economies of connection".

Under open strategy, technology and know-how will combine with each other beyond boundary of each enterprise. Chesbrough (2003) has been considered this open strategy as "Open Innovation" in terms of R&D activity. OSS is developed in community which is an organization outside an enterprise. Since OSS is released free, it is a kind of public goods. Under "Open Innovation", it is important for an enterprise to combine own development project with OSS in order to create new value and to enhance its competitiveness. "Open Innovation", needless to say it is equivalent to the "Bazaar Model". We think that the business model which uses OSS is based on "Open Innovation". This process enables enterprise to decrease its development cost by replacing own resources and OSS, or "connecting" both.

References

[1] Chesbrough, H.: Open Innovation. Harvard Business School (2003)
[2] Coase, R.H.: The Nature of the Firm. Economica 4(16), 386–405 (1937)
[3] Miyazawa, K.: The distribution system in a highly informative society. Toyo Keizai Inc. (1988)

I. Hammouda et al. (Eds.): OSS 2012, IFIP AICT 378, p. 396, 2012.
© IFIP International Federation for Information Processing 2012

FLOSS Survey 2013? A Proposal for Comprehensive Survey on FLOSS Developers

Masayuki Hatta

Surugadai University, Faculty of Economics, Room 710E,
10th Floor, The Di-ni Bldg, 698 Asu, Hannou Saitama, Japan 357-8555
hatta.masayuki@surugadai.ac.jp
http://about.me/mhatta

The year 2013 will mark the 10th anniversary of the renowned FLOSS surveys[1]. They were the first international efforts to conduct online (and offline) questionnaire surveys to collect comprehensive data on FLOSS developers, such as who they were, what motivated them, how they were organized, then aim at picturing an overview of what the FLOSS (Free/Libre/Open Source Software) development was all about. The outcome of FLOSS surveys has been considered as one of the most reliable sources on FLOSS ecosystem for researchers (especially in the realm of social sciences) who are interested in the FLOSS development process at large.

The FLOSS surveys provide us quite a complete outlook of the FLOSS world at that time. However, the following ten years since then were possibly the most rapidly evolving, dramatically changing days of ICT industries -- who could expect in those days, an yet another small tech startup which bore the strange name Google or an ailing niche computer maker named Apple would become the pinnacle of the world? It is highly possible that the landscape of FLOSS development is also radically different from the good old days of 10 years ago. Ever since, many researchers conducted smaller surveys, but most of them tended to be quite specific to their own research interest and not comprehensive, thus cannot be compared with the result of FLOSS 2002/2003 directly in its entirety.

In my poster, I propose a plan to conduct the second FLOSS survey. It will update the FLOSS 2002/2003 and give us a renewed view of what has become of the FLOSS world. Also, I intend to establish a good practice to conduct an online survey, using purely Free / Open Source Software.

Reference

1. http://flossproject.org/report/

I. Hammouda et al. (Eds.): OSS 2012, IFIP AICT 378, p. 397, 2012.

FLOSS Project Registration Strategies

Alexander Lokhman

Tampere University of Technology
alexander.lokhman@tut.fi

During the past decade open source software has gained increased popularity. A huge number of projects have been developed, published and widely used. Nevertheless, the idea that open source software is created and maintained by a loosely connected community working across the Internet remains suspicious. What is often overlooked however is that communities need support of different kinds. For instance, communities need basic environment to support project sources and documentation, as well as to monitor and to manage contributions, and to communicate with other members. In order to achieve this, community leaders (or supporting companies) often produce a website which contains information about the project. The website may also include facilities for issue tracking, managing communication between members (e.g. mailing lists, IRC, forums, chats, etc.), and access to source code.

Frequently it is difficult for community leaders to run and/or to support specified software (such as code repositories), and the best possible solution is to use external services. These services are mostly free, provide variety of features, and perform better than the locally installed. Moreover, well known code sharing services attract big number of developers all over the world which may bring more contributors to the managed project.

In our research we have identified three main strategies for OSS project registration using various code sharing services available. First identified is *Centralized scheme* which tends to become the most widely used scenario of project registration because of ease of support and single community concentration. Project source code is hosted in one forge, whereas other forges have stable link to the main one (usually via project website address). Centralized scheme is used by MySQL, PHP, Spring, Python, and many other successful OSS communities. *Syncing scheme* is not as popular as Centralized scheme but still it is adopted by many projects, which primarily use modern revision control systems (e.g. Apache HTTP Server). The main idea is to host source code in one forge and synchronize the repositories in other forges with the main one. The last *Doubling scheme* method is the rarest type because of the problems which this method entails, since the source code is copied to each forge repository.

Despite the fact that each strategy has its own technical features, from marketing perspective all bring enough effect for project promotion. However, marketing perspective and technical limitations are not the only forces for choosing suitable approach for project registration. Such dimensions of software engineering process as requirements, design, maintenance, and quality assurance applied to particular project may also bring new constraints.

I. Hammouda et al. (Eds.): OSS 2012, IFIP AICT 378, p. 398, 2012.
© IFIP International Federation for Information Processing 2012

Using the Eclipse C/C++ Development Tooling as a Robust, Fully Functional, Actively Maintained, Open Source C++ Parser

Danila Piatov, Andrea Janes, Alberto Sillitti, and Giancarlo Succi

CASE, Free University of Bolzano, Piazza Domenicani 3, Italy
{danila.piatov,ajanes,asillitti,gsucci}@unibz.it

Abstract. Open Source parsers that support contemporary C/C++, can recover from errors, include a preprocessor, and that are actively maintained, are rare. This work describes how to use the parser contained in the Eclipse C/C++ Development Tooling (CDT) as a Java library. Such parser provides not only the abstract syntax tree of the parsed file but also the semantics, i.e., type information and bindings. The authors used the same approach to obtain Java and JavaScript parsers.

Programming language parsers are used by industry and research to create compilers or interpreters, statical code analysis tools, code metrics tools, source code editors with code completion, etc.

Parsing C/C++ is particularly tricky (e.g., a construct a * b can be a multiplication or a pointer definition depending on the type of a). Generic Open Source parser generators do not alleviate this task since the ambiguities cannot be resolved by a parser alone but require type information.

We searched for Open Source C++ parsers that include a preprocessor, perform semantic analysis (resolve type information and name bindings), are robust, and support contemporary C/C++ features. Of the found parsers, namely cpp-ripper, Elsa, GCC using the "-fdump-translation-unit" option, GCC_XML, Clang, and the Eclipse CDT parser only the latter 2 fulfilled the requirements. We decided to opt for the Eclipse parser since the approach could also (and did) provide us with parsers for other languages like Java and JavaScript.

The actual parser is located in the file "org.eclipse.cdt.core_X.jar", in the Eclipse installation folder, where X stands for version of the file. The jar itself is an Eclipse plugin, however, it is possible to use it as a Java library, without initializing the Eclipse platform.

The instruction "org.eclipse.cdt.core.dom.ast.gnu.cpp.GPPLanguage. getDefault().getASTTranslationUnit(FileContent, IScannerInfo, IncludeFileContentProvider, IIndex, int, IParserLogService)" performs the actual parsing, returning an abstract syntax tree (AST).

This work deals with an (apparently) simple problem: to "find a working C++ parser". Eclipse CDT contains such parser, but there is no official documentation about using it as a library outside of Eclipse. We hope that our poster can fill this gap and be of help.

I. Hammouda et al. (Eds.): OSS 2012, IFIP AICT 378, p. 399, 2012.
© IFIP International Federation for Information Processing 2012

FLOSS Education: Long-Term Sustainability

Gregorio Robles[1], Jesús M. González-Barahona[1], and Wouter Tebbens[2]

[1] GSyC/LibreSoft, Universidad Rey Juan Carlos
{grex,jgb}@libresoft.es
[2] Free Knowledge Institute
wouter@fki.org

Summary

Learning in any environment has undergone major changes in recent times. Many of these changes are closely related or are similar to processes or solutions found traditionally in Free/Libre and Open Source (FLOSS) environments: peer to peer relationships, telematic support, use of new technologies, etc. [1]

The purpose of this workshop is to bring together free software experts to discuss challenges that we face in the educational world at present and and that we will face in the future and how they can be undertaken from a FLOSS perspective. A public call for papers has been made resulting in various contributions, as follows:

- Utilization of OSS Virtual Machines for the Hands-on Training Environment
- Free and Open Source Software in Project Based Service Learning
- Learning through analysis of coding practices in FLOSS projects
- Sustainable Open Source Systems for Education and Research in Health Care: The Case of Cuba
- Portable Educational Portfolios

Based on this contributions and on the over 20 registered participants, a series of topics will be discussed, and conclusions and remarks will be collected and published. The contributions to and outputs of the workshop can be downloaded at the workshop website at http://libresoft.es/flossedu. This workshop is supported by the eMadrid network of Excellence (S2009 TIC-1650) and by the Free Knowledge Initiative.

Reference

1. Weller, M.: The Digital Scholar: How Technology is Transforming Scholarly Practice. Bloomsbury Academic, Basingstoke (2011)

I. Hammouda et al. (Eds.): OSS 2012, IFIP AICT 378, p. 400, 2012.
© IFIP International Federation for Information Processing 2012

Developing Mobile Software with FLOSS

Anthony I. Wasserman

Carnegie Mellon University Silicon Valley
tonyw@sv.cmu.edu
http://sv.cmu.edu

Abstract. The goal of this workshop is to explore the challenges, issues and opportunities associated with the use of free and open source software (FLOSS) in mobile platforms and apps. As mobile phones and devices become more powerful, as cloud services and telecom infrastructure become richer, and as consumer expectations evolve, developers are faced with an array of challenges that affect how they should systematically build and deploy new applications and systems.

1 Introduction

Current mobile platforms and applications include both open source and closed software components. While development tools for mobile systems are largely open, the platforms and applications are largely closed. The mobile ecosystem is different from the traditional software ecosystem, since many developer decisions are affected by device manufacturers, mobile network providers, and application store requirements. Developers are, in general, more constrained the mobile environment than in traditional environments.

Beyond that, challenges to successful development of mobile applications cover a wide range of business and technical issues, including:

- Multiple hardware and software platforms
- Many development frameworks and programming languages
- Different operator restrictions and features
- Very short development cycles
- UI limitations and complexities of interaction with sensors and cameras
- Effective use of context
- Power management
- Security and privacy models and policies
- Computational and storage limitations
- Applications that depend on external services

Issues related to free and open source software (FLOSS) add some additional challenges, including:

- Rapid release cycles for FLOSS software
- Managing multiple FLOSS licenses within an app
- Complying with app store rules and restrictions related to FLOSS apps

I. Hammouda et al. (Eds.): OSS 2012, IFIP AICT 378, pp. 401–402, 2012.

2   Workshop Themes and Goals

The overall goal for the workshop is to develop an agenda for future research related to the development of mobile applications that use FLOSS. The workshop discussions will be built around several important questions and themes, including, but not limited to, the following:

- *How should developers address the increasing fragmentation of the mobile applications ecosystem, involving important decisions on how to address the plethora of devices, platforms, operators, languages and app stores?* Should a developer focus on only one combination of these, or use a toolkit or framework to mask (some of) the differences? What role can (or does) FLOSS have in helping developers create their apps?
- *How do traditional open source development practices relate to the engineering of mobile applications and systems?* Is it the same, different or a variant of conventional approaches? For example, should mobile software engineering employ the same methods and processes but with different patterns and heuristics? Which methods should be used? Are there new methods?
- *What are the distinguishing features of mobile software specification, architecture, development and testing that need special attention, skills, or innovation?* Are there specific categories of apps, such as native apps vs. mobile web apps, to address independently?
- *What new tools, if any, are needed to support the effective development of mobile apps that use FLOSS?* Is there a difference between the general needs for mobile app development tools and specific needs for FLOSS?
- *What are the needed business practices for developers to address the requirements of the mobile ecosystem?* For example, is the developer goal of "release early, release often" compatible with the inherent delay in gaining approval for the app from an app store? What are the mechanisms for releasing source code for FLOSS apps distributed from an app store?

Author Index